Jurij Murašov, Davor Beganović, Andrea Lešić(eds.)
Cultures of Economy in South-Eastern Europe

Culture & Theory | Volume 220

Jurij Murašov, born in 1952, is a professor for Slavic literatures and literary theory at Universität Konstanz. He has been Principal investigator in the Cluster of Excellence »Cultural Foundations of Integration« 2007-2019. He has published articles and books about literature, media, and culture in Eastern and Southeastern Europe and Central Asia.

Davor Beganović, born in 1959, is a lecturer for Bosnian, Croatian, and Serbian languages and literatures at Eberhard Karls Universität Tübingen. He has published books and articles about South Slavic literatures and cultures, narratology, theory of literature, and memory.

Andrea Lešić, born in 1972, is an associate professor of comparative literature and literary theory at the Philosophy Faculty, University of Sarajevo. She has published on literary theory, memory studies, South Slavic literatures, and popular genres.

Jurij Murašov, Davor Beganović, Andrea Lešić (eds.)
Cultures of Economy in South-Eastern Europe
Spotlights and Perspectives

[transcript]

Gedruckt mit der Unterstützung des im Rahmen der Exzellenzinitiative des Bundes und der Länder eingerichteten Exzellenzclusters der Universität Konstanz »Kulturelle Grundlagen von Integration«.

Bibliographic information published by the Deutsche Nationalbibliothek
The Deutsche Nationalbibliothek lists this publication in the Deutsche Nationalbibliografie; detailed bibliographic data are available in the Internet at http://dnb.d-nb.de

© 2020 transcript Verlag, Bielefeld

All rights reserved. No part of this book may be reprinted or reproduced or utilized in any form or by any electronic, mechanical, or other means, now known or hereafter invented, including photocopying and recording, or in any information storage or retrieval system, without permission in writing from the publisher.

Cover layout: Maria Arndt, Bielefeld
Cover illustration: Collage by Alexander Weber
Printed by Majuskel Medienproduktion GmbH, Wetzlar
Print-ISBN 978-3-8376-5026-6
PDF-ISBN 978-3-8394-5026-0
https://doi.org/10.14361/9783839450260

Contents

Cultures of Economy
Theoretical Perspectives
Jurij Murašov, Davor Beganović, Andrea Lešić 7

An Economic Survey of the Kingdom of Yugoslavia
Jelena Rafailović 35

Imagining the *zadruga*
Zadruga as a Political Inspiration to the Left and the Right
in Serbia, 1870-1945
Dubravka Stojanović 57

What Were the Outcomes of the Self-Managed Economy in Socialist Yugoslavia?
Aleksandar Jakir, Anita Lunić 79

Work as a Cure
Reana Senjković 97

Economy and the Cult of Relics
The Miracle-Working Icon of the Virgin and Financing
the Patriarchate of Peć Monastery
Ivana Ženarju Rajović 111

Artists and Merchants
Art "Patronage" in Carniola at the Beginning
of the Twentieth Century
Renata Komić Marn 123

Architecture and its Value(s)
The National and University Library in Ljubljana
Tina Potočnik 135

Fortunes and Misfortunes of Usury
Andrić's *Woman of Sarajevo*
against Balzac's *Eugenia Grandet*
Ivana Perica 143

The Socialist Robber-Baron as a Superfluous Man
Derviš Sušić's Novel *I, Danilo*
Andrea Lešić 169

Narration as Misunderstanding
The Economy in Borislav Pekić's
The Pilgrimage of Arsenije Njegovan
Davor Beganović 193

The End of the Socialist (An-)Economy, Money, and the Beginning of Literary Narration
On Miljenko Jergović's *Buick Rivera* (2002)
Jurij Murašov 207

Beyond Economy
Social Misery and Masochism in Post-Communist
Serbian Society (Nikola Ležaić's Film *Tilva Roš*)
Tanja Zimmermann 229

Economy on Stage
Theatrodicy and Revolution
Miranda Jakiša 247

Contributors 265

Cultures of Economy
Theoretical Perspectives

Jurij Murašov, Davor Beganović, Andrea Lešić

1. Introduction

The discussion on "culture" and "economy" is a result of an essential theoretical shift observable since the mid-90s, when one economic crisis began to follow another – namely the crises in connection with the transition process in Eastern Europe and the various and permanent Euro crises, not to mention the cyclical global financial crises. This theoretical shift towards "culture" in academia as well as in the public and political discourses is a reaction to neoliberal economic theories, which on the one hand proclaim the convergence of "capitalism and freedom", as Milton Friedman did in 1962 in his book of the same title, and on the other hand operate on the basis of concepts of rational choice and mathematics. This neoliberal concept has proven to be inadequate for an understanding of the historical contingence of real economic processes.

The irony of this "cultural turn" in economic discourses is that the very ideas that during the 19th and 20th centuries served as a theoretical basis for socialist or other anti-capitalist economies and seemed to be disqualified by the collapse of the communist systems in Eastern Europe are now celebrating a remarkable renaissance. This renaissance is obvious in various alternative and critical milieus, such as the *Occupy* movement, in which the anthropologist David Graeber features as one of the leading figures. In his books *Towards an Anthropological Theory of Value. The False Coin of Our Own Dreams* (2001) or *Debt – the First 5000 Years* (2012), Graeber presents a – more or less – explicit rereading of Marx and Engels, Marcel Mauss, Ernst Bloch and Bourdieu led by the intention to develop a new ethics-based economy. We find the same intention in Tomáš Sedláček's *Economics of Good and Evil. The Quest for Economic Meaning from Gilgamesh to Wall Street* (2011). Within a horizon of 4,000 years of cultural history, Sedláček shows that ethics, the question of good and evil, always remains an integral part of every economic discourse. Economy and ethics cannot be separated. His historical analysis ends in a critique of the recent attempts by advanced finance theories to represent economy exclusively via mathematical models.

This renaissance of socially, politically or ethically grounded economic theories is also taking place even in the inner circles of liberalism and mathematically based theories. One famous example here might be Joseph Stiglitz, the former Chief Economist of the World Bank (1997-2000) and one of the recipients of the Nobel Memorial Prize for Economic Sciences in 2001. Along with many articles and books on the global, American, Asian and European economies, the financial market and economic policy, Stiglitz wrote *Whither Socialism* (1996), one of the most important and instructive books about the socialist economy, showing that its failure was caused by the ignorance of information asymmetries in market procedures. The surprising point in this book is that Stiglitz argues that the same ignorance can be found in neoliberal visions of the free market. In the book *The Prize of Inequality: How Today's Divided Society Endangers Our Future* (2012), Stiglitz continues his critical analysis of deregulated markets, their liberalistic ideology, and the dominant role of the financial lobbies in American and European politics. A remarkable attempt to bring together history on the one hand and econometry and statistics on the other is Thomas Piketty's book *Le capital au XXIe siècle* (2013). Not only its title, but also Piketty's guiding thesis obviously refers to Marx's tremendous opus *Capital. Critique of Political Economy* (*Das Kapital. Kritik der politischen Ökonomie*, 1867, 1885, 1994). Analyzing an incredible wealth of statistical and economic data from Western capitalistic countries (mainly from France, Great Britain, Germany, USA) in a broad time frame from the late 19th century until the first decade of the 21st, Piketty shows how the capitalistic free market economy produces and increases inequalities on different levels of society and how the decades of the 1950s, 60s and 70s, when the neoliberal slogans about the interrelationship between the free market and social equalization and justice were proclaimed, must be understood as a brief exceptional period caused by the post-Second World War conditions. Piketty argues that beyond this period, the capitalist free market economy again started to work as an inequality-producing machine; the increasing inequalities in Western capitalistic economies after 2000 tend once again towards a situation resembling that of the last two decades of the 19th century.

This extension of the economic discourse by political, social, anthropological and historical perspectives is echoed by a new increasing interest in economics articulated by hermeneutic disciplines such as philosophy, sociology, history, and literature, art, film and media studies.[1]

---

[1] See in particular examples from film studies, such as Lizardo, Omar (2007) Fight club, or the cultural contradictions of late capitalism. In: *Journal for Cultural Research* 11(3): 221-243; Lynn, Ta. M. (2006) 'Hurt so good'. Fight club, masculine violence, and the crisis of capitalism. In: *The Journal of American Culture* 29(3): 265-277; Hamenstädt, Ulrich (2014) *Theorien der Politischen Ökonomie im Film*. Wiesbaden; for examples of economics in art, see: Sholette, Gregory/Charnley, Kim (2017) *Delirium and Resistance: Activist Art and the Crisis of Capitalism*. London; or the exhibition catalogue: Harten, Jürgen (2000) *Das fünfte Element – Geld oder Kunst. Ein fabelhaftes Lexikon zu einer verlore-*

Our book examines this hermeneutic engagement with economics in the Southeastern European region of the former Yugoslavia, which deserves special attention as a multilayered and to this day conflictual cultural space.[2] The complexity of this cultural space can be measured in three dimensions – the political, the religious and the linguistic.

Politically, for centuries the regions of the former Yugoslavia were hotly contested objects of various hegemonic ambitions – for the Habsburg Monarchy, Venice, Hungary, and the Ottoman Empire, until 1918, when the Kingdom of Serbs, Croats and Slovenes was established. With its foundation as the Socialist People's Republic in 1943, and in 1945, Yugoslavia entered the sphere of the political and ideological interests of the Soviet Union for several years, before stepping out on its own path to socialism in 1948, the so-called *third* way between the Western and Eastern political blocs. It followed this path until 1991, when the Federal Republic broke up into different tiny political entities. Since then, these political entities, Slovenia, Croatia, Serbia, Montenegro, Macedonia, Bosnia and Herzegovina, and Kosovo, have tried to renew their various historical relations to the spheres of the Austrian, Slavic-Russian or Islamic-Turkish cultures, but at the same time have gravitated with different intensity and success towards the European Union and/or NATO.

This turbulent political history comes along with and is embedded in different religious traditions, which have shaped the cultural space of the former Yugoslav regions to this day. Catholic Christians dominate today's Croatia and Slovenia, although the latter also had contact with the Reformation and Protestant movements of the 16th century, which essentially brought about the early codification of Slovenian language as a written language. There are Orthodox Christians in Serbia, Montenegro and also in Macedonia, where the remaining third of the population are Muslims, who also form the majority in Kosovo. Islam is also the leading religion (about 40%) in today's Bosnia and Herzegovina, besides Orthodox and Catholic Christians and around 1,000 Jews. This small remaining population of Jews, mostly Spanish Sephardi who migrated to Bosnia in the late 15th century and who

---

nen Enzyklopädie. Cologne; Kozioł, Monika/Piekarska, Delfina/Potocka, Maria (eds., 2013) *Ekonomia w sztuce. Economics in Art. Exhibition catalogue. Museum of Contemporary Art Krakow (MOCAK)*. Krakow; Widemann, Reinold (2018) *Artists' Conceptions of Money: Money Art and Artificial Money*. Soesterberg; in literary studies, see e.g.: Marsh, Nicky (2007) *Money, Speculation and Finance in Contemporary British Fiction*. London, et al.; Vogl, Joseph (2010) *Das Gespenst des Kapitals*. Zurich.

2 An instructive overview of Yugoslavia as a conflictual cultural space is given by Zimmermann, Tanja (2014) *Der Balkan zwischen Ost und West. Mediale Bilder und kulturpolitische Prägungen*. Cologne, Weimar, Vienna. Also, in Samuel Phillips Huntington's famous and controversially discussed book *The Clash of Civilizations and the Remaking of World Order* (1996, New York), the regions of Yugoslavia are identified as one of the main zones lying on the global inter-civilizational conflict line.

at the beginning of WWI still represented 10% of the inhabitants of Sarajevo, has declined. Many of them were victims of the Holocaust, initiated by the Independent State of Croatia, which existed between 1941 and 1945, and supported by the Germans.

In the cultural space of the former Yugoslavia we find three grammatically distinct languages, Slovenian, Serbo-Croat[3] and Macedonian; the last is a Bulgarian dialect, which was standardized in the 1930s and 40s and established as the official language in the region of Yugoslav Macedonia. What makes the linguistic situation so complex is the pragmatic use of the three languages and their varieties for creating political, nationalistic, ethnic and religious identities. Primarily due to religious traditions, the three grammatically distinct languages are represented using different script systems: Slovenian and Croat in the Latin alphabet and Serbian and Macedonian in Cyrillic; besides Cyrillic and Latin, Arebica, a variant of the Perso-Arabic script, was also used in Bosnia and Herzegovina until the 19th century.[4] At the same time, the common rate of illiteracy and the relevance of an oral tradition especially in the southern region were high by comparison with western parts of Europe. Both during and after the breakup of the Socialist Federal Republic of Yugoslavia, language questions played a crucial role in the national self-identification of the newly founded political entities, especially in Croatia and in Bosnia and Herzegovina, where the institutionalization of (new) official languages, Croatian and Bosnian, marks differences to the former Serbo-Croat by normalizing regional idiomatic and lexical characteristics or by etymological archaisation.

In examining this political-religious-linguistic complexity, our project on the "culture of economy" has a twofold task. The first is to spotlight in a series of articles from different hermeneutic disciplines how culture and economy interacted in the regions of Yugoslavia from the late 19th century to the post-socialist period and the first decade of the 2000s. At the same time, systematic positions are also taken by each of the articles, showing how "cultures of economy" can be fruitfully studied from the perspectives of economic and social history and literature, art and film studies. For this second task, which seeks to place the empirical analyses in a conceptual framework, the following explanation will outline the basic fields of mutual interdependence of culture and economics and try to open up some theoretical perspectives: *economy and ethics, money and language* (1), *calculating political, national and ideological identities* (2), *religion and economy* (3) and *aesthetics and money*

---

3 The Serbo-Croat language of the Yugoslav era is now taught in international university education as Bosnian-Croat-Serbian. The new denomination takes into acount the regional varieties and the political fact of three different state languages.

4 In post-Yugoslav Bosnia, a new interest in Arebica can be observed. See e.g. the comic book *Hadži Šefko i hadži Mefko* (2005) by the authors Amir Al-Zubi and Meliha Čičak-Al-Zubi. In 2013 Aldin Mustafić's book *Epohe fonetske misli kod Arapa i arebica (The Age of Phonetic Thought of Arabs and Arebica)* was published in Belgrade.

(4). Against this theoretical background, a final section will sum up the *topics and theses* (5) of the articles presented in the book.

2. Economy and ethics, money and language (Aristotle, Hamann, de Saussure)

In considering different attempts in various disciplines to reshape economic theory beyond algorithm-based econometry, one can find two main perspectives dealing with "cultures of economy". The first addresses ethical, the second semiotic and media issues.

The ethical issue is crucial for Aristotle's economic concept.[5] He distinguishes between two different forms of purchase or acquisition (*ktetike*). One form is a "natural part of economy (*oekonomia*)"; the purpose (*telos*) of this form of acquisition is dominated by the needs of the household and – in a wider horizon – by the political community (*koinonia*). The ethos of the community regulates the method (*techne*) of acquisition. The achieved wealth (*ploutos*) is limited by the welfare of the household and the political community. But there is also another form of purchase, which is called – as Aristotle claims – the art of gaining money (*chrematistike*). This monetary space is limitless, because it initiates a process of abstraction transforming all concrete utility items in formal and quantified values of exchange. A shoe – in the famous example Aristotle gives – is no longer a shoe, but now has a diabolic double function as an object of utility on the one hand and as an item indicating a value relation on the other. This monetary space is also infinite concerning the status of wealth (*ploutos*). The loss of its *telos* defined by the needs and the welfare of the household's or political community's monetary wealth causes infinite procedures of quantification and money trading based on the interest rate (*tokos*). Aristotle rejects this form of money-oriented purchase as unnatural – as an unnatural birth of money out of money. The point of Aristotle's argumentation is that economy is dominated by two operating modes which exclude but at the same time presuppose each other: the semiotic procedure of monetary abstraction and quantification, and the organization of the material reproduction of the human community as an ethical, social and political entity.

The second perspective, which is relevant for the cultural turn in economic theories, focuses on money as a medium of the economy and its semiotics. In this perspective, money is correlated with language. Referring to a long tradition reaching

---

5 For economy and ethics in Greek Antiquity and in Aristotle's philosophy, see Sedláček, Tomáš (2011) *Economics of Good and Evil. The Quest for Economic Meaning from Gilgamesh to Wall Street*. Oxford; Vogl, Joseph (2010) *Das Gespenst des Kapitals*. Zurich: 116-125.

back to Plato, the German Johann Georg Hamann pointed out this semiotic interrelationship between language and money in the late 18th century with a clarity that remains striking even today:

> Money and language are two things whose investigation is as deep and abstract as their use is common. Both are more closely related than one would expect. The theory of the one explains the theory of the other.[6]

Obviously, Hamann has in mind neither the language as such, nor the only spoken language idiom, but the written language as a system of signs. Taking into account the medial and semiotic considerations proposed by Marshall McLuhan, Niklas Luhmann and Jacques Derrida,[7] Hamann's idea about money and language can be concretized in four moments of convergence: a) in contrast to oral communication and trade as primary exchange of goods, money and the written word operate as abstract, arbitrary and material signs; their function of signifying immaterial semantic and economic values can only be produced within a defined closed language or monetary system. Relating the absent to the present, money and the written word as symbolic signs make social communication observable and produce new options of decision and praxis. That means that the written word, being no longer under the social control of an oral situation, proves to be a powerful instrument for cultural self-observation and also for fictional projections of the self. In precisely in the same way, money motivates and stimulates processes of material production, consumption and speculation. b) Money and writing, especially typography, increase procedures of generalization. The book supports the process of establishing common linguistic standards as well as common topics and notions. When books circulate as commodities, this generalization is essentially connected to the criteria of information value and originality. Similarly, "money makes the world go round", when in monetary space human skills, material goods, social functions and communication become commensurable and exchangeable. Both typography and writing and money generalize their effects in time and space. Yet

---

6 "Das Geld und die Sprache sind zween Gegenstände, deren Untersuchung so tiefsinnig und abstrakt, als ihr Gebrauch allgemein ist. Beyde stehen in einer näheren Verwandtschaft, als man muthmassen sollte. Die Theorie des einen erklärt die Theorie des anderen." Hamann, Johann Georg (1762, 1967) *Schriften zur Sprache. Einleitung und Anmerkungen von Josef Simon.* Frankfurt a. M.: 97. On the "close relationship" between money and language from the perspective of a history of semiotics, see: Rotman, Brian (1987) *Signifying Nothing. The Semiotics of Zero.* Stanford; also Shell, Marc (1978) *The Economy of Literature.* Baltimore.

7 McLuhan, Marshall (1964) *Understanding Media. The Extensions of Man.* New York, Toronto, London: 131-144 ("The Money: The Poor Man's Credit Card"); on money as a medium of a "symbolically generalizing communication", see Luhmann, Niklas (1997) *Die Gesellschaft der Gesellschaft.* Frankfurt a. M.: 347-351; see also Derrida's critiques of Marcel Mauss Essay *Le don* (1925) from the standpoint of semiotics: Derrida, Jacques (1992) *Given Time: I. Counterfeit Money.* Chicago, London.

time and space themselves now also appear calculable within rational procedures. c) Money and writing function as media of differentiation, forcing and perpetuating distinctions. They both distinguish between the human and the artificial, the spiritual and the material, past and present, present and future, between mental procedure and action, fiction and reality, between to have and to have not. Last but not least, they both function as media separating the common and the individual. d) This dimension of individualization is one of the leitmotifs in Georg Simmel's *Philosophy of Money*. Both money and writing function as media preconditions for all experiences and all concepts of individualization. While writing and typography transform language into an instrument of analytical self-reflection, introspection and speculation, money in the same way constitutes "spheres of inner experience" ("Sphären des Innerlichen")[8] by producing wishes and promising satisfaction and fulfillment.

This "close relationship" between language and money was complemented in most remarkable fashion by Ferdinand de Saussure's *Cours de linguistique générale* in the early 20th century. Here Saussure points out the similarity between structural, synchronic linguistics and monetary economic theory. Comparing the linguistic system (*langue*) with a system of currency, Saussure opens up a new perspective with the term "semantic value", which appears as a result of the inner functional structure of a language. Taking this seriously, one can say that literature and other aesthetic productions do not deal with linguistic meanings, but with these untranslatable "semantic values". Saussure also discovers the same diabolic double structure that Aristotle analyzed within the economic system in the space of the *polis*, inside language itself. In its communicational and performative dimension, language appears as a presupposition of the social; in this context Saussure uses the term *parole*. At the same time, language functions as a systemic entity (*langue*) working out procedures of abstraction, which – very similarly to the circulation of monetary signs – initiates a transformation of all communicational qualities in an endless process of fictionalization, especially increasing under the condition of literacy and typography, when language itself begins to circulate on the market as an economic object. In this perspective, "cultures of economy" appear as a mechanism based on the inner structure of language itself and manifesting itself in every moment when language is used. In this inner structure, opposing categories like individualization and the collective, abstraction and concretization, time and

---

8 Simmel, Georg (1900, 1989) *Philosophie des Geldes*. Frankfurt a. M.; on Simmel's *Philosophy of Money*, see Kintzele, Jeff/Schneider, Peter (eds., 1993) *Georg Simmels Philosophie des Geldes*. Frankfurt a. M.; on money and individualization in a historical perspective (mostly based on German literature), see: Breithaupt, Fritz (2008) *Der Ich-Effekt des Geldes. Zur Geschichte einer Legitimitätsfigur*. Frankfurt a. M.

space, quantification and quality, operate simultaneously excluding and mutually presupposing each other.

3. Calculating political, national und ideological identities

If we take into account this "close relationship" between money and language, then political, national and ideological identities prove to be results of a double calculation – both semantic and economic, linguistic and monetary.

Insofar as a monetary system cannot operate without confidence, trust and faith in a common semiotic and symbolic idea all participants in its economic procedures must share and foster, currency is able to create homogenous spaces of exchange not only of goods, but also of a common idea of value.[9] This common idea makes money function as a (self-) representation of political spaces, institutions and protagonists; in this way, political entities secure the currency system and always profit from it at the same time. This is quite evident on coins and paper money, where numbers as quantifying signs of value have been combined with portraits, pictures, symbols, emblems, words or text ever since they were invented. The stories they tell about political spaces and identities can be traced from Greek and Roman Antiquity to the present day. Such a common currency as an expression of a homologous political space can be found in the Mongolian Empire and its paper money of the Kublai Khan era (1260-1294), whose stability and value resistance is described by Marco Polo.[10] In a similar way, in the Ottoman Empire political power and integrity were affirmed by the currency *Akçe*, established under Orhan I in the 14th and remaining valid until the 17th century. In the last phase of its existence, in 1867 the Austria-Hungary Empire also decided to strengthen its political identity with the common currency of the *Gulden*. The *Rubl* dominated the Eurasian political space of the Russian Empire and even the USSR. Corresponding to this, the *Dinar* confirmed the first consolidation of Yugoslavia as a political entity under Serbian King Peter I. and even its political socialistic renewal after 1945 under Josip Broz Tito. The US Dollar, as the key global currency between 1945 and 1973, can be seen as a manifestation of political power and space. A very recent and evident example of creating political power space by currencies is the European Union proclaiming the supranational *Euro* as an integral part and a hypostasis of the idea of European political integration.

---

9 This "common value" is also a leading concept in Georg Simmel's *Philosophy of Money*.
10 See : Moule, Arthur Christopher/Pelliot, Paul (2011) *Marco Polo, Le devisement du monde. Le livre des merveilles*. Paris : 246-249.

In a different way, money promotes the creation of national identities.[11] While the integration of political identity via currency includes a contract-based idea of state entities, national identity has an essential linguistic component. As demonstrated by Marshall McLuhan and Benedict Anderson,[12] national identities (as a substance for policy-making) refer to language spaces homogenized by mass media, especially print media. Post-socialist countries in particular provide us with many examples of how the rebuilding of national(istic) identities is based on a strategic coincidence of language and currency politics: for instance, in Ukraine, where the reinvention of Ukrainian as the official state language came along with the change of currency from the Russian *Rubl* to the *Hrywnja*, alluding to a unit of value used in the Kievan Rus' in the 11th century, or in Kazakhstan, where the promotion of Kazakh as the official language coincides with the introduction of the currency *Tenge*, a Turkic word etymologically referring to "te", meaning balance or being equal.[13] We observe very similar forms of nation-building by coincident reforms of language and currency in the regions of post-Socialist Yugoslavia. While Serbia self-consciously remains in the Yugoslav tradition and has no reason to change its language and currency politics,[14] in Slovenia the declaration of independence of 1991 was immediately followed by a confirmation of Slovenian as the only and exclusive official language (in contrast to the former two languages Serbo-Croat and Slovenian) and by the change from the Yugoslav *Dinar* to the *Tolar*. It took its name from the German silver coin *Thaler*, which circulated in Western European regions until the late 19th century. By choosing the German word *Tolar*, the national Slovenian identity is defined and communicated as a common value in contrast to the other South Slavic language cultures.[15] Similarly, the national identity of Macedonia was

---

11 See Pointon, Marcia (1998) Money and nationalism. In: Cubitt, Geoffrey (ed.), *Imagining Nations*. Manchester: 229-254; Unwin, Tim/Hewitt, Virginia (2001) Banknotes and National Identity in Central and Eastern Europe. In: *Political Geography* 20: 1005-1028; Hymans, Jacques E. C. (2004) The Changing Color of Money: European Currency Iconography and Collective Identity. In: *European Journal of International Relations* 10/1: 5-31.

12 Benedict Anderson, (1983) *Imagined Communities: Reflection on the Origin and Spread Nationalism*. London, New York; McLuhan, Marshall (1964) *Understanding Media. The Extensions of Man*. New York, Toronto, London: 170-178 ("The Printed Word: Architect of Nationalism").

13 It is interesting to note that the Russian noun for money *den'gi* is taken from the Mongolian *tenge*.

14 On this Serbian identification with the Dinar see: Živančević-Sekeruš, Ivana (2012) Banknote Imagery of Serbia. In: Zimmermann, Tanja (ed.), *Balkan Memories. Media Constructions of National and Transnational History*. Bielefeld: 41-48.

15 A remarkable study in this context is a monograph on the history of the Slovenian language that appeared as early as 1989, published and supported by the Slovenian Academy of Science. It attempts to argue against the Slavic origin of the Slovenians and prove they originated from the Adriatic Veneti: Bor, Matej/Šavli, Jožko/Tomažič, Ivan (1989) *Veneti. Naši davni predniki*. Ljubljana, Vienna.

confirmed both by establishing the Macedonian language as the exclusive official language and by changing to the *Denar*, which refers to the Old Roman *Denarius*. In contrast to Slovenia and Macedonia, Croatia proclaimed its national identity by returning to Slavic traditions and choosing the medieval unit of value *Kuna* as the name for the new currency. It also pursued a strict language policy which tried to mark the difference to the modern, common Yugoslav Serbo-Croat idiom by archaizing the lexical structure with old or common Slavic expressions. In a polemical turn against the political role of Serbia in the history of the 19th and 20th century, Croatia seems to insist on a (newly invented) cultural primacy in the South Slavic region through its currency and language. Significantly, Montenegro, Bosnia and Herzegovina and Kosovo did not manage to develop a consistent language policy or their own currency. They went from the Yugoslavian *Dinar* to the European *Euro*, or to the *Euro*-based *Convertible Mark* in Bosnia and Herzegovina. The degree to which currency has symbolic power to create and strengthen language-based national identities can also be seen in the recent discussions in the European Union, where national, nationalistic and populistic challenges to the EU in Germany, Greece, France or Italy come along with demands to return to the former national currencies.

While political and national identities are endued with a symbolic and semiotic relation to money, ideologies include a substantial relationship to the economic sphere. Taking into account that ideologies deal with the pragmatics of selected knowledge and have to balance between individualization and the collective,[16] they can be separated into two categories which are based on different economic options. The first type of ideologies focuses on and proclaims the personal self as a protagonist to produce common welfare, consequently including the category of individual property and ownership and confirming the monetary effects of individualization and differentiation. The second type of ideology is based on the communitarian dimension as the telos of human society and the horizon for the individual. This type is related to the Aristotelian idea of the *oikos*, where the exchange of goods and services and the use of money is regulated by the ethos of the familial and social community. Looking back at the second half of the 20th century, we see both economic options not only as competing protagonists in the global economy and politics, but at the same time as powerful agencies for ideologizing entire spheres of knowledge and culture. This was more than obvious in the 1970s

---

16 There are many famous definitions of "ideology" and different attempts to categorize ideologies, e.g. Mannheim, Karl (1936) *Ideology and Utopia*. London; Eagleton, Terry (1991) *Ideology. An Introduction*. New York; or Hawkes, David (2003) *Ideology* (2nd ed.). London; Žižek, Slavoj (1989) *The Sublime Object of Ideology*. New York. Here, in our argumentation we refer to the Niklas Luhmann's concept of ideology based on communication theory; see: Luhmann, Niklas (1970; 1991) Wahrheit und Ideologie. Vorschläge zur Wiederaufnahme der Diskussion. In: Luhmann, Niklas (ed.) *Soziologische Aufklärung 1. Aufsätze zur Theorie sozialer Systeme*. Cologne, Opladen: 54-65.

and 80s in the Soviet Union, when after a short period of liberalization in the late 50s and early 60s the moral and collective key principle of the socialist planned economy was again and insistently extended as an ideological requirement to all parts of knowledge, science, education, culture, art and literature – as had happened in the 1930s under Stalin. We observe very similar processes of increasing ideologization of the whole cultural sphere in other Eastern and Southeastern socialist countries, which were part of the *Council for Mutual Economic Assistance*, dominated by the Soviet Union.[17] The situation in the Socialist Federal Republic of Yugoslavia was slightly different. It shifted away from the Soviet planned economy towards the concept of a socialist market and in the early 1950s the institution of workers' self-management was introduced, leading to competition not only between different industrial enterprises, but also between the regional economies of the republics. In this way, it undermined the socialist ideology of brotherhood and unity[18] and fostered national ideologies. The political breakdown and the following explosion of robbery capitalism of the 1990s made evident to what extent the Soviet and other socialist ideologies of collectivism persistently tried to suppress the individualizing effects of money. Precisely this suppressed dimension was called to mind by two of the first post-Soviet entrepreneurs, Leonid Nevzlin and Mikhail Khodorkovsky, and their programmatic book *The Man with the Rubl (Čelovek s rublem)* of 1992. In its critique of the Soviet collective ideology, the book proclaimed the opposite neoliberal ideology by expanding money to an existential and philosophical principle. Thus, Nevzlin's and Khodorkovsky's book corresponds with the ideological process of financialization and mathematization, not only of the economic sphere but of culture as a whole.

The cultural turn in economic theory as a reaction to the transition process in Eastern Europe in the 90s and to the financial crises of 2007 and the following years can be considered as an attempt to deconstruct neoliberalism as an ideology which not only dominates the economic sphere but also subordinates politics, education, culture, science and research under an econometric, quantifying logic and which categorizes regions, local places and public infrastructures as spaces

---

17 We also find an analogue mechanism politically enforced by the USA after WW II to permeate the sphere of cultural production by capitalist economics in Western Europe. One of the most remarkable attempts was the initiative of American economists to reform the European education systems. The agreement of European countries signed in Bologna in 1999, intended to unify the different national university systems through the so-called Bologna Process, appears to be a consequence of this American initiative from the 1950s.

18 On the media history of "brotherhood" in East European socialist and post-socialist countries, see: Zimmermann, Tanja (2014) Brüderlichkeit und Bruderzwist. Mediale Inszenierungen des Aufbaus und des Niedergangs politischer Gemeinschaften in Ost- und Südosteuropa. Göttingen.

for financial investments systematically excluding the point of view of human and social necessities.[19]

4. Religion and economy

In the world of the monotheistic, book-based religions, the semiotic convergence between language and money appears as a tricky but serious obstacle to achieving the essential religious task of transcendence, i.e. to overcome individual and material needs, their exchange and satisfaction and to escape from the mechanism which prevails in the economic sphere and which is driven by money signs.[20] Through their theological (and pragmatic) reflections, religions discover in their inner media constitution a semiotic-economic element which they had to eliminate from the point of transcendence. Book-based religions try to manage this semiotic self-purification on two levels, different religions and confessions choosing different ways. One can even presuppose that essential differences between various religions consist in the manner in which every religion solves its key semiotic questions and how religions thereby become involved in history and define their relation to the economic sphere. The first level directly concerns language, i.e. the material, graphic language signs, the second the text with its motifs and topics. Simultaneously, on every level there is the task of incorporating the (holy) text, its sense, in life, either in institutional forms, or in strategies of personal behavior.

---

19 These processes of financialization, economization and mathematization are analysed in Crouch, Colin (2004) *Post-Democracy*. Cambridge; and Crouch, Colin (2015) *The Knowledge Corrupters. Hidden Consequences of the Financial Takeover of Public Life*. Cambridge.

20 From an epistemological perspective, Niklas Luhmann provides a common and wide-ranging definition of religion: "Religion is immediately related to the peculiarities of the beholder. Any observation must distinguish in order to define something and demarcates an 'unmarked space' into which the final horizon of the world retreats. The transcendence which thereby accompanies all things that are ascertainable is relocated with every attempt to cross the boundary with new distinctions and denominations. It is always present as the opposite side of all ascertainable things, without ever being attainable. And precisely this unattainability 'binds' the beholder, who himself evades observation, to what he can observe. The reconnection of the undefinable with the definable is – regardless in which cultural formation – 'religio' in the broadest sense" (Niklas Luhmann, *Die Gesellschaft der Gesellschaften*, 232). This definition takes a remarkable turn of high analytical relevance from a media theory perspective and indicates the foundation of religion in writing: because only the materialization of acoustic language by graphic signs makes it possible to distinguish between sign and meaning, signifiant and signifié. This is the *condition sine qua non* to bring in motion the mutual mechanism of rational differentiation, on the one hand, resulting in the progression of "religio", i.e. relation to a transcendental sphere, on the other.

Like the analytical and technological dimensions of material language signs, i.e. how the written language transfers the production and exchange of meaning into the profane inner world sphere, every religion has to develop – on the first level – strategies to overcome this tendency towards profanation. We find this strategy in specific forms and rituals of oral teaching in all religions, in the comprehension and communication of religious meaning – reading and repeating aloud. This can be especially observed in Judaism and Islam, but also in Christianity, foremost in the Orthodox confession. At the same time, every religion elaborates pragmatics to overcome the materiality of written language. In Judaism this is carried out by the mystic and occult doctrine of the Kabbala, where the alphabet system and the combination of graphic signs are used to produce religious, transcendental, secret meanings. In Islam this function is taken over by calligraphy as a holy handcraft, which serves to transform the abstract, economic written signification into an aesthetic, i.e. corporal and sensitive, communion with the holy sphere. Islamic calligraphy thus discovers and makes evident the sacred meaning which is hidden behind the materiality of the graphic signs. Different strategies to overcome the materiality of the written word are used in Christian religions. On the one hand, a philosophical attitude towards the written form of the holy texts and the theory of the four meanings of scripture (*quatuor sensus scripture*) are developed here (under the influence of the Greek philosophical tradition such as in Augustine). On the other hand, in Eastern Orthodox Christianity, where the alphabetization of the Slavs directly coincided with Christianization, the written language obtains a holy status. In terms of its concept, the Church Slavonic language therefore does not allow any philological and grammatical treatment and reflection. That is the reason for the diglossic language situation in the Orthodox region, where the profane everyday language remained excluded from alphabetization for a long time, in Serbia until the reform initiative of Vuk Karadžić. From the perspective of Orthodoxy, reading and writing the Church Slavonic language are liturgical procedures requiring special mental and moral preparation.

The second level concerns the question as to how economic topics and the motif of money operate in the texts of Judaism, Islam and Christianity. First of all, we see that in all religious systems – like the written language form – money signs also prove to be problematic and ambivalent. On the one hand, money destroys prospects of transcendental grace by involving men in procedures of exchange of inner world necessities. On the other hand, it is impossible to get rid of money as a medium when goods and labor circulate. All religions and confessions more or less work with the semiotic function of money as a substitute for the concrete. However, in a certain moment of historical development they all articulate a strict veto when money itself appears as an instrument of acquisition and exchange in credit trading based on interest rates – as was already discussed and rejected by Aristotle. The significant nuance in this common religious prohibition is that in

Judaism this concerns only the Jewish community, but does not prohibit money trading with non-Jewish partners. This nuance stimulates the circumstance that, beginning in the early Middle Ages, the Jews found themselves in the role of the main national and international protagonists engaged in money and credit trading and banking. In this way, a tradition was established which continued to exist even when the religious prohibition of interest rates was later resolved by government-regulated credit markets.

In a closer and more detailed perspective, Judaism, Islam and Christianity show many differences in the way their texts handle economic topics. Judaism and Islam are explicitly concerned in their dogmatic teaching with economic – or, more precisely, anti-economic – issues and articulate prescriptions on how to overcome the secular and rational economy by an inverted practice of charity and gifts. These prescriptions as religious obligations to charity operate in Judaism and Islam in a manner analyzed by the French ethnologist Marcel Mauss in his book *The Gift* (1926), where the gift economy in primary societies is described as a "total exchange" involving both material goods and the spiritual personality of their participants.

In the Jewish tradition, the gift economy results first of all from the concept of justice as *tzedakah*, a religious obligation to give charity regardless of one's economic capacity. Since the Middle Ages and Maimonides' *Laws about Giving to Poor People* (in *Mishneh Torah*, 1170-1180), where donating anonymously to unknown recipients is one of the highest forms of religious charity, the *tzedakah* has functioned as a religious institution of the gift economy within the Jewish communities on a local, regional or even international level. It fostered social and cultural cohesion as well as economic solidarity among the Jewish population, especially during the catastrophes of the 19th and 20th centuries. To this day, *tzedakah* plays a significant role to the extent that some well-known NGOs are based on Maimonides' *Laws about Giving to Poor People*.

In Islam and its dogmatic teachings, we find two institutional forms in which religion and economy interrelate via a juridically based exchange of charity inside the secular economic world: *zakāt* and *waqf*. One of the "five pillars" of Islam, i.e. one of the five basic prescriptions a Muslim has to fulfill in his life, constitutes an economic issue insofar as this *zakāt* demands the interruption and transcendence of economic activities and interests. Similar to the Jewish *tzedakah*, the *zakāt* is a juridical institution defined by religious scholars which obligates every Muslim qualified as rich to contribute alms to the poor, whom at the same time *zakāt* gives the right to receive charity. This way, the religious *zakāt* institutionalizes an exchange of gifts and charity compensating the material and social effects of the economic mechanism (*zakāt* differs significantly from Jewish *tzedakah* in this regard). The Islamic institution of *waqf* is related to *zakat* and is also based on the gift economy. *Waqf* is a foundation which is set up by a personal and private donor, or even by the sultan, to fulfill a public purpose as stipulated by the Quran and which has to be registered by Islamic law. The institution of *waqf* is conceptualized as a mortmain and inalienable property whose owner is assumed to be God himself, who takes care of its administration. The purposes of the *waqf* are widespread – mosques, *madrassa* schools, Sufi convention (*khanqah* or *tekije*), but also hospitals, feeding of the poor and help for the pilgrims in Mecca and Medina or infrastructure projects like mills, soil irrigation and public fountains. Even after the end of the Ottoman Empire, *waqf* under the local name of *vakuf* continued to exist in the Balkans as juridical institutions until they were closed by Socialist Yugoslavia after 1945.

In Christianity, such religiously and juridically based obligations for a gift economy do not exist. Instead, Christianity discusses the problem of economy and money in its narratives of the New Testament. The key plot here is the betrayal by Judas, who sells out Christ to the Roman soldiers for 30 silver coins. The story is told in the Gospel according to Matthew (26, 14-16; 27, 3-10), Mark (14, 10) and Luke (22, 1-6). The point in this plot is that money, on the one hand, features as the main medium to fulfill the predicted and prophesied fate of Jesus Christ. Without money, this basic episode underpinning the holy history of salvation would not have happened. *Symbolically*, money relates the sphere of human weakness, represented by Judas, with the holy history of Christ the Redeemer. On the other hand, money evidently is evil, destroying confidence and solidarity between the disciples-apostles. In the strict sense of the word, money is a *diabolic*, i.e. separating medium. This way, Judas appears as a victim of this dissecting energy of money and as a tragic antihero, as is finally confirmed by his suicide, as told by Matthew (27, 5). Thus, here and in other episodes of the New Testament money is both an indispensable medium for the holy history of salvation and rejected as a diabolic, dissecting force. This ambiguity of money is treated in different ways in different confessional traditions of Christianity. Due to the semiotic approach to the Holy, the western – Catholic and Protestant – tradition outlines the symbolic function of money. From this point of view, sin and salvation coexist. In the Eastern Orthodox tradition, which is dominated by a liturgical orientation towards the sacred text, money is understood in terms of its diabolic function dissecting the human community and cutting off the prospects of salvation.

Mainly based on Christ's passion as revealed in the New Testament, Christianity develops modes of ascetic behavior which also imply specific economic strategies and even lead to institutionalized forms of dealing with economy within the religious claim of transcendence – very much like Jewish and Islamic asceticism.[21]

---

21 Inspired by Buddhism and Hinduism and Greek philosophy, all main book-based religions – Judaism, Islam and Christianity – have elaborated forms of asceticism as an integrative element of performing the Holy in the world of economic interests. Disrupting the logic of economic exchange, asceticism is disposed to provoking altruistic reactions and goes along with estab-

From the very beginnings of Christianity – which reacts to political circumstances, above all the fall of the Roman Empire – the powerful movements of monastic asceticism developed an intrinsic dynamic of cohesion and organization among their protagonists, leading to institutionalization in the form of monasteries. The organization of labor and activities by ascetic rules and orders which all monks have to share enabled the monasteries to act outwardly not only as spiritual, but also as economic and even political entities. This way, a mechanism of mutual legitimation of secular immanence and religious transcendence was installed: the economic (and political) success of the monastery (and also of the Church as a whole) confirmed its spiritual, religious and ethical authority, which – *vice versa* – sanctified and authorized its profane affairs. This is the paradigmatic situation which time and again provoked renewals of the monastic movement with its ideal of poverty. The most prominent and consequential of these is Francis of Assisi and his reformation of the monastic ethos, which includes proclamation of a Christian mission and an initiative for gift economy – to support people by practical means such as education and medical and economic aid. In this respect, the Franciscans played an important role in the Balkans, especially in the region of Bosnia and Herzegovina. They repeatedly came into conflict with the political institutions not only of the Ottoman Empire, but also the Vatican and later the Socialist Yugoslav authorities, where the Franciscans' ideal of poverty and their gift economy may have been perceived as rivaling the Socialist collective ideology. The cultural role of the Franciscans in

---

lishing anti-economies of gift and charity. Thus, asceticism not only remains in contact with the profane economic world it tries to overcome, but always establishes a specific relationship between calculated, rational economy and anti-economies of the gift (Durkheim). The modes in which asceticism subverts economy differ across the religions and confessions that are relevant in the cultural space of South-Eastern Europe – Judaism, Islam, Catholic, Protestant and Orthodox Christianity. In Judaism – because of the juridical relationship to God installed by the *Tora* – asceticism is partly an individual, but first of all a collective practice to support plees and prayers articulated in the dialog with God and to moderate divine retribution. In the context of the ideas of exile and of salvation as a historical inner world option, Jewish asceticism has a strong collective component and normally does not mean separation from society. In Islam, asceticism has been developed since the 9th century as the mystic movement of Sufism with the aim to overcome all profane desires. Significant aspects are its gnostic and arcane components. Their orders and conventions are sponsored by gifts and mainly by *waqf*. Their protagonists, the dervishes – meaning "beggars" in Persian – perform their experience of transcendence on holy dates and religious festivities via poetic texts, music and body practices (*semā*). Thus, dervishes in some way aesthetically react to the surrounding profane world with its economic, political and also religious rational and discursive order. There are moments of ambivalence and nonconformism that have accompanied the Sufi movement and their dervishes through history. In Socialist Yugoslavia, the dervish as an emblematic figure was remembered in Meša Selimović's novel *Death and the Dervish* (*Derviš i smrt*, 1966), which was read as an allegory of aesthetic resistance to the political and economic order of Socialist Yugoslavia.

Bosnia is impressively described in the novels and stories of Ivo Andrić.[22] The mutual legitimation of religious transcendence and economic (and political) power by the institution of the monasteries (and the Catholic Church as a whole) was also the target of the Reformation in the 16th century. As Max Weber has shown in his famous *The Protestant Ethic and the Spirit of Capitalism* (*Die protestantische Ethik and der Geist des Kapitalismus*, 1904-1920), the various Protestant movements (among them Calvinists, Lutherans, Pietists and Baptists) replaced the institutionalized procedures of religion with a personalization of religious faith facilitated by individual Bible reading and comprehension. This was followed by an ethic of secular "inner world asceticism", in which individual economic success is motivated and legitimized by religious transcendence. This "inner world asceticism" constitutes the basic mental and pragmatic disposition which initiated the capitalistic dynamic of future-oriented and transcendently legitimized profit-making and thereby opened up a new epoch of strategic organized capitalism.[23] In this perspective, to this day, especially in the North American milieus of Baptists, Presbyterians and Mennonites, economic success may indicate individual pretensions to spiritual redemption. This mutual institutional legitimation of religious transcendence and economy works in a different manner in Eastern Orthodox Christianity, where the asceticism of the monastic tradition is not essentially based on a philological, rational and semiotic treatment of the holy texts. Here the emphasis lies on the mystical praxis of an *imitatio Christi* and a simulation of the corporal passion of Jesus as a therapy for profane desires. The famous monastic prescription of the Order of Saint Benedict *ora et labora*, which made the organization of asceticism within monasteries as economic and political institutions possible, is turned to contemplative *ora in passionem* in the Eastern Orthodox tradition. Hence Orthodox monasteries (and the Church as a whole) establish and confirm their spiritual authority by the resoluteness with which they reject all forms of profane economic calculation.[24] The consequence of this strategic rejection of economic calculation was a specific form of gift exchange: the monastery (and the Church) as a religious institution offers spiritual goods by commenting on and interpreting the profane political and economic sphere, whose protagonists gratefully respond by supporting the religious institution with material goods. This division of labor and mutual dependence is the reason why the Orthodox Church did not develop autonomous social teaching

---

22 This is known as the Franciscansstories cycle, containing stories like *U zindanu, U musafirhani, Kod kazana, Ispovijed, Napast* or *Čaša* and the famous novel *Prokleta avlija*.
23 On "inner world ascetism" see: Weber, Max (1921; 1972) *Wirtschaft und Gesellschaft*. Tübingen: 329.
24 For more details on economics in Orthodox monasteries, see: Murašov, Jurij (2004) Irdischer Sinnmangel und göttliche Ökonomie. Wirtschaft, Schrift und Ethik in orthodoxen Heiligenviten. In: Guski, Andreas/Schmidt, Ulrich (eds.), *Literatur und Kommerz im Russland des 19. Jahrhunderts. Institutionen, Akteure, Symbole*. Zurich: 293-328.

like the Catholic and Protestant churches did in the 19th century and why from its very beginnings to the present day it has displayed a remarkable affinity to apologizing for economic and political power and structures and to giving absolution to their protagonists. Accordingly, within the Orthodox spiritual tradition all those who dare to critique secular economic and political power always tend towards religious heresy. A recent, instructive example of such corrupt cooperation between the Orthodox Church and neoliberal oligarchic and political power is Andrey Zvyagintsev's film *Leviathan* of 2014.

5. Aesthetics and money

Literature, art, cinema, i.e. aesthetic productions in general, are involved in a double relationship with the economic sphere. The first is extrinsic insofar as the aesthetic productions function as objects, as commodities of exchange and especially of the money-based market. This extrinsic relationship is well reflected in a poem by Alexander Pushkin, "The Conversation of the Bookseller with the Poet" (1825). The second relationship is an intrinsic one and consists of economic topics and motifs which are represented and developed by narration or by pictorial compositions. Like love, economy and money are the most significant catalyst for the plot. Great novels of the capitalistic 19th and 20th centuries like Fyodor Dostoevsky's *Poor Folk* (1846), Émile Zola's *Money* (1890/91) or Ivo Andrić *Gospođica* (1945) cannot be imagined without the motif of money. At the same time, these inner relationships between literature or any aesthetic production with the economic sphere have a remarkable formal component. This is the self-referential, semiotic orientation of the text or of an artistic or cinematic object, which results from their aesthetic function. This function, by which the question of *what* is represented, is shifted to the question of *how* it is presented, informs us how the aesthetic representation is related to the basic medium of sense-making, i.e. to language and to its structural and semiotic options as written, visual or oral, acoustic language. Working with this deeply language-based dualism of visuality and acoustics, literature, art and film tell us more by their aesthetic form than discourses do, which deal pragmatically with issues such as love, religion, law, science and economy. In a fundamental way, aesthetic productions make sense for the cultural horizon of human communities and societies by bringing to the surface of representation those semiotic and media mechanisms which function in the depth of the discourses and which must be excluded from observation and questioning here for pragmatic reasons.

In this way, aesthetic productions are not only deeply involved in the economic sphere, but can also serve as outstanding objects which may focus our view on the inner semiotic structures of economic procedures and thereby make us sufficiently sensitive to observe and analyze the cultural foundation of economy.

What aesthetic productions tell us about the semiotics of economy and about the "close relationship" between language and money can be illustrated by a rather famous work of art – Quinten Massys' picture *The Money Changer and His Wife* of 1514 (see fig. 1).[25]

Fig. 1 *The Money Changer and His Wife*, Quinten Massys (1514).

At first glance, Massys' picture confirms Max Weber's concept of *Protestant Ethics and the Spirit of Capitalism*, written about five hundred years later, in the early 20th century. The picture shows an interplay of language signs and money. Its composition is based on a well-calculated choreography of visual gestures leading from the written words in the holy book on the far right-hand side of the depicted table to the illustration of the Virgin Mary with her Son and from there, following the gaze of the wife dressed in red turning her attention away from the book, towards the

---

25 There have been many commentaries and much research on Quinten Massys' *The Money Changer and His Wife*. For art and economics in Massys' picture, see: Widemann, Reinold (2018) *Artists' Conceptions of Money: Money Art and Artificial Money*. Soesterberg.

money her husband is handling. The mental concentration of the money changer indicated by his lowered eyelids makes us focus on that green-colored and diffuse part of the table where the money changer is doing his job. At second glance, we discover the filigree scales testing the coins, whose inner and abstract value is approved by the well-balanced scales. The equilibration of money signs and the concrete physical weight on the one part of the table corresponds with the equilibration of graphic signs and the figurative illustration in the book. The very similar gestures of the hands operating with book and scales underline this correspondence. In our argumentation, Massys' picture performs the semiotic similarities of money and graphic signs in order to make us trust in the abstractions of both economic and graphic signs and belief in the spirit of the money and the book.

Massys' *The Money Changer and His Wife* illustrates the cultural foundation of capitalism and demonstrates the historical conditions of the semiotic mechanism, which produces the capitalist concept on the basis of a specific perception of written language and on the basis of a strict convergence of language and money. However, with regard to the evolution of language concepts and pragmatics fostered by communication technologies as it happened and still happens in the ages of typography, radio and television and in the present digital age, it also makes evident that this capitalist concept must be bound and limited to a defined historical segment and only to certain geographic regions.

6. Topics and theses

The spotlight on empirical constellations of "cultures of economy" in the regions of Yugoslavia covers four different fields – historiography, art, literature and visual media (film and theatre).

The field of historiography is explored by Jelena Rafailović's historical overview of the economic development of the Yugoslav regions. She chronologically follows the phases of subordinate (Slovenian and Croatian within the Austro-Hungarian empire), colonial (Bosnian and Herzegovinian in the same state, Macedonian in the Ottoman Empire), and independent (Serbian and Montenegran) political status. The second part of the article is dedicated to the economy of the Kingdom of Yugoslavia, a country that emerged from the process of unification after WWI. She meticulously studies the three economic sectors – agricultural, industrial and financial – to draw conclusions about the uneven development of the parts of Yugoslavia as well as necessary factors behind the construction of economic growth (particularly foreign investments). Rafailović stresses structural and infrastructural problems as the main obstacle for sustainable economic development – which did not change in the united Yugoslavia either.

Delayed economic development is also a leitmotif in Dubravka Stojanović's article dealing with *zadruga*, a very specific form of economic organization in agricultural Serbia which has attracted great interest in left as well as right-wing political circles. Stojanović begins with the historical fact that even in the time of the socialist Svetozar Marković *zadruga* was already an obsolete form of agricultural cooperative. In Marković's view it features as a utopian organization derived from the patriarchal structure of Serbian society but is capable of its reorganization. Quite different is the ideology of the Serbian Radical Party, which tries to establish *zadruga* as a conservative unit of agrarian (and economic) community. After WWI, *zadruga* appears in the discourse of the far right as the foundation of the popular state. In this part of political spectrum, *zadruga* is seen not as an economic but as an ideological factor. On the economic side, it was perceived as an autochthonous Serbian alternative to capitalism. In this way, it contradicts Western traditions and is close to Russian economic ideas of the "peculiar expression of Slavic civilization". As a social ideal, *zadruga* encompasses egalitarianism, collectivism and anti-individualism. In all of these senses, *zadruga* encompasses the similarities between popular socialism and far-right ideologies in Serbian society.

The later very specific form of socialist organization of labor and economy, the system of self-management and its structural problems, is analyzed and discussed by Aleksandar Jakir and Anita Lunić. The two authors detect in the system of self-management the nucleus of conflict between political and productive entities which defined the crisis of Yugoslav society until the early 90s. Still one more, extremely important component of this conflict is to be sought in the increasingly intensive relationship of those elites to the national core of decentralized society. This aporia inscribed in the system of self-management itself can be identified as one of the main reasons for the disintegration of Yugoslavia. The authors contend that it cannot be denied that the system of self-management was economically successful too in some areas. It brought some sort of market economy, at least partially freed the financial sector, or decentralized the economy. However, this decentralization itself was one of the main reasons for the (political) failure of the Yugoslav experiment. In the context of crisis, the authors concentrate on strikes, which they see as an illicit way of drawing attention to economic mismanagement.

The moral component of the socialist economy and especially the moral status of labor in youth brigades form the focus of Reana Senjković's article. Beginning with a novel by Pero Zlatar (1978), whose hero is the authentic figure of ticket scalper Vimpi, and a sociological study by Rudi Supek (1963), which was the source for Zlatar's novel, she poses the important question as to whether volunteer work was an economic, political or ideological component of Yugoslav social society. To solve this problem, she chooses the specific case of young delinquents sent to youth brigades – for correction on the one hand but also to create social consciousness on the other. It is indicative that the renewal of the federal Youth Work Actions coincided with the stronger introduction of the self-management economy in 1958. She further compares adolescent delinquency in East and West and concludes that stereotypes of rebels with and without a cause are not valid. Labor was used as a method of correction in both political and economic systems.

Three articles demonstrate how art production in a very wide scope spanning religious icons, painting and architecture becomes involved in different economic processes. A miracle-working icon from the monastery of Peć is the main protagonist in Ivana Ženarju's article. This icon also appears as a powerful instrument for the economic prosperity of the monastery due to pilgrimages to visit icons, a well-known phenomenon in Orthodoxy. The monastery earned money due to donations from believers, who placed it directly on the icon. A concrete example of this very worldly handling of the icon could be observed in times when the monastery was experiencing economic crisis, caused by the huge debt on the one hand and monasteries' inability to collect debts on the other. During a "holy expedition", the icon visited diverse places in Kosovo and enough money was collected to pay off the debts. This touring of sacrificial objects, and the possibility for the believers to come into direct contact with them, was a successful practice supporting the sometimes frail economy of the monasteries – a strange symbiosis of art, religion, and economy.

Renata Komić Marn takes another side of the relationship between art and economy into account. Her article focuses on the existential and financial situation of the Slovenian impressionist painter Ivan Grohar, who met with some approval from critics but did not have any success in selling his pictures and subsequently died in poverty. This is where the actual story begins, as told by Renata Komić Marn. She almost tells a detective story in which she tries to dismantle the relationship between the painter and the rich timber merchant who acted as his benefactor – but only acted! In fact, he allowed the artist to dwell at his house, without collecting rent and then, after his death, claimed the paintings to settle the debt. Komić Marn shows convincingly that the alleged beneficial help of the rich merchant for the poor artist is no more than a unpersuasive myth.

The national and economic self-representation of the state by architecture is examined by Tina Potočnik, who takes as her example the process of building the National and University Library in Ljubljana. As a national symbol, the library was built in two phases. The first started after WWI and was completed shortly before WWII. The architect was Jože Plečnik, the most renowned Slovenian architect. The second was a project of the independent Slovenian state founded after the breakup of Yugoslavia. The difference between the two projects lies in their uneven symbolic value. While the first, pre-war project contains the idea of national liberation, the second was a combination of pride in the newly won state and the necessity of obeying the laws of the liberal market. In this way it must be seen as a compromise between art and the market. Potočnik uses this premise to draw a broader conclusion on the place of architecture in the neo-liberal world.

The field of studies on literature and economy is opened by a crucial, even classical text dealing with money in Yugoslavia – Ivo Andrić's *The Woman from Sarajevo* (*Gospođica*), which Ivana Perica analyses in comparison with Balzac's *Eugénie Grandet*. She begins with the role of the miser in bourgeois society and sees him as an excessive part of the community in contrast to the usurer, who is typical of modern society. Perica first identifies the similarities between two novels: the peripheral position of the two cities in which the characters live and their apparent resemblance concerning the nature of the miser and usurer. However, the similarities appear to be superficial, while differences abound. Ultimately, Balzac's Eugènie becomes the capitalist who invests her money and Andrić's Rajka remains a prisoner of the idea of the miser who is unable to invest and remains an invaluable part of the community. In this sense, the two stories are about the successful or failed socialization of two women. Perica draws the final distinction between the two novels from their incomparable political, historical and geographic position. Eugénie Grandet had the opportunity to make a transition to modern capitalist society and seizes on it; Rajka Radaković remains a prisoner of her own position in colonial, patriarchal but not largely anti-capitalist Bosnia and later Yugoslavia. She does not accommodate to the society and remains a miser, a part of the community at the time when this very community is disappearing.

Andrea Lešić reads the novel *I, Danilo* by another Bosnian author, Derviš Sušić, as a paradigm of a literary text dealing with the economy in the system of Yugoslav socialism. Lešić begins her analysis with a critique of previous readings of the novel. The canonical interpretation sees in it a conflict between "idealistic humanity [and] dry bureaucracy". She dismisses this one-sided interpretation and shows that the protagonist Danilo balances existences as a socialist trickster and a conman who uses his power to bring progress to the background society without really gaining profit for himself. Lešić explains his final failure by placing him in the tradition of the character of the "superfluous man" in Russian realist literature. In the same way as his predecessor, he is not able to accept his counterpart – the "necessary woman" – and remains a prisoner of patriarchal society (and economy). That would not be the case if he succeeded in integrating the women into his allegedly new social construct.

Borislav Pekić's novel *Pilgrimage of Arsenije Njegovan* is interpreted by Davor Beganović as a complex narrative combining economic, juridical and literary discourse. The main theme of the novel is the transition from a peripheral rural community to capitalist society. The Njegovan family acts as a bearer of the process of urbanization of Belgrade, its transition from an Oriental town into a modern European metropolis. Arsenije, who is the town-builder and an economist with theoretical pretensions, is at the same time the loser of the next transition from the capitalist to the socialist economy. He spends the time after the war in a state of hibernation, completely excluded from every development in the country, only to wake up in the middle of the students' revolt in 1968. A déjà vu experience (he went "underground" after the demonstration against Yugoslavia's signing of a pact with the axis powers) can only bring him death. He dies, almost grotesquely, of a heart attack and never learns that his wealth is confiscated by the communists and consequently perishes. In this way, Pekić satirically describes the temporary breakdown of the capitalist economy into the socialist society.

In his article on the novel *Buick Rivera* by Miljenko Jergović, Jurij Murašov analyses the intricate structure of the Yugoslav economic mind and draws extensive conclusions comparing it to the theory of the gift developed by French anthropologist Marcel Mauss in his description of potlatch. According to Murašov, Jergović's novel is paradigmatic of the break-up of Yugoslavia, especially the economic background of its destruction. To prove this thesis, he begins with the analogies between the Yugoslav socialist economy and the specific economic mode that Mauss described with the concept of the gift. It is a phenomenon that unites diverse social dimensions. Much the same, the socialist economy is repulsed by possession and suspicious of money. Now, the two characters, the Bosnian Muslim Hasan and the Serbian Vuko, who came from the former Yugoslavia to the USA, meet and each of them, in his own way, exercises disconcertment with the rational American economy. Their uneconomic behavior can be seen in a collecting mania (Hasan) and mania for overspending (Vuko). In those two manic activities, symbolically generated and abstract entities such as money, law, love or politics lose their liability. Murašov cites Mauss, who stresses the violent potential of potlatch, again to show how the socialist economy has the same potential and to emphasize how Jergović exercises the power of this potential in the conflict between two paradigmatic proponents of that economic model. Their antagonism is metaphorically constructed as the process of destruction of Yugoslavia itself. This thesis finds its confirmation in the last scenes of the novel, when money comes into play. The cataclysm at the end of the novel denotes the defeat of Hasan's collecting and the victory of Vuko's overspending.

The book places two spotlights on economic issues in the sphere of visual media, film and theatre. In her article, Tanja Zimmermann turns to contemporary Serbia by analyzing the film *Tilva Roš* by Nikola Ležaić. She begins with an overview of the depiction of the poor in visual art from the 19th century on. Besides the common matrices of representation of the poor inherited from the realist tradition, the art dealing with them in the changed times of neoliberalism has to develop innovative approaches in order to cope with the changing conditions. One of these new approaches is tested in Ležaić's film. Drawing on Freud and Reik, Zimmermann contends that the masochistic principle is the central node of the new aesthetics of the poor. The main characters of the film seem to fulfill these preconditions. They come from a neglected environment, do not show any will for acting but passively endure the violence inflicted upon them. It is not by accident that Bor is chosen as a place of (un)action. The run-down industrial town is the symbol of the failure of the transitional economy. In particular, the youths that remained in the town are on the losing side. In order to represent their precarious situation, Ležaić uses authentic self-made videos, combining them with fictional material. Zimmermann shows how "[t]he boys work at inventing new ways of suffering and prolong their duration by repetition." Inflicting self-injuries is their strategy in the devastating fight against the consumerist economy that supplemented the industrial one of the socialist period. Miranda Jakiša deals with theatre production and explores the "economy theater" which emerged in Europe in the wake of the 2008 crisis and has remained virulent ever since. Her approach is twofold: on the one hand, there is a crisis of financing the theaters themselves, on the other hand, the financial crisis features as a topic in the plays. This situation is even more specific in the South Slavic region because of the aberrances caused by "transitional" capitalism. Jakiša chooses several exemplary plays to show how this situation is reflected in theatre: *That is not Us, it's Only Glass* by Ivana Sajko and *Workers Die Singing* by Olga Dimitrijević. Both plays are openly critical of the implementation of the doctrine of the free market economy in former socialist countries. At the same time, they do not try to offer a (revolutionary) solution to the crisis: the working conditions today do not allow for a revolution. Jakiša asks what the theater can do in changed times. She borrows from Jacques Rancière, for whom "theatre like any other art has to contour the border between the excluded and real dissent to be truly political". New theater should abolish the distance between the scene and the audience, let the audience take part in the play. That is what Sajko as well as Dimitrijević achieve in their plays, incorporating the rich experience of theater into their critique of the economy.

Bibliography

Al-Zubi, Amir/Čičak-Al-Zubi, Meliha (2005) *Hadži Šefko i hadži Mefko*. Sarajevo.
Anderson, Benedict (1983) *Imagined Communities: Reflection on the Origin and Spread Nationalism*. London, New York.
Bor, Matej/Šavli, Jožko/Tomažič, Ivan (1989) *Veneti. Naši davni predniki*. Ljubljana, Vienna.
Breithaupt, Fritz (2008) *Der Ich-Effekt des Geldes. Zur Geschichte einer Legitimitätsfigur*. Frankfurt a. M.
Crouch, Colin (2004) *Post-democracy*. Cambridge.
Crouch, Colin (2015) *The Knowledge Corrupters. Hidden Consequences of the Financial Takeover of Public Life*. Cambridge.

Derrida, Jacques (1992) *Given Time: I. Counterfeit Money*. Chicago, London.
Eagleton, Terry (1991) *Ideology. An introduction*. New York.
Graeber, David (2001) *Towards an Anthropological Theory of Value. The False Coin of Our Own Dreams*. Basingstoke.
Graeber, David (2012) *Debt – the First 5000 Years*. New York.
Hamann, Johann Georg (1762, 1967) *Schriften zur Sprache. Einleitung und Anmerkungen von Josef Simon*. Frankfurt a. M.
Hamenstädt, Ulrich (2014) *Theorien der Politischen Ökonomie im Film*. Wiesbaden.
Harten, Jürgen (2000) *Das fünfte Element – Geld oder Kunst. Ein fabelhaftes Lexikon zu einer verlorenen Enzyklopädie*. Cologne.
Hawkes, David (2003) *Ideology* (2nd ed.). London.
Huntington, Samuel Phillips (1996) *The Clash of Civilizations and the Remaking of World Order*. New York.
Hymans, Jacques E. C. (2004) The Changing Color of Money: European Currency Iconography and Collective Identity. In: *European Journal of International Relations* 10/1: 5-31.
Kintzele, Jeff/Schneider, Peter (eds., 1993) *Georg Simmels Philosophie des Geldes*. Frankfurt a. M.
Kozioł, Monika/Piekarska, Delfina/Potocka, Maria (eds., 2013) *Ekonomia w sztuce. Economics in Art. Exhibition catalogue. Museum of Contemporary Art Krakow (MOCAK)*. Krakow.
Lizardo, Omar (2007) Fight club, or the cultural contradictions of late capitalism. In: *Journal for Cultural Research* 11(3): 221-243.
Luhmann, Niklas (1970; 1991) Wahrheit und Ideologie. Vorschläge zur Wiederaufnahme der Diskussion. In: Luhmann, Niklas (ed.) *Soziologische Aufklärung 1. Aufsätze zur Theorie sozialer Systeme*. Köln, Opladen: 54-65.
Luhmann, Niklas (1997) *Die Gesellschaft der Gesellschaft*. Frankfurt a. M.
Lynn, Ta. M. (2006) 'Hurt so good'. Fight club, masculine violence, and the crisis of capitalism. In: *The Journal of American Culture* 29(3): 265-277.
Mannheim, Karl (1936) *Ideology and Utopia*. London.
Marsh, Nicky (2007) *Money, Speculation and Finance in Contemporary British Fiction*. London.
Marx, Karl (1867, 1885, 1994) *Das Kapital. Kritik der politischen Ökonomie*. Hamburg.
McLuhan, Marshall (1964) *Understanding Media. The Extensions of Man*. New York, Toronto, London.
Moule, Arthur Christopher/Pelliot, Paul (2011) *Marco Polo, Le devisement du monde. Le livre des merveilles*. Paris.
Murašov, Jurij (2004) Irdischer Sinnmangel und göttliche Ökonomie. Wirtschaft, Schrift und Ethik in orthodoxen Heiligenviten. In: Guski, Andreas/Schmidt, Ulrich (eds.), *Literatur und Kommerz im Russland des 19. Jahrhunderts. Institutionen, Akteure, Symbole*. Zurich: 293-328.

Mustafić, Aldin (2013) *Epohe fonetske misli kod Arapa i arebica (The Age of Phonetic Thought of Arabs and Arebica)*. Belgrade.
Piketty, Thomas (2013) *Le capital au XXIe siècle*. Paris.
Pointon, Marcia (1998) Money and nationalism. In: Cubitt, Geoffrey (ed.), *Imagining Nations*. Manchester: 229-254.
Rotman, Brian (1987) *Signifying Nothing. The Semiotics of Zero*. Stanford.
Sedláček, Tomáš (2011) *Economics of Good and Evil. The Quest for Economic Meaning from Gilgamesh to Wall Street*. Oxford.
Shell, Marc (1978) *The Economy of Literature*. Baltimore.
Sholette, Gregory/Kim Charnley (2017) *Delirium and Resistance: Activist Art and the Crisis of Capitalism*. London.
Simmel, Georg (1900, 1989) *Philosophie des Geldes*. Frankfurt a. M.
Stiglitz, Joseph (1996) *Whither Socialism*. Cambridge.
Stiglitz, Joseph (2012) *The Prize of Inequality: How Today's Divided Society Endangers Our Future*. New York.
Unwin, Tim/Hewitt, Virginia (2001) Banknotes and national identity in central and eastern Europe. In: *Political Geography* 20: 1005-1028.
Vogl, Joseph (2010) *Das Gespenst des Kapitals*. Zurich.
Weber, Max (1921; 1972) *Wirtschaft und Gesellschaft*. Tübingen.
Widemann, Reinold (2018) *Artists' Conceptions of Money: Money Art and Artificial Money*. Soesterberg.
Zimmermann, Tanja (2014) *Brüderlichkeit und Bruderzwist. Mediale Inszenierungen des Aufbaus und des Niedergangs politischer Gemeinschaften in Ost- und Südosteuropa*. Göttingen.
Zimmermann, Tanja (2014) *Der Balkan zwischen Ost und West. Mediale Bilder und kulturpolitische Prägungen*. Cologne, Weimar, Vienna.
Živančević-Sekeruš, Ivana (2012) Banknote Imagery of Serbia. In: Zimmermann, Tanja (ed.), *Balkan Memories. Media Constructions of National and Transnational History*. Bielefeld: 41-48.
Žižek, Slavoj (1989) *The Sublime Object of Ideology*. New York.

An Economic Survey of the Kingdom of Yugoslavia[1]

Jelena Rafailović

Economic trends in Europe during the 19th century resulted in the division into developed (industrial) and underdeveloped (agrarian) states in the first half of the 20th. The countries of Southeastern Europe, among which was the Kingdom of Yugoslavia, belonged to the category of underdeveloped agrarian states, which historiography characterized as a "periphery" whose economic development was seen as "evolution without development". State discontinuities, political instability, inability to adapt to modern technological and structural requirements, limited resources, lack of capital, inherited economic traditions, an insufficiently educated workforce, and variable attitudes in currency and finance policies were just some of the reasons for the weak economic development until the First World War. Economically backward relative to the countries of Western Europe, the Kingdom of Yugoslavia tried to close the gap. The problematic agricultural sector could not have an impact on economic growth, the industrial sector was in the early stages of its development, and financially represented all the weaknesses of the abovementioned sectors, due to which the economy followed a certain but limited development constrained by the realities of the Balkans and a complete lack of developed institutions (economic, social and political) which elsewhere originated in the 19th century.

The economic issue of Yugoslavia is a very open and insufficiently explored field of historiography. While it has attracted the interest of academics, it has yet to receive close analysis in the fields of political, ideological, military or cultural history. The absence of a specific model of development, the lack of good data, and the character of historiography after 1945 have resulted in the marginalization of questions on economic issues.

This paper presents a brief overview of the economic history of the Yugoslav countries in the period from the late 19th century to the First World War and the

---

1 The paper is part of the project Tradition and Transformation – Historical Heritage and National Identity of Serbia in the 20th Century, (№ 47019), which is financed by the Ministry of Education, Science and Technological Development of the Republic of Serbia.

Kingdom of Yugoslavia (1878-1939). First, I explain the basic economic characteristics of the Yugoslav territories until 1914, and then after unification through the analysis of the basic economic sectors (agrarian, financial and industrial).

1. The economy of the Yugoslav territories from the late 19th century to the First World War

Up to the Balkan wars, the newly founded Kingdom of Serbs, Croats and Slovenes was composed of the independent Kingdom of Serbia and Kingdom of Montenegro and territories under Austro-Hungarian authority (Vojvodina, Bosnia and Herzegovina, Slovenia, Croatia, Dalmatia and Slavonia) and Ottoman authority. These areas, although non-existent as such in political frameworks, represented invisible borders in economic terms from 1918 onwards. Hence I focus first on the main structural characteristics of the economy of the pre-Yugoslav area.

On the territory of the Austro-Hungarian Empire, Slovenia, as a constituent part of Austria proper, was the most developed and Dalmatia and Bosnia and Herzegovina were the least developed areas in economic terms. Vienna made efforts to fully integrate the territory of Slovenia into the Austrian economy by means of investing mainly Austrian capital into it, directing its trade towards Vienna and constructing the Vienna-Trieste railway in 1856. The trade in raw materials via Slovenian ports became unprofitable over time, and thus a vertical chain in the industrial processing of raw materials was established with Vienna as the final point for finishing. Subsequently, up to the First World War, Slovenia boasted textile and metallurgical industries, which were for the most part in Austrian hands (Pertot 1971: 5-6). Economic development was also influenced by a strong accumulation of trade capital from the late 18th century onwards, the gradual development of manufacturing, processing and finally heavy industry, the organisation of economic administration through the Court Trade Commission, industrial exhibitions, vocational education development, the introduction of steaming machines in light industry, maritime and railway traffic, and mining (Šorn 1974: 141-146).

Croatia and Slavonia had partial autonomy and limited jurisdictions in the economic sphere, accompanied by the constant divisions between Vienna and Budapest regarding their own spheres of interest. The Hungarian-Croatian Agreement of 1868 defined the responsibilities for economic development, according to which the Hungarian Assembly reserved the right to determine economic policies. The agreement envisaged the following joint affairs: industry, trade, credit institutions, domestic and foreign trade, traffic, the post office, state property, and particularly the railway. By means of railway tariffs and various technical regulations, Hungary contributed to the economic development on the Budapest-Rijeka line. However, a certain level of autonomy enabled them to develop their own consumer goods industry. There was also strong agricultural production in the area between the Sava and Drava rivers, which was owned and managed by landowners whose interests were in line with Hungarian agriculture and were thus part of the Hungarian export potential. In the second half of the 19th century, the chambers of commerce in Zagreb, Osijek and Rijeka played important economic roles along with the gradual creation of the processing industry by means of trade capital, primarily through manufactures in the mill and lumber industries and shipbuilding (Pertot 1971: 5-6; Karaman 1974: 37-59; Karaman 1991).

Vojvodina belonged to the Hungarian administrative area. Abundant in grain fields, its economy was based on agricultural production in mixed property structure, whereas its trade was oriented towards Budapest. Craft, manufacturing and industry were poorly developed, and the biggest factories operated within the food (sugar, alcohol, oil, mills etc.) and construction industries, whereas home craft was limited to local homesteads (Čehak 1974). Bosnia and Herzegovina belonged to the Ottoman Empire up to 1878, and its economic state at the time is best described by Kemalj Hrelja: "Bosnia and Herzegovina is immersed in the lethargy of Ottoman feudalism up to the second half of the 19th century, and its idyllic *kasaba* (small towns) are not even touched by the echo of important events from the turn of the 15th to the last quarter of the 19th century [...]." However, since 1878 and its annexation by the Austro-Hungarian Empire, the circumstances in the economic field had gradually changed and the territory of Bosnia and Herzegovina "became the subject of the particular Austro-Hungarian economic policy of the colonial type" (Pertot 1971: 8). Upon annexation, the construction of the railway network began, but it was a narrow gauge railway that was economically separated from other territories within the monarchy, as well as from the neighbouring countries. The investments in the extractive industry, mining, forests and the salt industry followed. Economic capital was primarily of Austrian, German and Hungarian origin, as domestic businesspeople were not able to start construction work on their own. At the very low level of economic development and very rich in raw materials, Bosnia and Herzegovina was not involved in the growth of Austria-Hungary, although it did belong to the customs territory of the Austro-Hungarian Empire (Hrelja 1974: 23-29; Pertot 1971: 8).

The monetary and financial system of the Austro-Hungarian territories was first based on the forint, then the krone, in Serbia the dinar, and in Montenegro the perper. The gold standard was in use in all the territories however. Thus at the dawn of the First World War, one krone was equal to 1.15 dinars. Financial institutions and the monetary system were more developed and stronger in Austro-Hungarian countries. In the Kingdom of Serbia there was an independent National Bank (1884), and just before the war, the total number of banks amounted to 187, with basic paid-in capital of 51 million dinars, savings of 65 million dinars, and loans of 96 million dinars. Led by the First Croatian Savings Bank (1846), there were 792 banks in Croatia, with 97 million krones in capital, 253 million in savings and 384 million in loans. In Bosnia and Herzegovina, there were 38 banks with 30 million krones of paid-in capital, 22 million in savings and 140 million in loans (Mirković 1958: 288-292).

Peripheral countries, such as those of South-Eastern Europe, were positioned far away from richer Central European states and this had a significant impact on the progress of certain regions (Aldcroft 2006; Berend/György 1982). The territories of Slovenia and Croatia, which were closer to Vienna, were much more developed than Dalmatia, Bosnia and Herzegovina and Vojvodina. This came as a consequence of an asymmetric integration into the Habsburg market in the second half of the 19th century. The process of total market integration began approximately in 1880 (up to then, differences in the economic market had not been visible), and developed asymmetrically: some regions were mutually integrated more rapidly and deeply than others. According to Max Schulze and Nikolaus Wolf's research, national differences played a crucial role in this matter. The creation of "borders within borders" was partially influenced by administrative barriers, physical geography and infrastructural changes, whereas the key reason was the ethno-linguistic composition of the population in regional capitals (Schulze/Wolf 2009: 117-118; Schulze/Wolf 2012: 671).

An independent economic development in the Yugoslav territories was not possible until 1918, except in the Kingdom of Serbia and Montenegro, which gained independence in 1878. Mari Žanin Čalić points out that "the acquisition of full political independence in 1878 was a turning point for Serbia in economic terms" (Чалић 2004: 108). Serbia was considered a poorly developed European country with an agrarian orientation and basic industrial development. The reasons for this categorisation were numerous, but the Ottoman economic legacy and its (semi-)dependent character were certainly dominant factors. Rulers of the Obrenović and Karađorđević dynasties encountered huge economic problems ranging from poverty and the completely agricultural character of the country to the impossibility of implementing their economic policies independently due to its position between the Ottoman and the Austro-Hungarian empires. Apart from primary problems in the agrarian sector, there were other obstacles too: the organisation of crafts into guilds, traders who did not invest in industry, and Austria with its trade agreements by means of which it ensured its leading position in the industrial sector (Vučo 1974: 79).

Several economic measures were crucial for the Serbian economy in the 19th century: the abolition of the Ottoman feudal system (1833, 1835) and solving the issue of ownership of land, with the effect that the Serbian peasant became the owner of the land he had hitherto cultivated without compulsory redemption (1838, 1839);

the Law on the Homestead (Zakon o Okućju, 1836),[2] which defined the agricultural minimum wage, i.e. the scope of their estates and land that farmers were not allowed to sell. In the literature, this regulation is seen as disabling the creation of big estates, influencing the credit ability of farmers and thus the amount of capital in the village, moving the population to the countryside, and finally reducing market competition;[3] and the Law on Stimulating Industry (1873, 1898), which encouraged the establishment of enterprises by providing various incentives to privileged industrial enterprises. The state of the Serbian industry in 1878 is best illustrated by the fact that apart from several factories of the military sector, only "one plant for baking bricks, two sawmills, two breweries and several steam mills" operated in Serbia. In the atmosphere of the weak domestic industry and the strong import of foreign competitive industrial goods, state authorities saw the possibility for initial industrialization in indirect intervention in economic policy. In order to implement the process of industrialization, they lacked technical knowledge, initial capital and an educated workforce, which legislators believed could be created via incentives (Чалић 2004: 149-150). However, it is important to note that the process of industrialization in the Balkans in the 19th century was not intensive enough to meet the criteria that would enable "sustainable" industrial development, and John Lampe writes: "according to any acceptable definition [...] the industrial revolution had not happened in any Balkan country before 1914. Mechanical power had just started to replace manual power" (Lampe/Jackson 1982: 237; Lampe 1975: 59).

The next very important economic question was the construction and development of the transport infrastructure, which depended on the financial and political situation. Based on the Treaty of Berlin of 1878 and due to German and Austro-Hungarian interests, Serbia undertook an obligation to construct the Belgrade-Niš-Vranje railway, which was ceremonially opened in 1883 with the assistance of a French company.[4] The Serbian Government repurchased the agreement on railway exploitation in 1889, on the basis of which management of the railway was transferred to the state.[5] According to the economic programme drafted by the Vladan Đorđević's government, the 1,100 km railway system was due to be constructed in the years to come (the National Assembly adopted the Law on Railway Construction and Exploitation) in an attempt to liberate the Serbian economy from Austro-Hungarian influence and to direct Serbian trade towards western and northern countries. This was meant to be achieved by building railways in eastern and

---

2 Чалић 2004: 42; Вучо 1955: 170-172, 177; Vučo 1974: 80; Миљковић Катић 2014: 27-28; Петровић 1930: 87-114.
3 Чалић 2004: 41; Gnjatović 2009: 46; Миљковић Катић 2014: 28.
4 "Железничка конвенција са Аустро-угарском", *Српске новине*, 128, XLVIII, 8.6.1880, 669-673; Вучо 1981: 128-129.
5 "Уговор о откупу експлоатације српских железница", *Српске новине*, 285, LVI, 29.12.1889, 1359-1361. Вучо 1981: 128-129.

western Serbia,[6] which actually occurred step by step after the First World War (Vučo 1974: 83-85).

Although independent after 1878, the Kingdom of Serbia was limited in implementing independent foreign trade and trade in general up to the Customs War with the Austro-Hungarian Empire (1906-1910). According to the *Trade Agreement* (1881-1882) and the *Veterinary Convention*, Austria-Hungary was granted the greatest privileges without reciprocity. Due to low customs tariffs on the import of particular goods, Austria-Hungary was in a privileged position on the Serbian market, with influence on the industrial and agricultural sectors, and thus able to exert political pressure when needed (Љушић 2008: 203; Вучо 1955: 230-232). Changes in the foreign trade and economic policy in general began in 1903, after the May Coup and the shift of dynasties from the Obrenovićs to the Karađorđevićs, resulting in the Customs War,[7] after which Serbia was more economically independent; its industry saw a certain progress, and the agricultural sector found new markets for its products.[8]

2. The economy of the Kingdom of Yugoslavia (the Kingdom of Serbs, Croats and Slovenes)

The newly founded Kingdom of Serbs, Croats, and Slovenes (the Kingdom of SCS, from 1929 onwards the Kingdom of Yugoslavia), was a heterogeneous economic unit in its essence, due to the aforementioned different political, social, economic, national and religious heritage of its regions. Those peculiarities of the pre-Yugoslav space led to different levels of development in different regions, with a loosely integrated market (Pertot 1971: 5; Đurović 1992; 1993; Singleton/Carter 1982: 75). Uneven and divergent regional development, alongside various modes of the economy without a clear economic evolution, were crucial to the Kingdom's economy throughout its existence (Dimitrijević 1962: 6).

---

6 "Закон о грађењу и експлоатацији нових железница", *Српске новине*, 281, LXV, 23.12.1898, 1; Вучо 1955: 222; Вучо 1981: 132-133.

7 The first economic measure towards independence was the introduction of a new autonomous customs tariff in the spring of 1904 by the adoption of the Law on General Customs Tariff. The Law envisaged superior customs provisions for the purpose of protecting domestic industry and reducing the strong Austro-Hungarian economic influence. After the introduction of the customs tariff, Serbia agreed to the Customs Alliance with Bulgaria in 1905, which, together with new German customs for the protection of their own agricultural products, Serbia's negotiations with France on armament, and general European political trends, led to the Customs War between Serbia and Austria-Hungary in the period 1906-1910 (Вучо 1955: 232-233; Чалић 2004: 157-158; Љушић 2008: 253-256).

8 Вучо 1955: 232-233; Чалић 2004: 157-158; Љушић 2008: 253-256.

On top of the existing problems inherited from the 19th century – lack of capital, an agrarian structure, a low level of technological development, a low level of education, undeveloped transportation infrastructure – new ones emerged as a consequence of the First World War: destruction and damage of basic capital, factories, mines, and agricultural land; the migration of minorities; repatriation of refugees; the burden of the war debt; uncontrolled inflation; a decrease in the already low agricultural and industrial production; the depreciation of the currency; and the problem of the restoration of a variety of state-owned, public, and private objects, transport infrastructure, melioration, nutrition, supplies, city dwelling, etc. (Mathias/Pollard 1989; Kaser 1968; Lampe/Jackson 1982; Đurović 1986; Чалић 2004). In general terms, the economic effects of the war were direct, but temporary, such as the aforementioned consequences of destruction, a decline in human and physical capital, and the redistribution of resources.

The area of the former Kingdom of Serbia suffered the most damage during the occupation and fighting. Its economy was ruined, while agricultural, industrial, and transportation sectors were devastated. The estimated material damage was 4.9 million golden dinars. Private companies in the cities lost around 30% of immovable property and 57% of movables, a particular problem being the Belgrade-Bar railway. The direct effects of war on the economy were much smaller in the regions of the former Austria-Hungary (Mitrany 1936; Đurović 1969: 168; Milenković 1972: 281-289; Dimitrijević 1962: 5; Jagodić/Radonjić 2015).

The Kingdom of Yugoslavia had to adjust to the new circumstances immediately after the war, since the trade routes of the regions that entered the common state were oriented towards Vienna, Budapest, and Istanbul (Mathias/Pollard 1989: 889). Western powers acknowledged the existence of the successor states, but they perceived them as a "cordon sanitaire" against the communist threat from Moscow and the Central European ambitions of Berlin, while economically the Balkans represented a single economic unit relative to the interests of the developed Western European countries (Berend 2009: 68; Mathias/Pollard 1989: 914; Ristović 1991: 10-13).

It should be pointed out that political changes, followed by the creation of a new country, influenced economic and demographic trends within the new borders, but not the structural transformation of the historic regions. Demographic changes in the Kingdom of Yugoslavia cannot be compared to the pre-war state of affairs. The long-term population growth rate was unprecedented because the mortality rate started declining in the late 19th century, while the birth rate remained at the same level, meaning that the territories of the Kingdom were in the second phase of demographic transition (Stavrijanos 2005: 567). By the First World War, the population was growing by 1.2% a year (Mirković 1958: 221-222), and that trend continued after the war.[9] At the beginning of the 20th century, Serbia had 2.9 million inhabitants, Croatia and Slavonia 2.7 million, Slovenia 1.3 million, Bosnia and Herzegovina 1.5 million, making a total of 12.8 million, and that trend continued after 1918. According to the first census of 1921, the Kingdom of SHS had 11,984,911 inhabitants; ten years later the number had grown to 13,934,038 million, while the estimated figure for 1939 was 15,703,000.[10]

The population was predominantly agrarian, around 77% in the interwar period. The total number of inhabitants who earned a living from agriculture in 1921 was 9.2 million (78.8%), and 10.6 million (76.5%) in 1931. In these ten years, the total population growth was almost two million, while the agricultural population grew by 1.4 million. Regionally, the largest agricultural population in relation to the total number of inhabitants can be noted in the Sava banovina with 14% (2,037,156), then in the Danube banovina with 12% (1,783,552), while the Drava banovina had the lowest ratio of the agricultural population, amounting to 4.95% (689,772).[11] Industrial workers and craftsmen made up 8.6% of the general employed population in 1921, while ten years later that number grew to 10% (717,002), a total of 19.2% (1.2 million) of the workforce together with those employed in state or private administration, trade, and transportation. As an absolute value, the population employed in industry grew by 194,911 (1.4%), indicating a certain level of industrialization and urbanization, but compared to the industrialized European countries that growth is imperceptible (Рафаиловић 2018: 260-261).

The workforce was an exogenous factor of agricultural production, and it was a double-edged sword in the economy since, on the one hand, available workforce meant the possibility of economic growth, while on the other hand, due to the undeveloped economy, it overburdened agriculture. The estimated surplus of the agricultural population in Yugoslavia was 43%, but averages hide the regional specificities. The Drava banovina had a surplus of 58%, the Zeta banovina 66%, the Primorska banovina 68%, while the Danube banovina had only a 2% surplus of agricultural population.[12]

---

9 The Kingdom of Serbia suffered the largest population losses. It lost one-third of the pre-war population not only in relation to the other Yugoslav territories, but also to all participants in the war. According to official data, the total number of dead from the territory of pre-war Serbia with Macedonia stood at 1,247,435, or 28% of the total population. This figure should also be added to 114,000 disabled war veterans and 150,000 people with reduced working capacity (Aldcroft 2001: 7; Bogart 1920: 299; Milenković 1972: 281-289; compared with estimates Јагодић 2015).

10 *Статистички годишњак 1929*, I: (Београд: Општа државна статистика, Краљевина Југославија, 1932) 57, 90; *Статистички годишњак 1932*, IV: 41; *Статистички годишњак 1936*, VII: 35; *Статистички годишњак 1938-1939*, IX: 111.

11 Cf. Vučo 1958: 15-16.

12 In Yugoslavia there were 112.6 inhabitants per 100 ha, in Romania 97, in Canada only 11, in America 17, in England 30, in Denmark 36, in France 48, in Germany 52 (Tomasevich 1955: 310-311; Vučo 1968: 44, 60; Stavrijanos 2005: 567; Berend 1968: 185; Поповић 1940: 48-50).

The surplus of agricultural population led to an agrarian overpopulation,[13] i.e. concealed unemployment, which resulted in various socio-economic problems, particularly influencing the creation of capital and the modernization of agriculture. Based on the population structure and demographic trends, it is easy to note the increase in the workforce in the agrarian sector and population pressure in rural areas because the undeveloped industry could not absorb them. Agrarian overpopulation thus caused low wages, low income, low productivity and modest consumption. Technical growth was also confined due to the lack of surplus capital for investing in the mechanization of agricultural production (Berend 1968: 184-185).

A peculiarity of industry workers, originating in the agrarian character of the regions, was the emergence of the what were known as "farmer-workers", i.e. workers who did not break with agriculture and had two jobs over the year: in the field and in the factory. They came from an agrarian background and were mostly either seasonal workers or held jobs for a few years. Entrepreneurs preferred employing these farmer-workers because they were easier to control and agreed to work for lower wages, having had income from the land as well (Kostić 1955: 106-119; Dimitrijević 1982: 191).

Yugoslavia had several serious structural problems, the most acute of which was the transportation network. It was underdeveloped and unadjusted to the significant territorial changes, thus leaving the regions poorly connected. The inherited railway infrastructure, as the most developed and significant mode of transportation when it came to the number of employees, investments, and its place in the economy, gravitated towards the centres in Austria, Hungary, and Turkey. The densest infrastructural network was in the north of the country, in the lands of the former Austro-Hungarian Empire, with 220 railway tracks around 9,000km long, while the pre-war Kingdom of Serbia had about 1,500km of track. The geographical centre of the country, Bosnia and Herzegovina, as well as the entire southern part of country, were either entirely disconnected from or loosely connected to the other regions; there was neither a transversal Ljubljana-Zagreb-Belgrade connection, nor a good connection between the coast and northern regions. By 1931, the railway network in the Kingdom of Yugoslavia was about 10,400km long, with the most developed infrastructure in Slovenia and Croatia, and the least developed in Montenegro (only 42km of the narrow-gauge track).[14]

---

13 See also Kopsidis 2012: 11.
14 The lengths of railway track in most developed countries in the 1920s were as follows (per 1,000 inhabitants): Sweden 27.5 km, Ireland 18.4 km, France 14.7 km, Denmark 14.9 km, Switzerland 14.8 km, Norway 14.6 km, Austria 12.5 km, Germany 9.3 km, Hungary 11.9 km; in the Balkan states, the situation was: in Yugoslavia 7.2 km, in Bulgaria 4.9 km, in Greece 5.1 km and in Romania 6.6 km (Đurović 1978: 183-188; Mirković 1950: 122-128; Lakatoš 1933: 165; Dimitrijević 1962: 6-7).

At the end of the First World War, the countries of South-Eastern Europe, including Yugoslavia, had great support from the western countries for the stabilization of their state systems devastated by the inevitable consequences of war – destruction of economic systems, material losses, deprivation, dislocation of industry and inflation. Through financial or trade ties with developed countries, they gradually entered the international market and thus became more sensitive to economic fluctuations, which further influenced their development.

The first positive economic boom in Yugoslavia took place during the period of reconstruction, from 1919 to 1924, in accordance with conjunctural inflation and the overall good economic climate. In the first post-war years, there was a global demand for agricultural products, which benefited predominantly agrarian countries. Under those conditions, the purchasing power of the rural population grew, as did the demand for consumer goods, causing the rise in prices of industrial products, which opened the door for high earnings in the industrial sector. The restoration of the damage caused by war and reconstruction of the wrecked industry resulted in the creation of new companies and greater import of production assets (Kukoleča 1941: 75-77). With its credit policies, the National Bank created inflation after the war to compensate for the lack of capital, thus creating the illusion of the abundance of capital in the country. Parallel to this monetary policy, the National Bank credited the industrial sector, leading to the founding of a significant number of shareholding factories, without real capital investments, through promissory notes and credits (Tomašević 1938: 163; Gnjatović 1991: 151-152; Тасић 1992: 151; Aleksić 2010: 5-7). In the following years, from 1925 to 1927, a certain stagnation took place as a consequence of the agrarian crisis, low agricultural productivity and the suspension of credit by the National Bank. This stagnation was followed by intense growth until the crisis of 1929. The average annual growth of the real gross national product was 3.48% from 1923 to 1929. During the Great Depression (1929-1934) the average rate of decrease in the gross national product stood at -2.42%. The fall in prices of agricultural products, the collapse of the Austrian credit bank (Kreditanstalt), and a whole range of protectionist measures in other countries led to price scissors in Yugoslavia, fewer export opportunities, rising unemployment, falling income, lower wages, a credit deficit, a fall in the volume of international trade, and deflation. The period from 1935 to 1939 is the age of a renewed rise in the real economy, with an annual growth in GNP of 7.84%. This period is characterized by a general rise in prices, a new economic direction under Milan Stojadinović, stronger state intervention in the economy, the stabilization of agriculture and growth in agricultural exports, a rise in employment, public works, support for the industrial sector, etc. (Kaser 1968: 223, 229-233; Stajić 1959: 6-17; Чалић 2004: 382-382).

Agriculture was the dominant sector in the real economy and the key economic issue on which industrialization, urbanization, social issues and modernization depended (Fischer-Galati 1992: 4). Agricultural production made for the largest part of the gross domestic product at 63.29%, while the agrarian population amounted to 76%, i.e. 10.7 million out of 13.8 million inhabitants (around 1929). Extensive production, pressure on land, agrarian overpopulation, small estates, the lack of capital and investment, and agro-technical backwardness were the main tenets of the agrarian sector in the interwar period. Agricultural growth, based on the rise in production of corn and wheat, did not come from investment in modernization of production, but from the expansion of arable land for those cultures, workforce growth, and the favourable climate (Petaković 2010: 45).

The ownership structure of the land matched those characteristics. In Yugoslavia there was 1.347 mil (67.8%) farmsteads with 0.01-5 hectares, owning 28% of arable land (c. 3,000,000ha). The ownership structure differed in different regions. In Serbia and Slovenia, small and mid-sized estates were dominant; Croatia, Slavonia and Vojvodina had more large estates belonging to a small number of landowners, and small peasant farms; Dalmatia was characterized by a whole range of inherited relations based on serfdom and colonates; Bosnia and Herzegovina still retained serfdom as a form of ownership structure, while in southern Serbia there was a čivija system based on Muslim hereditary landowning structures (Лазић 1999: 42-44; Ристић 1938: 36-37). The ownership structure was a result of the inherited political and economic systems, the aforementioned Law on Homestead valid in the territories of pre-war Serbia and Montenegro, and the agrarian reforms.

Small estates with a large number of inhabitants give rise to the issue of sustainability and overall possibilities of the agricultural development in such a system. Historians and economists generally agree that the estates under 5 ha were not sustainable and barely sufficient to feed families, often requiring additional non-agricultural work. Large farms had certain advantages – they could make better use of agricultural machines and more rational use of livestock and human capital, had better opportunities for the specialization of labour, and were more likely to obtain credits (Vučo 1958: 41).

The aforementioned agrarian reform, i.e. distribution of land to the poor population, was an attempt by the governing authorities to solve the existing problems, and it was primarily a social and political measure designed to appease social tensions and satisfy those who did not have land, rather than an economic policy. The agrarian reform was conditioned by political factors: promises that the Serbian Government and the National Council of Slovenians, Croats, and Serbs made during the war, the national structure of landowners (Hungarians, Germans, Austrians, Turks), as well as the existence of disparity between small estates in Serbia and big land ownership in the former Austria-Hungary (Stavrijanos 2005: 592; Vučo 1958: 23). In addition to that, there was a widespread "feeling" that peasants should get social justice (Berend 1968: 153; Lampe/Jackson 1982: 352-353; Stavrijanos 2005: 566).

The first measures predicted that during the agrarian reform, all the estates larger than 57ha should be redistributed, but the agrarian maximum was later raised to 288ha. The final results of distribution are estimated at 17% (1,700,000ha) of arable land, and around 12% of the total agricultural and forest area. The largest portion of distributed land was in Bosnia and Herzegovina, 1,200,000ha, then in the northern parts of the Kingdom, 589,000ha, followed by the southern regions, 540,000, while Dalmatia trailed with 50,000ha of distributed land (Ристић 1938: 72; Petranović 1980: 63). Large estate owners mostly kept their land, depending on the particular case.

After the agrarian reform, the issue of farmers' debt emerged (with approx. 710,000 debtors around 1932). It became a chronic problem for a large part of the agricultural population and worsened during the Depression. Drought, floods, bad yield years, and the rise or fall of the price of grain influenced the financial situation of the peasants. Growing farmers' debt during the Depression led to the passing of the Law on the Protection of Farmers in 1932, when a moratorium on agricultural debt was declared, and payments and forced sale of land were deferred. A temporary state of delayed debt payment ended in 1936, when the Regulation on Liquidation of Agricultural Debt was passed, transferring all the farmers' obligations towards banks (1.8 billion dinars) and cooperatives (1.2 billion dinars) to the Privileged Agrarian Bank. Farmers basically now owed money to the Privileged Agrarian Bank, that is, to the state (Mirković 1958: 347-349).

Agricultural production grew in the interwar period, but most of the agricultural work was done without the use of mechanization or chemicals. Grain production grew from 6.1 million tons in 1925-1929 to around 8 million tons in 1934-1939, i.e. by 30% (1,861,660 t), while arable land grew by 17%, but yield growth stagnated. The causes of high productivity and production were the geographic and climate traits of the terrain, and the expansion of cropped land, while the low yields can be explained with the whole range of the abovementioned problems in the agrarian sector. The tractor, a symbol of modern agriculture, was barely even used. It is estimated that of a total of 270,000 tractors in Europe before the Second World War, only 8,000, or 3%, were used in the Balkans, and only 2,000 in Yugoslavia. In most cases, farmers only saw the tractor after the war. In the interwar period, they were mostly used on large estates in Vojvodina and Slavonia; in the Drava banovina, there were only 22 tractors on 219,000 farming estates (Berend 1968: 194).

Small landowners mostly worked with agricultural tools, primarily primitive ploughs, while devices such as seeders, reapers, mowers or threshers barely existed (for more details, cf.: Поповић 1940: 67; Статистички годишњак 1936, VII, 136, 142; Vučo 1958: 57). Chemical devices for the increase in production were also almost unknown to the farmers. The basis for keeping the ground fertile was either manure or fallowing the land with the use of a two- or three-field system of crop rotation (Berend 1968: 194-196; Svennilson 1954: 99, 250; Vučo 1958: 62-63). Relative to arable land, the use of manure was 6kg per hectare, the smallest ratio in Europe (Vučo 1958: 22).

There were slight changes in agriculture from the mid-19th century until the First World War, even though production was low and stagnated compared to Western and Central Europe. Small farmsteads, unfavourable for the use of mechanization, were not capable of creating conditions for significant development and higher yields because modern agricultural technologies were made for large estates and were barely usable on small peasant farms (Berend 1968: 148-150). The lack of financial resources for investments in land and undeveloped banking system drove farmers towards loan sharks, further aggravating the situation. Agricultural production survived mainly due to the fertile ground and favourable climate.

The monetary system of Yugoslavia was based on a diverse historical heritage, which made heterogeneity, unevenness, and decentralization the main tenets of the financial sector (Тасић 1992: 152). The Ministry of Finance was the central institution that regulated this sector, and right after its foundation, the work on balancing financial legislation began. It was a relatively slow process, since it required evening out all the inherited regional particularities. A most important issue was the unification of the currency and tax systems.

The unification of the currency was one of the central political issues in the post-war years. Monetary chaos, reflected in the use of four different currencies – the dinar (pre-war Kingdom of Serbia), perper (Kingdom of Montenegro), krone (former Austro-Hungarian regions) and lev (eastern and southern Serbia) – was officially brought to an end on January 1st, 1923, when all the associations and institutions were obliged to pay and calculate in dinars. That was preceded by the unification of the currency by the following principle: 4:1 krone-dinar; 1:1 perper-dinar up to the value of 5,000 dinars, and 2:1 for higher amounts; the lev was exchanged through direct payment.[15] During the post-war inflation, the dinar fell from 20.41 (in October 1920) to 3.69 (lowest value in January 1923) Swiss francs for 100 dinars. Stabilization of the dinar was achieved in October 1925, when the ratio was fixated in Zurich at 9.135 francs, and that ratio was maintained for six years (Tomašević 1938: 162; Gnjatović 1991: 151-153; Nikolić 2003: 69-102; Мијатовић 2013: 102-104). The unification of the system of direct taxation was finalized by the Law on Direct Taxation of February 1928 and it was first applied on January 1st, 1929. Until that date, five different forms of taxation were used, and ways of levying taxes differed significantly depending on the region.

---

15 After the collapse of the Austro-Hungarian monarchy, the krone lost 60% of its value of 1914. After the war in Yugoslavia about 5 billion krone were in circulation, which influenced inflation. In order to establish a stable relationship between the krone, the levs and the dinar, in December 1918 the government banned the introduction of the krone and Bulgarians levs to the state in amounts greater than 1,000, and later issued an order to mark these currencies. The decline in the value of the krone was not stopped by these measures, and in January 1920 the value of the krone to the dinar was established at 4:1 (Mijatović 2014: 27-50; Gnjatović 1991: 129, 131, 132).

The banking system was mainly mixed-type. The number of banks operating in Yugoslavia went from 583 in 1921 to 700 in 1927, to 651 in 1929, and to 598 in the late 1930s (Gnjatović 1991: 151-152; Тасић 1992: 151). All the banks had both banking and trading roles, and their main source of income was savings accounts. A wide range of tasks banks performed were a consequence of the underdeveloped market and poverty, which made them unfit to keep track of "industrialization". The banking system at the turn of the decade consisted of: the National Bank of the Kingdom of SHS, mixed-type shareholding banks (around 60, two of which were privileged, and four branch offices of foreign banks), two state-owned money institutions (State Hypothecary Bank and Postal Savings Bank), between ten and twenty commercial banks, and credit cooperatives (around 3900). From the point of view of the financing of industry and other branches of the real economy apart from agriculture, shareholding banks were not of great significance (Anonymous 1930: 14; Тасић 1992: 150-156).

The central bank was the National Bank of the Kingdom of SCS/Yugoslavia. It was a formal heir of the Privileged National Bank of the Kingdom of Serbia founded in 1884, a fact corroborated by the Law of 26 January 1920.[16] As an issuing institution, its job was to regulate and enforce monetary policy (issuing banknotes and coins, regulating money circulation and payment transactions, etc.), but it also had a role in the short-term crediting of the real economy. Interest rates of the National Bank at 6-8% per year were the most favourable for short-term loans. By contrast, industrial loans by private banks and money institutions had 14% to 18% interest rates. That meant that an industrialist paid the entire sum of his loan in interest in four to five years (Kršev 2007: 194-196).

The industrial sector was a relatively small section of the real economy and therefore did not have a greater impact on its structure during the entire interwar period. Forestry accounted for 7.90% of national income, the extractive industry 1.8%, the manufacturing industry 11.6%, construction 1.10%, and crafts amounted to 10.6% (Ђуричић 1927: 265). There are also qualitative indicators on top of these

---

16 The Privileged National Bank of the Kingdom of Serbia was the only central bank and emission institution, with the right for printing/coining of the currency, from the territory of the former states that entered the newly established Kingdom. The National Bank returned from Marseille, where it was based during the war in 1919; with the expansion of territorial jurisdiction, it operated through its branches in other cities. The National Bank of Serbia, and later Yugoslavia, was established as a joint-stock company, according to the Belgian National Bank, with a capital of 180 million dinars, divided into 60,000 shares with a nominal value of 3,000 dinars, but it always operated under state control. According to the ownership structure, 20% of the shares belonged to the state privileged banks (State Mortgage Bank and Postal Savings Bank), 30% to private monetary institutions, 42% to small businessmen and individuals, and 8% to large businessmen whose package of shares exceeded 100 (Tomašević 1938: 144-152, 159-163; Kršev 2007: 193-195).

quantitative indicators: insufficient and outdated mechanization, the inadequacy of economic legislation, lack of capital and affordable loans, an unskilled workforce, dependence on foreign investments, small demand for and supply of industrial products, and poor infrastructure.

The mining and smelting industry, as a basic extractive industry, is a good example that reflected some of the problems, such as the absence of modern processing and transportation technologies. The largest companies that attracted interest both among the foreign investors and the state operated within the mining industry, employing the largest portion of industrial workers; they provided the undeveloped industry with raw materials. They were the greatest source of income for the state (due to lead export) and were the basis for "the industrialization of the country" (Đurović 1986: 32; Lakatoš 1933: 86). Mineral wealth was diverse (lignite, chrome, lead, zinc, and to somewhat lesser extent antimony, stone coal, copper and iron) and dispersed over 0.90% of the surface area of the Kingdom (Kukoleča 1941: 52; Đurović 1986: 32, 34; Lakatoš 1933: 86). However, due to the undeveloped economy, the character of the mining industry was extensive, i.e. products of Yugoslav mines were mostly exported as raw materials, and came back as finished or semi-finished factory products, which basically meant that industrialization in the area of heavy industry was unsuccessful.[17] A similar development can be noted in the textile industry too, with the (lack of) raw materials and the smaller but still significant role of foreign capital, etc.

The aforementioned structural flaws in the Yugoslav economy resulted in the fact that heavy industry and a larger portion of light industry remained at the same level as they were after the war. A. Gerschenkron's theory that late development enables industrialization based on the latest techniques did not hold up in practice in the Kingdom of Yugoslavia. The import of modern machines (both new and old) did not facilitate overcoming the gap in knowledge and technological processes, nor did it make sustainable industrial development possible. Modern technology in itself is not an indicator of industrial growth, since it does not encompass wider social issues of its application, the existence of a skilled workforce, delayed delivery of machines up to months at a time, or obtaining spare parts, lack of innovation in production, and good work organization.

We do not have continuous statistical data for the entire period until the second half of the 1930s. Therefore, the only thing that can be said with certainty is that from 1919 to 1938, 2,193 new companies were founded, with 4,335 million in invested capital, 145,000 employees, and 113,000 hp (without electrical power plants).

---

17 An example was the production of bauxite. Yugoslavia was among the five largest bauxite producers in Europe, but was its aluminium production was negligable (Димитријевић 1952: 9, 10, 27).

The lack of capital was the Achilles heel of Yugoslav industry. The agrarian sector, due to its undeveloped structure and overall poverty, did not contribute significantly to the accumulation of capital, while those farmers and traders who did own some capital mostly invested in production branches with simpler business models, and in small- or mid-capacity companies. Direct ways of creating cash, such as bolstering of the trade sector, industrial promissory notes, or the above-mentioned overflow from the agrarian to the industrial sector, were uncommon. Hence investments were mostly based on loans, financed by the state, private money institutions, or banks, with foreign capital playing the most significant role.

Banks participated in industrial development in several ways: through short-term loans, managing companies on their own, shareholding, engaging in consortium jobs, shares in industrial production, and rarely through long-term financing (Aleksić 2010: 7-11). Governing regimes did not do much in terms of measurements to facilitate industrial crediting and there were no special laws on crediting or money institutions that would provide for industrial loans. According to the data from 1937, shareholding banks participated in the economy with 2699.8 million dinars, 1699.8 million of which were invested in industry. The largest sum of credit was in forestry, the largest share of credit in mining, while the textile, metal-mechanical and cement industry also accounted for a large portion of loans (Тасић 1992: 193-194).

Due to the political instability, economic crisis, monetary and financial insecurity, deficiency of domestic crediting institutions and general lack of capital, foreign capital was of great significance for industry. However, its presence depended on the interests of foreign industrials. Foreign capital, mainly Austrian, Hungarian, and Czechoslovak, was particularly influential in the extractive industries, mining and cement, the chemical industry, forestry and the textile industry. The mining industry was mostly owned by foreign countries (65% overall, 88% in the production of metal ores, and the smallest portion in coal pits – 48%. Cf. Димитријевић 1952: 9-10).

Although most issues pertaining to the economic development of South-Eastern Europe are still relatively unknown or controversially discussed, there is a broad consensus among experts that before 1940 no process of industrialization resulted in self-sustainable modern growth. The Balkans countries did not manage to lessen the gap in GDP per capita in relation to Western Europe. For Lampe and Jackson, economic growth was "growth without development", and the very development of industry in the Balkans before 1940 was described as a sequence of industrial "mini-spurts", in contrast to Gerschenkron's "big spurts". On the eve of the Second World War, all countries in South-Eastern Europe were still territories on the periphery of the European economy (Kopsidis 2012: 3).

Production volumes lagged far behind those of developed countries. National income per capita in 1929 (based on the prices of 1937) stood at 86 US dollars in the

Kingdom of Yugoslavia, $60 in Bulgaria, $89 in Hungary, $181 in Czechoslovakia, $304 in Germany, $312 in France, and $372 in Great Britain (Mathias/Pollard 1989: 890).

Foreign trade was focused on the export of agricultural products and raw materials (wheat, corn, rye, hemp, tobacco, livestock, wood, ores, cement), and the import of industrial products. The countries with which Yugoslavia had the largest exchange were Austria, Czechoslovakia, Italy, and particularly Germany, especially in the 1930s, when its share in exports rose to 38% (in 1936), and imports 48% (1939). The Kingdom's goal was to maintain a positive balance in foreign trade, mostly successfully, but at a minimal level. From 1922 to 1939, it recorded 5 years with a negative balance and 13 years with a positive balance, 5.46 million to 5.58 million, with an overall gain of 115 million for the entire period (Mirković 1958: 373-377).

Consumer demand for industrial goods was higher than the production of domestic industry, which put pressure on imports. On the other hand, exports were not large enough to counterbalance imports and create a positive foreign trade balance, leading to interventionism, mainly through customs tariffs. The Law on the General Customs Tariff for Export and Import customs[18] came into force on June 20th, 1925, the goal being that the "import customs tariff protects domestic production" from foreign competition. Via the protective tariff, an average 32% of imported goods, the import of ready-made consumer goods was supposed to be completely unprofitable. Foreign trade was still carried out on the basis of the free market, but the new custom rates had a protectionist character towards domestic production. Protectionist policies of the state were supposed to enable "the birth of industry" through customs tariffs (Министарство финансија 1939: 114; Чалић 2004: 275; Dimitrijević 1982: 192). The general custom tariff defined two sets of rates, the maximum rate applied to imported goods from the countries with which the Kingdom of SCS had no tariff contracts or contracts of greatest privilege, and the minimum rate applied to the countries with which it had tariff contracts or contracts of greatest privilege (Мирковић 1932: 148). It should be noted that the issue of customs and industry is a part of the wider question, also posed by Mari Žanin-Čalić, as to whether Yugoslav industrialization was able to cover the import of industrial products with its own production and to what extent (Чалић 2004: 408-409).

Concluding this brief overview of the economy of the Yugoslav territories and the Kingdom of SCS/Yugoslavia in the period from 1878 to 1939, we can ascertain that structural problems remained unchanged throughout the period. The quality of the economy as a whole did not change, although there was certainly progress in quantitative terms, such as an increase in agricultural (grain) production and the

---

18 The bill on the General Customs Tariff was never ratified at the National Assembly and a temporary tariff was in force until 1951 (Pertot 1971: 36).

number of factories and workers and a positive foreign trade balance. However, deeper structural problems in the economy did not significantly change. They included insufficient financial capital, an underdeveloped and unadjusted transport network, a surplus of human capital, uneducated labour, and an underdeveloped agrarian sector that suffered from extensive production, pressure on land, agrarian overpopulation, small estates, lack of capital and investment, and agro-technical backwardness. This was compounded by the weak industrial sector, which itself suffered from the insufficient use of modern technology, its focus on the export of raw materials or basic processing, insufficient professional work, and insignificant export of industrial goods.

Bibliography

Aldcroft, Derek (2001) *The European economy 1914-2000*. London, New York.
Aldcroft, Derek (2006) *Europe's Third World, The European Periphery in the Interwar Years*. Burlington.
Aleksić, Vesna (2010) Foreign Financial Capital as the Catalyst of Serbian Economic Development before the Second World War. In: Hinić, Branko/Šojić, Milan/Đurđević, Ljiljana (eds.): *Economic and Financial Stability in SE Europe in a Historical and Comparative Perspective: conference proceedings. Forth Annual Conference of SEEMHN*. Belgrade.
Anonymous (1930) Jugoslovenski novčani zavodi. In: *Glasnik zavoda za unapređivanje spoljne trgovine 14*.
Berend, Iván (2009) *Ekonomska istorija u XX veku*. Belgrade.
Berend, Iván/György, Ránki (1982) *The European Periphery and Industrialization 1780-1914*. Cambridge.
Berend, Iván (1968) Agriculture. In: Kaser, M. C. (ed.): *Economic development for Eastern Europe: proceedings of a conference held by the International Economic Association*. London.
Bogart, Ernest (1920) *Direct and Indirect Costs of the Great World War*. New York.
Čehak, Kalman (1974) Neki aspekti i rezultati industrijalizacije Vojvodine do 1914. godine. In: *Acta Historico-oeconomica Iugoslaviae, Časopis za ekonomsku povijest Jugoslavije* I: 99-120.
Dimitrijević, Mira Kolar (1982) Osnovna obilježja industrijskog razvitka na području sjeverne Hrvatske od 1918. do 1929. godine. In: Kampuš, Ivan/Plećaš, Dušan (eds.) *Međunarodni kulturnopovijesni simpozij Mogersdorf 78*. Osijek.
Димитријевић, Сергије (1952) *Страни капитал у привреди бивше Југославије*. Београд.
Dimitrijević, Sergej (1962) *Privredni razvitak Jugoslavije od 1918. do 1941. godine*. Belgrade.

Ђуричић, В. М.; et al. (1927) *Наша народна привреда и национални приход.* Сарајево.

Đurović, Smiljana (1969) Industrija Srbije na početku privrednog života Kraljevine Srba, Hrvata i Slovenaca. In: *Istorija XX veka* 10: 167-226.

Đurović, Smiljana (1978) Razvitak železničkog saobraćaja i njegov uticaj na socijalne strukture Jugoslavije između dva rata. In: *Acta Historico-oeconomica Iugoslaviae, Časopis za ekonomsku povijest Jugoslavije* V: 183-188.

Đurović, Smiljana (1986) *Državna intervencija u industriji Jugoslavije 1918-1941.* Belgrade.

Đurović, Smiljana (1992) Da li su postojale ekonomske granice unutar jugoslovenskog istorijskog prostora 1918-1941? In: *Istorija 20. veka* 1-2: 111-123.

Đurović, Smiljana (1993) Problemi ekonomske integracije Jugoslavije 1918-1941. In: *Istorija 20. veka* 1-2: 179-189.

Fischer-Galati, Stephen (1992) Eastern Europe in the Twentieth Century: 'Old Wine in New Bottles'. In: Held, Joseph (ed.): *The Columbia History of Eastern Europe in the Twentieth Century.* New York.

Gnjatović, Dragana (1991) *Stari državni dugovi: prilog ekonomskoj i političkoj istoriji Srbije i Jugoslavije: 1862-1941.* Belgrade.

Gnjatović, Dragana (2009) Prva mera kreditne politike u Srbiji. In: *Bankarstvo* 38, 11/12: 42-61.

Hrelja, Kemal (1974) Razvoj ndustrije u Bosni i Hercegovini do Drugog svjetskog rata. In: *Acta Historico-oeconomica Iugoslaviae, Časopis za ekonomsku povijest Jugoslavije* I: 17-36.

Јагодић, Милош (2015) Процена демографских губитака Срба у периоду 1910-1921. In: *Српске студије* 6: 11-65.

Jagodić, Miloš/Radonjić, Ognjen (2015) Pyrrhic Victory: The Great War and its Immediate Consequences for Serbia's Economy. In: Vujačić, Ivan/Arandarenko, Mihail (eds.): *The Economic Causes and Consequences of the First World War.* Belgrade: 219-234.

Karaman, Igor (1974) Osnovna obilježja razvitka industrijske privrede u severnoj Hrvatskoj do Prvoga svjetskog rata. In: *Acta Historico-oeconomica Iugoslaviae, Časopis za ekonomsku povijest Jugoslavije* I: 37-59.

Karaman, Igor (1991) *Industrijalizacija građanske Hrvatske 1800-1941.* Zagreb.

Kaser, M. C. (ed., 1968) *Economic development for Eastern Europe: proceedings of a conference held by the International Economic Association.* London.

Kopsidis, Michael (2012) Missed Opportunity or Inevitable Failure? The Search for Industrialization in Southeast Europe 1870-1940. In: *EHES working papers in economic history* 19: 11.

Kostić, Cvetko (1955) *Seljaci industrijski radnici.* Belgrade.

Kršev, Boris (2007) *Finansijska politika Jugoslavije: 1918-1941.* Novi Sad.

Kukoleča, Stevan (1941) *Industrija Jugoslavije: 1918-1938.* Belgrade.

Lakatoš, Joso (1933) *Jugoslovenska privreda*. Zagreb.
Lampe, John (1975) Varieties of Unsuccessful Industrialization: The Balkan States Before 1914. In: *The Journal of Economic History* 35(1): 56-85.
Lampe, John/Jackson, Marvin (1982) *Balkan Economic History 1550-1950, From Imperial Borderlands to Developing Nations*. Bloomington.
Лазић, Милан (1999) *Пољопривредна производња у Краљевини Југославији*. Београд.
Љушић, Радош (2008) *Српска државност 19. века*. Београд.
Mathias, Peter/Pollard, Sidney (eds., 1989) *The Cambridge Economic History of Europe from the Decline of the Roman Empire Volume 8: The Industrial Economies: The Development of Economic and Social Policies*. Cambridge.
Мијатовић, Бошко (2013) Економска политика и конјунктура у Југославији 1919-1925. године. In: *Годишњак за друштвену историју* 3: 99-118.
Mijatović, Boško (2014) Zamena austrijskih kruna za dinare 1920. godine. In: *Историја 20 века* 32(1): 27-50.
Milenković, Milica (1972) *Ekonomske prilike u Srbiji i problemi besposlice u svetlu posledica prvog svetskog rata*. Slavonski Brod.
Миљковић Катић, Бојана (2014) *Пољопривреда Кнежевине Србије: (1834-1867)*. Београд.
Министарство финансија (1939) *Министарство финансија Краљевине Југославије 1918-1938*. Београд.
Мирковић, Мијо (1932) *Спољна трговинска политика*. Београд.
Mirković, Mijo (1950) *Ekonomska struktura Jugoslavije: 1918-1941*. Zagreb.
Mirković, Mijo (1958) *Ekonomska historija Jugoslavije*. Zagreb.
Mitrany, David (1936) *The effect of the war in southeastern Europe*. New Haven.
Nikolić, Goran (2003) *Kurs dinara i devizna politika Kraljevine Jugoslavije 1918-1941*. Belgrade.
Pertot, Vladimir (1971) *Ekonomika međunarodne razmjene Jugoslavije, knjiga 1, analiza razdoblja između 1919 i 1968 godine*. Zagreb.
Petaković, Jelena (2010) Komparativna analiza poljoprivrede na Balkanu od 1925. do 1939. na osnovu statističkih izveštaja Društva naroda. In: *Tokovi istorije* 2: 24-46.
Petranović, Branko (1980) *Istorija Jugoslavije 1918-1978*. Belgrade.
Ristović, Milan (1991) *Nemački novi poredak i jugoistočna Evropa 1940/1941-1944/1945*. Belgrade.
Schulze, Max-Stephan/Wolf, Nikolaus (2009) On the Origins of Border Effects: Insights from the Habsburg Empire. In: *Journal of Economic Geography* 9: 177-136.
Schulze, Max-Stephan/Wolf, Nikolaus (2012) Economic Nationalism and Economic Integration: The Austro-Hungarian Empire in the Late Nineteenth Century. In: *Economic History Review* 65(2) 652-673.
Singleton, Fred/Carter, Bernard (1982) *The Economy of Yugoslavia*. New York.

Šorn, Jože (1974) Doprinos proučavanju problema "industrijska revolucija u jugoslovenskim zemljama" (s osobitim obzirom na Sloveniju). In: *Acta Historico-oeconomica Iugoslaviae, Časopis za ekonomsku povijest Jugoslavije.* I: 141-146.

Stajić, Stevan (1959) *Nacionalni dohodak Jugoslavije 1923-1929 u stalnim i tekućim cenama.* Belgrade.

Stavrijanos, Leften (2005) *Balkan posle 1453. godine.* Belgrade.

Svennilson, Ingvar (1954) *Growth and stagnation in the European economy.* Geneva.

Tomašević, Jozo (1938) *Novac i kredit.* Zagreb.

Tomašević, Jozo (1955) *Peasants, politics, and economic change in Yugoslavia.* Stanford.

Општа државна статистика, Краљевина Југославија (ed.): *Статистички годишњак:* 1929, I; 1932, IV; 1936, VII; 1938-1939, IX. Београд.

Петровић, Јеленко (1930) *Окућје или заштита земљорадничког минимума, (§ 471 тач. 4а грађ. суд. поступка и односне одредбе пореских, царинских и монополских закона).* Београд.

Поповић, Ратибор (1940) *Аграрна пренасељеност Југославије.* Београд.

Рафаиловић, Јелена (2018) *Текстилна индустрија у Краљевини Срба, Хрвата и Словенаца и Бугарској 1919-1929.* Београд.

Ристић, Теофан (1938) *Борба за земљу и наша аграрна реформа.* Београд.

Српске новине 128, XLVIII, 08.06.1880; 285, LVI, 29.12.1889.

Тасић, Антоније (1992) Југословенско банкарство између два рата. In: *Глас САНУ* 26, CCLXVI: 147-208.

Вучо, Никола (1955) *Привредна историја Србије до Првог светског рата.* Београд.

Вучо, Nikola (1958) *Poljoprivreda Jugoslavije: 1918-1941.* Belgrade.

Vučo, Nikola (1968) *Agrarna kriza u Jugoslaviji 1930-1934.* Belgrade.

Vučo, Nikola (1974) Pogled na industrijsku revoluciju u Srbiji u XIX veku. In: *Acta Historico-oeconomica Iugoslaviae, Časopis za ekonomsku povijest Jugoslavije* I: 79-98.

Вучо, Никола (1981) *Развој индустрије у Србији у XIX веку.* Београд.

Чалић, Мари-Жанин (2004) *Социјална историја Србије 1815-1941, успорени напредак у индустријализацији.* Београд.

Imagining the *zadruga*
Zadruga as a Political Inspiration to the Left and the Right in Serbia, 1870-1945

Dubravka Stojanović

The concept of *zadruga* could be called the ideological subterranean river of Serbian political history. It appeared in public discourse and disappeared from it, only to pop up on the political stage once again in completely different historical circumstances. By changing contexts it also changed its meaning, gaining new features and losing some older ones. However, research conducted for the Sorbonne's project "The Political Legacy of Zadruga in the South Slavic Area" has shown its persistence over a long historical period and on completely opposite sides of the political spectrum. The *zadruga* was positioned as the key political ideal for Svetozar Marković's early socialists from the early 1870s onwards, but it was also the key ideal of the extreme right in the 1930s and 1940s. Both Milan Nedić, the prime minister of the Serbian collaborationist government during the Nazi occupation, and Dimitrije Ljotić, the leader of the most important section of the armed forces that cooperated with the occupiers, found their primary political inspiration in the *zadruga*.

This presence of *zadrugas* in different positions and different contexts is all the more interesting for the fact that extended families, the family *zadrugas*, were quite uncommon in Serbia even in Svetozar Marković's days, and even then it was clear that they were breaking down under the sway of the widespread national and social modernization. It therefore seems legitimate to pose the following questions: to what extent was this a utopian model that held up an already finished past as the future? To what extent was it just a demagogic narrative whose purpose was practical politics: winning over the poor rural masses, who, until the Second World War, had constituted the vast majority of the population? Was this a political project that grew out of underdevelopment, became its reflection, but also hindered further development?

This chapter will present data from unusual comparative research. It will compare political phenomena which are temporally very distant. Furthermore, it will compare phenomena from different and opposite ends of the political spectrum, those on the far right with those on the far left. Persisting as the key political term, *zadruga* was employed in very different contexts – from an imaginary idyllic socialist society of equals in the mid-1800s to the cornerstone and bulwark of racial purity almost a century later. This chapter will primarily take into account those different contexts, since it would otherwise entail simplifications and equalizations of the movements which were, both temporally and in terms of their ideological affiliation, very far apart. That would be methodologically inaccurate and would not lead us to a justifiable conclusion. With all the methodological precautions, comparisons will be drawn around the basic axis – the ideal of the family *zadruga* as a political and social utopia.

The research has shown that the *zadruga* ideal arose in numerous discussions when the participants in the political struggle spoke about politics, society, and economic organization. For this reason, the use of the term in this chapter will be confined to these three broad fields, which will best demonstrate the similarities and differences in its use.

1. The *zadruga* as a political ideal

The fundamental political question in Serbia since the 19th century concerned which type of state would emerge after it gained first autonomy and then independence. Among the issues to raise conflicting opinions was the issue of which state model was to be emulated and, in the 19th century, several political movements arose which advocated the adoption of different European models. First of all, in the early 1870s, there emerged the socialist movement led by Svetozar Marković, who held that these conditions – considering the idiosyncrasies of Serbian society, with poor farmers constituting almost ninety percent of its population – were most suitable for creating a special model of the popular state, different both from the liberal and the absolutist concepts. This ideal of the popular state in Marković's works, despite all the social and political changes, would persist for a long time in the Serbian political discourse, and would dominate the politics of the People's Radical Party (founded in 1881), which found its ideological underpinning in the very principles developed by Svetozar Marković. What is particularly interesting is that the ideal of the popular state also found support among extreme right-wing ideologues in the interwar period. Hence the concept deserves special attention, and what is particularly important for this project is the fact that the people's state model found its main inspiration in the family *zadruga*.

2. The popular state

The ideology of the popular state came about as a reaction to the early formation of the modern state, the first signs of class disintegration of the peasant nation and the decline of traditional institutions (Perović 2006: 101), primarily the family *zadruga*. The first ideologue of the popular state concept, Svetozar Marković, said that such a state is the same as society, that it abolishes the division between those who govern and those who are governed, that it should be a federation of municipalities, an extended family *zadruga* in which the people govern themselves (Perović 2006: 12): "The popular state is based on the principles of popular sovereignty. The people must try to eliminate all the ideological professions in society, such as judges, legislators, lawyers, as well as policemen and soldiers. Every citizen must be a defender of his county and, with education expanding, the manufacturing worker should at the same time be capable of doing the types of jobs that are done today by "specialists" from the ideological professions (Perović 1985: 310).

Marković clearly saw the popular state as an antithesis to the modern state that at the time was pioneering institutions in Serbia. Thus, he insisted that the main objective of his program was: "to completely abolish the current bureaucratic system of state administration and replace it with popular self-government in all the domains of our social system."[1] According to Marković, only the popular state could deliver his other ideal – social equality, which was, again, a prerequisite for attaining political freedom. According to him, this freedom could not exist without a society of complete equals. In addition, for him such a society and such a state were the preconditions for national liberation, at which point Marković's social and political platform merged with the national one.

In 1881, the year the People's Radical Party was formed, conditions in Serbia had changed somewhat. A series of factors led the newly formed party to abandon Marković's revolutionary concept and to opt for a peaceful road to the popular state by expanding voting rights and using parliamentary institutions. This is how the Radicals gave up on the leap forward and accepted the idea of social and political reform. The central question for our topic is whether the change of political means also meant changing political goals; that is to say, whether, in the final two decades of the 19th century, the Radicals genuinely dropped Marković's platform and with it the political ideals derived from the patriarchal *zadruga*.

Analysis of historical sources setting out the Radical Party's programmatic principles indicates that throughout this stage, from 1881 to the early 1900s, Marković's ideals were retained regarding the fundamental issues, such as ownership, types of production, and forms of state. The central axis of the radical ideology remained the creation of the popular state as the antithesis to the liberal, legal, and civil state. The popular state was understood as the collective owner of capital and the organizer of national production; like the *zadrugas*, it had the duty of ensuring

---

[1] Marković, Svetozar (1875) Narodna partija. In: *Oslobođenje*, no. 16, 5 February 1875, cited after: Perović, Latinka (2006) *Između anarhije i autokratije. Srpsko društvo na prelazima vekova, XIX-XX*. Belgrade: 103.

the equal distribution of wealth. The party's first ideologue, Pera Todorović, wrote: "Our party knows that by using the power of the state, this country can create such economic institutions which would lead the people to prosperity, so the party is striving to take this power away from the bureaucracy and give it to the people, so that general welfare can be achieved in which universal enlightenment and freedom in the true sense of the word can be developed."[2]

There are numerous documents, both public and confidential, that can confirm the survival of ideological continuity over the final two decades of the 19th century. Among the documents outlining the political platform are Pašić's 1872 letters to the minister of education, a secret draft constitution from 1882, letters to Metropolitan Mihailo from 1884, and especially the letter to the head of the Russian Ministry of Foreign Affairs, Ivan Zinoviev, from 1887. In this letter, Pašić sketches out his political conceptions and writes, directly referring to the *zadruga*: "The main point of our political struggle is to maintain the fine institutions agreeable to the Serbian character and to stop implementing new Western institutions which would undermine the sovereign life of our people and subvert the popular movement and life" (Pašić 1995: 241). Apart from numerous documents, the most important piece of writing is Pašić's position paper "Sloga Srbo-Hrvata" (The Harmony of Serbo-Croats), most likely dating from the late 1880s (Pašić 1995). The text expressed the essence of his Slavophilic understanding of state and society, which primarily places the *zadruga* as the central political inspiration.

The last stage covered in this paper begins with the coup of 1903, after which the Radicals almost continuously remained in power for the next 23 years, and lasts until Pašić's death, although the party did not lose power even after that. Pašić himself spoke a lot less frequently during this period, and political principles were primarily discussed by the Radical deputies, who held 80% of the Assembly seats. For them, the state was still primarily a socio-economic category (Popović-Obradović 2008: 329) which, until the First World War, they had described as a large *zadruga* (Popović-Obradović 2008: 287). One of the most active deputies in the Assembly, Aleksa Ratarac, said: "Serbia is a large *zadruga*, and we are the representatives of this *zadruga*, and it is better when more people decide what is to be done."[3]

The party's evolution and its coming to power did not produce changes in the social structure of its parliamentary deputies, who were mostly representatives of poor rural communities. It is true that, at this stage, a new generation of European-educated, young and modern politicians emerged, but the majority of them were technocrats and did not discuss party principles. On the contrary, rural deputies

---

2 "Zapisnik rada Glavne skupštine Narodne radikalne stranke, III sastanak", in: *Samouprava*, 27. July 1882; Perović (1995: 123).

3 *Stenografske beleške narodne skupštine*, 12 May 1910, Belgrade, 1911, 2997.

remained the main speakers, and they still argued for "equality in poverty", retaining the basic ideas of early Serbian socialism in their discourse.

Even though they expounded on their principles less frequently after coming to power, the Radicals reaffirmed the most important tenets of their faith with their political actions. The only thing that changed from when they took power was that the ideal of the popular state turned into the practice of the party state, erasing any difference between the nation as a politically homogenous entity and the mass ruling party, which controlled 80% of the parliamentary seats. The party state meant that the power of the ruling party was greater than the fundamental laws of the country, which undermined the laws, but also the state itself. The concept of the party state is best seen from how the power of the majority was understood, with the opposition describing it as the "majority terror". The party ideologue Stojan Protić repeatedly argued that a government which holds the majority has the right to violate laws, "When it comes to the national interest, the government (backed by the majority) not only can, but sometimes must do something outside the law."[4] While commenting on such positions, the opposition weekly *Nedeljni pregled* wrote: "The Radical Party has subordinated the state to itself in all things and, under the pretentious slogan that the party is more important than the state, it is using Serbia as a cash cow whose exclusive owner is the People's Radical Party."[5]

Several decades later, after the great changes brought by the First World War, the founding of the Kingdom of Serbs, Croats and Slovenes, the constitutional debate on the form of the state and the economic collapse of 1929, the *zadruga* ideal also appeared on the Serbian extreme right. In the writings of Dimitrije Ljotić and later, during the Second World War, in the speeches and writings of Milan Nedić, the prime minister under occupation, we again find the ideal of the *zadruga* state, which was supposed to be the foundation of the popular state. These two models were somewhat different, but the key word that binds them – *zadruga* – was present in both names. Nedić referred to his state as a *zadruga*-peasant state, while Ljotić called his a professional-*zadruga* state. (Ljotić used the archaic term 'stalež', which literally translates as 'estate', but for convenience we will call them professions or associations). Already evident in these phrases, the crucial difference is that Ljotić saw the future society as organized into professions, approaching the ideal of the Italian fascist corporate state, while Nedić emphasized the peasantry as a collective agent of the future social and political system.

Although doctrinal differences are clear, these two models had a visible common feature – the *zadruga*. This similarity was not merely terminological, because a closer analysis of what the two leaders said and wrote about the *zadruga* reveals that this institution was what they saw as the foundation of the future state and

---

4 "Samostalci ruše parlamentarizam", in: *Samouprava*, 29 May 1907.
5 *Nedeljeni pregled*, no. 2, 1908: 35.

society. It should be noted that it was a *future* structure, because Ljotić, despite the *zadruga* being a rarity at the time, often insisted that the return to it does not mean a return to the past, but that it is a concept of the future, which speaks about the utopian nature of this ideology, comparable to the ideology of Svetozar Marković.

It was in the *zadruga* that both Nedić and Ljotić saw the Serbian uniqueness and authenticity compared to related movements. Emphasizing this specificity, Nedić wrote that "Serbia has its own national socialism epitomized in family *zadrugas*."

Ljotić also emphasized in a series of texts the difference he found important between his movement and fascism and Nazism. He insisted that the understanding of professions in his ideology was "neither Hitlerian nor Mussolinian, but purely national, Yugoslavian", underlining that the institutions of the new state should be created from the "national spirit".[6] In addition, he wished to avoid terminological misconceptions that could arise from the modern usage of the term *zadruga* (cooperative): "Here we must stress that the *zadrugas* of our spirit, of our ideology, are not cooperatives that emerged in England or Germany, but cooperatives that grew from the roots of the Yugoslav family *zadruga* and the Yugoslav racial spirit".[7] Nedić also insisted on authenticity, declaring: "We do not need a foreign seed. We Serbs have the finest social structure in the old Serbian *zadruga* system. It is not founded on platitudes or pleasant slogans [...]. We wish to draw on the interpretations of the old Serbian *zadruga* system. We want this old Serbian family *zadruga* spirit to become the faith, knowledge, and understanding of the whole Serbian nation. The most perfect order is to be found in the *zadruga*".[8]

It is interesting that, although there were scarcely any *zadrugas* at the time, Ljotić insisted that they had survived, that they were still there. This is why he insisted that his concept did not mean a return to the past, but that it was real, claiming it could not be undermined either by capitalism or legislators or sociologists who "sounded the death knell" for it, because "to this day it lives in the Yugoslav countryside".[9] In insisting on its continued existence, Ljotić sought to underline the uniqueness of his movement, emphasizing that, in both Italy and Germany, it was the state and the party that organized those corporations and professions while, in the case of Serbia, they emerged from the old social structure based on *zadrugas*, which facilitated "freedom and self-government".[10]

The state, for which both Nedić and Ljotić stood, similar to Svetozar Marković and later the Radicals, had several basic functions: it was supposed to solve social

---

6 Dimitrije Ljotić, "Čemu težimo?", in: *Sabrana dela*, 3: 139.
7 Dimitrije Ljotić, "Staleži i Zbor", in: *Sabrana dela*, 3: 114.
8 Quoted after: Milosavljević, Olivera (2006) *Potisnuta istina. Kolaboracija u Srbiji 1941-1944*. Belgrade: 268.
9 Dimitrije Ljotić, "Staleži i Zbor", in: *Sabrana dela*, 3: 113.
10 Dimitrije Ljotić, "Staleška demokratija", in: *Sabrana dela*, 3: 147.

and economic problems (to be discussed in more detail in a separate section), abolish the existing institutions of parliamentary democracy and, finally, bring about national unity. In its characteristics, it was the opposite of a liberal state, because in it people should govern directly, and not through institutions described as "slow and cumbersome".[11] Ljotić said that democracy was the government of numbers, that parliamentarism meant irresponsibility, and that parties divided the people. In contrast, his concept meant "an organic life, the people, the state".[12] He wrote that Zbor stood for "the professional-*zadruga* state in which the people, through professional associations, will take matters into their own hands. The people want to control and handle all the means of national production, and not leave them to individuals".[13] He saw this type of state organization as superior, as one that went beyond the interests of social groups, which he sought to merge into one: "Our road is the rule of the people, a total state, a total national policy instead of the petty, partisan one".

Ljotić dedicated one article precisely to this matter, differentiating between the popular and the national state in its very title: "The national or the popular state". In the article he insists that every national state is not at the same time a popular state, that it can become one only if it "suits the origin, spirit, and destiny of the nation, if it expresses its deepest feelings and beliefs".[14] The popular state is Ljotić's vital idea, because such a state would also have a national function, alongside the social and economic, based on his key concept – the organic unity of the nation. According to Ljotić, this unity was crushed by liberal democracy, which tore society apart into groups and individuals. A popular state would allow the organic unity based on cooperative principles that would solve all human relations: "to harmonize human relations and produce the hormone of harmony and mutual solidarity".[15] Only such a state could answer the people's needs: "The state needs to emerge from the people's needs and draw its strength from the national characteristics".[16]

3. Political parties

The question at hand is the perception, both on the left and the right, of the relationship between the people and the popular state. It is interesting that both sides of the political spectrum found the same solution: the popular state was the one to "draw in the entire people and form the unbreakable bond between the people

---

11 Dimitrije Ljotić, "Veliki zbor g. Dimitrija Ljotića u Vršcu", In: *Sabrana dela*, 3: 65.
12 Dimitrije Ljotić, "Naš nacionalizam", in: *Sabrana dela*, 5: 105.
13 Dimitrije Ljotić, "Kakvu politiku hoćemo?", in: *Sabrana dela*, 3: 103.
14 Dimitrije Ljotić, "Nacionalna ili narodna država", in: *Sabrana dela*, 5: 88.
15 Dimitrije Ljotić, "Staleži i Zbor", in: *Sabrana dela*, 3: 114.
16 Dimitrije Ljotić, "Veliki zbor g. Dimitrija Ljotića u Vršcu", in: *Sabrana dela*, 3: 65.

and the state." It is a populist movement aiming to incorporate the entire people, it is the connective tissue of the popular state (Perović 1985: 136). Such movements are the opposite of modern parties, whose purpose is to represent the interests of particular parts of a society. Popular movements or popular parties seek to cover the entire people, abolish social division, unite the nation, defy political pluralism, and become the foundation of a monolithic regime. This is the crucial feature of populist movements. In fact, many other movements refer to the people, but populist movements are different in that they speak of themselves as representatives of the entire nation understood as a homogeneous whole, an organism, in Ljotić's terminology, which cannot be divided. Accordingly, such movements are bitter enemies of political parties, and even of representative democracy, because they see it as an instrument for dividing a homogeneous national body. The "movement" is also a reflection of the essence of anti-pluralist political thought. Its task is to draw in the entire nation, and those who find themselves outside of it cannot be either legitimate or legal. Movements assign themselves historical missions, they are characterized by fanaticism and exclusivity toward every political other (Perović 2006: 129), which is derived from the concept of the popular party and the popular state, which do not tolerate political divisions. The other can only be a traitor, the one who divides the monolith.

The Radical Party saw itself only in that light: "The great Radical Party, which the people do not separate from its name [...] the Radical Party, or better yet the Serbian people [...]. In ten years, the Radical Party will be the same as the Serbian people".[17] They kept insisting that they were not an "ordinary political phenomenon",[18] but an expression of the "people's soul",[19] its essence. They wrote that their party best reflects the needs of the Serbian people, that it is a guarantee for survival.[20] They explained the founding of the party itself as a natural phenomenon, like a geyser: "Its power erupted strongly from the people itself, and it erupted so strongly that the organizers of the party barely managed to channel all the movements in it into a single course."[21]

The cornerstone of the party state was the People's Radical Party, which was commonly described by its members as a church, an army (Stojanović 2013: 40), or, precisely – a *zadruga*. Referring to the Independent Radical Party split in 1911, the radical newspaper *Samouprava* wrote: "Reasonable people must know that true and devoted friends of a *zadruga*, should they disagree with its line, will not work on splitting up the *zadruga* [...]. The Independents left the common house [...] and star-

---

17 "Pisma seljaku. Od jednog starovremskog radikala", In: *Samouprava*, 6 May 1908.
18 "Pisma seljaku. Od jednog starovremskog radikala", In: *Samouprava*, 6 May 1908.
19 "Narodna svest", in: *Samouprava*, 14 June 1906.
20 "Biračima", in: *Samouprava*, 13 April 1908.
21 "Tridesetogodišnjica Narodne radikalne stranke", in: *Samouprava*, 25 December 1911.

ted working against their old *zadruga*, the Radical Party."²² In internal party debates too, members of the central committee identified their party with the *zadruga*, often evoking that ideal. For example, in a lively debate about the relationship between the party organs, it was said: "Indeed, there should be order in a house, and everyone who comes to that house, that is to say that *zadruga*, should and must respect its order [...]. It should be known that in union there is strength [...] otherwise, as soon as one member of this community reaches for dictatorship, the community breaks up and the *zadruga* is stranded."²³

Dimitrije Ljotić held a very similar view of his political organization. It is true that in the 1930s this type of political organization was dominant on the European right and that the Italian fascists began as a movement and only subsequently morphed into a political party, while the German Nazis began as a party and later became a movement (Mitrović 2009). But it should be noted that the idea of the popular movement had strong roots in the Serbian political tradition. It was an expression of defiance against the institutions of parliamentary democracy and political parties as their key drivers, but also a way to undo the plurality of "the people", which Ljotić, like Pašić, understood to be breaking up or dividing the nation. In several speeches and articles he insisted that Zbor was not a political party, but a moral and spiritual movement. His arguments were similar to those of the Radicals, and the basic idea was to deny the possibility of pluralistic thinking in society and to reduce the entire society and nation to a single line, a popular movement, the movement under his leadership.

As a popular movement that did not recognize differences, Zbor, according to its leader, was supposed to connect fragmented popular forces and discipline special interests. He said that a popular movement grows from below, from the people,²⁴ that this was a genuine organization and not a party. Similar to the Radicals, the members of Zbor saw their movement as a natural phenomenon that occurs in an eruptive manner and draws its power directly from the people: "the people's movement will swell like an unstoppable life current".²⁵

By portraying their movements and parties almost as natural phenomena, these political groups reaffirmed their respective ideological tenets. If political movements connected the people with the popular state, then this meant strengthening, even institutionally, the monistic character of these ideological systems, which see a threat in all the pluralism, and see an enemy in any "political other" (Perović 2006: 387-400). A different opinion appeared as something antagonistic to the desired natural unity, a foreign object against which, as the opposition claimed, "any

---

22 "Narod u jedinstvu u Radikalnoj stranci", in: *Samouprava*, 11 May 1906.
23 "Rad zemaljske radikalne konferencije održane 21 i 22 novembra 1911" (1912) *Stenografske beleške Narodne skupštine*, 1875-1876, Belgrade: 44.
24 Dimitrije Ljotić, "Razmišljanja o vladama", in: *Sabrana dela*, 4: 40.
25 Dimitrije Ljotić, "Stranke ili pokreti", in: *Sabrana dela*, 1: 68.

means are allowed" (Stojanović 2013: 107). Apart from other social and historical factors, this ideological axis was one of the foundations of authoritarian regimes, which were repeated in Serbian political history, as well as in the history of political violence, as one of its key features (Stojanović 2013: 103-125).

4. The *zadruga* as an economic ideal

As we mentioned earlier, the basic functions of popular states were social and economic ones. From Svetozar Marković onward, it was seen as a way to avoid capitalism (Perović 1985: 121) and prevent the division of society into, as Nikola Pašić later said, "those who govern and those who are governed" (Pašić 1995: 98). The main objective of the popular state was to prevent the penetration of capitalism, private property, and the free market. As a state – a union of communities, an expanded *zadruga*, in which the people govern themselves, in the belief of its ideologues – it could help Serbia avoid replicating the Western European path of development (Perović 1985: 125).

In Marković's works, the *zadruga* was primarily a model for solving the property question. He opposed private property and argued for shared labor and common ownership, which would allow everyone in Serbian society to remain equal by way of redistributing social wealth. It was Marković himself who put it succinctly: "Our task is not to destroy capitalist production, which in fact does not exist, but to transform the small patriarchal property into a common good and thus skip an entire epoch of economic development – the epoch of the capitalist economy."[26] This type of social and political development was to be realized by the popular state, which would, according to Marković, abolish the division between the governing and the governed as a union of communes, an extended *zadruga* in which the people govern themselves.

Marković's program began transforming from position papers into political practice when the first members of the parliament close to these ideas, especially Svetozar's brother Jevrem Marković and Adam Bogosavljević, turned the ideological agenda into a political demand in their Proposal to the National Assembly in 1876, opposing the construction of railways and seeking to disband the gendarmerie, close down forestry schools, the National Theater, the teacher training school, and the only three diplomatic missions Serbia had, cut clerical salaries and ban schools that taught foreign languages, rhetoric and music. The Proposal clearly expressed fears that such institutions would change both society and individuals: "If you wish to create a bunch of soft weaklings out of a nation, let it have such schools, let those schools teach many different languages, poetic and oratorical styles, let them teach

---

26 "Inaugural address", *Gesammelte Politische Schriften*, 2nd edition, Tübingen 1955, 23.

painting, dancing, music, singing [...] in a few decades you shall see an outgrowth of a difficult class of people on the national body."[27]

In his treatise *Sloga Srbo-Hrvata* (The Harmony of Serbo-Croats), Nikola Pašić proved his conceptual continuity in relation to his "political fathers", arguing for the adoption of economic relations to the *zadruga* ideal: "Serbian *zadrugas* can become a model in production." This model primarily meant protection against capitalism (Perović 2006: 134), which in the Harmony of Serbo-Croats was clearly stated and adapted to his Slavophile understanding of state and society, primarily by placing the *zadruga* as the central ideal: "The Serbian *zadruga* is the social institution which is closest to the Russian 'obshchina' and behind this Serbian *zadruga* stands the Serbian commune which has not dropped or abandoned the demand for its 'communal self-government' and which still has ample communal land, belonging to the whole commune, to all its members" (Perović 2006: 134). He did not see the *zadruga* as something ancient or utopian, but as a real economic future for the common state of Serbs and Croats: "The Serbian *zadruga* can serve as a role model in production, and the Serbian commune will be an example of civic life in the Serbo-Croatian state."

But the *zadruga* was more than that. From the time of Svetozar Marković, the *zadruga* was understood as a peculiar expression of Slavic civilization, its protection against the West, and a profound link with Russian civilization. This was again expressed most consistently by Pašić in *The Harmony of Serbo-Croats*: "The *zadruga* is an advantage of the Slavic civilization because it solves the socio-economic problem, which the West did not resolve. In the *zadruga* there is collective ownership of land, because collectivism protects us against the West" (Perović 1985: 126). This demarcation was extremely important to Pašić, it was one of his program's vital features that tied him firmly to his ideological predecessor – Svetozar Marković. It was a model of economy and society different from those provided by Western Europe through its mode of development, and the idea that this road can be avoided, that one does not have to take it, is unequivocally expressed in Pašić's crucial work. Again, the *zadruga* is seen as the framework for this autonomous path: "The Radical Party wants to prevent the people from adopting the errors of Western industrial society, where a proletariat and immense wealth are created, but instead wants to build industry on the basis of association. It wants to introduce full self-government as opposed to a bureaucratic system. Instead of capitalist enterprises, there should be workers' *zadrugas*" (Popović-Obradović 2008: 329; Pašić 1995: 43-44, 51).

Half a century later, with completely altered historical conditions, the Serbian radical right made the fight against liberal capitalism its main economic objective.

---

27 "Predlog Narodnoj skupštini" (1912) *Stenografske beleške Narodne skupštine*, 1875-1876, Belgrade: 1568; Perović 2006: 87.

It is interesting that Svetozar Marković had fought against capitalism even before it developed in Serbia, while the rightists developed their thinking when it looked like capitalism had reached its end, after the Great Depression of 1929. This breakdown sparked new lines of thinking throughout the world about the fate of capitalism, its crisis, and alternatives. The Serbian right wing tapped into this thinking when speaking about the end of capitalism, blaming the system of producing crises, and writing that "capitalism is unable to resolve the crisis, because the source of the crisis is the basis of the capitalist system, free play with human interests, which is why capitalism leads only to chaos."[28] This otherwise often repeated criticism was gradually complemented, especially as the thirties progressed, by racist and anti-Semitic elements of their ideology, and they wrote that capitalism was as it was because it was "the lever by which the Jews govern",[29] which brought them closer to *Action française* and the German National Socialists.

What is pertinent to this paper is the fact that Dimitrije Ljotić, in contrast to capitalism, and similar to Marković and the Radicals, saw the solution in the popular state, because only such a state could, according to them, enable politics and economy to unite to form an organic whole. He expressed this succinctly in one sentence: "*Zadrugas* must form the basis of the political system [...], the basis of the economic and national order. Only then will the state become an organism".[30]

The starting point was that the political form of the popular state can guarantee better property and economic relations than a liberal-democratic state, primarily because it would install full control: "we want state intervention to regulate relations between labor and capital".[31] This is supposed to be the basis of the planned economy Ljotić advocated: "We are against liberal capitalism, injustices, disorder. We seek the intervention of the state. In contrast to the liberal economy, we advocate the *zadruga*-type, organic, national economy where all the relations are regulated."[32]

Another important point for this chapter is the fact that the right wing also assumed Serbia had an authentic, traditional solution to the capitalist crisis that had shaken the world. Nedić said: "The spiritual foundation of our economic cooperatives stems from the family *zadruga*. And this originates from our distinctive products, the racial-biological and ethnic realities" (Milosavljević 2006: 301) Ljotić also unequivocally argued that the spirit of *zadrugas*, which he promoted as the antithesis to the capitalist free market spirit, had special roots in Serbia, writing that "the

---

28 Dimitrije Ljotić, "Kapitalizam", In: *Sabrana dela*, 11: 102.
29 Dimitrije Ljotić, "Skupština glavnog saveza", in: *Sabrana dela*, 9: 171.
30 Dimitrije Ljotić, "Zadrugarstvo u staleškoj državi", In: *Sabrana dela*, 3: 134.
31 Dimitrije Ljotić, "Kakvu politiku hoćemo?", in: *Sabrana dela*, 5: 61.
32 Dimitrije Ljotić, "Zadrugarima glavnog saveza", in: *Sabrana dela*, 3: 74.

spirit of the *zadruga* movement originated in the family *zadruga*, so it is different from others. It is a deeper community than is usually understood."[33]

In his speeches and writings, Dimitrije Ljotić remained vague regarding ownership, not giving a clear answer to the question whether the people's property, which he advocated, also meant the property of the state. He wrote: "The people want to take their affairs into their own hands. Zbor wants to return the entire land and wealth of the nation into the people's hands. The people want to run and handle all the means of national production, and for them not to be handled by individuals, groups, cliques, trusts, cartels."[34] This is where he saw the crucial role of *zadrugas*, as a link between the state and the people, in the transmission of ownership: "We are fighting for the people to be handed back, through professional and *zadruga* organizations, the right to deal with their social and economic difficulties".[35] Apart from the ownership question being regulated through professions and *zadrugas*, although he did not say how this would work, the system would look like this: "fair taxation, a radical exchange of goods, transition from an anarchist to an organized planned economy, socialization of large enterprises",[36] which clearly inferred nationalization or partial abolition of private property.

By setting such an economic system as his goal, Ljotić came dangerously close to his greatest ideological enemies, the Marxists, which probably led him to unequivocally embrace private property in a series of long articles. However, this was contrary to his previous works, in which he had advocated collective ownership. In these texts he called private property the "basis of our society",[37] trying to balance between irreconcilable ideological doctrines: "a planned economy will, along with the *zadruga*, limit the play of private interests and subordinate them to general ones, without destroying private property".[38]

The primary purpose of the *zadruga* both on the left and the right was to provide protection against the penetration of the capitalist system, seen as a product of the West and, therefore, foreign. In capitalism they saw the potential for exploitation within Serbia, but also for Serbia to be exploited by developed countries. But the primary motive for opposing capitalism was the attempt to preserve the premodern order, which was still dominant in the undifferentiated Serbian society. It was believed that the free market would provoke tectonic changes in the social structure. This is why the *zadruga* ideal was, first and foremost, a social ideal which was to be achieved or safeguarded by constructing a popular state and preventing

---

33 Dimitrije Ljotić, "Staleži i Zbor", In: *Sabrana dela*, 3: 113.
34 Dimitrije Ljotić, "Naša pobeda", In: *Sabrana dela*, 3: 117.
35 Dimitrije Ljotić, "Zadrugarstvo u staleškoj državi", in: *Sabrana dela*, 3: 131.
36 Dimitrije Ljotić, "Nekoliko osnovnih misli", in: *Sabrana dela*, 6: 32.
37 Dimitrije Ljotić, "Veliki zbor druga Dimitrija Ljotića u Petrovgradu", in: *Sabrana dela*, 3: 54.
38 Dimitrije Ljotić, "Veliki zbor druga Dimitrija Ljotića u Petrovgradu", in: *Sabrana dela*, 3: 54.

the capitalist development on the Serbian borders. The values of Serbian society they wanted to preserve were the values of the family *zadruga*.

5. The *zadruga* as a social ideal

Apart from being a political and economic ideal, the *zadruga* was, possibly most of all, a social ideal. It was this social thought of different political elites throughout Serbian history that was behind many political activities, and it constituted, as will be shown, the main ideological obstacle to Serbian modernization and Europeanization. In this regard too, the family *zadruga* remained the main inspiration politicians on both the left and the right turned to whenever they portrayed an ideal society. Their motives differed and the emphases they placed were diametrical, but the *zadruga* narrative as a social ideal persisted in very remote historical situations, different times and national frameworks. The basic components of this ideology, which can be found on the left and on the right, are egalitarianism, collectivism, and the glorification of the Serbian village as a guardian of the social and national identity, and its last defense.

5.1 Egalitarianism

In a society of negligible social differences, such as Serbia, a singular ideology was created and it emanated from a fear of change and reflected a desire for social petrification, preventing changes brought on by development. This ideological system connected patriarchal conservatism with European left-wing ideas (Stojanović 2003: 183), creating an amalgamation that would dominate the public discourse, but also influence the implementation of actual political decisions.

These ideas could primarily be heard in the National Assembly from the members of the ruling People's Radical Party, whose representatives proudly pointed out that it never became a "party of bosses", a testament to their egalitarian ideal included in the basic principles of their movement. They continued to advocate the philosophy of "equality in poverty", retaining the basic ideas of early Serbian socialism in their discourse.

The main representative of this line was the priest Milan Đurić, who was virtually a spokesman for Pašić himself. While arguing for the adoption of the law which would prevent the division of the *zadruga*, Đurić revealed his strong anti-Semitism: "We do not need wealth. The Serbian tribe is not an Israelite tribe and it does not run on money. We are all equal, not divided into classes like other nations."[39]

---

39 Speech by Milan Đurić, *SBNS*, 1910-1911, II, 12.

This ideal could be found not only among rural representatives, but also among elite intellectuals and scientists. Thus, a Belgrade University professor and government minister Jovan Žujović, asking for money for pensions, said in the Assembly: "Most probably I would not have been forced to ask for farmer's pensions today had a fairly equal division of property been preserved; had strong family *zadrugas* and a patriarchal life in them been preserved, had the taxes remained insignificant, the need for money would be slight. Today, unfortunately, this is not the case" (Žujović 1905: 755-756).

Apart from these speeches that could be described as lamenting the past, the egalitarian ideal continued to dominate the Assembly and directly influence the legislation. The problem with the traditional concept of social equality was not that it was rationally trying to prepare the country for modernizing transition and to reduce the price that had to be paid (Stojanović 2003: 187), but that it fought these changes and tried to prevent them. This type of egalitarianism proved to be anti-modernizing, an impediment to development. The most important argument was the fear of stratification. Thus one deputy pointed out when comparing Serbia to Russia: "I believe that it is not an exaggeration to say that the sudden application of cultural achievements to these two Slavic nations, related by faith, blood, and tradition, gave quite the same results: tattered tail-coats and torn elbows [...]", and again, discussing the egalitarian concept of society: "There are no conditions among the Serbian people for creating classes in the form we know in the West, because we are all children of the same class, the peasant class."[40]

It should be emphasized that the Radicals did not stop at the anti-modernizing narrative; rather the egalitarian ideal continued to dominate the Assembly and directly influence the legislation. The overwhelming parliamentary majority consisting of deputies from the countryside kept Pašić's government in power almost continuously from 1891 until his death in 1926. Within that time, Pašić formed 25 governments. Many reform laws were postponed or permanently rejected on the grounds of egalitarian arguments. That is why it seems accurate to claim that the Socialists and the Radicals in Serbia were an expression of "the original contradictions of a society faced with modernization, the contradictions between the patriarchal substratum and European forms which provoked resistance, frustration, and hostility" (Perović 2015: 20) There are many examples from the decade before the First World War which reveal that egalitarian discourse had not been limited to political demagogy and propaganda, but had represented a practical policy which had held back Serbian development in many ways. We can mention the decade-long debates on approving the funds for basic public works in Belgrade, which delayed the construction of the sewerage system in the capital for 35 years. The argument repeated every time was very similar to the one in the Proposal to

---

40 Speech by Đorđe Genčić, *SBNS*, 1903-I, 530.

the National Assembly of 1876: "If we embellish (!) Belgrade to the detriment of the people, we will be unable to bring out to the battlefield the kind of soldiers that we should."[41] In the 1930s and 40s, the far right was also dominated by similar, egalitarian social ideas, but the motives and objectives were different. Right-wing ideologues saw in social stratification a threat to the nation understood in an organicist manner. They saw a threat to its homogeneity, which was one of Dimitrije Ljotić's central ideas. He viewed all the stratification as "grinding down the social organism",[42] to which he opposed his organicist conception of collectivism: "With our class understanding we wish to unite all the fragmented parts and assemble them into a single organ of our country – the association – and unite these newly created organs into a single organic Yugoslav state".[43]

For Ljotić, the relation between associations and cooperatives was crucial, because they were the solution to what the Marxists called the problem of class. The association was for him a senior social category and a community, which, as he said, had determined our independent social development through the centuries.[44] According to Ljotić, *zadrugas* stood above associations, bringing together people from different associations, and he especially insisted on their civilizational, almost racial distinction, calling them the cornerstone of the Slavic social order.[45]

In the social sense, it was supposed to become the institution, under the corporate state, that produces "harmony and mutual solidarity for settling differences",[46] a necessary element for "harmonizing class and interpersonal relations."[47] Ljotić perfectly conveyed this unique economic, social, and national function of the cooperative in a single sentence: "Cooperatives must form the basis of the political system [...], the basis of the economic and national order." In such a state, the cooperative will be, as he wrote in a biologistic manner, a 'hormone'[48] providing solidarity to reconcile contradictions between classes and enabling the functioning of the planned economy.[49]

There is one striking difference between the leftist and rightist understanding of the cooperative which is also ideologically critical. The Serbian left imagined the cooperative as an egalitarian community of equal individuals, the cornerstone of a future classless society without inequality. In contrast, the right described a diametrically opposite notion of the cooperative. For Ljotić and Nedić, it was a

---

41 Speach by Miloš Ćosić, *SBNS*, 1909-1910, 1591.
42 Dimitrije Ljotić, "Staleži i Zbor", in: *Sabrana dela*, 3: 113.
43 Dimitrije Ljotić, "Čemu težimo?", in: *Sabrana dela*, 3: 141.
44 Dimitrije Ljotić, "Je li majka rodila junaka?", in: *Sabrana dela*, 3: 102.
45 Dimitrije Ljotić, "Izvori naših osnovnih načela", in: *Sabrana dela*, 3: 145.
46 Dimitrije Ljotić, "Zadrugarstvo u staleškoj državi", in: *Sabrana dela*, 3: 133.
47 Dimitrije Ljotić, "Zadrugarstvo u staleškoj državi", in: *Sabrana dela*, 3: 133.
48 Dimitrije Ljotić, "Nekoliko osnovnih misli", in: *Sabrana dela*, 6: 32.
49 Dimitrije Ljotić, "Kakvu politiku hoćemo?", in: *Sabrana dela*, 3: 73.

strictly hierarchical community, with a strong authority in the form of a head or elder leading it. Nedić, who was called both the leader and master of the house, transplanted the family cooperative model directly into the state: "The new Serbia will be a patriarchal, corporate, theocratic state, organized as a family where the leader is obeyed without question" (Milosavljević 2006: 39). Although in a much less patriarchal vein, Ljotić's *zadruga* is ideal also because of its hierarchy, order, and discipline, as opposed to democracy, which he defined as the main root of the global crisis: "In this cooperative the head of the house (elder) was the leader not only of material things, but also a spiritual and moral drive. An authority!"[50]

5.2 Collectivism

One of the fundamental political values which was read in the *zadruga* ideal was collectivism, that is to say a condition in which the community is superior to the individual and its interests are more important than the interests of each of its members. The format of that community could vary – from a society to a nation – but what bound them together was the emphasis on the collective over the individual, or more precisely, the annulling of the individual and his or her immersion in the collective. Such ideas could often be held by the deputies from the countryside, but also by prominent intellectuals, those with degrees from Western universities who formed the social and political elite of the country. Thus a leading ethnographer of his day and one of the pioneers of the field in Serbia, Sima Trojanović, writing in the most influential intellectual journal of the time – *Srpski književni glasnik* – with some glumness and resentment, described the practices in the *zadruga* and the changes brought about by its disappearance. He portrayed the *zadruga* almost mechanistically, as a well-oiled machine whose main advantage lay precisely in the fact that all its parts were subordinated to it: "In the *zadruga* the person is always subordinated to the community, and everything he does looks like the operation of a sprocket or some other part of the machine. With this dependence on the entire *zadruga* everything ran smoothly, until one day the person was *individualized*, that is to say until he began calculating for himself and his power separately and believing that he and his wife would do better separately and would acquire larger property" (Trojanović 1907: 742). There evidently is regret about the fact that individuals placed themselves above the collective and a certain reproach of the "scramble" for property, ownership, and self-interest, which the author more than likely would rather see subordinate to the interests of the community.

This issue was discussed even more explicitly in the newspapers belonging to the two strongest parties. While writing about the new project of creating agricultural cooperatives, the Radical *Samouprava* voiced resentment concerning the

---

50 Dimitrije Ljotić, "Staleži i Zbor", in: *Sabrana dela*, 3: 114.

organization and position of individuals in earlier patriarchal communities. What is clearly expressed is a commitment to the patriarchal model of society in which one does the thinking for all, and the collective protects the individual, who surrenders his or her individuality to the community, sacrificing it on the altar of collective security, "Moving from the patriarchal life, in which the *zadruga* elders, either by virtue of their age or intellect, took upon themselves the responsibility for the progress and the well-being of the entire *zadruga*; therefore, moving from this life to another one in which every member had to handle their own affairs, every individual became more fallible not only as a worker or creator of wealth, but also in upholding what he had already gained. He felt various harmful effects more strongly when he became autonomous than he had while he was in the *zadruga*, and his income scale was declining day by day."[51]

While it is true that the authors concluded the period of such relations had passed, the way they wrote about it reveals that they regarded a modern society, the atomized family, and self-conscious individuals as unwanted necessities. They openly stated that the concept was foreign to them, imported from the West, and extraneous. This could not reintroduce the *zadruga* or ossify the society, but such a discourse could become a hindrance to development.

These attitudes are especially visible in discussions about different types of freedom, which were often conducted on the pages of newspapers and magazines, and in the Assembly. While freedom and democracy were constantly invoked as principal and sacred political ideals, comparing discourses at different levels clearly shows that, when it came to national matters, the collective took precedence over the individual, while so-called external freedom (the freedom of the nation and its unification) was placed above internal freedom (the political freedom of the individual). That was actually the toughest test of the degree of society's democratization, which always came down to prioritizing ideals, and instead of the necessary balance between freedom, equality, and fraternity, an order was established with brotherhood on top, understood as a collective (the nation): "They [Serbs] need to work together, uniformly, unanimously. We need to think, feel, and work as one",[52] wrote *Odjek*, the Independent Radical Party daily, a splinter group of the old Radicals. The even more liberal *Dnevni list* wrote in similar fashion: "The political struggle that had either crushed or is now crushing separate units of our people should stop once and for all."[53]

A strong anti-individualism and reliance on the collective can be found in a series of articles by Ljotić, who often reflected on this subject. He wrote without reluctance that "all misfortune comes from individualism", repeating several times

---

51 "Bogatstvo naroda", in: *Samouprava*, 23 February 1908.
52 "Posle razočaranja", in: *Odjek*, 25 March 1909.
53 "Crnogorska emigracija", in: *Dnevni list*, 3 December 1910: 236.

that human society is not the sum of individuals, but a "being of a higher order, primarily a moral and historical being that lives and acts." Individualism was for Ljotić the essence of Westernism, which for him was a "frantic game of individual interests in economy, politics, and social relations".[54]

At the core of his organicist concept, the human individual could not have "primarily personal interests, but the interests of the community".[55] Individuals were seen only as parts of the whole, "fragments and limbs of the national body",[56] and in their historical totality in which all the generations, "the dead, the living, and those to come",[57] form the community. For Ljotić, the general interest must not be the sum of personal, individual interests, because the general was "something else. The nation is a collective being."[58] This was precisely the essential role of the *zadruga* spirit that was to "unify the fragmented parts of the nation and assemble them into a single organ."[59]

This new type of community was also a common feature with Nedić. Fiercely opposed to any plurality and particularism, he often defined society and the nation as homogenous entities: "My dear *zadruga* brothers, allow me to address you this way, following an old Serbian custom, when we were all brothers, all Serbs, not divided into parties, or coteries, when we were led by a single spirit, the spirit of our great ancestors and the spirit of mother Serbia" (Milosavljević 2006: 303).

This comparative study has revealed deep similarities between the populist socialism and extreme right-wing ideologies of the 1930s and 40s. Although those concepts were temporally and ideologically distant, there was a single conceptual pattern that united them, and which can be summed up in a single word – the zadruga. In those imageries, the zadruga was attributed different, often diametrically opposite features, but this actually confirms the hypothesis that a myth is a preferred depiction of the past, or that its long-term strength and persistence depends on the flexibility, extensibility, and ability to simultaneously communicate entirely different, even conflicting things, just like the myth of the zadruga. It was this ideological flexibility and adaptability that allowed it to play the role of the ideological subterranean river over a long historical timespan, to disappear from the discourse and reappear again, to be an inspiration in so many different contexts and to so many different political systems. It was neither a utopia nor demagogy. On the contrary, the concept of the zadruga was a persistent ideological cornerstone, the foundation of anti-pluralist, anti-liberal, anti-Western, and

---

54 Dimitrije Ljotić, "Dva izlaza", in: *Sabrana dela*, 3: 41.
55 Dimitrije Ljotić, "Ideali savremene omladine", in: *Sabrana dela*, 6: 203.
56 Dimitrije Ljotić, "Jedinka i zajednica", in: *Sabrana dela*, 11: 86.
57 Dimitrije Ljotić, "Dok još nismo roblje", in: *Sabrana dela*, 3: 30.
58 Dimitrije Ljotić, "Zbor i partije", in: *Sabrana dela*, 6: 108.
59 Dimitrije Ljotić, "Ni fašizam, ni nacizam", in: *Sabrana dela*, 3: 147.

anti-modernizing political orders. It was a concentrated ideological essence, a synthesis. But it was also a symptom which can open up a deeper understanding of Serbian society. The constant returning to the patriarchal, pre-modern ideal is a testament to the attempts by various political groups to hinder development and prevent changes. Returning to the zadruga is not proof that history is repeating itself, but that when there is a choice between the present and the past, it is the latter that is chosen.

Bibliography

"Biračima", In: *Samouprava*, 13 April 1908.
"Bogatstvo naroda", In: *Samouprava*, 23 February 1908.
"Crnogorska emigracija", In: *Dnevni list*, 3 December 1910, 236.
"Inaugural address", *Gesammelte Politische Schriften*, 2nd edition, Tübingen 1955, 23.
"Narod u jedinstvu u Radikalnoj stranci", In: *Samouprava*, 11 May 1906.
"Narodna svest", In: *Samouprava*, 14 June 1906.
"Pisma seljaku. Od jednog starovremskog radikala", In: *Samouprava*, 6 May 1908.
"Posle razočaranja", In: *Odjek*, 25 March 1909.
"Predlog Narodnoj skupštini" (1912) *Stenografske beleške Narodne skupštine*, 1875-1876, Belgrade: 1568.
"Rad zemaljske radikalne konferencije održane 21 i 22 novembra 1911" (1912) *Stenografske beleške Narodne skupštine*, 1875-1876, Belgrade: 44.
"Samostalci ruše parlamentarizam", In: *Samouprava*, 29 May 1907.
"Tridesetogodišnjica Narodne radikalne stranke", In: *Samouprava*, 25 December 1911.
"Zapisnik rada Glavne skupštine Narodne radikalne stranke, III sastanak", In: *Samouprava*, 27. July 1882.
Ćosić, Miloš, speech at *SBNS*, 1909-1910, 1591.
Đurić, Milan, speech at *SBNS*, 1910-1911, II, 12.
Genčić, Đorđe, speech at *SBNS*, 1903-I, 530.
Ljotić, Dimitrije (2001) *Sabrana dela*, 1-12. Belgrade.
Marković, Svetozar (1875) Narodna partija. In : *Oslobođenje*, No. 16, 5 February 1875. Quoted after : Perović, Latinka (2006) *Između anarhije i autokratije. Srpsko društvo na prelazima vekova, XIX-XX*. Belgrade.
Milosavljević, Olivera (2006) *Potisnuta istina. Kolaboracija u Srbiji 1941-1944*. Belgrade.
Mitrović, Andrej (2009) *Fašizam i nacizam*. Belgrade.
Nedeljeni pregled, No. 2, 1908.
Pašić, Nikola (1995) Pismo Nikole Pašića A. I Zinovjevu. In: Perović, Latinka/Šemjakin, Andrej (eds.) *Nikola Pašić. Pisma članci i govori*. Belgrade.
Pašić, Nikola (1995) *Sloga Srbo-Hrvata*. Belgrade.

Perović, Latinka (1985) *Srpski socijalisti 19 veka*, 3. Belgrade.
Perović, Latinka (2006) *Između anarhije i autokratije. Srpsko društvo na prelazima vekova, XIX-XX*. Belgrade.
Perović, Latinka (2015) *Dominanta i neželjena elita*. Belgrade.
Popović-Obradović, Olga (2008) *Kakva ili kolika država. Ogledi o političkoj i društvenoj istoriji Srbije 19-20 vek*. Belgrade.
Stenografske beleške Narodne Skupštine, 12 May 1910, Belgrade, 1911, 2997.
Stojanović, Dubravka (2003) *Srbija i demokratija. Istorijski ogled o "zlatnom dobu srpske demokratije" 1903-1914*. Belgrade.
Stojanović, Dubravka (2013) *Iza zavese. Ogledi iz društvene istorije Srbije*. Belgrade.
Trojanović, Sima (1907) Zadruga i inokoština. In : *Srpski književni glasnik*, X : 742.
Žujović, Jovan (1905) Misli o fondu za zemljoradničke penzije. In: *Srpski književni glasnik*, X: 755-756.

What Were the Outcomes of the Self-Managed Economy in Socialist Yugoslavia?

Aleksandar Jakir, Anita Lunić

The integration, functioning, and dissolution of Yugoslavia are issues that still produce very different scholarly assessments, as the Slovenian sociologists Sergej Flere and Rudi Klanjšek have recently put it (Flere/Klanjšek 2014). In this chapter, we seek to address the economic system of socialist Yugoslavia. Officially, the Yugoslav economic system from the 1950s onwards was labeled *workers' self-management*, and it seems that its role in the developments that led to the Yugoslav tragedy is still not fully understood. We argue that this system, which was gradually applied at all levels of society after Yugoslavia's split with the Stalinist Soviet Union, was a system imposed from above when the party-state leadership initiated a process of controlled decentralization of power. In fact, the communists under Tito did so to maintain power as long as possible. However, in times of economic crisis the imposed system became out of control – with fatal consequences for the whole country and the people living in that self-managed "market" socialism. We argue that the economic crisis and reforms triggered a slide towards political disintegration in socialist Yugoslavia. We hold that the beginning of the process of disintegration of the central governmental authority, which ultimately resulted in the breakdown of political order, can be traced back to the implementation of the social and economic system of self-management that was supposed to function within *market socialism*.

From the devolutions of the early 1960s until its end, socialist Yugoslavia was convincingly described, for example in the works of Sabrina P. Ramet, as a nine-actor balance-of-power system that consisted of a federal actor (the federal government or, alternatively, the League of Communists), six socialist republics (Bosnia-Herzegovina, Croatia, Macedonia, Montenegro, Serbia, and Slovenia), and two socialist autonomous provinces (Kosovo and Vojvodina). Yugoslavia was certainly a very fragmented country with, as a famous saying went, two alphabets, three religions, four languages, five nations, and six *states*. However, the labeling of the Yugoslav republics as "states" in the context of socialist Yugoslavia, even before the Constitution of 1974 defined the republics as such, referred to the large degree of autonomy of the then six constituent Yugoslav republics. What is often forgotten is that this qualification primarily referred to the large degree of autonomy of the republics in *economic* terms (Horvat 1970; 1982).

It could be said that the republics had viewed themselves as rival centers of legitimate interests since the (initially economic) reforms in the 1960s. Regional demands were aggregated along ethnic lines and articulated by republican and provincial authorities. National rivalries, of course, had their historical sources (Banac 1984). However, in the mid-1960s, many observers would have agreed that the unsolved 'national question', which was blamed for the break-up of the first centralist Yugoslav state in the years between the World Wars, had been successfully put to rest in the second socialist and federal Yugoslavia (Plaggenborg 1997). How then did these nationalist rivalries resurface, and when did they become a threat to the stability of the now (con)federal state itself?

1. The Yugoslav economic system: the historiographical and sociological perspective

It seems reasonable to ask about the role of self-management, self-managed enterprises and the functional elite, the directors of these enterprises, in the different republics in shaping that system. The political and economic decision-making system in Yugoslavia shows how its functioning generated certain tensions between and among governmental and productive entities, tensions that led to unintended and undesired economic consequences. New research based on a great variety of archival sources on big investment projects in Yugoslavia, for example the railway connection between Belgrade and Bar on the Adriatic coast in Montenegro, clearly shows how difficult it was to finance and finish such a project under the circumstances of the decentralized Yugoslav self-managed economic system (see Kežić 2012, and the forthcoming publication of his dissertation on this topic).

As can be demonstrated, from the mid-1960s on, national problems were discussed on hundreds of pages in reports and confidential documents to Tito and the members of the Central Committee and presidency, and they were often related to 'economic' arguments. Focal points of national interests in socialist Yugoslavia first developed out of particular economic interests of individual industrial concerns because the development of enterprises in the individual republics was interlinked with national well-being. Thus, under the conditions of a federal Yugoslavia (after the Constitution of 1974, it can be called without doubt *confederal*) the republics competed for resources and investment, and economic problems turned into national rivalry. This rivalry, again, was first expressed in economic terms. Then, in the second step, it became combined and emotionally charged with all the well-known historical, linguistic and cultural arguments (as became clear in the movement in

Croatia between 1967 and 1971, later called the 'Croatian Spring', without losing the economic aspect (for a detailed argument and sources see Jakir 2011; 2012; 2013).

In his analysis of the promise and the failure of the system, Peter Liotta states that the innovation of Yugoslav self-management, once considered a benchmark in creative economic reform within a socialist society, proved to be a major contributing factor in the death of Yugoslavia (Liotta 2001). Others note that this peculiar system, "invented" by Edvard Kardelj and introduced to the Yugoslav political system in 1950 after the Tito-Stalin split, made a significant and largely unrecognized contribution to the ethnic violence and disintegration of Yugoslavia because it transformed the country from a community of nations into a community of nation-states through permanent constitutional engineering and decentralization. Despite the "Yugoslav experiment's" extremely critical balance sheet, there are also voices arguing that the experiences were not all negative. As Boris Kanzleiter puts it, the country and the society managed the leap from a peripheral agrarian country to a relatively modern industrial nation and although no producers' democracy was developed under the slogan of "workers' self-management", it was still a relatively open society, and important social rights were successfully enforced in socialist Yugoslavia (Kanzleitner 2011). However, the debate is still open as to whether Tito's Yugoslavia was a totalitarian state, a politocracy (Denitch 1990) or "almost impossible to slot into a classification of political systems" (Flere/Klanjšek 2014), which some authors still bring to peculiar qualifications of the essence of Yugoslav socialism, describing it as "something playful" (Ćosić 2015). Alas, there can be little doubt that after their victory in 1945 the Yugoslav communists introduced a system with key totalitarian features such as a one-party system, mass extra-judicial executions immediately after the war, control of mass media with the propagation of the official communist ideology, the establishment of an "political armed force" subordinate to the Communist Party etc.

However, when it comes to the political order and politics of Yugoslav socialism, we can still find many more studies analyzing these features than research dealing with the specific economy. One difference that is often stressed, also in recent works, is the complexity of decision-making in the Yugoslav case of a federal state and a federal party, and some sociologists go almost so far as to label the Yugoslav system "a full-fledged polyarchy", adding: "[...] there was no blind, unconditional and unquestioning following of the leader by the basic actors" (Flere/Klanjšek 2014: 239). Indeed, it seems to be true that a "strong defense of particularistic interests took place" in Tito's Yugoslavia, and we would like to concentrate here on some remarks on the economy of socialist Yugoslavia. As long as it existed, the "Yugoslav model" was of interest to researchers belonging to very different disciplines and backgrounds, and was often presented as best proof of the hybrid nature of the system, apparently much closer to the Western model than other socialist countries in South-East Europe.

2. The system of self-management: concept and implementation

In theory, the Yugoslav system was designed to place ownership in the hands of "society", and workers were supposed to have the right (and duty) to manage the means of production (Jakir 2005). It was claimed that in such a system, with power and control promised neither to be in the hands of individual capitalists nor state-socialist bureaucrats, the state would 'wither away' (see the thorough discussion of this concept in Jović 2003). The idea was that the *withering away of the state* would lead to a juster society with no alienation. Dejan Jović argues that the commitment of the Yugoslav political elite to the Marxist ideology of the "withering away of the state" had a central place in Yugoslav politics and fostered the trend towards decentralization based on the Marxist belief that the state should be decentralized and weakened until it was finally replaced by a self-managing society. In the Yugoslav system of self-management, in theory at least, the production unit or factory was meant to be an autonomous and competitive organization. The worker's council was the basic operational unit and had to decide how much and whom to pay, how best to reallocate profits after taxes etc. This idea was grounded in councils that existed during the war and were called people's committees (Zukin 1975: 55), already established in 1945 as special institutions, officially to protect workers' and social rights. When the whole program was presented to the Yugoslav public in 1949, it was described as a final step in establishing the direct participation of workers in the economy to ensure their real political and economic power, but also to increase productivity. From the very beginning, the aim was clear: it was not only an attempt to establish an ideal model, but to motivate the individual development of enterprises. This also meant implicitly that enterprises were supposed to compete on the market and boost their own growth, which was supposed to ensure higher profits and meant less responsibility for the central authority (Lanyan 1986: 28). This aspect of obligations is clearly expressed in Tito's introduction to *The Draft Law on Workers' Management* presented to the Federal Assembly in 1950, which stated: "The slogan *the factory to the workers, the land to the peasants* is not an abstract propaganda slogan, but one with deep meaning. It encompasses the whole program of socialist relations in the sphere of production and also in regard to social property and the rights and obligations of the workers, and therefore it can and must be realized in practice, if we really desire to build socialism" (Wachtel 1973: xvi). The National Assembly of Yugoslavia adopted the Worker's Self-Management Act on 26 June 1950, and the very first enterprise that formed a workers' council as a new body according to the new law was the cement factory in Solin (near Split, Croatia) on 13th of December 1949. Over the next six months, 520 workers' councils were formed across Yugoslavia. But it was not until 1952 that relevant portions of the Act took hold in the economic transition that attempted to give enterprises more independence, broaden workers' rights, and introduce market elements. The bill titled "Basic Law on the Management of State Enterprises and Holding Companies by Work Collectives" stated that all factories, mines, communication enterprises, transportation systems, and agriculture and forestry enterprises, as public property, were to be managed by work collectives, and carry out this management via workers' councils and management boards, the management boards being elected by the workers' councils. As the *Handbook of Yugoslav Socialist Self-Management* later stated: "Social ownership banishes all forms of exploitation, monopolistic appropriation and control over the means of production and products of social labor, encourages the rapid development of productive forces and creates the prerequisites for the implementation of Marx's idea about the association of free producers in a communist society" (Trifunović 1977: 178-179).

However, to put it briefly, the Yugoslav Socialist Self-Management resulted not in a utopia of free associations of producers in self-managed enterprises, but polycentric étatism which ended in national chauvinism. Studying the economic system of the former Yugoslavia can be helpful when searching for explanations for the disastrous demise of the country in the early 1990s. Many studies on the "Yugoslav model" were published during the Cold War. It is quite obvious that many authors were then fascinated by the unique economic system between capitalism and a planned Soviet-style economy (see the bibliography in Jakir 2005 and 2011). For quite a long time, workers' self-management in enterprises was considered an alternative to both capitalistic and Soviet-style authoritarian work relations (Horvat 1982). Ideas of workers' control and self-management have long been a matter of public debate in the Scandinavian countries as well as in the so-called "Third World" (Bayat 1991), and as long as societies are organized on the basis of inequality in power and property, the desire of individuals to control their own lives and work is likely to remain, and the idea of workers' control and self-management thus may still represent an organizational form which gives expression to that desire.

However, the concrete Yugoslav system of workers' self-management that existed in reality passed through four distinct systemic phases during its existence: *administrative socialism* (1945-1952), *administrative market socialism* (1953-1962), *market socialism* (1963-1973), and so-called *contractual socialism* (1974-1988), followed by its collapse. These phases in a timespan of four decades mark the shift from an agricultural, capitalist society to an industrial socialist society. For example, in 1948 the percentage of the population living in villages in the countryside in Croatia was 66.3%, while in 1971 only 36% of all citizens in the Socialist Republic of Croatia lived in rural areas.

3. Competition between the "developed" and the "underdeveloped"

During none of the above-mentioned four phases did the self-managed economy of the former Yugoslavia find an answer to the problem of competition between so-called "developed" and "underdeveloped" republics. For example, statistics clearly show that Slovenia already had an income index of 175.2% in 1947 (the Yugoslav average being 100), whereas Kosovo was listed at only 52.2. That ratio became even worse in the following decades, when the index for Slovenia in 1970 reached 191.6%, whereas Kosovo dropped to 31.2% (Jovanov 1979: 142). Under these conditions, the competition (and the results of this competition) between the industries and enterprises located in the different parts of Yugoslavia and competing within the system of self-management was recognized very early as a threat to the stability of the country.

However, the warnings went unheeded. It can even be argued that most of the disputes between the republic elites within the Communist party were based on economic issues and related to the unequal distribution of wealth (Korošić 1983). Susan Woodward seems to make the point when she states that, in the first instance, it was *market socialism* (as the Yugoslav system was often labeled) that failed; in the second it was *decentralization* – to the great disappointment of the many who continue to support both (Woodward 1995).

Historically, the decision to introduce workers' self-management was made in difficult economic circumstances. Production in Yugoslavia between 1950 and 1953, after the break with the Soviet Union under Stalin, was even lower than in 1949. As much as 24% of national income was spent on defense. Self-management became a key point of the ideology of the Party after the Tito-Stalin conflict. But until the late 1950s, the government still played a dominant role in managing the economy and society. Investment funds were centralized, allowing the state authorities to distribute almost the entire surplus labour. The proclaimed economic reform in 1961 was supposed to resolve the distribution of the social product between enterprises and the state. It was announced that the changes were introduced to overcome all the contradictions existing in capitalism and state socialism, and the planned changes were publicly praised as being "revolutionary" and the "last battle with étatism". After the establishment of a socialist economy through nationalization in 1946 and the introduction of self-management in 1950, the economic reforms in the 1960s were meant to create a new type of successful socialist economy. However, the implementation of the reform measures proved difficult. The reform was partly blocked due to the resistance of those party structures that feared the consequences of an entirely free market. Thus, its implementation was slowed down. One side wanted to preserve and strengthen bureaucratic centralism, whereas the other side advocated decentralization and changes in the state structure. Decentralization was predominantly favoured by communist cadres from Slovenia and

Croatia seeing in it the possibility of achieving real federalism and autonomous decision-making by the republics. Étatism had its stronghold in the federal structures and in Serbia, building up resistance to the new changes. Soon the division of federal funds was on the agenda, which gave rise to the unsolved problem of how to balance the obvious differences in wealth among the so-called developed and underdeveloped parts of Yugoslavia. This seems to be the key question the Yugoslav socialist economy had to solve. Part of the attempted solution was that the Party, officially renamed as the "League of Communists", retained control over the 'self-managing' system, which is why some authors describe this model as a self-managing statist model based on a dualist conception of coexistence of the state and workers' management (Marković 1986: 98).

However, since the economic reforms in the mid-1960s, the representatives of divergent national interests (reflecting particular situations of economic concerns in individual republics) were engaged on the federal level in fierce competition for limited economic resources. Thus, it seems that the history of the disintegration of Yugoslavia can be better understood when we examine the connection between the economic reform, decentralization, ethnic differentiation and prosperity or poverty.

4. Decentralization: Socialist republics and provinces as political and economic (f)actors

The republics certainly became increasingly important in Yugoslavia (Ramet 1992), first economically, then politically (Bićanić 1973). The end of state centralism established 'new relations between the (Yugoslav) nations', as Dušan Bilandžić stated. Reforms at the beginning of the 1960s opened the Yugoslav economy to world markets and the international division of labor, which partly decentralized the financial system, at the same time giving enterprises and workers a greater degree of control over the determination of wages. The pursuit of regional economic interests was both facilitated and justified with the reform of 1965. The Development Fund, created as a compensating institution, enabled Slovenia and Croatia to convince the less developed republics to vote with them in favor of the reform (Pleština 1992). The Reforms in 1965 were intended to further liberalize the economy and provide a solution to the emerging crisis of corporate and national indebtedness. Banks were given freedom to run along capitalist lines, and to use their discretion when granting credits to individual enterprises. Socialist Yugoslavia indeed evolved a particular economy, and given the immanent decentralized structure of self-management, it seems to make sense to ask if there is a connection between the economic system of self-management and the emergence of a new nationalism in socialist Yugoslavia (Plaggenborg 1997).

Especially the consequences of self-managed "market" socialism, implemented in the mid-1960s, have to be considered with respect to the balance within the federation. The decentralization of economic power to the enterprises and the broadening of self-management rights of workers' councils went hand in hand with greater decentralization of political power to the different territorial units of the Yugoslav federation. In our opinion, it can be argued that different economic interests of the Yugoslav republics, on the basis of the finally vastly decentralized system, were of vital importance in the process of Yugoslavia's disintegration (see different contributions in Rusinow 1988). From the outset, the polarization between the developed northwest (Slovenia, Croatia and Vojvodina), which stood to gain from the liberalization and a market-orientated economy, and the less developed southeast (Bosnia-Herzegovina, Macedonia, Kosovo and Montenegro), which stood to lose from it, threatened to make economic decentralization a political issue. At the same time, some in Serbia saw their interests parallel to those of the less developed regions. As is well known, the ruling party decided to open Yugoslavia's economy to the world market, and it therefore became the first socialist country where so-called 'joint ventures' between 'socialist' Yugoslav enterprises and those from abroad were allowed. The increasing importance of the republics and provinces as political and economic actors since the end of the 1950s seems beyond doubt. Often the implementation of the system of labor-managed firms in Yugoslavia and their independence in decision-making is seen only as an economic success story, merely implying the development of a market economy with high growth rates (around 9 percent yearly until the middle of the 1960s). As long as it was possible to develop the institutional structure of a market economy and economic democracy, the argument goes, the Yugoslav economy was highly successful and one of the fastest-growing economies in the world, with a significant and continuous improvement in the welfare of the population. Reforms in the early 1960s in fact opened the Yugoslav economy to world markets and the international division of labor, partly decentralized the financial system, and gave enterprises/workers a greater degree of control over wage determination.

After the 1965 attempt to introduce economic reform, which failed and brought several years of very slow growth with increasing inflation, attitudes towards economic policy were increasingly shaped by liberalization, although the preconditions for it were non-existent (Jakir 2012). Liberalization of an economy without factor markets, as economists concluded, could not succeed. Hence the economic debates in the early 1960s can in our opinion be seen as "the beginning of the end" of socialist Yugoslavia (Zečević 1992).

Conflicting interests between the more advanced republics and the underdeveloped ones could not be overlooked, and neither the partisan myth nor promises of a bright future on the basis of "brotherhood and unity" of the Yugoslav nations, nor the coercive force of the ruling Communists could hide that. The determination of the party apparatuses of the Republics to pursue their own interests was demonstrated on many different occasions from the 1960s onwards. Certainly, the republics viewed themselves as rival centers of legitimate interests (Ramet 2013). The forecast of one of the masterminds of the Yugoslav socialist economic system, Boris Kidrič, that the underdeveloped and the developed parts of Yugoslavia would reach the same level of development in the year 1964 turned out to be an "illusion", as a Serbian journalist put it at the end of that decade. In fact, the regional economic inequalities were not leveled but grew instead. The political consequences were that the more developed republics, Croatia and Slovenia, transformed economic issues – decentralization of economic decision-making, dismantling of central planning, and curtailment of aid to unprofitable enterprises in the south – into political issues, in opposition to Serbian hegemony and support of "liberalization". Quickly the question emerged in different Yugoslav Republics: "who is exploiting whom?" (Madžar 1996).

5. The position of workers within the system of workers' self-management

Despite the ideas of solidarity and equality, and despite the concept of wage determination based on expertise and working hours, a salary scale that privileged higher-ranking workers was still retained in many cases. It also affected productivity, the low and insufficient salaries combining with easy access to annual and/or sick leave. This motivated at least some of the workers to work as little as possible at their official work place, and to focus instead on additional sources of income and engage in 'moonlighting' (Bićanić 1973: 80, 102; compare Lowinger 2009). This phenomenon illustrates not only workers' perception of their role within the self-managing system and power relations within the factory (as many clearly did not consider the success of the enterprise something crucial for themselves), but also the economic situation that required side jobs to make ends meet. Vušković's report of 1976 suggests that as many as 23.9% of workers lived below the poverty line, while 36.5% were around it (Vušković 1976: 41). That is probably also the reason why enterprises preferred to raise salaries than invest in employing new workers.

The problematic social status of workers within the system is also visible from the statistics on productive workers in leading positions, which in general were significantly under ten percent. The stratification of society was also apparent in the distribution of property, the level of education and the figures on workers' presence in governing bodies (Vušković 1976: 26-44), despite the constant growth of the number of workers in the overall population and despite the reduction in the proportion of the agricultural population. Moreover, the change in the structure of the population was followed by an absolute increase of unemployed persons: from

82,000 in 1953 to 320,000 in 1970 (Jovanov 1979: 73). According to the Federal Bureau of Statistics, the number of unemployed was between 110,000 and 170,000 for the period between 1964 and 1971. Moreover, since "working abroad", mostly in Germany and other capitalist countries of Western Europe, became legal in 1965, the size of the unemployed workforce within socialist Yugoslavia is even higher than 850,000 if we also count those temporarily working outside the country. By the end of 1967, around 750,000 workers were unable to find a job in Yugoslavia (McClellan 1969: 149; Vušković 1976: 37). These numbers are important to keep in mind when discussing the decrease in the number of non-workers in works councils and other self-management bodies. According to research on works councils from 1960 to 1972, there was a noticeable drop in the total number of members: from 156,300 to 135,171 over 12 years, which constituted a general decline of 13.5%. At the same time, the decline in the number of workers in works councils (including the unskilled, semi-skilled workers, highly skilled, qualified workers and apprentices) was 10.7%. During that period, the only increase in the proportion of workers was that of highly qualified workers, from 15.1% to 17.4% in 1972. We can conclude there was an absolute drop in workers' participation, which also had a direct impact on their possible influence in resolving the issues of labor collectives.

The decrease in the share of workers in central administrative boards in the same period was even greater: while the number of board members increased from 51,261 in 1960 to 54,156 in 1972, the percentage of workers in central administrative boards decreased from 67.2% to 46.9%. A similar decline was also recorded regarding specific positions within the councils. In 1972, only every third president of the workers' council was in fact a worker, and workers accounted for only 27% of presidents of administrative boards.

In addition to the bodies directly related to their own work, the proportion of workers was also constantly decreasing in the political and social bodies in general. Although the share of workers in local councils remained more or less constant, around 13%, at higher levels this share was steadily decreasing. In 1958, workers accounted for 9% of the members of parliament in the republics, and 8% of the deputies in the Federal Assembly, and in 1970 their share in both political bodies was only 1%! The increase in the share of highly educated persons in general meetings at senior levels decreased the relative representation of workers, and the same process helped to increase the share of economic officials (which is why the Federal Assembly was informally called 'the Council of Directors'). A similar tendency is visible even in the Congress of Self-Managers of Yugoslavia, in which the number of workers also dropped in favor of an increase in technicians, engineers and highly educated people (Jovanov 1979: 78-81).

These data show that self-management as an idea of establishing an economic system from below was in reality a system imposed and directed from above (Dabčević-Kučar 1997: 185).

6. Strikes: From economic inequalities to political conflict

Both the socio-economic and the political position of the workers led to increasing dissatisfaction, resulting in strikes across Yugoslavia. From 1958, when the first strike occurred, until 1969, 1,906 strikes were registered with more than 77,000 participating workers. After 1969, the number of strikes increased. In the 1980s the increase was immense. In the year of Tito's death, 1980, 247 strikes took place with 13,507 workers involved (Marinković 1995: 83). In 1984 the number increased to 384 (violations of the Helsinki accords: Yugoslavia 1986: 49), whereas in 1988 a total of 1,851 strikes took place, in which 386,123 workers were involved (Marinković 1995: 83). This enormous growth culminated in 1990, when no fewer than 470,000 workers were involved in 1,900 strikes (Liotta 2001: 133). This growth not only reflected the awareness that strikes were a successful method to obtain better payment and working conditions, but also shows the growing political crisis in the country. Comparing the reasons and results of the strikes and analyzing the economic progress of the area where these strikes took place provides us with clues as to why so many strikes took place in a self-managed type of socialist economic system that was officially run by workers. It also points to certain economic structures in Yugoslavia that triggered first social and later political conflicts.

On the basis of the aforementioned differences in the level of regional development, it is interesting that most strikes took place on the territory of the better-developed federal units, i.e. Slovenia and Croatia. In fact, the smallest number of strikes took place in the less developed agricultural areas of Kosovo, Macedonia and Montenegro. For example, the first strikes in Kosovo, a region with a high percentage of villagers, began a whole decade after the first strike took place in the already industrialized republic of Slovenia. The reasons are surely, on the one hand, the number of enterprises and the proportion of members of the working class in the population, but on the other hand, we can also observe different economic interests: while developed regions were likely to object to different policies that functioned to ensure investments in underdeveloped regions, workers in the southern republics had no reason to protest against such policies.

Besides those specific issues related to their level of development, all republics and regions shared many basic economic problems, such as the inadequate distribution of rights and income as a result of bureaucratization, the strengthening of technocratic-managerial power relations, and what was considered an insufficient material and institutional basis for self-management. Jovanov listed more reasons for strikes such as the lack of information and communication in resolving workers' problems, irregular salaries, illegal extensions of the working day, irregularities, etc. (Jovanov 1979; 1983; 1989).

Yet when did economic reasons for dissatisfaction within an enterprise turn into political ones? If we compare data on workers' participation in the Communist

Party (LCY), it is obvious that the number and the importance of workers in the Party fell steadily. According to the publication *Consulting on the Social Structure of Yugoslav League of Communists*, workers accounted for 28.8% of the total number of Party members in 1971. In the same year, Vinko Hafner published a study that showed that as many as two-thirds of the total number of LCY members were from the middle and higher strata of society (Jovanov 1979: 84).

However, it was not until the deep political and economic crisis that hit Yugoslavia in the 1980s that the nationalist agenda became dominant. When we look at the data concerning workers' strikes outside the enterprises, with rallies on streets and squares of the local and federal centers (Zagreb, Belgrade), and compare it with data on local support and solidarity movements, there seems to be hardly any evidence until the end of the 1980s that war was on its way. For example, strikes against IMF agreements or laws based on them – such as the new law freezing wages in 1988 (Lowinger 2009: 99) pointed more to the unwillingness to change current relations in any radically new direction. But, because of decentralization and the "peculiar and complex governing structure adopted in Yugoslavia after the death of Tito [...] the federal governance structure" was left "vulnerable to manipulation by regional political elites, who were able to turn this impasse to their advantage in promoting a narrow nationalist interest", as Jake Lowinger observes (Lowinger 2009: 2-3).

7. Inability to surpass differences

As is well-known, Yugoslavia went through several constitutions, enacted in 1946, 1953, 1963 and, finally, in 1974. Each of these constitutional changes has been interpreted as a promise to further establish a general system of socialist self-management, one that went beyond workers' self-management to include self-management decision-making councils in every walk of life: social, political, and economic. Self-management was not supposed to be limited only to the sphere of production, but was meant to comprise all aspects of society. As far as the economy was concerned, the 1974 constitution promised a *dogovorna ekonomija*, an "economy of agreement" in all spheres of Yugoslav life. Self-management and "social ownership" (*društvena svojina*) were trusted to solve all problems. Unfortunately, however, problems in all segments of Yugoslavia's society and economy became more and more serious. In the context of the general crisis of socialist Yugoslavia in the 1980s after Tito's death, the reassessment of self-management proceeded on different analytic levels (Ramet 1985). Among all the questions posed about its efficiency, its autonomy from political and economic pressures, and its real contribution to the creation of a new society, it was not asked whether perhaps the system itself brought some unanticipated and dysfunctional consequences concerning the immense regional inequalities, as shown in these statistical figures:

Fig. 1: National product per capita, level of consumption, and public spending in Yugoslavia in 1980 in %.

Republic/province		GDP per capita	Level of consumption per household		Public spending: level of expenditure per capita in %
			Workers	Peasants	
Bosnia-Herzegovina		64	91	73	66
Montenegro		78	72	82	85
Croatia		125	107	89	125
Macedonia		67	79	89	75
Slovenia		206	140	155	192
Serbia	Serbia	101	96	112	93
	Serbia proper	101	97	97	104
	Kosovo	28	64	81	45
	Vojvodina	115	101	161	99
Yugoslavia		100	100	100	100

Figures from Sirotković, Jakov (1996) *Hrvatsko gospodarstvo: Privredna kretanja i ekonomska politika*. Zagreb: 33.

Fig. 2: Gross domestic product per capita 1953-1979 (Yugoslavia = 100).

Republic/province		1953	1961	1971	1979
Bosna-Herzegovina		84	73	67	66
Montenegro		62	65	72	60
Croatia		114	122	127	130
Macedonia		61	62	66	67
Slovenia		174	195	187	197
Serbia	Serbia proper	94	95	96	97
	Kosovo	47	33	32	30
	Vojvodina	109	102	118	123
Yugoslavia		100	100	100	100

Figures from Lydall (1984): 175.

Fig. 3: Basic indicators of development of federal units of Yugoslavia 1952- 1990.

GDP per capita in thousands of dinars prices in 1972								
Year	YU	B-H	Monte.	Croat.	Maced.	Sloven.	Serb. p.	Kosovo	Vojvod.
1952	3.36	3.21	2.94	4.07	2.40	6.10	3.42	1.56	3.00
1955	4.63	3.85	3.57	5.67	3.27	8.09	4.20	1.97	4.33
1960	6.43	4.89	4.22	7.68	4.11	11.61	6.20	2.40	6.93
1965	8.50	6.09	6.47	10.26	5.67	15.60	8.17	3.10	9.54
1970	10.92	7.38	8.34	13.72	7.64	21.15	10.45	3.76	11.56
1975	14.10	9.31	9.62	17.63	9.86	28.71	13.53	4.63	16.18
1980	17.76	11.72	14.03	22.51	11.96	35.23	17.45	5.01	20.03
1985	17.72	12.43	13.75	22.37	11.54	35.56	17.52	4.85	20.74
1990	15.31	10.32	10.99	19.42	9.76	30.82	16.06	3.35	18.67
Fixed assets of working age population in thousands of dinars, prices in 1972								
Year	YU	B-H	Monte.	Croat.	Maced.	Sloven.	Serb. p.	Kosovo	Vojvod.
1952	9.36	8.08	3.43	10.60	5.54	20.95	8.06	4.02	7.69
1955	10.97	11.64	4.22	12.77	6.19	25.25	8.28	4.15	8.10
1960	15.89	15.36	12.78	19.22	10.97	32.52	12.59	6.06	12.02
1965	23.32	20.10	29.20	27.35	16.67	44.52	18.51	11.11	22.64
1970	31.66	26.11	37.11	37.66	22.90	61.47	25.47	15.93	32.68
1975	44.01	34.07	51.19	53.17	32.59	88.26	36.91	21.69	43.90
1980	58.72	46.21	68.01	73.22	41.95	116.80	48.17	27.65	61.01
1985	67.35	53.72	80.97	86.09	45.27	137.64	54.28	28.02	72.39
1990	72.71	56.29	86.56	94.90	47.63	150.88	59.71	28.73	80.03
Number of employees in self-managed enterprises in 1000								
Year	YU	B-H	Monte.	Croat.	Maced.	Sloven.	Serb. p.	Kosovo	Vojvod.
1952	161.80	165.83	130.43	183.45	123.10	270.33	133.57	89.59	145.81
1955	199.07	185.77	196.17	226.67	174.90	332.32	166.84	95.98	186.20
1960	257.51	215.36	223.57	288.97	234.71	418.75	221.39	141.88	284.49
1965	299.27	240.04	250.30	343.11	269.64	494.36	259.61	157.16	338.94
1970	293.88	231.52	250.09	331.56	261.81	493.60	279.95	150.89	306.23
1975	344.74	272.59	293.96	388.49	307.82	591.68	325.01	184.88	358.01
1980	393.35	306.27	344.30	458.88	350.56	645.72	378.64	208.61	402.73
1985	423.54	357.58	391.52	495.92	382.03	654.71	414.89	216.03	434.96
1990	418.22	337.92	383.13	495.24	370.31	620.39	432.14	184.94	450.38
Unemployment rate in %								
Year	YU	B-H	Monte.	Croat.	Maced.	Sloven.	Serb. p.	Kosovo	Vojvod.
1952	0.43%	0.27%	0.24%	0.54%	0.82%	0.52%	0.34%	0.12%	0.46%
1955	0.64%	0.34%	0.39%	0.75%	1.27%	0.75%	0.49%	0.57%	0.60%
1960	1.41%	0.91%	1.36%	1.63%	2.72%	0.84%	1.37%	2.20%	1.13%
1965	1.98%	1.24%	1.43%	2.09%	4.23%	0.90%	2.12%	2.83%	1.66%
1970	2.49%	1.72%	2.08%	1.64%	5.74%	1.55%	2.73%	4.88%	2.34%
1975	3.99%	3.53%	5.09%	2.32%	8.28%	0.89%	4.77%	5.68%	4.31%
1980	5.44%	5.11%	6.05%	2.61%	9.79%	0.90%	7.18%	8.14%	5.82%
1985	6.90%	8.39%	9.66%	3.93%	10.56%	1.18%	7.25%	11.72%	6.96%
1990	7.81%	9.19%	11.25%	4.59%	10.96%	2.23%	8.32%	12.61%	7.52%

Figures from Radelić (2006): 515-516.

Among other authors, Harold Lydall (Lydall 1984) also dealt with the economic policy and relations between the republics in Yugoslavia, and argued that the Communists believed that after a few decades the differences between the republics would disappear. However, quite the opposite happened: the differences increased, as can be seen when we look at the data for gross domestic product per capita:

If we compare the data for comprehensive indicators concerning development and inter-republic relations in Yugoslavia, the figures clearly show that the differences between the republics increased during the socialist period.

8. Conclusion

Todor Kuljić, in his assessment of Yugoslavia's workers' self-management, calls the system a social as well as a national laboratory with structural problems because it "arose in a relatively underdeveloped Balkan state" without a modern working class, with no industrial culture but an immature political culture, and he stresses the contrast between the idea of direct democracy and control by the cadres of the League of Communists. Indeed, the "important, structural problem", as he calls it, points to "the contrast in Yugoslavia between the rich and the poor areas, the rich and the poor republics, which later became the rich and poor nations" (Kuljic 2003).

This brings us to the conclusion that it seems necessary to re-examine the system of self-management in the light of the fact that the socio-political system obviously produced increasingly greater inequalities. At the same time, this economy provided the political and economic elites in all republics with the possibility of obtaining a kind of "legitimation" from their "basis" by pointing to the given contradictions that were caused, and by stirring up national sentiments as the easiest way to explain why the results were far from expected.

For a better understanding of the history of the disintegration of socialist Yugoslavia, we have to consider the connection between ethnic differentiation and prosperity or poverty. Thus, under the conditions of federal Yugoslavia and the Republics which were competing for resources and investment, it is not surprising that economic problems turned into national rivalry which was first expressed in economic terms. It seems worth noting that it was not until economic conflicts had taken hold that we can find evidence of national mobilization of large parts of the population. So it seems justified not only to research historical, linguistic and cultural arguments in the process of disintegration but also the specific economic system of Yugoslavia's socialist self-management economy.

Bibliography

Banac, Ivo (1984) *The National Question in Yugoslavia: Origin, History, Politics.* Ithaca.
Bayat, Assef (1991) *Work, Politics and Power. An International Perspective on Workers' Control and Self-Management.* New York, London.
Bićanić, Rudolf (1973) *Economic policy in socialist Yugoslavia.* Cambridge.
Bilandžić, Dušan (1985) *Historija SFRJ. Glavni procesi 1918-1985. III dopunjeno izdanje.* Zagreb.
Brown, Michael B. (1960) Workers' Control In A Planned Economy. In: *New Left Review* 12: 28-31.
Ćosić, Bora (2015) Wie der Stahl gehärtet wurde. In: *Neue Zürcher Zeitung*, 24.01.2015: 53.
Dabčević-Kučar, Savka (1997) *'71. Hrvatski snovi i stvarnost.* Zagreb.
Denitch, Bogdan D. (1990) *Limits and Possibilities: The Crisis of Yugoslav Socialism and State Socialist Systems.* Minesotta.
Dimitrova, Dimitrina/Vilrokx, Jacques (2005) *Trade Union Strategies in Central and Eastern Europe: Towards Decent Work.* Budapest.
Erić, Zoran (2009): *The Third Way: The Experiment of Workers' Self-Management in Socialist Yugoslavia.* URL: https://www.academia.edu/4223251/The_Third_Way_The_Experiment_of_Workers_Self-Management_in_Socialist_Yugoslavia (retrieved July 23, 2019).
Flaherty, Diane (1992) *Self-Management and Requirements for Social Property: Lessons from Yugoslavia.* URL: https://www.nodo50.org/cubasigloXXI/congreso/flaherty_15abr03.pdf (retrieved July 23, 2019).
Flere, Sergej/Klanjšek, Rudi (2014) Was Yugoslavia totalitarian? In: *Communist and Post-Communist Studies* 47: 237-245.
Goldstein, Ivo (2008) *Hrvatska povijest.* Zagreb.
Hoffman, G.W./Neal, F.W. (1962) *Yugoslavia and the new communism.* New York.
Horvat, Branko (1970) *The Economic System and Economic Policy of Yugoslavia.* Belgrade.
Horvat, Branko (1982) *The Political Economy of Socialism.* New York.
Human Rights Watch (1986) *Violations of the Helsinki accords: Yugoslavia. A report prepared for the Helsinki Review Conference.* Vienna.
Jakir, Aleksandar (2005) Worker's Self-Management in Tito's Yugoslavia Revisited. In: *Mitteilungsblatt des Instituts für soziale Bewegungen* 33: 137-155.
Jakir, Aleksandar (2011) The Economic Trigger – The Satus of 'Nationality' in a 'Self-Managed' Economy During the 1960s and 1970s in Socialist Yugoslavia. In: Calic, Marie-Janine/Neutatz, Dietmar/Obertreis, Julia (eds.): *The Crisis of Socialist Modernity. The Soviet Union and Yugoslavia in the 1970s.* Göttingen: 134-155.
Jakir, Aleksandar (2012) Nemoguća misija i početak kraja? Gospodarske reforme u SFR Jugoslaviji tijekom 1960ih godina. In: Iveljić, Iskra/Matković,

Stjepan/Lazarević, Žarko (eds.): *VPOGLEDI 4. Iz hrvatske povijesti 20. stoljeća – Iz hrvaške zgodovine 20. stoletja.* Ljubljana: 91-110.

Jakir, Aleksandar (2013) Wirtschaft und Wirtschaftsreformen im sozialistischen Jugoslawien. In: Grandits, Hannes/Sundhaussen, Holm (eds.): *Jugoslawien in den 1960er Jahren. Auf dem Weg zu einem (a)normalen Staat?* Wiesbaden: 83-108.

Jovanov, Neca (1979) *Radnički štrajkovi u SFRJ od 1958. do 1969. Godine.* Belgrade.

Jovanov, Neca (1983) *Dijagnoza samoupravljanja: 1974-1981.* Zagreb.

Jovanov, Neca (1989) *Sukobi.* Nikšić.

Jović, Dejan (2003) *Jugoslavija – država koja je odumrla: uspon, kriza i pad Kardeljeve Jugoslavije 1974-1990.* Zagreb.

Jović, Dejan (2008) *Yugoslavia. A State that Withered Away.* Glasgow.

Kanzleitner, Boris (2011) Workers' Self-management in Yugoslavia – An Ambivalent Experience. In: *transform,* 09/2011. URL: http://www.transform-network. net/journal/issue-092011/news/detail/Journal/workers-self-management-in-yugoslavia-an-ambivalent-experience.html (retrieved July 23, 2019).

Kardelj, Edvard (1977) *Pravci razvoja političkog sistema socijalističkog samoupravljanja.* Belgrade.

Kežić, Danijel (2012) Die Eisenbahn Belgrad-Bar 1952-1976. Eine Geschichte der Finanzierung des größten Eisenbahnprojektes Jugoslawiens. In: *Südost Forschungen,* Band 71: 285-309.

Korošić, Marijan (1983) *Ekonomske nejednakosti u jugoslavenskoj privredi.* Zagreb.

Kovač, Oskar (1995) Foreign Economic Relations. In: Ramet, Sabrina P./Adamovich, Ljubiša (eds.): *Beyond Yugoslavia. Politics, Economics, and Culture in a Shattered Community.* Boulder, San Francisco, Oxford: 281-300.

Kuljic, Todor (2003) *Yugoslavia's Workers Self-Management.* Belgrade. URL: http:// www.ressler.at/workers_self-management (retrieved July 23, 2019).

Kuzmanić, Tonči (1988) *Labinski štrajk rudara: paradigma začetka konca.* Ljubljana.

Lanyan, Chen (1986) *The Yugoslav Experiment with Self Governing Market Socialism.* Canada.

Liotta, Peter H. (2001) *Dismembering the State: The Death of Yugoslavia and why it Matters.* Lanham.

Liotta, Peter H. (2001) Paradigm Lost: Yugoslav Self-Management and the Economics of Disaster. In: *Balkanologie,* V(1-2/2001). URL: http://balkanologie. revues.org/681 (retrieved July 23, 2019).

Lowinger, Jake (2009) *Economic reform and the 'double movement' in Yugoslavia: An analysis of labor unrest and ethno-nationalism in the 1980s.* Baltimore.

Lydall, Harold (1984) *Yugoslav Socialism: Theory and Practice.* Oxford.

Lydall, Harold (1989) *Yugoslavia in crisis.* Oxford.

Madžar, Ljubomir (1996) Ko koga eksploatiše. In: Popov, Nebojša (ed.): *Srpska strana rata. Trauma i katarza u istorijskom pamćenju.* Belgrade.

Marinković, Darko (1995) *Štrajkovi i društvena kriza.* Belgrade.

Marković, Živko (1986) Neki uzroci krize političkog sistema. In: Dejanović, Jovan (ed.): *Rasprava povodom kritičke analize funkcionisanja političkog sistema socijalističkog samoupravljanja*. Belgrade.

McClellan, Woodford (1969) Postwar Political Evolution. In: Vucinich, Wayne S. (ed.): *Contemporary Yugoslavia: Twenty years of socialist experiment*. Berkeley, Los Angeles: 119-153.

Plaggenborg, Stefan (1997) Die Entstehung des Nationalismus im kommunistischen Jugoslawien. In: *Südost-Forschungen* 56: 399-421.

Pleština, Dijana (1992) *Regional Development in Communist Yugoslavia: Success, Failure, and Consequences*. Boulder.

Radelić, Zdenko (2006) *Hrvatska u Jugoslaviji 1945.-1991.: od zajedništva do razlaza*. Zagreb.

Ramet, Pedro (1985) *Yugoslavia in the 1980s*. Boulder, London.

Ramet, Sabrina P. (1992) *Nationalism and Federalism in Yugoslavia, 1962-1991*. Second Edition. Bloomington, Indianapolis.

Ramet, Sabrina P. (2006) *The Three Yugoslavias: State-Building and Legitimation, 1918-2005*. Indianapolis.

Ramet, Sabrina P. (2011) *Die drei Jugoslawien. Eine Geschichte der Staatsbildungen und ihrer Probleme*. Munich.

Rusinow, Dennison (1988) *Yugoslavia. A Fractured Federalism*. Washington.

Shoup, Paul (1964) *Communism and the Yugoslav National Question*. New York.

Singleton, Fred/Carter, Bernard (1982) *Economy of Yugoslavia*. London, Canberra, New York.

Trifunović, Bogdan (1977) *A Handbook of Yugoslav Socialist Self-Management*. Belgrade.

Unkovski-Korica, Vladimir (2016) *The Economic Struggle for Power in Tito's Yugoslavia. From World War II to Non-Alignment*. London.

Vanek, Jan (1972) *The Economics of Workers' Management: A Yugoslav Case Study*. London.

Verba, Sidney/Shabad, Goldie (1978) Workers' Councils and Political Stratification: The Yugoslav Experience. In: *The American Political Science Review* 1: 80-95.

Vušković, Boris (1976) Social Inequality in Croatia. In: *New Left Review* 1: 26-44.

Wachtel, Howard M. (1973): *Workers' Management and Workers' Wages in Yugoslavia: The Theory and Practice of Participatory Socialism*. Ithaca.

Woodward, Susan L. (1995) *Socialist Unemployment. The Political Economy of Yugoslavia, 1945-1990*. New Jersey.

Zečević, Miodrag (1998) *Početak kraja SFRJ. Stenogram i drugi prateći dokumenti proširene sednice Izvršnog komiteta CK SKJ održane od 14. do 16. marta 1962. Godine*. Belgrade.

Zukin, Sharon (1975) *Beyond Marx and Tito. Theory and Practice in Yugoslav Socialism*. Cambridge.

Work as a Cure

Reana Senjković

1. Prologue[1]

In early spring of 1958, an "unexpected guest" entered Inspector Mane Brzica's office at the Department of Juvenile Delinquency in Zagreb:

– Long time no see, my man ... – Brzica greeted him [...]. Old furniture which, according to the office fashion rules, should have been trashed long ago, contrasted with freshly painted white walls. Vimpi felt a loose spring rub him annoyingly beneath the armchair he crawled into.
– You did not expect me, did you? – started the visitor questioningly, indirectly. Brzica would rather laugh in his face.
– I did. To be honest: I did. Only I was not sure when. Nor on which side of the lock we'd meet? This one or the other one ... I much prefer that we do not see each other on the side I lock and unlock!
Vimpi laughed with restraint.
With his professionally streamlined manner, Brzica opened a notebook, took his pen, coughed, cleared his throat and asked slowly with his silent bass:
– So, what brings you here, Vimpi?
Vimpi inhaled and talked, talked, talked ... It seemed to him that he would not be able to stop. The Inspector's silence was a reliable sign that he was listening attentively [...].
[Vimpi] did not forget to complain that his plan for setting up a brigade of black angels failed when he set it forth to 'these jaded guys from the City Youth [Committee]'.
Brzica openly told him that what he had thought out was more than brilliant. He did not guarantee a positive response, but he gave his word that he would set to work, that he would knock on every door and dial each and every telephone number in order to obtain permission to found a brigade of stigmatized bums:

---

[1] This work has been fully supported by Croatian Science Foundation under the project Transformation of Work in Post-transitional Croatia (IP-2016-06-7388).

– A feeling tells me (and you, Vimpi, know all about policemen's heightened sense of smell) that this will be a good thing. (Zlatar 1978: 88-89)

The event described by writer and journalist Pero Zlatar in his novel *Bitange, mirno!* is also mentioned in the famous Croatian sociologist's study on voluntary Youth Work Actions (*Omladinske radne akcije*, ORA; hereafter YWA) *Bratstvo i jedinstvo* (Brotherhood and unity):

> In the midst of agitation for the first renewed federal work action in 1958 in the City Committee of the League of Communists of Yugoslavia in Zagreb came a young man called "Vimpi", who enjoyed a reputation of one of the "chiefs" of Zagreb's young ticket scalpers. Vimpi, whose real name is Vilko Kokalj, is a typical representative of a postwar youth gone astray. His father, being a forced laborer, took him when he was still a child to Nazi Germany, where, amidst the deported workers, he was witness to the demoralization and decline of a social system where, in fact, all the means of self-sustainment had been good and legitimate. There, as a child, he learned that fists and craftiness are the main means of sustaining life. After he came back to his homeland he continued with a similar way of life and by virtue of his strength, although small in stature, his energy and intelligence, he imposed himself as a leader of young ticket scalpers. He served several sentences for affray and tyranny, until he realized while serving his last sentence that in socialist society such a path leads to nowhere. He was thinking about his destiny and about his friends' destiny, and decided that he would take the path of social rehabilitation. So in the spring of 1958 he came to the Committee and proposed to the secretary that he would himself organize a brigade composed of young people with whom society did not know how to deal. He set two conditions: first, that employment be guaranteed for each of the participants, and second, that they be assured of an apartment. [...] And so it was. In 1958 "Vimpi" even organized two brigades named Polet and the next year, 1959, two more. (Supek 1963: 275-276)

Vimpi's fictionalized character in Zlatar's novel addresses his friends (who were startled by the idea that they should join the brigade that would build a section of the highway between Zagreb and Ljubljana) as follows:

> This is the last day I belong to the world, our world, which is well known in Zagreb. I don't want to remain a man with no future, dumped by the people and sitting where I grew up and where I intend to stay. I am too old to be delirious with shallow stories about an easy life out there in some land of false promises. In order to stay here, in order to survive and find a job – a job because of which I won't get goose pimples when I hear the screech of tires in front of the house for fear that cops are coming to bust me – I need to change. And I will! But I also want for all of you I invited to come with me. The highway is our prime chance. And even bigger temptation. I beg none of you and I force nobody to join me. There will be no

problems if somebody decides to drop out. We should let those who aren't able to find the strength to put a cross ... a thick cross ... against everything they have done so far withdraw. Whoever wants to stay on the street, if anyone does, will balance freedom and jail like a clown. I am convinced that he, or she, all the same, will, sooner or later, end thoroughly outlawed ... You should know that there will be no mercy on the highway. They will monitor us from all sides because we are coming already marked. For that reason I repeat once more: those who think they won't be able to go through with it should stay! And those who will listen to me should be ready for the greatest sacrifices ... For the greatest discipline, for life to a schedule, for backbreaking toil. Only that way will we be able to become visible to people who gave us a chance and who will, when we come to Zagreb after two months, continue to lend a helping hand so we are able to find a decent job ... (Zlatar 1978: 97-98)

Rudi Supek is particularly interested in Vimpi's brigade's behavior, its achievements and its prospects. Vimpi, who was appointed commander of the brigade, as Supek discovers, maintains strict discipline, although at times by his own "methods". Eventually, the brigades are awarded shock brigade medals (Supek 1963: 276). On that occasion, the work actions' newspaper recalls:

When, a month ago, a brigade whose arrival was not scheduled came to the "Ivan Milutinović" youth work camp, now it can be said openly, many shook their heads doubtingly. Young men who made up the brigade carried their reputation as uncared-for delinquents, numbering various members of Zagreb's underground groups, and all kinds of things. How would these people, who had never done anything in their lives, perform construction duties here, how would they who are not used to any discipline and order obey a strict regime of community life and our camp rules – many wondered. Wasn't it too risky to bring such a brigade to the camp which is considered the best [of all the camps during the highway building activities]? [...] In the end, when summing up their one-month stay and work in the actions was done, it turned out that they committed fewer violations of discipline and order than some of the other brigades, that they were, all in all, good brigadiers.

[...] Exactly that is the greatest success of their stay on the highway. Tomorrow, when these young people, determined to take the other path, which is better than the one they were treading in recent times, get a job in working companies, the first days will not bring with them the usual disappointments. They are already accustomed to efforts, they have learned to work honestly for their living.

Furthermore, during the month of community living in the camp, young men from the "Polet" brigade came together with hundreds of boys and girls from all over the country. They found much in common – they rejoiced and were excited because of the same things, in a word, they are not separated by some unbridgeable gap. (cf. ibid.: 276-277)

However, Vimpi did not come from nothing: the archeology of literature on the Yugoslav YWAs, including its fictional corpus, uncovers Radža, the main character in Josip Barković's 1947 short story. He went through a cathartic transformation similar to Vimpi's: coming from a very poor family and used to spending his days on the street, involved in petty theft and occasional fighting, he joined the Zagreb youth brigade in building the Šamac-Sarajevo railway. Finally, he became an exemplary brigadier (Barković 1947).

2. The framework

The milieu of Yugoslav voluntary actions has been perceived not only as a place, or *mis-en-scène*, where the prime values of Yugoslav socialism were displayed,[2] but also as a kind of social laboratory where these values could be observed and tested. As early as during the first phase of construction of the *Bratstvo i jedinstvo* highway from 1946 to 1950, the idea that work would cure social ills was brought to life: in order to rid the town of Zagreb of female down-and-outs, but also in order to re-educate them and involve them in building the country, a number of them were joined in a brigade that had the duty to clean the roadways of sand, to neaten the verges and the like (Celmić 2006: 175). Moreover, in May 1951, Yugoslavia freed 1,097 political prisoners jailed on charges of supporting the Russian-led Cominform. "The former prisoners will go to work", as one of the American newspapers reported, "on a 'volunteer' basis to prove their loyalty by building a railway line between Breza and Vareš, two industrial centers in Bosnia" (Anonymous 1951: 10).

During the late 1950s and early 1960s, the projects of "re-socializing" juvenile delinquents were encouraged by changes to the concept of the YWAs (which resulted in changes to their organization), but also by contemporary shifts in social psychology theory. In the early postwar years in socialist Yugoslavia, as well as in other newly founded European socialist states, it was expected that all sorts of criminal behavior, including juvenile delinquency, would gradually disappear together with the remnants of the political system that had supposedly caused them. However, not only did they not disappear, they actually grew in number, so that society was compelled to adopt a "more realistic approach" (Špadijer-Džinić 1968: 269). Otherwise, as Slovenian psychologist Leopold Bregant noticed as early as 1954,

---

2 "Participation in the youth work actions represents the inclusion of the new society's material basis in such a way that the ideal of that society is already given in the very organization of the working actions as anticipation" (Grgić-Bigović 1978: 18).

"[i]n parallel with the introduction of social management in public life, interest increased in phenomena such as behavior of juveniles coming into conflict with the normal perspectives and demands of society" (Bregant 1954: 51).

From 1952 to 1958, only local YWAs were organized, following the assumption that a period of the country's reconstruction had been completed (and that the foundation for its industrialization was provided), but also as a consequence of the findings that voluntary youth work was economically unjustifiable. The 1958 revival was thus announced by moving the emphasis away from the economic to the social sphere, or, as Rudi Supek put it: "Youth Work Action finds its justification primarily in bringing together young people, in its educational significance, which will always reimburse losses in economic terms" (Supek 1963: 14). However, as could be detected in the then American newspapers, the reasons were somewhat more complex:

> Teenage Yugoslavs, often accused of apathy and waywardness, are being drafted for road-building in the hope hard work will keep them out of mischief. The Yugoslav Communist Party is so anxious about the younger generation it has decided to revive a postwar system of labor brigades, in which youngsters will be enrolled for building tasks. (Anonymous 1958: 8A)

Only three years later, the principles of self-management were introduced to the YWAs too: in 1958 they were organized and supervised the same way as immediately after the war, "semi-militarily" and "authoritatively", but from that year onwards "we notice gradual liberalization [...] and the introduction of various democratization measures that, in 1961, logically led to the adaptation of a new ideal of governance – social self-government" (Supek 1963: 177). Interestingly enough, the first Yugoslav film on the topic of juvenile delinquency is Toma Janjić's *Crni biseri* (Black Pearls) of 1958, the same year the federal YWAs were renewed. The film follows the efforts of a new head of the juvenile correctional home on the island of Badija to positively affect the lives of his protégés, the boys that had hitherto been considered incorrigible. His success is presented as the result of a different, relaxed, softer and friendlier approach to children.

3. Is hard labor really that bad?

The "socially neglected youth's self-rehabilitation" case of Vilko Kokalj and his gang was, for Rudi Supek, "probably one of the most interesting" among a number of attempts at "correcting" (socially rehabilitating) the delinquent youth at the YWAs. Moreover, it was a case that "induced responsible social factors to field-test the problems of juvenile delinquency [...], also by sending them to youth brigades" (Supek 1963: 275, 271-272).

The same year Rudi Supek published his study on *Bratstvo i jedinstvo YWAs* Alojz Majetić published his novel *Čangi*. After having fun with his friends and drinking a lot, Majetić's main character steals a car and hits a passer-by. In order to find a safe haven from the police chase, he chooses to join the work actions. However, Čangi does not feel very secure while staying in the camp: his fellow brigadier Flor, a young man with a perfect socialist biography, doubts his genuine desire to participate. Eventually, we find out that Flor was witness to Čangi's outrage. After a while, the tensions between the two break out in a fist fight, but, ultimately, Čangi decides to measure his strength against Flor's by dumping soil from trucks. Quite unexpectedly, he finds himself enjoying heavy physical work under the hot sun and, at the same time, he finds meaning in "serving the common goal". Thus, although he does not avoid legal punishment in the sequel to the novel (which was published seven years later; Majetić 1970), he was, at least for a time, converted to a person on the verge of a meaningful life.[3]

The phenomenon of Yugoslav voluntary YWAs alone, not to mention the idea of sending the youth who had gone astray to the actions in order to re-socialize them, undoubtedly belongs to a set of past experiences that are prone to interpretation from a highly normative perspective designed at the peak of the Cold War: "The best way for the Western world to face this war was to establish itself as the champion in the struggle against the new totalitarianism, which was labeled as the necessary and inevitable consequence of Communist ideology and programme" (Losurdo 2004: 30). Hence, although it became one of the core "explanatory" categories concerning the socialist countries, the category of totalitarianism is not devoid of serious flaws, as Domenico Losurdo admonishes: "[...] it transforms an empirical description tied to specific characteristics into a general logical deduction" (ibid.: 50).

Thus, if we wish to reflect on efforts to "bring back" delinquent youngsters from the margins of society to its mainstream or, as we may also put it, from materially and socially unproductive to productive activities, we need to take a closer look at the concepts of delinquency and labor in a somewhat wider context.

Delinquency is commonly defined as an offence or misdeed, usually of a minor nature, especially one committed by a young person, or as conduct that is out of line with accepted behavior or the law. A bottom-up view sees delinquency as a way to obtain material possessions, along with popularity and admiration within a certain social group. As such, it opposes not only socially accepted behavior, but also undermines the accepted and preferred mode of earning a living. The crime that

---

3 Nonetheless, Majetić's novel was banned immediately after it was published due to "pornography and incorrect representation of youth", but this official ban actually ensured Majetić's status as a rebel in literary and pop-cultural circles at that time, which led to greater interest in his work.

continued to exist in the European socialist states after 1945, which was not only an economic problem, but also a threat to internal discipline and morale, was interpreted, according to Eric Buchholz, as "a hang-over ('a worm continuation') of the non-socialist past, or [as] a direct consequence of capitalist efforts to undermine the socialist system" (cf. Sperlich 2007: 194).

On the other hand, the concept of labor (which was yet to become, in Marxian terms, the *need*) was one of the most important defining concepts in all socialist countries, although even Karl Marx's concept of labor, on which they relied, proved to be "highly complex and heterogeneous", containing a tension between alienated and non-alienated work activity – between integrated organic craft work and atomized, mechanical fragments of activity (cf. Berki 1979: 35).

When it comes to reflecting on juvenile delinquents who were included in voluntary youth work brigades, the term *voluntary*, already prone to interpretation by means of the ideological signifiers, would most likely be immediately questioned. At the very least, the idea of volunteering for the actions, if scrutinized from today's perspective and within the Yugoslav context, demarcates a clear line between voluntary labor and labor that is forced by whatever means, including labor aimed at re-education or punishment. Yet, it seems that this line needs to be wide enough to form a sort of no-man's land and to include cases where people decided that they had better choose to take part in work actions for whatever reason, including their future prospects,[4] but also those in which people took part in the actions only because they had no other way to spend their summer vacation. Likewise, during the late 1950s and early 1960s, the problem of juvenile delinquency preoccupied not only socialist authorities, astonished by its persistence in spite of supposedly unconducive social circumstances, but also the "general public's attention" in the West. In 1962, the Coordinating Committee for International Voluntary Service suggested that, in industrialized countries:

> Juvenile delinquency is largely a reaction to unprecedented material wealth and the orderly, often boring society that produced it. And delinquents will not be bribed back into the fold by offers to teach them the techniques and graces of that society. On the contrary, what is needed is something exciting, something involving physical challenge, something that can bring delinquents together with other

---

4 Alternatively, as one of the characters in the early Yugoslav film *Život je naš. Ljudi s pruge* (*Life is Ours. People from the Railway [Building Actions]*), directed by Gustav Gavrin in 1948, put it straightforwardly: "A shock-worker or not, it is all the same. You'll receive the medal for the action, and the medal for taking part in digging the tunnel, the most difficult object. And whether you've been working or not, that is not written on your forehead. You come back, the medal is shining ... 'Well ... I've been to the actions ...' And all the doors are open. And they say: 'Here you are, do you want a scholarship?'"

energetic [...] young people in a situation where they face together the necessity for some sort of even rudimentary social order. (cf. Gillette 1968)[5]

Moreover, the Executive Board of UNESCO expressed at its 78th session in 1968 "the hope that the Director-General will be able to submit to the General Conference at its fifteenth session proposals on the measures that UNESCO might take in 1969-1970 to reinforce its youth programme" ("Report on Youth" 1968: 1). Although this urge was the outcome of the worldwide "student revolt movement", the report clearly stated that "the problem of juvenile delinquency has been attracting the general public's attention [...] for some fifteen years past" (ibid.: 9). In addressing the multiplicity of causes that led to the profusion of the phenomenon, the countries in which "radical and far-reaching social and economic changes, socialist or otherwise in type, were initiated either as a sequel to the Second World War or in the process of decolonization" were mentioned too. As was noted, "time and again hopes of economic, social and cultural progress, and above all of structural change, have run into material difficulties, or suffered from dilatory execution". Therefore the spectrum of what was recognized as "protest from the young" was attributed to "this situation, and more particularly [to] the tension between those who fought for independence and those who had no part in the struggle" (ibid.: 8).

However, UNESCO's carefully weighed opinion was an exception in observing what was clearly defined as an issue. Only five years prior to the UNESCO report, Carl Leiden, visiting professor of government at the University of Texas, wrote somewhat spitefully on the problem of juvenile delinquency in state socialist countries:

> We think of long sideburns and uncut hair, leather jackets and narrowed trousers as the hallmark of western delinquency, but visitors in the communist countries have observed similar grooming and attire there. One should make no mistake of the fact – delinquency is to be found in Moscow, Leningrad, and other Soviet cities, along with East Berlin, Poznan, Budapest, and Peking. Guarded references in the communist press and fuller comment from political refugees and western visitors have lent substantial support to this contention. Young Soviet hoodlums carry guns and knives and act very much like their western counterparts, performing all the while only perfunctory lip service to communism. They commit crimes of violence; they steal and cheat; they pride themselves upon their ability to live on the fringe of excitement. They riot occasionally, as in Vladivostok two years ago, and they are a happy reminder that the Soviet Union has its problems, too. (Leiden 1963: 152)

---

5 URL: http://www.ourstory.info/library/5-AFSIS/Gillette/volunteers05.html (retrieved July 23, 2019).

For this author, "the existence of delinquency in the Soviet Union [was] an indication that youth has not been brain-washed there" (ibid.: 153). Yet, for him, this does not imply that juvenile delinquents were not brainwashed on the other side of the Iron Curtain too. They, unlike their Eastern counterparts, as the author explicitly states (by referring to one of the most popular series of 1950s American films that shifted the youth rebellion closer to the mainstream), were "rebels without a cause", since "a stable, politically free state produces little need for [...] revolt and rebellion" (ibid.: 153, 155). Along these lines, and given Leiden's competence evident in his assistance in composing the 1968 American Juvenile Delinquency Prevention and Control Act, we may speculate that the delinquency that existed in Western countries was not expected either.

Yet the idea that labor has healing powers was neither new nor innovative, as was demonstrated by *Time* magazine's Washington correspondent in his 2009 article entitled "Is Hard Labor Really That Bad?". Alex Altman presented his version of its history beginning with Sisyphus, then skipping to Oscar Wilde's sentence to two years' hard labor and then to the Soviet gulag, Nelson Mandela's imprisonment on Robben Island and the U.S. military's sentencing of Army Private John Suarez in 2008 and the late Sergeant Santos Cardona in 2006 (2009). Indeed, and also in relation to young delinquents, the idea seems more vital today than in most periods of its history. Filip Coussée summarizes recent research on youth work and organized leisure activities as follows:

> Academic research in Flanders – as in UK, Germany, USA, [...] – underpins the belief that youth work (especially if it concerns structured programmes) produces positive outcomes for its participants. Participation in structured youth activities contributes to academic results (Fredricks & Eccles 2006), to the development of social and cultural capital (Dworkin, Larson & Hansen 2003), to mental health (Mahoney, Schweder & Stattin 2002), it promotes a sense of citizenship (Williamson 1997), contributes to the process of achieving independence whilst maintaining a good relation with the parents (Larson, Pearce, Sullivan & Jarret 2007), prevents all kinds of risk behaviour (Mahoney, Stattin & Lord 2004), leads to a stronger position in the labour market (Jarret, Sullivan & Watkins 2005), nurtures democratic skills and attitudes (Eccles, Barber, Stone & Hunt 2003), [...] Developmental and community psychologists and sociologists seem to find each other promptly in further unravelling the relation between participation and positive outcomes. (Coussée 2009: 45)[6]

---

6 Coussée's list of youth work's positive outcomes, but also his rhetoric, resemble those used in discussing the issue in the public discourse of the Socialist Federal Republic of Yugoslavia.

4. Delinquency vis-à-vis labor

In order to come closer to interpreting the attempts at "re-socializing" Yugoslav juvenile delinquents at the YWAs, Alexei Yurchak's insight into the everyday life of the last Soviet generation, and more precisely, his thesis that the authoritative discourse by that time had become generally performative and lost its constative dimension, thus allowing the dispersion of meaning(s), may be instructive. Following Austin's, Derrida's, Bourdieu's and Butler's germane discussions while also using the respective proposals of Amy Hollywood and Saba Mahmood, Yurchak points out that "the performative reproduction of the form of [late Soviet] rituals and speech acts actually *enabled* the emergence of diverse, multiple, and unpredictable meanings in everyday life, including those that did not correspond to the constative meanings of authoritative discourse" (Yurchak 2006: 25).

In the Soviet case, the *performative shift* "at the level of concrete ritualized forms of discourse" began, as Yurchak asserts, as "a byproduct of the changes – beginning in the 1950s – in the conditions under which Soviet authoritative discourse was produced, circulated, and received" (ibid.: 26). Yurchak's persistent insistence on scrutinizing the adjustments that were made to Soviet authoritative public speech would help us anchor the second phase of the Yugoslav YWAs' history in a time category comparable to that of the "last Yugoslav generation". Accordingly, we need to raise the question whether Yugoslav YWAs are to be considered successful performances (meaning that they were successful in performing what was meant to be performed), or whether they were misperformed. In order to provide an answer we should examine the very idea that first guided the project. In doing so, we should surely stress the difference between "after the war" actions (that were designed to unite the need to rebuild the country's infrastructure with the "enthusiasm" that sprung out of stepping into a "new future") and the actions that followed (insisting on the concept of brotherhood and unity). Here, we could offer data on the Yugoslav YWAs' failure in terms of their economic profitability, first stated publicly in 1952. We could even try to insist on elaborating the possibility of (a certain) resistance or, at least, negotiating practices in participating in the efforts already made during the postwar reconstruction of the country, but also during the history of the Yugoslav YWAs. There would doubtlessly be enough evidence to prove such an interpretation (or interpretations), ranging from almost anecdotal evidence about parents forbidding their daughters from taking part in the actions "because only hooligans gather there" to severe cases in which some working organizations required their young workers to participate. In addition, one will find confirmation that the actions tended to become deprived of their content, in particular towards the 1980s:

Even today our work-site is poorly organized. They are moving us from one ground to another; again, there is not enough work for all of us. [...] We gather stone that was left after mining and we carry it away to the piles. [...] Several soldiers punched the rocks not far away. They told us that all we are doing is useless since tomorrow the terrain will be mined again. (Jilek et al. 1981: 16)

When I came out of my tent, I noticed some commotion in the camp. Television Zagreb, while shooting a half-hour broadcast about the work actions, filmed the scouts in front of our camp. [...] After that, the cameraman entered the camp to film our brigade. [Our commander] tried to make an atmosphere of joy, song and content, thus helping the people from television, who had been largely directing (or producing) the scenes of this documentary. (Ibid.: 79)

Thus, considering both Čangi's fictional and Vimpi's actual experience, one could concentrate on cultural performance alone, guided by the idea that "successful performance depends on the ability to convince others that one's performance is true" (Alexander 2006: 32). This may prove to be in line with Evgenii Aleksandrovich Dobrenko's recent perspective on the *Political Economy of Socialist Realism*:

[...] the ideology that not only dominated economics, but also gave it meaning, was shaped in Socialist Realism itself. [...] Socialist Realism's basic function was not propaganda, however, but rather to *produce reality by aestheticizing it*. [...] To aestheticize is to re-create the world, to transform it 'according to the laws of beauty and harmony'. (Dobrenko 2007: 4)

For Dobrenko, since "an enormous rift" existed "between the original reality of socialism and the socialist ideal", socialist realism became "a mechanism for bringing them into correspondence" (ibid.: 8). Thus, "the basic function of Socialist Realism [was] to create socialism – Soviet reality, and not an artifact" (ibid.: xii). Dobrenko found the idea to be in accord with what Clifford Geertz discovered while examining the state ceremonials of Bali. Geertz called them "'metaphysical theatre', 'theatre designed to express a view of the ultimate nature of reality and, at the same time, to shape the existing conditions of life to be consonant with that reality; that is, theatre to present an ontology and, by presenting it, to make it happen – make it actual'" (ibid.: 21). In the same vein, the famous Georgian philosopher Merab Mamardashvili argued that Soviet history "had created a 'self-imitating man, in whom a historical man might well not recognize himself'". For him, this new person's consciousness has been led "'into an antiworld of shadows and images that cast no shadows of their own', 'a world behind the looking glass, made up of imitations of real life', a world of 'illusory illusions' and 'life imitating life'" (cf. ibid.: 16).

Each of these ready-made possibilities for interpreting the Yugoslav YWAs, together with potentially introducing Foucault's idea of heterotopias, Arnold van

Gennep's and Claude Lévi-Strauss's idea of the *rite de passage*, or Jean Baudrillard's observation that the "mode of production" has transformed into a "code of production", lead us to understand the actions as detached from reality (if defined as the totality of what is, as opposed to what merely seems to be). We would see them as a stage in which the defining concepts of socialism/communism were to be performed, where the illusions were to be imitated, where the idea of transition from socialism to communism was ritualized by inscribing it onto the brigadiers' bodies, also (or even more so) onto the young delinquent participants' bodies...

However, we should consider yet another possibility offered by Saba Mahmood, who draws on Butler's Foucauldian point that "the possibility of resistance to norms [is located] within the structure of power itself rather than in the consciousness of an autonomous individual", while "agentival capacity is entailed not only in those acts that result in (progressive) change but also those that aim toward continuity, stasis, and stability" (Mahmood 2001: 212; cf. Yurchak 2006: 28). Indeed, while paving her way to posing the question whether "[t]o endure is to enact?", she clearly states that "if the ability to effect change in the world and in oneself is historically and culturally specific (both in terms of what constitutes 'change' and the capacity by which it is effected), then its meaning and sense cannot be fixed a priori" (ibid.).

Hence, in rethinking the proposal to interpret the "last Yugoslav generation's" voluntary work actions in terms of the participants' resistance to what was announced in the invitation to them to partake, we need to return to the lesson we learned from Alojz Majetić's *Čangi*. Although the novel already gained the aura of being "unsuitable" for "the regime" shortly after it was published, we should not overlook the main character's change that followed his conflict with Flor, the character personifying "the regime" itself. This observation could be reinforced by the quotation from the *Bratstvo i jedinstvo* YWAs' newspaper Rudi Supek used to demonstrate Vimpi's brigades' success: not only did they go to the actions voluntarily, but the brigadiers were highly motivated to prove themselves within the reigning value system. In keeping with this, a parallel interpretation could be proposed that would bridge the gap between our "impartial" post-insight(s) or "induced" interpretation(s) and the mere fact that today, more than 1,700 former brigadiers (belonging to the "last Yugoslav generation") found the Internet to be friendly enough to host them (at bilten-ora-sfrj.com) in their wish to warn that "Maybe we'll be very old the day we'll meet beside the track [...] on both sides of what we've done", and to preserve what they believe to be their community and, more importantly, their values. With this in mind, one should assume (at least) that we should not be too eager to conclude that Yugoslav voluntarily work actions were nothing more than yet another "totalitarian" misperformance.

Bibliography

Alexander, Jeffrey C. (2006) Cultural pragmatics: social performance between ritual and strategy. In: Alexander, Jeffrey C./Giesen, Bernhard/Mast, Jason L. (eds.) *Social Performance: Symbolic Action, Cultural Pragmatics, and Ritual*. Cambridge, 29-89.

Altman, Alex (2009) Is Hard Labor Really That Bad? In: *Time*, August 12, 2009. URL: http://content.time.com/time/nation/article/0,8599,1915823,00.html#ixzz2RCdqDs8f (retrieved July 23, 2019).

Anonymous (1951) Yugoslavia Frees Political Prisoners. In: *The Milwaukee Journal*, May 7, 1951: 10.

Anonymous (1958) Yugoslav Teen-Agers Again in Labor Gangs. In: *The Miami News*, March 29, 1958: 8A.

Barković, J. (1947) Radža. In: *Na pruzi. Zbornik radova književnika iz Hrvatske o pruzi Šamac-Sarajevo*. Zagreb: 95-107.

Berki, R. N. (1979) On the Nature and Origins of Marx's Concept of Labor. In: *Political Theory* 7/1: 35-56.

Bilten ORA SFRJ: *Leksikon omladinskih radnih akcija*. URL: http://www.bilten-orasfrj.com/public_html (retrieved November 12, 2014).

Bregant, L. (1954) Sociološko-psihološko istraživanje besprizornih maloletnika. In: *Socijalna politika* IV/7-8: 51-62.

Celmić, I. (2006) Kako smo gradili Autoput Beograd-Zagreb. In: *Ceste i mostovi* 52/1-6: 156-175; 52/7-9: 93-106; 52/10-12: 105-107.

Coussée, F. (2009) Youth work and its forgotten history. A view from Flanders. In: Verschelden, G./Coussée, Filip/Van de Walle, Tineke/Williamson, Howard (eds.): *The History of Youth Work in Europe*. Strasbourg: 45-61.

Dobrenko, E. A. (2007) *Political Economy of Socialist Realism*. New Haven.

Gavrin, Gustav (1948) *Život je naš. Ljudi s pruge*. Belgrade.

Gillette, A. (1968) *One Million Volunteers. The Story of Volunteer Youth Service*. New York. URL: http://www.ourstory.info/library/5-AFSIS/Gillette/volunteersTC.html#TC (retrieved July 23, 2019).

Grgić-Bigović, J. (1978) *Maloljetni delinkventi i radne akcije*. Zagreb.

Janić, Svetomir (1958) *Crni biseri*. Sarajevo.

Jilek, M./Kokot, M./Potočnjak, Ž./Tadej, P./Vidušić, M. (1981) *Četiri priče s 'Otoka mladosti'*. Zagreb.

Leiden, C. (1963) A Gold Medal for Delinquency. In: *Crime & Delinquency* 9: 152-157.

Losurdo, D. (2004) Towards a Critique of the Category of Totalitarianism. In: *Historical Materialism* 12/2: 25-55.

Mahmood, S. (2001) Feminist Theory, Embodiment, and the Docile Agent: Some Reflections on the Egyptian Islamic Revival. In: *Cultural Anthropology* 16/2: 202-236.

Majetić, A. (1963) *Čangi*. Novi Sad.
Majetić, A. (1970) *Čangi off Gottoff*. Zagreb.
Špadijer-Džinić, J. (1968) Sociološki pristup istraživanju maloletničke delinkvencije. In: *Sociologija* 10/1: 269-280.
Sperlich, P. W. (2007) *The East German Social Courts: Law and Popular Justice in a Marxist-Leninist Society*. Westport.
Supek, R. (1963) *Omladina na putu bratstva. Psiho-sociologija radne akcije*. Belgrade.
UNESCO (1968) *Report on Youth*. 15th General conference in Paris on October 21, 1968. URL: https://unesdoc.unesco.org/ark:/48223/pf0000160212 (retrieved July 23, 2019).
Yurchak, A. (2006) *Everything Was Forever, Until It Was No More: The Last Soviet Generation*. Princeton.
Zlatar, P. (1978) *Bitange, mirno!* Zagreb.

Economy and the Cult of Relics
The Miracle-Working Icon of the Virgin and Financing the Patriarchate of Peć Monastery

Ivana Ženarju Rajović

The Patriarchate of Peć monastery was established by Archbishop Arsenije in the 13th century. He was buried in this monastery, as was his successor Archbishop Sava II, brother of King Uros I and other Serbian archbishops and patriarchs. In the 14th century, it was the seat of the Serbian Archbishopric, and the seat of Patriarchate between 1557 and 1766, when it was merged to form the Patriarchate of Constantinople. In the 19th century, the monastery of Peć was part of the Diocese of Raška and Prizren, one of many in the Patriarchate of Constantinople.

As a complex structure, the monastery consists of three separate churches with a common western part and a chapel on the south side. Archbishop Arsenije built the Church of the St Apostles that is now in the centre. On the north side, Archbishop Nikodim constructed a church dedicated to St Demetrios between 1316 and 1326. A few years later, Archbishop Danil II erected a church dedicated to the Virgin on the south side of the St Apostles Church, a narthex for three churches, and a chapel of St Nicholas, on the south side of the southern church.

The focal points of the piety in the Patriarchate of Peć in the 19th century were the grave of Archbishop Arsenije, and the miracle-working icon of the Virgin, believed to have been painted by St Luke the Evangelist and brought to the monastery by the first Serbian archbishop, St Sava, from Jerusalem or Mount Athos as a major relic. The icon from the monastery of Peć shows the Virgin holding the Child in her right hand. She is flanked by 12 small images of the apostles, six of them on each side. Also, the icon has a rich silver votive frame. The icon had its own liturgical service called Служба сретењу чудотворне иконе пресвете Богородице зване Пећске (*The Service of Presentation of the Miracle-Working Icon of Peć*), written by the priest Nikodim Dimitrijevic Svetogorac and published in 1812 thanks to a donation by one of the faithful from Prizren (Anonymous 1902: 325). The Akathistos was published later in 1894 due to the Serbian metropolitan Michael.

After traveling through Bosnia and Herzegovina and Old Serbia, Aleksandar Giljferding published his travels in 1856, in which he recorded seeing the miracle-working icon of Peć. He wrote that this icon was held in the Church of the Virgin in Peć Monastery and that it was carried into the homes of believers to heal the sick (Гиљфердинг 1859; 1996: 134). In a letter addressed to the metropolitan, Abbot Miron of Peć asked for support for the monastery, describing it as the Monastery of Saint Arsenije and claiming the importance of the saint. He wrote that holy relics of various Serbian clergymen were placed near the miracle-working icon of The Virgin of Peć, which was brought from Jerusalem by Saint Sava (Archives of Serbia, MID-PPO 1906: 932).

Fig. 1 Miracle-working Icon of Peć.

Unfortunately, we have no scientific study related to this icon, most probably painted at the end of the 17th or beginning of the 18th century, and all we know concerns its wooden Baroque throne that was constructed by the famous Macedonian wood engraver Dimitar Stanišev from Kruševo in 1863 (Корнаков 1986: 153). In the lower part of the throne, on its left-hand side, the artist engraved his own portrait. He represented himself while making the throne, beside two figures of the monks who commissioned it, Jerotej and Maxim, all of them flanked by two angels. On the other side of the throne, he engraved portraits of St Arsenije and St Nikodim, saints whose relics are kept in the monastery. This construction has rich wooden decoration in the form of anthropomorphic, zoomorphic and vegetable motifs. There are scenes of The Ascension of Christ and the Birth of the Virgin, figures of angels, evangelists, eagles and lions, and motifs such as acanthus leaves, roses, grapes, etc.

Also, there are some painted parts on this throne, by the painter Kostadin Krstev from Veles (Корнаков 1986: 154). Firstly, a Baroque medallion is placed beneath the place where the icon is held. Kostadin Krstev painted on this medallion a composition that conveys a visual understanding of the legend of the icon. He depicted the scene *Presentation of the Miracle-Working Icon*. On the right side, there is St Sava, dressed in episcopal robes, holding the miracle-working icon in his hands, and escorted by two clergymen. St Arsenije is presented in front of St Sava. He is also dressed as bishop and accompanied by his escort. It is clear that Kostadin Krstev painted the moment when, according to the legend, St Sava brought this icon to the monastery. This pictorial construction, probably designed by patrons, was invented in order to assure the faithful of the authenticity of the story in which they believed. Above this medallion, there is a painted rectangular panel with portraits of St Danil and St Sava II, also saints whose relics are in the monastery. Between them, there is a text explaining who commissioned this wooden throne and who made it. Above the miracle-working icon, there is a medallion with the presentation of Christ as the Great Archpriest.

Fig. 2 Presentation of the miracle-working icon.

This icon, as well as the grave of the founder of the monastery, as evidence of God's presence in the community, was a core of the sacred space (Lidov 2009: 9). The relics, which include all items directly related to the figures of the heavenly hierarchy, were the subject of the theological exegesis and liturgical rites, and of a strong expression of devotion (Поповић 2006: 208). They had protective and healing powers and were also considered a palladium of the town (ibid.: 209). Thus the miraculous icon of the Virgin was regarded as the patron of the city of Peć, with healing powers that made it an object of worship, especially in the area of female piety. The Orthodox Christian world is familiar with many miracle-working icons, and the majority of them were of the Mother of God (cf. Lidov 1996: 2000; Shevzov 1999; 2000; 2007). The popularity of these icons derived from the visual image of the depicted saint, as well as from narratives behind the icon. Those narratives pointed to events that led to the icons' special veneration, from their creation to the miracles they performed (Shevzov 2000: 613). Concerning the creation of miracle-working icons, Orthodoxy attributed many of them to St Luke as their painter, even if it was clear that they were post-Byzantine due to the style and iconography, as in the case of the Peć icon (cf. Bacci 2000: 79-89). In that way, miracle-working icons played the role of a mediator of divine energy radiating from the most sacred spaces (Lidov 2004: 291-321).

Miracle-working icon form the monastery of Peć and its cult made a great contribution to the economic prosperity of the monastery through the donations of the faithful. They donated money to the monastery and bestowed votive offerings to the holy image when visiting it as pilgrims. Members of other religions visited this miraculous icon too, seeking salvation and comfort. For example, among Muslims it was known as St Merima (Петровић 1995: 168). Besides those living in the vicinity of the monastery, there were many pilgrims who had to travel long distances to venerate relics in the monastery. The pilgrim of the 19th century was usually one who venerated, rather than one who traveled, due to the limited possibilities of traveling through certain parts of the Ottoman Empire (cf. Weyl Carr 2002). Also, the faithful donated money on occasions when the icon visited their homes. The miraculous icon usually left its sumptuous throne in times of great and prolonged droughts and epidemics (Поповић 1995: 168). This is a specific kind of icon veneration which has been called 'pilgrimage in reverse' (Shevzov 1999: 36).

This phenomenon of icon visitations was well known in the Orthodox world. In Russia, it was a widespread practice within a parish, district, diocese, or even between dioceses. Usually, these visitations were initiated upon requests from local communities, since pilgrimage was not possible for many social groups. A large number of Russian communities sponsored annual miracle-working icon visitations to commemorate such events as droughts, epidemics, floods and fires. Icon visitations were organized in the form of processions with a focus on the particular icon that was being carried (Shevzov 1999: 34-36). In Bulgaria, the miracle-working icon of the Virgin from the monastery of Rila was also carried into the homes of the faithful on several occasions. Great credit was attributed to this icon in preventing the spread of the plague in the late 1820s (Kоюмджиев 1998: 52).

In the ceremonial processions in which it was carried, the miracle-working icon of the Virgin from the monastery of Peć was accompanied by believers, priests and monks. During Lent and in cases of long droughts and epidemics, the icon was carried into the homes of the faithful (Петровић 1933: 6). The icon entered the home in the evening, in a specially equipped room, with a large table decorated with flowers and vigil lamps. The table was oriented to the east, and surrounded by chairs for many people, friends and neighbors of the hosts. The entrance to the house was decorated too. Once the icon entered the room, an old cross was placed on it so people could venerate both of them. They then placed vigil lamps and candles near to the icon, as well as parts of clothing of their sick relatives, and they stayed all night in the room praying. Since this event was considered a great honor and ceremony, on this occasion housewives would prepare food that was served during the night (ibid.: 6). It is interesting that people used to treat this icon as a living person. They did not speak as if the icon had been brought to their home, but as if she had come alone and spent the night. Gathering around the icon contributed to the good social relations in the community. Also, there was another social dimension to venerating this icon, due to the belief that the icon punished violations of moral and hygienic rules (ibid.: 6). The icon played its most significant role in the economic life of the monastery in 1907.

Besides being spiritual, educational and cultural centers, Orthodox Christian monasteries functioned as economic entities. This multi-functional monastic role was immanent to every monastery in the vast territory of the Patriarchate of Constantinople in the time of Ottoman rule. The economic life of the great monasteries in the Diocese of Raška and Prizren in the 19th century was shaped by their financial means and properties, which included metochia, arable land, vineyards, meadows and pasture areas, forests, houses, shops etc. Via the rational management of monastic properties, they were able to generate income for fraternities.

Properties were arable land, pasture areas and real estate. The most profitable monastic asset in the period of Ottoman rule was land. Land could be cultivated by members of a fraternity, or it could earn income in the form of rent. Pasture could also be used for monastic stock or could be rented for a fee. Land was usually exploited by local villagers, who were obliged to pay an annual percentage of their income. There were also many cases when land generated no income. Many monasteries had real estate in the form of houses, schools, shops and taverns, and often had houses on monastic land in other dioceses, which served as resting places for monks traveling in order to collect donations to the monastery. A very important category of monastic property was *metochia*, monastic land that was usually not located in the vicinity of the monastery and that had its own church or monastery (Roudometof/Michael 2010: 61). The monastery could acquire estates in several ways, including purchase from timar owners who sold public land, or purchase with complete ownership. More often, the monastery could earn properties from donations and dedications from the faithful (Roudometof/Michael 2010: 62). Besides managing assets, it could also earn income from regular parish taxes.

In the late 19th century, in 1894, the monastery of Peć had three estates in the vicinity of Peć and Gnjilane (Archives of Serbia, MID-PPO 1894: 440; 1904: 150). It had three taverns, six shops and four houses in Peć, as well as vineyards and a large brewery in Orahovac. The monastery earned regular annual income from the collection of regular parish taxes, rent, mills and livestock. Many people gathered twice a year at the monastery, on the day of Assumption of the Virgin and St Peter's day, and they also contributed to the economic well-being of the economy. The monastery also earned donations from believers who venerated to the miraculous icon of the Virgin (Archives of Serbia, MID-PPO 1894: 440).

Money was spent on salaries for the brotherhood, servants and guard, on feeding the fraternity and monastery guests, on maintenance of the church and buildings within the complex of the monastery, and on the lawsuits conducted against some members of the local Albanian communities (Archives of Serbia, MID, Consulate in Priština 1909). Bad management by Abbot Sofronije in the late 19th century put the monastery into heavy debt. He sold monastic land in Goraždevac at half price to a Bišara Bey. He also sold three shops, and one of them, in the prominent part of Peć, was bequeathed by the merchant Staniša Đukić. Abbot Sofronije built a two-storey house at the cost of a monastery for a son of a man who managed the church and school community (Archives of Serbia, MID-PPO 1894: 440).

In 1907, during the time of Abbot Miron, the monastery fell into huge debt, which was added to old debt due to his poor management of money and estates. There were problems between the church and school community as well as between the priest and monks. They were negligent in taking care of accounting and bookkeeping, and the monastery cash was used for costs of various kinds (Петровић 1995: 166-167).

When Metropolitan Nićifor visited the monastery in 1907 as head of the Diocese of Raška and Prizren, he found that various persons owed a total of 160,000 coins to the monastery. Many of them could not be traced, because some were no longer alive and some were bankrupt. Therefore only 4,000 groš could be raised. At the same time, the monastery owed around 59,000 groš, and all the creditors, including citizens of Peć and surrounding villages, demanded their money back. It was difficult to pay back all the debt, because annual monastic income stood at approximately 60,000 groš at the time (ibid.: 167).

Fig. 3: *The Patriarchate of Peć Monastery (around 1925)*.

At that time, the monastery earned income from everyday parish activities to the tune of approximately 16,000 groš. Those activities involved the consecration of water and oil, baptism, memorial services and funerals, reading prayers for healing and so on. The faithful also used to place money and various contributions next to the miracle-working icon as well as on other icons in monastery churches. In addition, they were obligated to pay parish taxes, and at that time the parish consisted of between 800 and 900 homes. The monastery had annual earnings of over 20,000 groš from land, its most profitable source. Income from letting different facilities, including houses, shops and taverns, amounted to around 8,000 groš. The monastery also owned water mills through which it earned about 3,500 groš, and livestock that could bring in more than 7,000 groš (Archives of Serbia, MID, Consulate in Priština 1909).

Given that at the time of his stay in the monastery there was not enough money to pay off all debts, the Metropolitan had an idea how to collect the amount owed as quickly as possible. He ordered sending the miraculous icon of the Virgin throughout the Diocese of Raška and Prizren, hoping for a high amount of donations. Although this miracle-working icon had left the monastery before, this time its tour was supposed to produce concrete financial benefits for paying monastery debts.

During this "holy expedition" in 1907, the miraculous icon visited the monasteries of Dečani and Gračanica and the towns Đakovica, Prizren, Uroševac, Gnjilane, Priština, Lipljan, Vučitrn, Mitrovica, Novi Pazar, Sjenica, and Nova Varoš. During the transport of the icon, the monastery had two abbots, Joanikije and Maxim, who escorted the icon, and they were greeted very solemnly in each town (Петровић 1995: 168). The icon was exhibited to the faithful in the parish churches, where they could venerate it and donate money. This endeavor proved to be very profitable, the icon raising enough money to cover the monastery's debts.

After being displayed in the monastery of Gračanica, the miracle-working icon visited the town of Lipljan. There the icon was exhibited in the center of the Church of the Presentation of the Virgin. The welcoming committee consisted of a local priest in ceremonial dress, deacons, teachers and the faithful. The icon spent a night in the church and early in the morning the priest went through the parish to collect money. Money was also placed on the icon, as well as offerings in the form of socks, scarves, and fabric, which was later sold (Archives of Serbian Academy of Science and Arts: E-469-II-131; E-469-II-132). Beyond those offerings, people endowed the icon with 1,033 groš.

In the cities of Raška and the Lim Valley, the icon was endowed with tens of thousands of coins (Шалипуровић 1972: 183). The highest amount was collected in the town of Nova Varoš, where the faithful donated 61,543 groš, which was enough to pay back the monastery debts. For unknown reasons, this amount never reached the monastery of Peć, but was kept in the church school community in the town (Шалипуровић 1972: 188). The second largest amount was collected in the town of Sjenica, where believers donated 40,000 coins, even though the community of Sjenica was known to be very indigent. Of these, about 6,000 coins were left in Sjenica for the completion of the school building with the permission of the Metropolitan (Петровић 1995: 154).

The usual annual income from the miraculous icon of the Virgin in the monastery of Peć was between three and four thousand coins. The decision by Metropolitan Nićifor for the icon to tour the Diocese in 1907 resulted in 250,747 coins. There was enough money to pay monastery debts, as well as to finish some necessary construction work that had already been started within the monastery complex. With that money the fraternity also initiated new constructions in the complex, built a tower in a field near the monastery, and helped repair some buildings in the city that had been damaged due to extreme weather conditions (Archives of Serbia, MID, Consulate in Priština 1909).

Fig. 4: The community awaiting the return of the icon to the monastery, 1907

It is interesting that during the very same year of this great icon visitation by the Diocese, the Trust of the Holy Virgin was founded at the monastery. The founding of trusts under the church authority was a common practice among the Orthodox population in the Ottoman Empire. Church and school communities took care of ecclesiastical properties in the 19th century and established church trusts modeled on the trusts of guilds, which were the primary form of monetary mergers of Serbs within Ottoman society (Чемерикић 1937: 697-698; Ракић 1985: 113; Микић 1988: 314). Those trusts served to lend money with interest, for which there were two active Ottoman banks on the territory of the Diocese of Raška and Prizren, but their credit conditions were not suitable for Serbs (Храбак 1982: 58). Therefore, under the auspices of the church, trusts were founded based on the shareholdership principle, which attracted a large number of investors as well as large capital (ibid.: 68).

After the Balkan wars and the liberation of the territories of Old Serbia from Ottoman rule, church trusts were transformed into banks. For example, the Trust of St Sava Church in Kosovska Mitrovica, founded in 1902, was transformed into the Bank of Kosovo in 1913 (Пантовић 1996: 16). The Trust of St Uroš' Church in the town of Uroševac, which was founded with capital of 3,000 napoleons (324,000 groš) in 1907, was turned into the Bank of Uroševac in 1914 (Храбак 1982: 79; Секулић 1991-1992: 69). In 1907, the Trust of the Holy Virgin was established in the monastery of Peć, as mentioned above. The fund sold shares, and it was later advertised in newspapers as a collection of charitable contributions. Joining this fund, the Bank of Montenegro created the Bank of Peć (Храбак 1982: 65, 74).

The dislocation of sacred objects, relics and icons from the sacred to the profane environment was a common practice associated with solving the economic problems of monasteries. Monks often traveled through the places inhabited by Christians, carrying monastic relics, which at the same time could invoke the sanctity of monasteries and appeal to religious feelings of the faithful. In order to gain financial support for their fraternities, they frequently traveled to Russia to visit great monastic centers, the patriarch or even the tsar. On these occasions, they carried icons, often the most precious ones, or even holy relics, which they gave as a gift of gratitude (Петковић 1997: 123). It is well known that monks from Mount Athos used to travel to Russia carring miracle-working icons aiming to collect money for their monastic communities (cf. ibid.: 122-153). During their stay in Russia, two representatives of the monastic brotherhood from the Dečani monastery carried the cross of Tsar Dušan (Ристић 1864: 62). Monks from Dečani used to carry this cross while collecting charity in the Diocese of Raška and Prizren too.

The dislocation of relics, especially those with healing powers, enabled a greater number of believers to directly encounter them, which also meant more gifts of gratitude addressed to the saint and to the monastery as his habitat. As we have seen in the case of the miraculous icon of the Virgin in the Patriarchate of Peć Monastery, this kind of extensive use of relics was a way for monasteries to gain economic prosperity.

Bibliography

Anonymous (1902) Срби и Српкиње у Призрену. In: *Братство* 9-10: 324-358.
Archives of Serbia (1894) MID-PPO: 440.
Archives of Serbia (1904) MID-PPO: 150.
Archives of Serbia (1906) MID-PPO: 932.
Archives of Serbia (1909) MID, Consulate in Priština.

Archives of Serbian Academy of Science and Arts, E-469-II-132.
Archives of Serbian Academy of Science and Arts, E-469-II-131.
Bacci, M. (2000) With the Paintbrush of the Evangelist Luke. In: Vassilaki, M. (ed.): *Mother of God. Representations of the Virgin in Byzantine Art.* Milan, Athens: 79-89.
Гиљфердинг, А.Ф. (1859, 1996) *Путовање по Херцеговини, Босни и Старој Србији.* Београд.
Ќорнаков, Д. (1986) *Творештвото на мијачките резбари на Балканот од крајот на XVIII и XIX век.* Прилеп.
Куюмджиев, А. (1998) Ритуали и стенопис в главната църква на Рилския манастир. In: *Проблеми на изсукството* 3: 52-57.
Лидов, А. (1996) *Чудотворная икона в Византии и Древней Руси.* Москва.
Lidov, A. (2000) Miracle-Working Icons of the Mother of God. In: Vassilaki, M. (ed.): *Mother of God. Representations of the Virgin in Byzantine Art.* Milano, Athens: 47-57.
Lidov, A. (2004) The Flying Hodegetria. The Miraculous Icon as a Bearer of Sacred Space. In: Thunoe, E./Wolf, G. (eds.): *The Miraculous Image in the Late Middle Ages and Renaissance.* Rome: 291-321.
Лидов, А. (2009) *Иеротопия. Пространственные иконы и образы парадигмы в визнатийской культуре.* Москва.
Микић, Ђ. (1988) *Друштвене и економске прилике косовских Срба у XIX и почетком XX века, од чифчијства до банкарства.* Београд.
Пантовић, Љ. С. (1996) *Храм Светог Саве у Косовској Митровици.* Приштина.
Петковић, С. (1997) О култу светогорских чудотворних икона у Русији. In: *Друга казивања о Светој Гори.* Београд: 122-153.
Петровић, Д.М. (1933) Пећка чудотворна икона Мати Божје. In: *Вардар, независан привредно-културни преглед*: 6.
Петровић, М.Ф. (1995) *Документи о Рашкој области 1900-1912.* Београд.
Поповић, Д. (2006) *Под окриљем светости: култ светих владара и реликвија у средњовековној Србији.* Београд.
Ракић, М. (1985) *Конзулска писма 1905-1911.* Београд.
Ристић, С. (1864) *Дечански споменици.* Београд.
Roudometof, V./Michael, M.N. (2010) Economic Functions of Monasticism in Cyprus: The Case of the Kykkos Monastery. In: *Religions* 1/1: 54-77.
Секулић, М. (1991-1992) Оснивање и развој новчаних завода и банака у Гњилану и Урошевцу до арпилског рата 1914. године. In: *Зборник радова Филозофског факултета.* 21-22: 39-92.
Shevzov, V. (1999) Miracle-Working Icons, Laity, and Authority in the Russian Orthodox Church, 1861-1917. In: *Russian Review* 58/1: 26-48.
Shevzov, V. (2000) Icons, Miracles, and the Ecclesial Identity of Laity in Late Imperial Russian Orthodoxy. In: *Church History* 69/3: 610-631.
Shevzov, V. (2007) Scripting the Gaze: Liturgy, Homilies, and the Kazan Icon of the Mother of God in Late Imperial Russia. In: Steinberg, M. D./Coleman, H.J.

(eds.): *Sacred Stories: Religion and Spirituality in Modern Russia*. Bloomington: 61-92.

Храбак, Б. (1982) Почеци банкарства на Косову. In: *Историјски гласник* 1-2: 54-84.

Weyl Carr, A. (2002) Icons and the Object of Pilgrimage in Middle Byzantine Constantinople. In: *Dumbarton Oaks Papers* 56: 75-92.

Чемерикић, М. (1937) Трговина, занатство, индустрија, кредитне установе од 1875. до 1937. Године. In: *Споменица двадесетпетогодишњице ослобођења Јужне Србије 1912-1937*. Скопље: 685-732.

Шалипуровић, В. (1972) *Културно-просветне и политичке организације у Полимљу и Рашкој 1903-1912*. Нова Варош.

Artists and Merchants
Art "Patronage" in Carniola at the Beginning of the Twentieth Century

Renata Komić Marn

1. Introduction

Art patronage is a specific activity narrowly linked to the question of the patron's wealth, taste and reputation. The patronage of a famous artist and especially of an artist of distinctive national significance should be well researched and studied. However, the case of the Slovene impressionist painter Ivan Grohar (1867-1911) and the wealthy merchant from Upper Carniola Franc Dolenc (1869-1938), who at the time of his death owned nine paintings by Grohar that today are very famous and who can therefore be considered one of the painter's most important patrons, has only rarely piqued the curiosity of art historians. Consequently, scholars have overlooked the fact that the merchant obtained these paintings only after the artist's unfortunate and premature death in 1911. Moreover, Grohar tried in vain to sell the paintings in question during his lifetime, but it was not until after the Second World War that they gained the reputation of masterpieces of Slovenian art. It is true that some excellent painters, such as El Greco, Vermeer, Claude Monet, Paul Gauguin or Vincent van Gogh, had to deal with rejection and criticism during their lives. The reasons for their posthumous recognition lie mainly in the quality of their work, alongside their influence on and significance for the history of painting, partly also in transformations of public taste. However, in contrast to common belief, not all artworks created by a skilled artist who died relatively young or in deprivation – as Ivan Grohar did – increase in value. Recognition sought in vain throughout such an artist's lifetime follows his death only in exceptionally favourable socio-economic or socio-political circumstances. This paper aims firstly to examine the way in which Dolenc came to be the owner of Grohar's paintings and thus his supposed patron. There then follows an analysis of the subsequent fate of these paintings and their present status in order to explore the specific conditions in which their economic and symbolic value increased.

2. Slovene impressionists and their struggle for success

The most prolific period of Ivan Grohar's artistic career coincides with the era in which the foundations of Slovenian impressionism were laid. Together with his fellow painters Rihard Jakopič (1869-1943), Matija Jama (1872-1947) and Matej Sternen (1870-1949), Grohar tried to transcend traditional landscape realism in order to create impressionist paintings full of emotional power and national character.[1] The number of visitors who came to see the great Ljubljana exhibition (more than 100,000)[2] a century later indicates the importance of the four impressionists for Slovenian art history and national identity. However, in the early years of the twentieth century, these modern painters rarely managed to sell their work (Smrekar 1997a: 14, 24).

At that time, the territory of modern day Slovenian was part of the Austro-Hungarian Empire and it comprised the Inner Austrian hereditary lands of Carniola and (parts of) Carinthia and Styria. Carniola was marked not only by modernist tendencies in fine arts and literature – the most renowned Slovenian literary modernist was Ivan Cankar (1876-1918), but also by accelerated economic and technological progress. The years following the great earthquake (1895) represent an age of changes for Ljubljana, the capital of Carniola. In 1896-1910, during the mayoralty of Ivan Hribar (1851-1941), many new bridges, monuments and parks were built and over 1,000 buildings erected or renovated,[3] and reforms were implemented in the municipal administration, healthcare, the education system and the tourist trade. The economic circumstances seemed favourable for presenting national paintings: in 1900, the first Slovenian exhibition was set up in Ljubljana and Grohar and his colleagues showed their work, together with other Slovenian artists. The critics were quite appreciative and the exhibition was very successful, but over 5,000 enthusiastic visitors bought only five of the 192 paintings (Žerovc 2002: 60). At the second exhibition (1902), when the impressionists put forward the "modern manner" more determinedly, their work was severely criticised and they did not sell a single painting (Žerovc 2002: 60). The local public, which had in fact expected to see some grand historical paintings (Zgonik 2008: 105), was not appreciative of the impressionist manner and did not want to accept these modern painters as the representatives of national art.

This was very discouraging for Grohar, whose only income was from painting. Consequently, he decided to seek recognition in Vienna, the imperial capital.[4] Tog-

---

1 On Slovenian national identity represented in fine arts, see for example Zgonik 2002.
2 See *Slovene impressionists* 2012 (April 23, 2008-February 15, 2009). The works of the four Slovenian impressionists were also presented in Paris (April 18-July 13, 2013); see *Les impressionnistes slovènes* 2013.
3 On Ivan Hribar and his time, see Grdina 2010.
4 See Modern Gallery (MG), IIc, Grohar to Jakopič: 31.05.1903, 26.07.1903, 20.08.1903, 12.09.1903.

ether with his colleagues, he exhibited in the famous Miethke Salon (1904).[5] The critics expressed great appreciation and the local Carniola papers slowly began to recognise the value of Slovenian modernist art. Numerous exhibitions followed the Vienna success: by 1908, Grohar had exhibited his work in Vienna (1904, 1905), Belgrade (1904, 1907), Berlin (1905), London (1906), Sofia (1906), Trieste (1907) and Warsaw (1908).[6] All of this brought him moral satisfaction but did not improve his financial situation. After his return to Carniola in 1904, he lived in deprivation, constantly hoping for better times, but in 1911, he became ill and died without proper recognition.[7] Soon afterwards, articles appeared in which the authors pointed out that the painter had died in misery because the competent authorities and local public had not appreciated his work.[8] The outbreak of the First World War temporarily interrupted these efforts. However, the War had a significant impact on shaping the taste of the local public. Although impressionism had already asserted itself with a considerable delay in the Slovenian lands, the public needed additional persuasion and a sufficient temporal distance to learn to value it (see Žerovc 2002: 219). Moreover, the new political circumstances also influenced public taste. In the newly created state – the Kingdom of Serbs, Croats and Slovenes – scholars started to acknowledge the impressionists' paintings as the carriers of the Slovenian national character. On the fifteenth anniversary of his death, they honoured Grohar with the first Slovenian retrospective exhibition (1926),[9] and he was the first Slovenian artist to have been studied in an extensive monograph (Podbevšek 1937). In the following years, numerous exhibitions were dedicated to him or to all four Slovenian impressionists.[10] In the late 1950s, Slovenian impressionism was presented as "one of the cardinal movements in the history of modern Yugoslav art" (Stele 1960: 7, 26). After the importance of Grohar's work had been officially confirmed, his best works, such as *Sower, Larch, Škofja Loka in a Snowstorm, Kamnitnik* and *The Štemarje Garden*, then the property of Franc Dolenc's heirs, changed owners.[11] However, nobody knew how Dolenc had acquired these paintings. They were already in his possession in 1926 at the first retrospective exhibition of Grohar's work.[12] In the

---

5 See *Ausstellung* 1904; Mikuž 1985; Brejc 1997: 29-31.
6 See Smrekar 1997: 18-19; *Ivan Grohar* 1997: 223-224.
7 For the painter's biography, see Stele 1960: 8-18; *Ivan Grohar* 1997: 210-221.
8 See especially the necrologies: Jakopič 1911: 297-298; Kristan 1911: 127-131; Mantuani 1911: 228-229; Zorman 1911: 504-505. See also Vavpotič 1921: 4-6.
9 In June and July 1926, all known works by Grohar were exhibited in Ljubljana. See *Ivan Grohar* 1926.
10 See for example *Slovenski impresionisti* 1949; *Ivan Grohar* 1954; *Začetki slovenskega* 1955; *Slowenische Impressionisten* 1979.
11 In 1958, they belonged to a certain Danica Slanc from Preddvor near Kranj; see *Ivan Grohar* 1958, cat. 184, 197, 198, 222, 223.
12 See *Ivan Grohar* 1926, cat. 106, 141, 144, 149, 150, 151, 152, 162, 166.

literature on Ivan Grohar, scholars regularly mention this timber merchant and industrialist from Stara Loka near Škofja Loka as the painter's patron and benefactor. According to them, Grohar lived at Dolenc's residence in Škofja Loka over a longer period, but no one tried to verify or at least elucidate this commonly accepted information.[13] It is only recently that scholars have shown interest in the relationship between the deprived artist and the wealthy merchant and the circumstances in which the paintings in question came into Dolenc's possession.[14] On the basis of newly discovered archival sources, it is possible to explain in more detail how the paths of the modern painter and the speculative merchant were intertwined.

3. Ivan Grohar in Škofja Loka

In comparison to Ljubljana, Škofja Loka was then just a little medieval town surrounded by rural suburbs. Nevertheless, it was the first town in Carniola with an electric circuit and research shows that it kept up well with the provincial capital in terms of development (Gašperšič/Vozel 1994: 72-74; Podnar 1995).[15] In the Loka region, economic growth was the most obvious at the turn of the century. The crafts, which originated from the medieval trade corporations, gradually developed into small industrial plants (Logar 1955: 87).[16] In accordance with the local tradition combined with the abundance of forests in the area, textile and especially timber industries prospered (Tušek 1976: 123). Franc Dolenc was a well-known timber merchant.[17] He continued his father's trade and created his own enterprise in Škofja Loka in 1905 (Tušek 1976: 124; Štukl 2000: 40). Ivan Grohar, who originated from a small village in the Loka highlands, was already staying in Škofja Loka at that time.[18] In autumn 1904, he went there to find refuge and inspiration and remained there, with short interruptions, until his death (*Ivan Grohar* 1997: 217). From 1926 onwards, Grohar's biographies state that between 1904 and 1910 he resided

---

13   See *Ivan Grohar* 1926; Armič 1931; Stele 1958: 3, 12; Stele 1960: 16, 29; Stele-Možina 1962: 15.
14   See Štukl 1987: 70, 74; Štukl 1996: 125-126; Smrekar 2008: 48-51; Komić Marn 2014. Andrej Smrekar tried to explain Dolenc's ownership as being due to a relatively high sum that Grohar owed Dolenc at the time of his death, but could not support this plausible hypothesis with archival sources; see Smrekar 1997b: 115; Smrekar 2008: 50.
15   For the economic development of Škofja Loka at the turn of the century, see for example Smrekar 2008: 47ss; Štukl 2011: 13; Smrekar 2011: 27; Smrekar 2013: 25.
16   See also Štukl 2000: 31-44.
17   He was one of the four most productive private entrepreneurs in Drava province (roughly today's Slovenia) in 1937; see statistical data on the Drava province timber industry in *Krajevni leksikon* 1937: 631-635.
18   In the summer of 1905, he resided at Homan's, the renowned Škofja Loka inn; see Štukl 1987, 73-74.

permanently at Franc Dolenc's residence in Štemarje Manor near Škofja Loka.[19] Art historians France Štukl and Andrej Smrekar recently pointed out that Dolenc did not buy the Štemarje property until 1908 (Štukl 1987: 73; Smrekar 2008: 48, 50) and their findings call into question Dolenc's patronage. It is true that in a town as small as Škofja Loka was then, Dolenc and Grohar must have known each other well.[20] According to local oral tradition, Grohar changed several domiciles in Škofja Loka, yet it seems that he never stayed at Dolenc's prior to 1908 (see Štukl 1987: 73-74). In fact, the research hitherto shows that in the contemporary documents and periodicals there is no mention of the merchant in connection to Grohar before 1911, not even in Grohar's or Jakopič's correspondence. So when and how did Dolenc become Grohar's patron and benefactor?

4. Dolenc's "patronage"

As artistic life – previously dominated by external sources of legitimacy – progressively freed itself from aristocratic and ecclesiastical protection and its aesthetic and ethical demands (Bourdieu 1993: 112), the question of finding or creating a market for art products became increasingly important. In nineteenth-century France, dealing in contemporary art thus emerged as a distinctive and remunerative economic practice (Green 1987: 60).[21] This did not diminish the importance of individual or collective art patronage. The practice of supporting artists financially, by commissioning their works or by providing the m with lodgings and sustenance, remained very welcome. In late nineteenth-century Carniola, important commissions were given mainly by the Church or Municipality of Ljubljana, whereas individuals often commissioned portrait paintings. Art exhibitions, which had played such a crucial role in the market for new art in European metropolises, were not very remunerative in Carniola. Nevertheless, a new clientele, consisting of wealthy industrialists, entrepreneurs and bourgeois amateurs began to form,[22] and Franc Dolenc belonged to this group. This is why Dolenc's ownership of Grohar's paintings fits well with the story of Grohar's long stay on his property in Štemarje. Inviting the artist to live in one's own home in order for him to produce artworks is

---

19 *Ivan Grohar* 1926; Armič 1931; Stele 1958: 3, 12; Stele 1960: 16, 29; Stele-Možina 1962: 15.
20 For example, Grohar's friend Rihard Jakopič actually lived at Franc Dolenc's residence in Stara Loka from 1904 to 1906, but there is no patronage-related evidence regarding this fact. Jakopič was Dolenc's lodger, living there together with his future wife's family; see Podbevšek 1983: 222; Štukl 1987: 73-74; Štukl 1996: 126.
21 For the art market during the period in question, see for example Brown 1993: 262-264, with further literature.
22 They began to act more visibly as buyers of art after the First World War, see for example Komelj 2005: 166-168; Žerovc 2012: 213, 222.

actually one of the most defined forms of art patronage (see Roeck 1999: 13), creating close interaction between the artist and the patron. Thus, a romantic vision of Grohar finding refuge at some rural property of the wealthy industrialist emerged, based on the early biographies of the artist. However, several facts contradict this vision. First, Dolenc did not buy the modest Štemarje Manor (Stemmerhof), renovated as a hotel, until February 1908 and he let it out on lease in the June of the same year.[23] This confirms Štukl's and Smrekar's statements that Grohar could not have lived at Dolenc's residence in Štemarje prior to February 1908 (see n. 30). Second, recent research shows that Grohar spent the winter of 1909-1910 in Škofja Loka, in a rented room at Kašman's residence, who threw him out together with his paintings in the spring of 1910.[24] Finally, it is only in November 1910 that we can locate Grohar in the Štemarje hotel.[25] However, he was still not benefiting from Dolenc's hospitality, because he was paying rent to the innkeeper, who was Dolenc's tenant.[26] Only three months later, Grohar went to Ljubljana, where he completely wasted away; instead of going to Italy with the scholarship finally granted to him by the Provincial Council, he went to the Ljubljana hospital, where he died of tuberculosis in April 1911 (Jakopič 1911: 648-649; Podbevšek 1937: 309-310).

Grohar's death certificate states that at the time of his death he was residing at Franc Dolenc's residence in Štemarje in Škofja Loka.[27] This means that Grohar stayed in an unheated attic room[28] in Štemarje until the end of February, when he had to go into hospital. Surely, these three months spent at the Štemarje hotel cannot substantiate the claim that Grohar lived at Dolenc's from 1904 to 1910 (see note 29). What about the benefactor element? Even if Dolenc did let Grohar stay there gratuitously for three months, the artist would never have given him nine paintings in exchange. A monthly rent for a room did not amount to more than 25 crowns at the time.[29] It is therefore surprising that only a few weeks after Grohar's death, Franc Dolenc claimed an unsettled debt of nearly 1,118 crowns, which was

---

23 See *Gorenjec*, 9/9, 29.02.1908: 5; *Slovenec*, 36/51, 02.03.1908: 6; *Slovenec*, 36/144, 25.06.1908: 4.
24 The reason seems to have been the unpaid rent; see Komić Marn 2014: 217. Some scholars have vaguely mentioned this forcible removal, but it looks like a mythologised episode in the painter's life because to this day it lacks key information: on the identity of the uncomprehending lessor, see Petrović 1912; Stele 1960: 16; Stele-Možina 1962: 17, 28.
25 In his letter to Jakopič of 18 December 1910, he wrote that he owed rent for two months to the innkeeper who was leaving Štemarje; see MG, IIc, Grohar to Jakopič, 18.12.1910.
26 MG, IIc, Grohar to Jakopič, 18.12.1910. See also Podbevšek 1983: 288, who cited Stenarje instead of Štemarje.
27 Ljubljana Historical Archives (SI-ZAL), ŠKL 173, Škofja Loka Court, 149, A156/11, 3.
28 Catering and hotel services in Štemarje were available only in summer season when tourists, mountaineers and holidaymakers visited Škofja Loka; see Žužek 1968: 100. On the fact that the room was not heated, see Pirnat 1911: 206; Podbevšek 1937: 309.
29 Compare the prices in Žužek 1968: 100.

almost a third of the entire sum Grohar owed to nine creditors altogether.[30] The artist's legacy consisted mainly of paintings (Berčič 1955: 135), but it was difficult to research their fate because the legacy records are incomplete.[31] Since several pages are torn out, the inventory with the legal valuation of the paintings is missing. For this reason, it was suggested that before Grohar's death Dolenc might have acquired some of the paintings he possessed in 1926.[32] However, the newly discovered inventory of Grohar's estate lists all of the paintings which later came into Dolenc's possession.[33] This means that during the seven years of the artist's stay in Škofja Loka, Franc Dolenc never bought a single painting of his.[34] He also could not have obtained them as a debt settlement since the legal value of the paintings in question (2,475 crowns) exceeded more than twice the amount of his claim. Thus, we can assume that the shrewd merchant "smelled" a good investment and bought an exquisite collection of the dead artist's paintings for a relatively low price. This was a very wise investment, for the value of these paintings grew slowly but steadily in the decades following Grohar's death.

The answer to the question as to how Grohar accumulated such a debt to Dolenc[35] was hidden until now in Grohar's tiny notebook, which contains a list of Grohar's creditors.[36] Grohar noted for Franc Dolenc (Fr. Dol.) the sum of 500. Thus, in the summer of 1909, Grohar owed Dolenc 500 crowns. By 1911, he must have asked Dolenc for a few more loans to reach the amount of almost 1,118 crowns. When Grohar complained in 1910 that his paintings would have to qualify as "sport"[37] for private individuals to buy them, he must have been thinking of Dolenc, who was then donating large sums to the Škofja Loka gymnastics society (Sokol).[38] At any rate, it is surprising that Dolenc lent money to the painter. He must have been anxious about getting it back. Perhaps that is why a friend of his wrote an article in 1911 about Grohar's room in Štemarje and described some of the paintings, the

---

30 For the list of creditors, see Podbevšek 1937: 323.
31 Already noted by Štukl 1987: 75, n. 24. See also Smrekar 2008: 50, n. 18.
32 Suggested by Smrekar 2008: 50. In 1926, Dolenc had nine of Grohar's paintings altogether; see *Ivan Grohar* 1926, cat. 106, 141, 144, 149-152, 162, 166.
33 National and University Library (NUK), Ms 1761, personal maps, 27.
34 About twenty paintings by Grohar were listed in his room in Štemarje and in the exhibition pavilion in Ljubljana in May 1911. All the paintings that Dolenc had in 1926 were there or available for sale in June 1911; see NUK, Ms 1761, personal maps, 27; *Vl. umetniška razstava* 1911: 6.
35 The amount sufficed for at least forty months of rent; see Žužek 1968: 100.
36 NUK, Ms 1078, Č, various material.
37 See a letter to an unknown addressee cited in Berčič 1955: 148.
38 Dolenc was one of the most prominent members and the most generous patron of the Škofja Loka liberal Sokol society, which was founded in 1906 in his own house in Stara Loka; see *Spominski spis* 1931: 15.

painter's only legacy.[39] Besides this, the article referred to Dolenc's connection to Grohar and his paintings at an early stage.

In the 1920s, Dolenc started to invest in things other than industry or "sport". Together with his partner, he bought, renovated and furnished Brdo Manor and then sold it to the then Yugoslav regent Pavle Karađorđević (Slana 2004: 139-140).[40] In 1930, he bought Stara Loka Manor together with a small collection of old paintings.[41] After 1924, he lived in Hrib Manor in Preddvor near Kranj. His extensive legacy records from 1938 reveal him to have been an important landowner and his legacy was estimated at 4,322,209 dinars.[42] His daughter inherited the Hrib Manor[43] and this is how Danica Slanc, née Dolenc, came into possession of many precious paintings, which she gradually sold to various institutions after 1945 (see Komić Marn 2014: 223-224).

5. The long road to recognition

A palpable irony accompanies the story of these paintings' fate: Grohar painted them between 1904 and 1911, his most prolific period, but nobody wanted to buy them during his lifetime. Even *Sower*, already regarded by his contemporaries as "the most popular painting of our people",[44] was lying around in Grohar's atelier for some years. Moreover, when Grohar died and the paintings were put on sale in order to settle the claims of the creditors, the competent local institutions failed to realise the great potential of Grohar's work. The paintings could have been bought for the municipal gallery or the land museum's collections. Instead, a wealthy timber merchant acquired them in order to decorate his salon.[45] It took (now) national institutions almost half a century to obtain these paintings, and even then they were not all earmarked for the public galleries. In 1960, *The Štemarje Garden* was in Belgrade, in the private collection of Edvard Kardelj, one of the most influential Slovenian politicians in post-war Yugoslavia (see Smrekar 1997b: 101).[46] The National Gallery in Ljubljana bought *Kamnitnik* (Smrekar 1997b: 81, 87). The so-called Fund of the Socialist Republic of Slovenia acquired *Sower* in 1963, together with *Škofja Loka in a Snowstorm* (Smrekar 1997b: 89, 115), and the Central Committee of the Communist

---

39 The author of the article visited Grohar's room on 26 April, five days after Grohar's death; see Pirnat 1911: 206.
40 The manor was the state protocol centre in the Kingdom of Yugoslavia (1935-), Socialist Yugoslavia (1945-) and still is in Slovenia (1991-).
41 He sold the manor a few years later, but kept most of the paintings; see Komič 2009: 193-197.
42 SI-ZAL, ŠKL 173, Škofja Loka Court, 190, O240/38.
43 SI-ZAL, ŠKL 173, Škofja Loka Court, 190, O240/38: 4-5.
44 Cited by Zgonik 2008: 106.
45 For display of the paintings, see Gaber 1929: 3.
46 The inheritors donated the painting to the National Gallery in Ljubljana in 1990.

Union of Slovenia obtained *Larch* the same year (Smrekar 1997b: 77). The paintings – today exhibited in the permanent collection of the National Gallery in Ljubljana – are exceptional achievements of Slovenian painting that have preserved their artistic authority and wide social persuasiveness for over a hundred years (Smrekar 2011: 27). Grohar's *Sower* became Slovenian national myth (*Ivan Grohar* 1997: 7), whereas Grohar, the "poet of the Slovenian landscape", represents one of the principal and most characteristic pillars of Slovenian impressionism (Stele 1960: 7, 26). On the other hand, the artist's death in misery, which became a crucial element of his biography, came to serve the needs of others. Already Grohar's colleagues emphasized his poverty and his significance for Slovenian art in order to draw attention to the art market problem they were confronted with.[47] Later, Grohar's biographers successfully used the story of his sinister fate to create public sympathy. Even the title of the first study of his life and work is meaningful: *Ivan Grohar. A Tragedy of a Slovenian Artist* (Podbevšek 1937). His biographies became compilations of so many unfortunate episodes that the true significance of his hardship somehow diminished.[48] Moreover, when Slovenian art historians pointed out that Grohar's contemporaries had neglected his importance,[49] was it only to distance themselves from those "past errors"?

Franc Dolenc, who opportunistically obtained nine of Grohar's paintings, is yet another exploiter of the artist's misery. His ownership of the paintings, his financial loan to Grohar and numerous mentions of the artist's sojourn "at Dolenc's in Štemarje", enabled him to later pass for Grohar's benefactor and patron. The image was fostered not only by the local tradition but by Slovenian art historians too.[50] Grohar actually sojourned at Dolenc's residence in Štemarje only in the months before he went into hospital. The merchant's support for the artist must have been restricted to financial loans, which were later settled in the legal process. Therefore, the story of his patronage is actually the mythologized part of Grohar's biography, whereas the painter's financial difficulties and housing problems, which often have an anecdotal ring to them, represent the hard truth.

6. Conclusion

The quality and significance of Ivan Grohar's work for Slovenian painting is undisputable today. The fact that his paintings gained national symbolic value only long after his death is linked to specific circumstances. As the public taste in Slovenia

---

47 See for example Jakopič 1911: 651-652; Smrekar 2011: 27.
48 See for example Stele 1960, Stele-Možina 1962.
49 See for example Stele 1960: 8-9.
50 See Armič 1931: 50; Gaber 1929: 3; Stele 1960: 16; Stele-Možina 1962: 15; Štukl 1987: 74.

conformed to the notion of impressionism in the decades after the end of the First World War, the economic and symbolic values of Grohar's paintings started to rise. Yet it was not until after the Second World War that Slovenian art historians firmly recognised Grohar's significance for the evolution of Slovene national art. When creating the image of its national identity, the new Yugoslavia needed to establish the history of national painting and determine its landmarks. Grohar and his paintings with their symbolic value served well. Moreover, the painter's miserable life story corresponded entirely to the then prevalent strategy of creating national myths and heroes to educate the masses and intensify national awareness. Thus, Ivan Grohar's posthumous success proves to be due to the needs of others: not only the needs of his fellow painters and (so-called) patrons but also the needs of art historians and the relevant authorities.

Bibliography

Armič, Josip (1931) *Ivan Grohar, Zbornik za umetnostno zgodovino*, 9: 44-50.
Ausstellung der Künstlervereinigung "Sava" (Slowenische Künstler). Galerie Miethke, Wien, Dorotheergasse 11., März-April 1904. (1904) Vienna.
Berčič, Branko (1955) Drobtine iz Groharjeve zapuščine. In: *Loški razgledi*, 2: 134-156.
Bourdieu, Pierre (1993) *The field of cultural production. Essays on art and literature* (ed. Randal Johnson). New York.
Brejc, Tomaž (1997) Mitologija krajine. Esej o impresiji in »štimungi«. In: *Ivan Grohar (1867-1911). Bodočnost mora biti lepša*. Ljubljana: 29-38.
Brown, Marilyn R. (1993) An entrepreneur in spite of himself: Edgar Degas and the market. In: Haskell, Thomas L./Teichgraeber III., Richard F. (eds.): *The culture of the market. Historical essays*. Cambridge, New York, Melbourne.
Gaber, Ante (1929) Francek Dolenc šestdesetletnik In: *Jutro*, 10/178, 02.08.1929: 3.
Gašperšič, Janez/Vozel, Mile (1994) Škofja Loka – mesto s prvo javno razsvetljavo v Sloveniji. In: *Loški razgledi*, 41: 72-74.
Gorenjec, 9/9, 29.02.1908.
Grdina, Igor (2010) *Hribarjev zbornik*. Ljubljana.
Green, Nicholas (1987) Dealing in temperaments. Economic transformation of the artistic field in France during the second half of the nineteenth century. In: *Art History*, 10/1, March 1987: 59-78.
Grohar, Ivan (1926) *Spominska kolektivna razstava, Narodna galerija*. Ljubljana.
Grohar, Ivan (1954) *Študijska razstava, Mestni muzej*. Ljubljana.
Grohar, Ivan (1958) *1867-1911. Retrospektivna razstava, Moderna galerija*. Ljubljana.
Grohar, Ivan (1997) *1867-1911. Bodočnost mora biti lepša, Narodna galerija*. Ljubljana.
Jakopič, Rihard (1911) Ivan Grohar. I, Pogreb; II, Spomini. In: *Ljubljanski zvon*, 31/5: 297-298; 648-655.

Komelj, Milček (2005) *Kronika Marjana Pogačnika o zaljubljencih v umetnost*. Ljubljana.

Komič, Renata (2009) Po sledeh Strahlove zbirke. In: *Zbornik za umetnostno zgodovino*, 42: 185-216.

Komić Marn, Renata (2014) Ivan Grohar in njegov "mecen" Franc Dolenc v luči arhivskih virov. In: *Acta historiae artis Slovenica*, 19/2: 209-226.

Krajevni leksikon dravske banovine. Krajevni repertorij z uradnimi, topografskimi, zemljepisnimi, zgodovinskimi, kulturnimi, gospodarskimi in tujskoprometnimi podatki vseh krajev dravske banovine. (1937) Ljubljana.

Kristan, Etbin (1911) Ivan Grohar. In: *Naši zapiski*, 8/4-5: 127-131.

Les impressionnistes slovènes 2013 : Les impressionnistes slovènes et leur temps (1890-1920). Petit Palais, Musée des Beaux-Arts de la Ville de Paris [18 avril-13 juillet 2013], Éditions Paris-Musées, Paris 2013.

Logar, Vladimir (1955) Kratek prerez loškega gospodarstva. In : *Loški razgledi*, 2 : 87-92.

Mantuani, Josip (1911) Akad. slikar Ivan Grohar. In : *Carniola*, 2/3 : 228-229.

Mikuž, Jure (1985) Les impressionnistes slovènes à Vienne. Une exposition politique. In : *Revue d'esthétique*, 9 : 169-174.

Petrović, Nadežda (1912) Četvrta jugoslovenska izložba u Beogradu. In: *Bosanska vila*: 199-200; 249-251.

Pirnat, Makso (1911) V Groharjevi sobi. In: *Slovan. Mesečnik za književnost, umetnost in prosveto*, 9/7 : 206-208.

Podbevšek, Anton (1937) *Ivan Grohar. Tragedija slovenskega umetnika*. Ljubljana.

Podbevšek, Anton (1983) *Rihard Jakopič*. Ljubljana.

Podnar, Franc (ed., 1995) *Sto let električne razsvetljave v Škofji Loki*. Škofja Loka.

Preininger, Kristina/Smrekar, Andrej (eds., 2012) *Slovene Impressionists and Their Time 1890-1920. A guide to the exhibition, 23 April 2008-8 February 2009*. Ljubljana.

Roeck, Bernd (1999) *Kunstpatronage in der Frühen Neuzeit*. Göttingen.

Slana, Lidija (2004) Utrinki iz zgodovine Brda. In: *Kronika*, 52/2: 131-142.

Slovenec, 36/144, 25.06.1908.

Slovenec, 36/51, 02.03.1908.

Slovenec, 66/222a, 27.09.1938.

Smrekar, Andrej (1997a) Ivan Grohar. Daljave in bližine. In: *Ivan Grohar (1867-1911). Bodočnost mora biti lepša*. Ljubljana: 11-27.

Smrekar, Andrej (1997b) Katalog razstavljenih slik v Narodni galeriji Ljubljana. In: *Ivan Grohar (1867-1911). Bodočnost mora biti lepša*. Ljubljana: 39-137.

Smrekar, Andrej (2008) Kamnitnik – ikona slovenskega Barbizona. In: *Loška krajina v podobah zapisana*. Škofja Loka: 44-52.

Smrekar, Andrej (2011) Grohar in slovenska kultura. In: *Železne niti*, 8: 13-30.

Smrekar, Andrej (2013) La première peinture moderne en Slovénie (1880-1920). Modernisme, impressionnisme, identité. In : *Les impressionnistes slovènes et leur temps (1890-1920)*. Paris : 17-67.

Spominski spis Sokolskega društva v Škofji Loki ob 25 letnici. 1906-1931 (1931) Ljubljana
Stele, France (1958) Ivan Grohar. In: *Ivan Grohar (1867-1911). Retrospektivna razstava.* Ljubljana: 1-13.
Stele, France (1960) *Ivan Grohar*, Ljubljana 1960.
Stele-Možina, Melita (1962) *Ivan Grohar*. Ljubljana.
Štukl, France (1987) Slikarja Rihard Jakopič in Ivan Grohar v Škofji Loki. In: *Loški razgledi*, 34: 69-76.
Štukl, France (1996) *Knjiga hiš v Škofji Loki III. Stara Loka in njene hiše.* Ljubljana, Škofja Loka.
Štukl, France (2000) Prispevki k privatni proizvodnji v Škofji Loki od cehov do leta 1941. In: *Loški razgledi*, 47: 31-44.
Štukl, France (2011) Grohar in loški utrip na prelomu v 20. Stoletje. In: *Moč pogledov*. Škofja Loka: 13-17.
Tušek, Janez (1976) Poskus orisa razvoja lesne industrije na Trati pri Škofji Loki. In: *Loški razgledi*, 23: 123-127.
Vavpotič, Ivan (1921) Ivan Grohar. In: *Vesna*, 2: 4-6.
VI. umetniška razstava 1911: VI. umetniška razstava v paviljonu R. Jakopiča. Spomladanska razstava, Jakopičev paviljon. (1911) Ljubljana.
Žerovc, Beti (2002) *Rihard Jakopič – umetnik in strateg*. Ljubljana.
Žerovc, Beti (2012) *Slovenski impresionisti*. Ljubljana.
Zgonik, Nadja (2002) *Podobe Slovenstva*. Ljubljana.
Zgonik, Nadja (2008) Podobe mladega naroda. In: Jaki, Barbara/Breščak, Mateja/Smrekar, Andrej (eds.) *Slovenski impresionisti in njihov čas 1890-1920*. Ljubljana: 102-110.
Zorman, Ivan (1911) Ivan Grohar. In: *Veda*, 1/5: 504-505.
Žužek, Vladimir (1968) Razvojna pot turistične dejavnosti v Škofji Loki. In: *Loški razgledi*, 15: 95-122.

Architecture and Its Value(s)
The National and University Library in Ljubljana

Tina Potočnik

Architecture and culture are interconnected on several levels. Or at least they should be if we consider the definition provided by Alberto Perez-Gomez, a Mexican-born architectural historian and theorist, who perceives *architecture* as a reflection of a certain *culture*: "When we speak about architecture, we refer to significant buildings that frame diverse cultural situations" (Perez-Gomez 2008: 158). Vice versa, some architecture, especially that of national importance, such as a national library, has (or should have) a special, formative role in a culture or in the process of cultural recognition, as the National and University Library in Ljubljana does for Slovenians. This is surely not only because of the institution itself, i.e. the function of the building,[1] but also due to the structure that houses it. The same applies to many edifices with this function, in cities all over the world, but also in the Slovene capital, as the Ljubljana national library building was designed (1930-1931) and built (1936-1941) by Jože Plečnik,[2] the most renowned Slovenian architect, who put Slovenia on the architectural world map.

Today some of Plečnik's works are perceived not only as an essential part of Slovene culture but also as national symbols. The silhouette of the national parliament building he planned (named "The Cathedral of Freedom"), but which was never realised, is depicted on the national side of the Slovene 10 cent euro coin. Despite the resistance of the authorities in Belgrade to the demand for a new Slovenian university library, which was followed by persistent student protests and demonstrations

---

1 The library was established by a decree issued in 1774 by Maria Theresa and made more than 600 books available for public use in the nearby establishment. After World War I, when it was renamed the State Library, it received the deposit of publications from all the regions of former Yugoslavia. With the foundation of the first Slovenian university in Ljubljana in 1919, the library also served as the central university library. URL: http://www.nuk.uni-lj.si/nukeng1.asp?id=123006838 (retrieved October 14, 2013).
2 Jože Plečnik (1972-1957), who studied under Otto Wagner and worked in his architecture office in Vienna, was a founding member of the Ljubljana School of Architecture and the most important Slovene architect of the first half of the 20th century. His most notable works are located in Ljubljana, Prague and Vienna.

in its favour (cf. Prelovšek 2010), Plečnik's building has housed the library since 1941. After liberation in 1945, it was renamed the National and University Library and has held similar cultural and symbolic value. It is therefore understandable that the competition for the *new* (additional) National and University Library building, known as NUK II, which came to a close in March 2012, has been denoted as one of the most important architectural competitions in the history of our independent state. This is also supported by the fact that almost two hundred architectural offices and individuals participated in it (National and University Library NUK II 2012: 9).

However, the competition for the additional library building, concurrent with the increasing global economic and financial crisis and the end of what American architecture critic Robert Campbell has called "the era of severe architectural recession on the one hand, and grotesque architectural luxury on the other", i.e. the "Bilbao decade"[3] (Campbell 2009), was already the second in succession. It followed an earlier competition that coincided with the fall of the Berlin Wall in 1989, with the beginning of the transition process towards global capitalism in Eastern and Central Europe and, again, with severe economic and other crises.

There are many studies that focus on the life and work of Jožef Plečnik and also consider his library building (cf. Charney 2011; Prelovšek 2008; Hrausky/Koželj/Prelovšek 2007; Prelovšek 2005; Krečič 1997). The other two (still unrealized) projects have been discussed mostly in daily newspapers. The winning project of 2012 presented in the catalogue was more detailed and accompanied the exhibition of the competition entries prepared by the Ministry of Education, Science, Culture and Sport and the Chamber of Architecture and Spatial Planning of Slovenia in July 2012 (Narodna in univerzitetna knjižnica NUK II 2012). Thus this paper focuses above all on the competition entries for the *new* National and University Library building. More precisely, the emphasis is placed on the relationship between the formal aspect of architecture and specifics of the location and culture, the relationship between the local and the global that is reflected in those two designs. The cultural and symbolic values of architecture are – with the case study of NUK II in comparison to Plečnik's library building – confronted with *market value*, gained through a universally likable, *contemporary* form.

Following the general crisis in society, which had culminated in the late eighties with the collapse of the former federal state, the transformation process from the once centrally planned economy to a free market economy and from the socialist

---

3 The term "Bilbao decade" is linked to the "Bilbao effect", which refers to an iconic building becoming the catalyst for reviving a distressed area, as occurred with the Guggenheim Museum in the Spanish city of Bilbao. The museum, which became iconic and helped the city achieve a successful economic and cultural revival, was designed by the "star architect" Frank Geary.

regime to a democratic one took place simultaneously to the development of information technology. This led to a situation in which architecture was confronted with the process of globalization, and subsequently also with the changes in the internal spatial and physical structure of cities. This is most evident in the Central Eastern European capitals, including Ljubljana (Hamilton/Dimitrovska Andrews 2005: 160). Miha Dešman, the editor of the AB magazine, explained it in his own words: "The period of Slovene [...] transition was a turbulent one that challenged many paradigms previously held sacred, and architecture was no exception. The restrained modesty, the social righteousness, the rationality of function and expression, the honesty of construction, etc. all had to give way to new requirements: the prevalence of the private over the public, the architecture of the spectacle, the architecture of media dynamism, lifestyle and trend architecture, the emergence of architectural celebrities, etc." (Dešman/Lobnik 2006: 1).

The beginning of that period brought about the first architectural competition for NUK II, carried out to obtain the most suitable architectural solution for the new library building. In 1989, when national libraries had already been built in most of the Yugoslav capitals, the project by architect Marko Mušič was selected. However, due to financial complications, issues relating to the acquisition of building plots, and finally because of unsuitable plans which became out-of-date two decades later, the selected winning project was never realized. Instead, another invitation to an international architectural competition for the solution most suitable for a modern, technologically up-to-date library was issued in 2011.

The winning design, which in the opinion of the evaluation committee was economically most favourable due to its structure, was the work of the architecture office Bevk-Perović arhitekti. The latter represents a new generation of architects who emerged in establishing and adapting to the new market relations, as the transitional period brought on the collapse of big architectural firms, consequently changing the investor structure. The state continues to remain an important investor, yet private capital has substantially gained ground on the market. While the design by Mušič from the late eighties was chosen among the other 26, the winning design from 2012 beat over seven times more competitors. Yet the greater number of competition entries in public architectural competitions, and numerous unrealized and incomplete projects (such as the multipurpose Emonika complex in Ljubljana)[4] are only some of the "local" consequences of the global crisis. In the case of the NUK II project, the construction of which is estimated to be worth 38 million euros and which depends on the financial perspective of the European Union in the

---

4 The construction of a multipurpose complex combining a business tower, a shopping and an entertainment centre, a hotel and a congress centre, including a residential complex, was planned to begin in spring 2012, yet it still has not begun. URL: http://www.emonika.si/en/citycenter/concept (retrieved January 12, 2014).

period 2014-2020 (Brkić 2012), the crisis is also reflected in the relatively low value of the first prize. The amount of the first prize was 36,000 euros; there were 13 authors working on the winning project in 2012 (Narodna in univerzitetna knjižnica NUK II 2012: 15).

The situation in architecture, influenced by the socio-economic transformation of the former socialist country into a pluralistic democracy and market economy on the one hand, and changes towards globalization along with the increasing significance of information technology on the other, is reflected in both winning designs for the new library building. The *visual* that gained its primacy in postmodern art, culture and architecture saturates contemporary architectural *creativity*. "Less is a bore" was already evident in the form of the NUK II from the 80s. Mušič foresaw a typical postmodern architectural complex in the manner of the 1970s and 1980s, based on the critique of modernism and the re-interpretation of the traditional architectural motifs. Several different volumes are irrationally arranged and characterized by a vivid modern paraphrasing of the classical architectural elements such as arches, galleries, and pilasters. Furthermore, the planned building is typified by a parody of these elements (for example with the mushroom-shaped windows) and also by strange concepts, among them the demolished corner and the rotunda with a corner cut out. Yet all this is associated with the then topical postmodern style, to which we cannot attribute the fact that, firstly, the height of the building is not adjusted to the historically built environment and, secondly, the architectural complex does not take archaeology into consideration. Most obviously, the axis of this architectural complex does not concur with the Cardo of the ancient town of Emona beneath it.

If postmodernism in architecture started at three in the afternoon, on July 15, 1972, as American architectural theorist Charles Jencks precisely determined,[5] is then this library building the last sigh of Slovenian postmodern architecture? In his book *The Language of the Post-Modern Architecture* Jencks (1977: 101) states that the architect's role is: "to express the meanings a culture finds significant [...]", and adds, "No other profession is so specifically responsible for articulating meaning and seeing that the environment is sensual, humorous, surprising and coded as a readable text. This is the architect's job and pleasure and not, let us hope, never again his problem." Continuing with this focus, does the final decline of the postmodern mentality of the global structure manifest itself only in the NUK II design from last year? The plastic treatment of the façade of the huge volume, the perimeter structure, comprising pre-cast hollow and reinforced concrete columns of two different diameters alternating with one another characterize the building, which

---

5 Jencks was precise in determining the time of the "death of modernism", linking the latter to the demolition of the Pruit-Igoe scheme (several blocks) in Saint Louis by the Japanese and American architect Minoru Yamasaki, a symbol of unsuccessful urban renewal projects of modernism.

actually reveals a global, universal computer-generated architectural language. A syncopated plastic effect across the surface of the entire building is interrupted by two full-height picture windows on the main axes that correspond in width to the respective dimensions of the Cardo and Decumanus and represent an echo of the windows in the old NUK building nearby.

Mušič stated that his NUK II design represented an "intersection of time and culture" (Bilten UKL 2001: 6) and the evaluation committee also appreciated the contextual approach through his architectural interpretation and the integration of elements from the historical surroundings. Yet would this building be able to communicate cultural values or be the prop for cultural identity and for cultural recognition? It seems there is no point in searching for the answer in the framework of this case, as the same question arises in the case of the topical design for the new library building. As was pointed out some years ago in the architectural journal AB, analyses of the plural layering of recent Slovene architecture show a duality of standpoints: "Some remain in keeping with the Slovene school and its continuity (particularly the older and middle generations) and see architecture as culture embedded in a space and context, which could be national, geographical, historical – the Mediterranean, the Alps, wood and stone, etc., as it were. Frampton's term *critical regionalism* may also apply. Other, particularly younger architects, think differently, *glocally*, to use a neologism, turning and returning to the local from their global position. They are interested in the media, the architecture of sensual experience rather than cultural distinction, commercial efficacy rather than ethical validity" (Dešman/Lobnik 2006: 1). Of course, there are numerous positions between these two basic directions, but it still seems that the latest NUK II design supports rather the latter, especially when analyzing the relation of the planned building to the location: to the archaeological site, the historic town core, and the works of Plečnik, in short, the built fabric and built heritage, as an essential part of every nation's culture and identity. Is the planned library building going to be, as American social theorist David Harvey would say, "only the mask, covering the decay of everything" (Harvey, cited after Featherstone 1991: 201).

Another interesting question arising from this situation is whether the financial and economic crisis that has deeply affected the construction sector and consequently that of architecture as well could be perceived as an opportunity for the rebirth of the art form. In order to develop this point, an argument on the necessity of this rebirth is required. While Slovene philosopher Rado Riha (2010: 84) describes "the time of global disorientation, when capitalism seems to be our destiny", the built environment follows almost exclusively the logic of the market, as it is integrated into the economy on several levels – with the primary message that it has to be profitable (Bentley 1997: 101-102). Perez-Gomez stresses: "In this predominantly scientistic world, what gets built reflects little else but the enshrined, supposedly objective (and at best hedonistic) values of economy and efficiency that instantiate monetary or political power" (Pérez-Gómez 1991: 3). By contrast, Finnish architect and theorist Juhani Pallasmaa (cf. Pallasmaa 2007 and 2009), who emphasizes the primacy of the visual over other senses (and all consequential losses for architecture due to this primacy), mentions in this context that "the image of built environment has become the object of free production and daily consumption as any other goods" (Harvey 1992: 293). Several respectable architectural theorists and architects, for example British architect and critic Kenneth Frampton, who was also on the evaluation committee for the NUK II, but also British architectural historian William Curtis, Australian architect Glenn Murcutt, Pallasmaa and others, do find that the current crisis is an opportunity to become disillusioned and to take greater responsibility in the sphere of architecture and built environment. Also, Peter Gabrijelčič, the dean of the Faculty of Architecture in Ljubljana and a member of the evaluation committee for the NUK II, stressed that "The task of architecture is much more than providing spectacular images and daring icons in the town silhouettes, as it has to serve the entire society, not merely the financial elite [...]. It carries a responsibility to settlements, tradition, urban culture and the natural environment" (Interview: Kriza spodbuja večjo ustvarjalnost, 2013).

Architecture really does hold a mirror up to society, thus putting us in a situation that forces us to ponder upon the future, which I personally see not in the global unification of the formal aspect of architecture, but rather in the architecture that mirrors cultural diversity and leads to the reestablishment of an individual cultural stance in architecture. Frampton (1983) proposes critical regionalism and not the universal civilization as a solution to preserve culture(s). Plečnik's library might be seen as an example of how to design a contemporary building without losing the link to culture and its characteristics. If architecture has the ability to communicate the values of a certain culture and the time it belongs to, which value(s) should it communicate? In contrast to the old NUK, there is a righteous doubt as to whether the planned new library building will be able to set the prop for cultural belonging. Then again, does the crisis enable the rebirth of architecture and is the *crisis* a moment of decision as the Greek origin of this word denotes?

Bibliography

Bentley, I. (1997) Profit and Place. In: *Urbani izziv* 30-31: 101-107.
Brkić, V. (2012) Ministrstvo ni še niti izplačalo nagrad za podobo NUK II. In: *Dnevnik*, August 29, 2012. URL: https://www.dnevnik.si/1042548958/slovenija/1042548958 (retrieved July 23, 2019).
Campbell, R. (2009) Marking the end of "The Bilbao Decade". In: *The Boston Globe*, January 11, 2009. URL: http://www.boston.com/ae/theater_arts/articles/2009/01/11/marking_the_end_of_the_bilbao_decade (retrieved July 23, 2019).

Charney, N. (2011) *The Descent and Rise of Jože Plečnik: Plečnik's Self-Sacrificing Career Decisions for his Nation & the Critical Reception of Them*. Ljubljana. (Padec in vzpon Jožeta Plečnika: Plečnikovo poklicno odpovedovanje za voljo svojega naroda in kritični sprejem njegovih poklicnih odločitev.)

Dešman, M./Lobnik, U. (2006) Uvodnik', AB: 169-171, 2006, 1.

Emonika City Center. The Concept. URL: http://www.emonika.si/en/citycenter/concept (retrieved January 12, 2014).

Featherstone, M. (1991) *Consumer Culture and Postmodernism*. London.

Frampton, K. (1983) Towards a Critical Regionalism: Six Points for an Architecture of Resistance. In: Foster, H. (ed.): *The Anti-Aesthetic: Essays on Postmodern Culture*. Seattle.

Hamilton, I./Dimitrovska Andrews, K./Pichler-Milanović, N. (eds., 2005) *Transformation of Cities in Central and Eastern Europe: Towards Globalization*. Tokyo.

Harvey, D. (1992) *The Condition of Postmodernity*. Cambridge.

Hrausky, A./Koželj J./Prelovšek Damijan, D. (2007) *Jože Plečnik: Vienna, Prague, Ljubljana*. Ljubljana.

Intervju: Kriza spodbuja večjo ustvarjalnost v slovenski arhitekturi. In: *Finance*, 48, March 11, 2013. URL: https://gradbenistvo.finance.si/8335584/Intervju-Kriza-spodbuja-vecjo-ustvarjalnost-v-slovenski-arhitekturi?cctest& (retrieved July 23, 2019).

Jencks, C. (1977) *The Language of Postmodern Architecture*. London.

Krečič, P. (1997) *Jože Plečnik: branje oblik*. Ljubljana.

Narodna in univerzitetna knjižnica NUK II (2012) *Javni arhitekturni natečaj. Natečajni katalog*. Ljubljana. (National and University Library NUK II: public architectural design competition. Competition catalogue.)

National and university library NUK II (2012) *An open, anonymous, public, one-step architectural project competition to select the most suitable professional solution for the building with corresponding external arrangement. Final report*. Ljubljana. URL: http://www.zaps.si/system/download.php?dir=115&file=final+report+koncno_ang2 (retrieved May 20, 2013).

National and University Library. History. URL: http://www.nuk.uni-lj.si/nukeng1.asp?id=123006838 (retrieved October 14, 2013).

Pallasmaa, J. (2007) *The Eyes of the Skin: Architecture and the Senses*. Chichester.

Pallasmaa, J. (2009) *The Thinking Hand: Existential and Embodied Wisdom in Architecture*. Chichester.

Pérez-Gómez, A. (1991) The Modern City: Context, Site, or Place for Architecture. In: Quantrill, M. W./Webb, B. C. (eds.): *Constancy and Change in Architecture*. Texas.

Pérez-Gómez, A. (2008) *Built upon Love: Architectural Longing after Ethics and Aesthetics*. Cambridge.

Prelovšek, D. (1997) *Jože Plečnik: 1872-1957: architectura perennis*. New Haven, London.

Prelovšek, D. (2001) *Architekt Josip Plečnik: práce pro presidenta Masaryka*. Prague.

Prelovšek, D. (2005) *Jože Plečnik: 1872-1957*. Milan.
Prelovšek, D. (2008) *The architect Jože Plečnik: guide to monuments*. Ljubljana.
Prelovšek, D. (2010) *NUK. Narodna in univerzitetna knjižnica*. Ljubljana.
Riha, R. (2010) Arhitektura in nove ontologije. In: Bickert, J./Čeferin, P./Požar, C. (eds.): *Projekt arhitektura: Kreativna praksa v času globalnega kapitalizma*. Ljubljana.
UKL Bilten (2001) *Univerzitetna knjižnica v Ljubljani*. Ljubljana.

Fortunes and Misfortunes of Usury
Andrić's *Woman of Sarajevo* against Balzac's *Eugenia Grandet*

Ivana Perica

1. Financial capitalism as the birthplace of usury

Around 1800, mercantilist and cameralistic economics of the 17th and 18th century were superseded and the ruling apparatus of the absolutist state was supplemented by a completely new realm – society. This new form of societal organization was structured by the dichotomy of 'private' and 'public', understood both in terms of the 'private man' vs. the 'public citizen' and the (self-regulating) 'market' vs. the (restricted) 'state'. Concomitantly, with the supersession of Thomas Hobbes' *statism* by Adam Smith's model of *market liberties*, a new social subject came into being: *homo oeconomicus* (Pulcini 2001: 10; Rost 2008; Vogl 2004: 12). This new subject, accompanied by the philosophical idea of the *individual*, consists in two main passions, the one *social* ("passion for acquisition"/"la *passione acquisitiva*", Pulcini 2001: 12), the other *private* ("passion for the self"/"la *passione dell'Io*", 12).[1] From the very onset of modern political economy, the idea of the *individual* is fissured between these two passions. Hence, the 18th-century politico-theoretical division between the *private man* and the *public citizen* becomes practically unsuitable to socialized life: the public citizen (*citoyen*) cannot be separated from the private man (*bourgeois*), nor can the newly established society function without continuously transgressing and subverting the dividing line between private life and the public sphere. The unavoidable intersection of private interests with the interests of the social environment makes the Hegelian (and Habermasian) ideal of the separation of private life and the public sphere practically impossible. It lays bare the interlocking of market economy and the economy of social exchange, of the *market* and *society*.[2] In the given

---

1 All italics are by the authors if not specified otherwise.
2 As Marx has shown in his critique of Hegel's separation of the private citizen (*Bürger*) and the public, i.e. state, official (*Staatsbeamte*), this distinction is possible only on the basis of its mitigation and obfuscation. Two persons and two types of interest (political, economic) overlap in

context, *political economy* comprises the wide "realm that in the modern era has occupied the space between the old public sphere (equating to the sphere of politics) and the sphere of privacy" (Vollrath 1987: 146). At the same time, in this era of *society*, control and governance, typical of the Hobbesian *state*, do not disappear: if earlier the mechanisms of constraint and surveillance were employed by the state, it is now 'society', i.e. its 'political economy', that controls the behavior of individual agents (Vogl 2004: 55). Privacy as tantamount to "secrecy" (*arcanum*) abates. With the shift from a *Leviathan*-like regime to the regime of Smith's "invisible hand" (45), the state control apparatus re-enters the society itself, encompassing economy *and* family, public *and* private life. Invaded by the economy, social intercourse becomes restructured by the logic of supply and demand.

Still, albeit fundamentally privatistic, social life preserves the idea of sociability and mutual support. Contrary to Hobbesian conjecture of the 'war of all against all', the self-regulating society does not consist of outright privatistic, selfish actions. In order to suppress belligerent social impulses, it involves a new form of sociality: given that earlier the absolutist state was the supreme guarantor of social stability and protection, after its decline the *"self-preservation of the individual"* (*"autoconservazione dell'individuo"*, Pulcini 2001: 41) must be guaranteed by individuals as peers. As a result, subjects of social exchange "are not constrained to follow their *self-interest* in atomistic isolation but act according to a behavior pattern that takes into consideration the expectations of the other" (85).[3] The very idea of the modern individual – and the modern market – thrives on this idealized balance of privatism and public benefit, of profit and responsibility, of entrepreneurship and sociability, of the capacity to steer one's chances and opportunities – and to reconcile private interests with the expectations of others. Therefore, *society* that is shaped by the economic model of the market has to be understood as a two-faced realm concurring with state control on the one hand and with outright privatism on the other. Simultaneously, this historical trajectory from mercantilism to free market capitalism is accompanied by a shift from the *Enlightenment subject* (who is eager to subject nature and to transform the environment after his – mostly not her – rational cause) towards a *bourgeois* (who is earnest, diligent, self-contained). The sociality of the latter consists in the justification of his/her accumulated wealth by means of actions that make private wealth seem socially fruitful and thus useful in the eyes of others.

If the necessity of social justification of capital is ignored, then the 'passion for acquisition' (12) lays bare its darker side: avarice, greed. In this case, one distin-

---

one function: thus, the state official never ceases to be a private citizen; he is constantly trying to govern public interests for his own benefit (Marx 1981: 249). Cf. Vogl (2004: 132).
3 "I soggetti dello scambio non si limitano infatti a perseguire atomisticamente il loro *self-interest*, ma agiscono secondo uno schema di comportamento che tiene conto delle aspettative dell'altro."

guishes two types of avaricious characters: the eager, predatory but still self-contained *miser*; and the socialized, sometimes even erratic type of the *usurer*. Now, in the discussions on the assumed historical transgression from the community (*Gemeinschaft*) to society (*Gesellschaft*), the *miser* is seen as an excessive part of the *community*.[4] Although he/she is its negation, he/she is an exemption the community is, nevertheless, able to tolerate. By way of contrast, the miser's historical successor, the *usurer*, is already typical of modern *society*. The usurer is not a type or an exception but a constitutive element of society, a character trait lurking in every corner and in each social agent. There is yet another pertinent difference between the miser and the usurer: whereas the miser is not conditioned by a particular mode of production and is thus present and possible in every form of social coexistence, the usurer as a specifically new social type can exist only in structures of financial capitalism. It is only in the framework of financial capitalism that the usurer "is able to socialize his private passion in order to meet the others as material he can suck out" (Dolar 2002: 24). Therefore, in contrast to the miser, who withdraws from community in order to prove its very existence, the usurer *makes* the society by way of overriding the community:

> On the one hand, we encounter the person Marx calls the 'hoarder of money' (*der Schatzbildner*), a miser who piles up his fortune, puts it into his pot and his trouser legs, under the bed, etc.; on the other hand, this person realizes that the fortune can best be accumulated if given away as soon as possible, if circulated, or if invested. In other words, one should buy the paradoxical commodity that can produce an excess of value over its proper value, that is, over the value of the workforce that produced it in the first place. Finally, it is only spending that bears results on the market. (Dolar 2002: 51)

As miserliness is, by way of sublation (*Aufhebung*), superseded by usury, it changes only its outer form but not its substance. It endures and perseveres, echoing as a ventriloquist's voice in the hollow corpus of the usurer. According to Dolar and Pulcini, in late capitalism the passion for acquisition ceases to exist as a private sin and becomes a collective, superindividual social obsession,[5] as expressed for

---

4 In her discussion of political economy and modern conceptualizations of money and individuality, Elena Pulcini points out that the translation from miserliness to usury is concomitant with the loss of community (*Gemeinschaft*) and the emergence of society (*Gesellschaft*). Similarly, in his study on avarice Mladen Dolar locates the usurer at the historical and phenomenological juncture where community is superseded by society (2002: 22-23, 168).

5 When depicting Felix Grandet's character, Balzac points precisely to this *universality of greed*. Here, the narrator maintains as follows: "every spectator has a touch of sympathy for these personages, they reflect on the whole of human sentiment, because in themselves they comprise the whole. Where is a man without desire? And what desire can he indulge without money?" (13).

instance in 'Geiz ist geil' ('Tight is right'), a popular marketing slogan of the German chain store Saturn.[6]

This is how the progressive narrative of world history goes (Chakrabarty 2000: 50). This "stagist" (ibid.: 9) or evolutionary approach to the history of capitalism suggests, furthermore, that there are 'more developed' and 'less developed' spaces of capital, that the latter tend to follow the former, and that the developed areas even help the underdeveloped to reduce global discrepancies (cf. Kopsidis 2014). This evolutionary approach relies on a malleable distinction between progressive (Marx' 'historic') nations and those who are lagging behind (the 'non-historic' nations). In his pertinent study *Provincializing Europe: Postcolonial Thought and Historical Difference* (2000), Dipesh Chakrabarty exemplifies this by juxtaposition of *History 1* and *History 2*. Within the paradigm of a "stagist" (Chakrabarty 2000: 9) or evolutionary approach to the history of capitalism it is assumed that *History 1*, "posited by capital", necessarily sublates *History 2*, which does not belong to capital's "life process" (ibid.: 50), into itself. The latter is sublated into the former in a similar way as 'society' is sublated into 'market society', and the "inter-est" (Arendt 1998: 182)[7] of the 'world' into the 'interests' of entrepreneurs.

When taking into account, first, the interlocking of this 'evolutionary' history of capital with the history of literature and, second, the *"ortgebunden*, place-bound nature of literary forms" that in turn affects the *"internal* logic of narrative" (Moretti 1998: 5), then one may observe how particular literary narratives, their protagonists, and whole narrative patterns function within the world system of market economy. In what follows, I propose a contrastive reading of Honoré de Balzac's *Eugenia Grandet* (1833) and Ivo Andrić's *Gospođica (The Woman from Sarajevo*, 1945) that unfolds the disparities and asynchronies within the narrative of capitalist progress. The contrastive reading of the two novels not only displays disparities in the history of capitalism but also reveals the essentially different logic of literary narratives that are related to their distant positions in the global literary geography. Namely, Balzac and Andrić share an interest in the troublesome modes of sublation (in the progressivist manner called 'transition') of one production and value system into another. Both reflect the vestiges of miserliness in its historical translations to usury, as well as the fortunes and misfortunes these transitions, i.e. sublations, bring. However, Balzac's novel functions as a narrative of a *successful* sublation of pre-capitalist miserliness into the usurious lifeworld of modern political economy. By way of contrast, Andrić's novel is an example of 'another', *unsuccessful* outcome of the dialectics of privatistic avarice and capitalist social ethos.

---

6 Cf. https://de.wikipedia.org/wiki/Geiz_ist_geil (retrieved July 23, 2019).
7 "These interests constitute, in the word's most literal significance, something which *inter-est*, which lies between people and therefore can relate and bind them together" (Arendt 1998: 182).

Balzac's and Andrić's novels portray lifeworlds of capital in two distinct transition periods: Balzac's narrative is situated in post-revolutionary France, in the period when capital takes its ultimate sway on social life. In contrast, Andrić's novel touches upon the political and social upheavals during the demise of Austro-Hungarian imperial rule and the lack of social certainty, which offers no sound foundation for auspicious social embedding for lucrative business. Separated by a time span of approximately one hundred years (in 1814 Eugenia Grandet turns 18, and a hundred years later Archduke Franz Ferdinand is assassinated, which brings about both socio-political and private turnabouts and determines the life of Andrić's heroine Rajka Radaković), the two narratives demonstrate the complex mechanisms of the "uneven development" (cf. Chakrabarty 2000: 12) of capitalism, i.e. the historical and spatial factors that determine its successful or failed progress and, of course, the fortunes and misfortunes of its protagonists. Where Balzac depicts France with regard to unevennesses between the center (Paris) and periphery (the provincial town of Saumur), Andrić's novel is similarly positioned between the capital (Belgrade) and the province (Sarajevo). An additional fulcrum is provided by the fact that both Sarajevo and Belgrade function as peripheries of their own, frontiers of capital within the system of *History 1*. This reading explores the tales of two cities, i.e. of two remote city constellations – Saumur and Paris, Sarajevo and Belgrade – and in two distinct periods of the history of capitalism.

The political and economic subjects of Balzac's and Andrić's novels cannot be sufficiently reflected upon if one approaches their greed only in terms of avarice as an individual character trait. Namely, this line of interpretation would remain entangled within the paradigm of methodological individualism. That is why I choose to read the novels as narratives on easy-uneasy coming to terms with socialized greed as typical of financial capitalism.[8] Even if the individual novel, when read separately, could be interpreted as a "psychological study" (Hawkesworth 1984: 170), the two narratives reveal more than case studies on avarice. Precisely, Balzac and Andrić, when set against each other, disclose a series of political and social landmarks that allow for scholarly reflection on the enabling or disabling conditions of miserliness and usury. In other words, the fortunes of a 'wealthy' heroine who is living in *History 1*, when judged by moral standards of 'private happiness' (not 'private fortune'), may not seem more favorable than the misfortunes of a usurer who partakes in the alleged *History 2*. If judged by a sentimental stance, the life narratives of Balzac's Eugenia Grandet and Andrić's Rajka Radaković are surely

---

8 This reading of Andrić's novel goes against the grain of the probable intention of the author himself, who said that he was primarily "interested in a vice called avarice. I do not know when exactly it happened but one day [...] I asked myself: why are only men avaricious? As far as I know, this vice makes no distinction between men and women. And then somewhere I decided to introduce a female character governed by money" (cit. in Jandrić 1982: 137).

comparable narratives of alienation. But sentimental pity is not the purpose of this article. The aim is to investigate the social setting of Balzac's and Andrić's female characters, to question whether their positions can be interpreted as partaking in the 'progress' of *History 1* or just belonging to the 'state' of *History 2*, and, finally, to discern whether the novels merely depict the idea of a two-stage history or if they support or subvert it in any way.

2. Private vices, private benefits

Notwithstanding the fact that both novels are situated in a time when the "great dichotomy" (Bobbio 1989) of private and public is imagined to still have functioned in its traditional vein, by 'private' I do not refer to the realm of 'private space' or 'secrecy'. Similarly, the term 'public' does denote the 'public sphere' as an institutionalized media landscape. Deriving its meaning from the Latin 'privus' (French: 'privé'), 'private' primarily refers to a state of exemption from or deprivation of something, e.g. of the possibility or right to appear in the public sphere or to act as a recognized subject. It also refers to the privatistic and profit-oriented socialization that conditions the political reduction of the idea of the common, public "inter-est" (Arendt 1998: 182) towards economically informed 'interests'. Along this trajectory, the idea of a social commonality that would exceed the private and privatistic desolation gets lost. Subjects who conceive themselves and act as private competitors can only fabricate a society of competition and rivalry; they aspire not to the 'world' but adhere to the "sheer necessity of life" (117), that is, to the sheer necessity of the life of capital.

Although his study is more focused on the discussion of avarice as one of seven capital sins and less on spatial and historical prerequisites for the sublation of miserliness into the usurious frame of financial capitalism, Dolar correlates important elements of avarice that will prove useful for the present study. He sets out from the traditional, antique type of miser as known from Plautus and Shakespeare. When observing the miser in his paradigmatic *topos* – the secret place where he hides his treasure – he describes him as follows:

> [C]arefully and precisely the miser closes the door, locking it with at least double bolts and some other padlock; he hermetically closes the window shutters, lowers the blinds, draws the curtains, breaks every connection to the outer world, precisely clogging every vent through which a view from the outside could penetrate. Thereafter, in the artificial light, closely listening to possibly suspicious noises, he fetches his shrine [...]. Thus he is finally alone with his fortune; he begins to sweat and jiggle, and with accelerated pulse and rapid and deep breath he opens the shrine with his subtle fingers. What joy: he counts the talers, the banknotes,

counts over and over again, perhaps letting a couple of them fall on the floor, but only to put them back in order, in the appropriate system; he shares them out in one way, thereafter trying out another one, constantly in ecstasy, in perfect excitement, with a sharp ear, with all his senses in the most heightened state of alertness. But the delight of counting is simultaneously the road to discontent: the fortune may be twice as big, and still it will always be too little. (21)

From a comparative perspective, *Eugenia Grandet* and *Gospođica* deal with the phenomena of miserliness and usury in a seemingly similar manner. In what follows, I will outline the specific characteristics of miser and usurer that can be found in both novels. As can be seen from the above quotation, miserliness is a private matter, isolated and hidden in the dimness of one's private chamber. It is non-social, precisely an "antithesis of sociality" (23).[9] It is also conservative: whereas other sins (lust, sloth, or wrath) undoubtedly present a state of excess, revolutionary disorder, subversion, and distortion of norms, miserliness is bound to preserve the present state, to keep the treasure untouched and the situation under perfect control.

In *Eugenia Grandet* and *Gospođica*, the description of a miser withdrawn in his private chamber, warmed by the treasure ("that warms me again!" says Grandet, 21) is given in an almost identical manner. Nevertheless, the father-daughter relationships are laterally reversed: whereas in Balzac's novel it is the father who is avaricious, in Andrić's novel this role is given to the daughter Rajka. In Balzac, it is not the heroine Eugenia (the "miser's daughter", as indicated by the book title) but her father Felix who withdraws to his chamber, where he dwells alone "like an alchymist in his study" (7). Furthermore, it is not Eugenia's but Felix Grandet's house that resembles Rajka's dim and cold abode, "a bleak, cold, and silent house, situated above the town, and sheltered by its ruined ramparts" (3). Similarly, Rajka's is a "mute and joyless house, empty of laughter and conversation, of warmth and ornament, avoided even by beggars" (56); its bleakness only reflects Rajka's psychic coldness (8-10). Although Grandet may be compared to Gobseck, a famous usurer from Balzac's novella *Gobseck* (1830), he is not a usurer in the modern sense of the word but still an old-fashioned miser.[10] His social behavior is outlined as unmistakably pathological: "As a financier, Mr. Grandet partook of the nature of both

---

9 I use the term "non-social" similarly to Kristin Ross, who in *The Emergence of Social Space* employs a distinction between a poet who is "nonsocial" and a poet who is "asocial". Whilst the "non-social" refers to someone who "is not at home to anyone" (Ross 2008: 20), Ross interprets the "asocial" character as "indifferent to conforming to conventional standards of behavior – be they moral, sexual, national, artistic, or lexical" (20).
10 In comparison to Gobseck, Grandet represents the old type of a provincial usurer who accumulates his fortune but still stays very connected to the rural landscape and agriculture. Gobseck is no longer of that kind: being a metropolitan type of usurer, he is not obsessed with the physical touch with money. The presence of gold is no longer important; rather it is all about the exchange of the added value that comes to life by means of the mere self-referentiality and

the tiger and the boa. He knew how to crouch and watch patiently for his prey; and then to spring, open the maw of his purse, and engulf a mass of crowns; this done, he would lay himself quietly down, like the serpent when gorged, impassible, cold, and methodical" (2). Similarly, Rajka walked past the people "as if they were dead" (72) and from their talk, gossip and assumptions "she could hear and grasp only the part connected with her dream: the endless, intricate, and perpetual talk of income and outgoings" (72). Her predatory character interpreted society as a "hunting ground" (55) and was inclined "to lose sight of everything except her craving for prey" (55). Rajka, hesitating over every piece of bread,[11] and Felix Grandet, inspecting the reasonableness of every mouthful that is taken in his household,[12] obtain in the figures of their respective father and daughter *adversaries* – the non-social father Radaković and the non-social daughter Eugenia.

In the modern era, the bourgeois knows that "private vices" ought to be in perfect concord with "public benefits" (Vogl 2004: 43). Here, even an old miser like Grandet has learned that "money without honor is a canker" (*Eugenia* 15). He built his fortune thanks to cautiously outbalanced participation in the public life of Saumur, fulfilling both public obligations and obtaining advantageous private benefits. This warranted him the title "Mr.": after occupying the position of mayor in times of the Consulate, and after being removed from office under the Emperor (in 1806), Grandet became "Mr. Grandet" – or even "Father Grandet" (2). At the very beginning of the novel, the reader is acquainted with the history of Grandet's success, which relied on his excellent taste for historical changes. Still a master cooper in 1789, Grandet married Eugenia's mother, a daughter of a rich wood merchant who in 1806 inherited the fortune of her deceased mother. Gradually he gained property over "thirteen granges; an old abbey, the windows of which he walled up for economy; one hundred and thirty acres of meadow, containing three thousand poplars planted in 1793; and, finally, the house in which he resided" (7) – all in all, financial property which only two people in Saumur (the notary Cruchot de Bonfons and the banker des Grassins) could roughly estimate.

One important trait of the bourgeois is the capability and willingness to enter into relations with others. Although driven by the need for profit and success, the

---

self-reproduction of money in the long chains of transactions and transmutations of wealth. He does not live from the accumulation of wealth but from its *socialization* (Dolar 2002: 193).

11 When giving alms to the beggar, Rajka takes old bread: while cutting it into small slices, she is "trying to convince herself that she had not made a mistake and given him too much" (49).

12 Grandet refuses to spend additional money on food, especially on bread. In his conversation with the maid Nanon, who reminds him that they have a guest, Eugenia's cousin Charles ("There are five of us to-day, sir", 9), he says as follows: "That's true, [...] but your loaves weigh six pounds, so there will be some over. Besides, young men from Paris never eat bread" (9). After Nanon suggests that she could prepare "frippe" (a sort of spread), he says: "No, [...] they eat neither frippe nor bread: they are like young misses engaged to be married" (9).

bourgeois knows that only outbalanced exchange and earnest credibility can secure his gains. Given the fact that in bourgeois society the rule of money – "the only deity to whom modern mortals bow the knee" (5) – affects even what in the course of the Romantic Movement was considered to be a matter of the heart, it becomes logical that marriage serves as a means to guarantee a person's financial standing and social existence. Now, if one makes the claim that both Felix and Eugenia Grandet partake in the great history of the bourgeoisie, and that Rajka Radaković presents a failing of the bourgeois ideals imported from *History 1*, then this claim can be examined precisely via the characters' marital decisions and sexual lives. Here, the distorted sociability of Balzac's and Andrić's characters is equally reflected in their self-inflicted limitations on food and comfort as in their (un)fortunate 'scenes from a marriage'. Dolar completes the remarks on the infelicitous libidinal economy of the miser withdrawn to his chamber with the following comment: "It is apparent that this scene bears sexual connotations, there is something orgiastic and orgasmic about it; and it is also apparent that the joy it brings cannot be promulgated or in any way shared with others" (2001: 21). Due to the fact that the miser's sexuality is self-involved, it is closely connected to the libidinal drive of inhibited life, of *thanatos*: Grandet serves his nephew not with chicken, turkey or pork but with crows, birds that "eat dead people" (9). Although crows are birds that eat the dead, Grandet considers them entirely apt: "They eat, as every one does, just what they can get. Don't we all live on dead people? What are inheritances?" (9) In a similar manner, Rajka's *death drive* is fixated on her father's grave, and it is precisely the cemetery where her necrophilous attachment to the ancestor reaches its climax. She makes pilgrimages to the grave on a regular basis, never letting her mother come along (79). There "the last link between her and the multitude was cut. Here she was detached and sheltered from everything" (79). It is only in front of the tomb where she lets her feelings run freely: "Choking with emotion, Raika gasped and whispered into her clenched fists: 'You! You! You!'" (80). In her topography of passions, the grave plays a similar role to the chamber in which she keeps the money. Not only does her desolate house begin looking like a tomb (72), even her enjoyment in counting the savings resembles the "orgiastic and orgasmic" passion described by Dolar (2002: 21).

Despite the fact that the comparative reading of the novels exposes the laterally reversed structures of fathers and daughters, allow me to refer to one decisive point of comparison: both novels are named after a female inheritor who is "curbed by the will of a dead father" (cf. Dolar 2002: 101).[13] Felix Grandet's advice to

---

13 In Shakespeare's *The Merchant of Venice*, Act 1, Scene 2, Portia says: "The brain may devise laws for the blood, but a hot temper leaps o'er a cold decree. Such a hare is madness, the youth, to skip o'er the meshes of good counsel, the cripple. But this reason is not in fashion to choose me a husband. O me, the word 'choose'. I may neither choose whom I would, nor refuse whom I

his daughter reads as follows: "Take care of all! [...] you shall render a strict account to me *there!*" (*Eugenia* 24) While saying this, Grandet points upwards, thus "proving that Christianity ought to be the religion of misers" (24). Rajka's father makes a similar statement: "You must understand once and for all, and don't ever forget it, that a person who does not know how to strike a balance between his income and his expenses according to the demands of his life is headed for certain ruin" (*The Woman* 21). Beside the words that bind the daughters likewise to money and to their fathers, the fathers' legacy subverts the genealogical principle that is a precondition of biological reproduction. Rajka is explicitly called "son" ("sinak", *Gospođica* 22, 24), or a "big son" ("veliki sin", 25), which is an idiomatic phrase for a child used independently of a child's sex but is linguistically still gendered. The dying father speaks to his "son" as follows: "From now on you'll have to be your own father and mother, because your mother ... well, you know what she's like, a good woman but soft" (*The Woman* 20). Rajka's greedy and rigid behavior turns out to be a result of a perfect misunderstanding of her father's dying words: thus she makes amends both for her mother's 'softness' and for the father's economic unwariness. After his sudden death, at the age of 15 she experiences rapid maturation and begins to manage business on her own, rejecting the well-meant advice of her guardian Mihajlo, friends of the family, and relatives. Additionally, the unmourned death of the father is extended with the death of Uncle Vlado, who was only four years older than Rajka. Generous and jovial, Vlado "passionately loved to give presents" and was "deft in choosing exactly the gift that best accorded with the wishes of the recipient, one that was bound to give him the most pleasure" (26). And this "lust to squander" was in Rajka's eyes a vice "graver than any sin and blacker than death itself" (28). Thereafter, burdened by unmourned grief over the loss of her father and her beloved Vlado, Rajka builds her character over a void. Her "taming of the emotional life" ("l'addomesticamento della vita emotiva", Pulcini 2001: 132) suppresses and replaces the social economy of interpersonal interaction and the physical economy of the body. By incorporating and exaggerating the will of the dead father and thus adhering only to the "perverted 'sexuality' of money" (Dolar 2002: 119), Rajka becomes a miser, scrooge, "tvrdica" (meaning someone "hard" or "rigid", *Gospođica* 218). Occupying time and space that is far remote from the productive ethos of the 19th-century bourgeois, she skips a whole historical phase in the development of capitalism – namely, the production phase, or the phase of real economy – and applies herself to usury as an activity that, in fact, does not need production, workers, or society, but consists only in helping money to self-referentially reproduce itself, to "breed" (56). It is only after many years, after her flight from Sarajevo to Belgrade, that she senses the "motherly tenderness" (27) she

---

dislike, so is the will of a living daughter curbed by the *will of a dead father*. Is it not hard, Nerissa, that I cannot choose one, nor refuse none?" (16, italics mine)

had once had towards Vlado. Deluded by his physical resemblance to Vlado, she lends money to Ratko Ratković, a charlatan or trickster who mimetically adopts the habits of dandyism he becomes acquainted with in Paris, Vienna, Brussels, or Biarritz. She never gets the money back. Remote from Sarajevo society that despised her usury and unaccustomed to the habits of Belgrade's lavish bourgeoisie, Rajka dies a lonely death.

In Eugenia's case, another type of death marks her coming of age and defines her social trajectory. Her rite of passage consists in the great disillusionment with Charles, a cousin from Paris whose father (another Grandet!) commits suicide due to his sudden bankruptcy. Here, the enamored Eugenia offends her father's thrift because she tries to prepare a breakfast that could keep up with her cousin's Parisian habits. Soon after, at the age of 23, she secretly bestows upon Charles all her savings (her father's fortune). However, Charles, who hereafter sets off into the wide world, ceases to be a "fallen dandy" (*Eugenia* 14) and becomes a successful entrepreneur, thus forgetting about his enamored cousin from the province. He remembers her only as "a *creditor* to whom he owed six thousand francs" (25). Consequently, Eugenia's disenchantment with love becomes "a malady controlling her destiny" (13). Here, it is precisely Charles who makes her realize that love and marriage are two separate phenomena, the first a matter of the heart, the second a matter of business: "Love, in marriage, is certainly a chimera, and my experience tells me we are bound to obey all the laws of society, and unite all the compatibilities required by the world, when we enter into that state" (26). Significantly, this does not lead Eugenia away from society but, in fact, only introduces her into the realm devoid of inefficient sentimentality. As Michael Lucey remarks, in *Eugenia Grandet* the "discourse of economic utility never stops" (Lucey 2001: 20): while Rajka rejects the very idea of courtship and marriage and remains a lifelong 'mademoiselle',[14] Eugenia decides to conclude a marriage contract. After Felix Grandet's death she marries her longtime suitor Cruchot de Bonfons and thanks to her dowry becomes his fully-fledged partner. Here she no longer acts as a 'good match' (an object of matrimonial transaction) but as an experienced, rational agent that enters a lucrative deal. As she is not married by her parents, she is 'her own father and mother' (cf. *The Woman* 20), i.e. the bride and the bride's guardian. Thus if Rajka's gender identity hovers between masculinity and femininity, and therefore between a woman and a witch,[15] Eugenia's female identity, if judged by her social endeavors, remains undisputed. However, Eugenia chooses to remain childless –

---

14 In the English text, "gospodica" is translated as "madam", which is not the exact equivalent to the original wording. Meaning both "madame" and "spinster", "gospodica" has a slightly pejorative connotation.
15 Newspapers depict her as a "modern-day witch" (76), and people turn away from her bewitching, horrifying sight (139). Rajka thus reminds us of a middlesex identity or a gender that is "hors-sexe" (Dolar 2002: 190).

to be "*both married and a virgin*" (Schor 98) – but only on condition that this is socially and canonically acceptable. So if one can argue that both Rajka and Eugenia are not 'successful' in terms of sexual reproduction, one also has to agree that whilst Rajka's social identity is considered thoroughly 'reprehensible', Eugenia reconciles her private, emotional misfortune with the fortunate accumulation of wealth and with social esteem. Thus, the question is not whether Eugenia and Rajka live what one may call a 'fulfilled life'. The question is rather what kind of fulfillment of the "high duties toward society" (*Eugenia* 26) is expected within the *chronotope* of the particular novel, i.e. within the certain time and space in the multilateral history of capitalism (cf. Moretti 1998: 70-71). Finally, let me consider Karl Marx' observation "The less you *are*, [...] the more you *have*" (Marx/Engels 1988: 119; cf. Dolar 2002: 50) and discuss it with regard to 'having' and 'being' in the inspected novels. In both novels, the reduction of the 'self' is proportional to the accumulation of wealth. This reduction of the 'self' is compensated by a secondary, alienated self-assertion, exerted over possessions. However, whilst Eugenia's reduction of the self enables the accumulation of wealth, so that her story functions as a narrative of gradual liberation from an outdated, conservative, and non-social greed, Rajka's narrative shows the impossibility of traditional miserliness in the shift from a traditional merchant economy to the epoch of a new, financial capitalism.

By way of conclusion to this section, one may point to John Maynard Keynes' ideas on saving, investment, and economic community (Keynes 1964; cf. Padua 2014: 98-101). In *The General Theory of Employment, Interest and Money* (1936), Keynes considers individual investments to be actions that enable the whole economic community to prosper.[16] However, the 'community' in question is not 'community' as opposed to 'society' and as discussed by Ferdinand Tönnies, Roberto Esposito, or Elena Pulcini. Instead, Keynes speaks of a *community of consumers*, which is unequivocally a "utilitarian" idea (Padua 2014: 98). Departing from the claim that in an outbalanced economic system every consumption would also be an investment, Keynes speaks of saving and spending as a "two-sided affair" (Keynes 1964: 84). However, Keynes' understanding of spending does not bear the meaning of *donum* (a gift that is "potentially unilateral", Esposito 5) but of *munus*. And *munus* is not simply "goods", "wealth", or "interest" (6), but a remuneration for the initial "debt" that every member of a community always already owes to this selfsame community. Paradoxically, society as a utilitarian, economic community expects of an in-

---

16 In the words of Roberto Esposito, *munus* is the precondition of belonging to the community. Esposito does not speak, of course, of capitalist community. However, his observations on *communitas* (as opposed to *immunitas*) may structurally correspond to Keynes' idea of social capital, according to which investment is a *gift* that "one gives, not what one receives" (Esposito 5). As in Keynes, this gift is always a "pledge" or a "tribute" that creates gratitude and demands new donations (5).

dividual that he/she fulfill certain duties he/she owes to this society. In this line of argument, Keynes claims that only savings that are translated into consumption are considered to be investments in the "community" (Keynes 1964: 85). In his view, the saving is not problematic as long as it does not turn into saving for saving's sake. The problem arises only when money and goods remain enclosed in the miser's chamber unintended for spending. This kind of saving blocks the cash flow in the 'community': if everybody tries to top up their savings without the intention of spending, then the volume of value left to circulate diminishes. The community 'freezes' due to reduced consumption, which halts production and, in turn, does not result in new goods that will be sold on the market: "Every such attempt to save more by reducing consumption will so affect incomes that the attempt necessarily defeats itself" (84).

The accordance of these observations with the late-capitalist pressure on private individuals to consume in order to stimulate the economy is striking. In the world of advanced capitalism, it is not sufficient to merely keep the money. In order to carry yields, *homo oeconomicus* has to socialize and thus to justify his greed. In Balzac's novel, Mandeville's pragmatic maxim, according to which "private vices result in public benefits" (Pulcini 2001: 74),[17] has been successfully passed from the father to the daughter and inheritor: although Eugenia "carefully accumulated her surplus revenues", she was cautious enough to disarm criticism "by noble and perpetual charities" (27). She founded hospitals, schools, public libraries, and made donations to the churches. If translated to today's circumstances, Eugenia, who decides to "invest" in the 'community' of Saumur by way of giving money to the poor and the church, already paves the way towards the deceitful idea of "communism of capital" (Marazzi 2011: 111). According to the latter, it is exactly the paradoxical reversal of Marx' statement – 'The more you *give*, the more you *have*' – that Eugenia accomplishes and Rajka fails to realize. In contrast to Eugenia, Rajka erroneously intensifies the perverse tendency of finance capital that likes to hive off and dissociate from any idea of the common – even of that minimum of 'community' that money needs to 'breed'.

3. Social expectations regarding capital

I have already pointed out that the two narratives develop downright adversatively: *Eugenia Grandet* depicts a trajectory of a person's coming of age, beginning with the obedient daughter, intermitted by juvenile abandonment to a loved one, followed by a phase of disenchantment, after which life arranged by the maxim 'business as

---

17 "Da vizi privati nascono pubblici benefici[.]"

usual' can begin. Although it is a narrative of an intimately infelicitous and sorrowful disenchantment, its heroine ultimately becomes what one may characterize as a successful and recognized member of society. The novel thus contains elements of a *Bildungsroman* that – similarly to Goethe's *Wilhelm Meister's Apprenticeship* – reaches its end with the realization of a perfectly socialized, i.e. market-determined, identity. If in her youth she was a sentimental provincial girl (*Eugenia* 8), willing to bestow on Charles "the treasures of her pity" (13), in the end Eugenia acts as a person who – similarly to her cousin – has successfully internalized the basic principles of the new political economy that is described by Pulcini as follows:

> Individuals are united solely through provisional contractual relations and through the impersonal bonds of money that [...] remains perfectly indifferent to the singularity of the other and that substitutes the personal bonds through an abstract objectivity of material relations. (Pulcini 2001: 143)[18]

Another pertinent difference between Rajka and Eugenia lies in the modus and pace of their transition from the "time of poetry in her life" (*The Woman* 30), i.e. from the "springtime of love" (*Eugenia* 17) to "the endless, intricate, and perpetual talk of income and outgo" (*The Woman* 72). While Rajka was not expected to command the father's legacy so that her rite of passage to the world of finance and coerced maturity occurs as abrupt and unforeseen (her life "began at a dark point, and with a bitter experience", 16), Eugenia's sublation of Christian sentimentality into the lifeworld of capital is prepared and trained in timely fashion. Moreover, Eugenia even has enough time to stage a conflict with the will of the father, that is, to "negotiate" (Schor 98). Expectedly, this conflict is not over the addressee of her love; rather, it is over the way she commands the fortune that is given to her.[19] Therefore, it is not a 'simple' conflict between father and daughter but a conflict of two financial ethoses: the former conservative, sadist, and contemptuous, the latter sentimental, religious, and socialized. In other words, if the father as the representative of the older generation is "sterner, narrower, profit-driven", he is also by far more "independent" and "uncompromising" (Moretti 2013: 113). By way of contrast, Eugenia's financial ethos is obedient, subservient, and patient: "Eugenie is no longer a minor, but she submits to the imprisonment anyway" (Lucey 2001: 4). While displaying ignorance of the legislative novelties brought by the Code Napoleon in

---

18 "Gli individui sono uniti unicamente dalla provvisorietà di rapporti contrattuali, dai vincoli impersonali del denaro che, come ben mostrerà l'analisi marxiana, è del tutto indifferente alla specificità dell'altro, e sostituisce ai vincoli personali l'oggettività astratta di rapporti cosali."
19 In the conflict, the will of the father is clearly coded as the 'will of gold'. So Grandet says as follows: "You despise your father, eh? You don't know what a father is! If he is not everything to you, he will be nothing. Where is your gold?" (20)

1804,[20] she proves, paradoxically, to be 'progressive' in her submission to Grandet's conservative paternalism,[21] in her patient waiting, after which she does not simply follow the 'will of a dead father' but, indeed, adapts it to the new circumstances. Eugenia's financial education (which overrides the mother's sentimental education[22]) is a long-term process that progresses only by making mistakes and learning from them. One could even conclude that Eugenia *needs* a dead father in order to further his legacy. Thus, when Michael Lucey poses the rhetorical question whether Eugenia learns from experience (2001: 10), the answer is undoubtedly positive.[23] The early mistake regarding her savings could thus be interpreted as a painful examination the usurer must pass in the present in order to impeccably bargain in the future.[24] Finally, Eugenia chooses the "melancholic solution" (Schor 99) and, meandering between the 'will of a dead father', her own disillusionment and the inclination to enter a convent, she takes the path of "evolution" (99). Although Naomi Schor touches upon this evolutive element in Eugenia's personal trajectory, she does not interpret it as a historical compromise within the given social and political context. I will return to this evolution at the end of the text.

20 Before the introduction of the Napoleonic Code, marriage was exclusively regulated by canon law. After its promulgation in 1804, the Civil Code "established for the first time in France a uniform set of laws concerning marriage and inheritance" (Lucey 2001: 15). According to the Code, after her mother's death Rajka gained the right to take into command her savings and her mother's inheritance. On this occasion Eugenia shows that she is sufficiently conservative (she does not disobey her father's will) and at the same time sufficiently modern (she successfully socializes her inherited avarice).
21 "My father is master of his own house, and while I remain beneath his roof, it is my duty to obey him" (22, cf. Lucey 2001: 15).
22 Felix Grandet trains Eugenia in being emotionless too. After the death of his brother he says to her: "You did not know your uncle! [...] why do you cry?" (9)
23 Lucey expects Eugenia to learn about the possibilities of political action: "Might she not have learned something from watching her mother's death at her father's hand? Might she not have learned something from the way Charles values a woman with an aristocratic name over her? Might she not have learned something – about, perhaps, the political economy of modern heterosexuality, and her own affective participation in it – from the forms of attention her various suitors pay her, and the kinds of marriage contracts they would agree to? Might she not learn something, at the very end of the novel, from the choice of her faithful servant Nanon to marry only reasonably late in life?" (Lucey 2001: 10-11) Although granting Naomi Schor's reading perspicaciousness, Lucey finds the interpretation of Eugenia as "a case" (Schor 1985: 98) unsatisfactory and rather expects a reading that gestures towards Eugenia's possible liberation.
24 At this point, one should remember that not even Grandet's fortune emerged out of nothing and without obstacles. Even the 'grand' Grandet has experienced a business failure: he was once deceived by a Jew pretending to be deaf. While striving to speak loudly and to explain every detail of their business transaction, Grandet forgot his own hidden intentions and conducted the worst business ever. But he has internalized this failure – similarly to how his daughter will – and learned from it. Pretending to be deaf and stammer himself, Grandet thereafter used the same ruse when he did business (2).

Furthermore, while Radaković's death is coded as a great emotional loss, the deaths in *Eugenia Grandet* are predominantly connected to matters of inheritance. Grandet interprets the death of his own brother and Charles' father in terms of a financial catastrophe, not of an emotional loss. When his brother dies, he says to Charles "you have lost your father" (11) and underlines this statement with "you have not a penny in the world" (11). If at this moment Charles is still perfectly unconcerned with the questions of inheritance (he answers with "What is that to me? [...] Give me back my father!" 11), soon the reader is informed that "[t]he blood of the Grandets at length asserted its dominion in him; he became avaricious and cruel. [...] He exacted usury on a large scale [...]." (25)

Beside the 'will of a dead father' there are other factors that determine the daughters' habits and attitudes. The reversed trajectories of Eugenia's and Rajka's life narratives can be tracked via both the educational policy of their fathers and their biological and financial inheritance and the "institutional support" (Lucey 2001: 2) that is necessary for the reproduction of the social order. If one takes a closer look at the type of inheritance that is passed over to the daughters, one may observe that not only "social structures left over from a past social dispensation" (2) engender Eugenia's and Rajka's trajectories; their biological inheritance already proves to be determinant. As the narrator extensively elaborates, in Grandet's family the strength of biological inheritance is certain to such a degree that its materialization proves inevitable. When speaking of Charles, the narrator remarks that although he was not obliged to follow the "Parisian morality" (16), he had so thoroughly imbibed its principles "that it required nothing but the occasion to cause the seed sown to germinate in his heart" (16).[25] When Eugenia outlives her husband, she is redeemed by the genetic inheritance of her maternal ancestors, La Bertellières. It is thus not surprising that Grandet's sole heiress displays a sophisticated business sense, an improved version of Grandet's attachment to wealth ("She is more of a Grandet than I am myself", he observes, 21). If in her childhood biological inheritance was only an imperfect genotype, still containing too much of her mother's Christian bequest, it was perfected by her father's "educating the avarice of his heiress" (4). That is why Grandet trains his daughter to be thrifty and asks her frequently for "an account of her treasure" (4). Finally, the biological genotype and the education of avarice are completed by the expectations of Eugenia's social surroundings, which are exemplified by the pastor's words: "If you wish to secure your salvation, you

---

25 Eugenia's maternal grandparents ensured the legacy of misery from the other side of the family as well. Even here, one can observe the generational shift from old-school miserliness towards modern usury. Namely, the miserliness of Mr. La Bertellière, Eugenia's maternal grandfather, was so keen that he "considered an investment in the light of a prodigality, for he reaped a larger interest in looking at his gold than in the gains of usury" (2).

have but two courses open for your choice; leave the world; or, conform to its usages. Fulfil your earthly destiny, or your heavenly one" (26). Ultimately, while Rajka's 'social economy' is based on naïve, clueless repetition, intensification and exaggeration of the unmourned loss, Eugenia is taught to put aside her melancholy and to do what is expected to be done.

Although Andrić's narrative provides very little information about Rajka's father, the reader learns that Obren Radaković was among those merchants who moved to Sarajevo in order to swiftly become the town's major businessmen. Although not a native of the city (he "hailed from one of the frontier districts", 16), Master Radakovich was "one of Sarajevo's most respected Serbian merchants" (16). Having come to town immediately after the Austro-Hungarian Empire established the protectorate in the 1880s, he "had quickly, by dint of acumen and a few lucky breaks, established himself as one of the more solid businessmen" (16). Nevertheless, he was a person of great social esteem, known for his helpfulness and humanity. He married "a gentle good-looking blonde girl from the old and reputable Sarajevo family of Hadzi-Vasich" (16). And although it is said that his mother's grandfather, Master Ristan, was a scrooge too, he "was also known to loosen the purse strings and spend money to entertain and be a host when this could not be avoided or when the prestige of his house demanded it" (75). That is why in the case of Miss Radaković people exclamatorily ask, "How is it possible *those* parents produced *this* – thing?" (74). Moreover, if one considers that the people of Sarajevo at that time still partly adhered to inherited Ottoman customs and beliefs according to which "all interest was considered usury, and usury was outlawed by the Sharia" (Sugar 1963: 17; cf. Terzić 2009: 80-81), then it becomes obvious that Rajka pursues a passion that must have been considered not only an excess and an anomaly but also a symptom of social pathology.

The legacy of the father involves money; it steers the daughter's social philosophy. When lying on his deathbed, Rajka's father makes several remarks on the culture and customs of "[o]ur life here" (22): people are "decent and conscientious only toward those who don't depend on them or ask anything of them; because the moment you bind yourself and put yourself in a position of dependence, it's the end of everything, friendship and kinship, reputation and respect" (22). In order to protect herself from the endangering influence of the insidious "multitude" (79), Rajka follows the advice to "be merciless with [her]self and others" (22). She thus incorporates her father's advice never to become entangled in social relations that could make her dependent on people. This retreat from society not only calls for a spatial withdrawal: it means "suppressing those so-called higher considerations, those lordly habits of inner gentility, delicacy, and high-mindedness" (22). By turning her father's advice into a philosophy of ascetic strictness, she rejects society in a way the father probably never did.

By way of contrast, after Grandet's death Eugenia opens her salon up to society and exposes herself to the flattery she was explicitly warned about. Flattery, Balzac does not omit to mention, "never emanates from great minds – it is the prerogative of small ones which even reduce their own diminutive proportions, the better to enter into the sphere of the person around whom they gravitate" (24).[26] Although Eugenia does not embrace the gatherings and the flattery of the 'interested' at once (e.g., praise makes "her blush at first", 24), she eventually becomes accustomed to "hear[ing] her beauty lauded", and finally learns to like the "homage". (24) Step by step she improves the "lordly habits of inner gentility, delicacy, and high-mindedness" (*The Woman* 22) to such an extent that she becomes "a queen, and the most skillfully adulated of queens" (*Eugenia* 24).

Whereas the conception of social success in Balzac's narrative is closely connected to financial liquidity (so that "to fail" simply means "to commit the most dishonorable act of which a man is capable", 11), in Andrić's universe the word for 'society' – 'svet', meaning 'world',[27] 'multitude', and 'people' – does not always coincide with *society* as elaborated in the introductory part of the paper and as set out by Obren Radaković in the above quotation. Sometimes it is closely connected to the notion of solidarity and mutuality. One should remember that after Radaković's death, people helped Rajka not as entrepreneurs but as friends and relatives. Similarly, their expectations were based on the concept of the 'world' waiting for her to be or become 'human' (have mercy, be helpful). Further on in the novel, Rajka listens to voices of drunken men who walk beneath her window and say that "[k]illing her would be a public service" (146). And she is warned by Veso that "[a] person is not alone in this world. You can't ignore the living" (76). This 'world' explicitly expresses critique of Rajka's non-social usury, reflecting upon its own 'worldliness' as the "core and meaning of life" (105), which to her presents only "a mere obstacle to orderly existence and gainful functioning" (105).[28] In her perspective, this world of

---

26 Rajka was given similar advice: "Train yourself not to feel the least bit flattered when the people praise you, and don't let it bother you when they call you a tightwad, a heartless and selfish creature" (23).

27 This is another idiomatic expression that entails a dimension of the ubiquitous and universal validity of 'society', which changes its meaning if one translates it as 'multitude', a somewhat negatively connoted term used in the English translation of *Gospođica*. This 'svet' should not to be confounded with Hardt and Negri's concept of multitude as "an antagonistic and creative positivity" (Hardt/Negri 2000: 61).

28 Similarly, Rajka is instructed by a young army doctor, Dr. Roknić, about the development in international politics and that the Central Powers will lose the war, which is "good for all humanity", and especially "for all of us South Slavs, because otherwise we would disappear from the face of this earth" (123). While Dr. Roknić quotes the speeches of the South Slav national delegates in the parliament at Vienna, Rajka remains uninterested and even frightened by these developments.

people is directly opposed to the precious world of money: "This shadowy, antipodal side she regarded as the true face of the world; the other side, the dark reverse of it" (73). From this distorted view of society, Rajka concludes that not the market, but the 'people' were to blame for the father's misfortune: it is the people who have taken everything from her (226). To conclude, whereas in times of economic expansion the *chronotope* of Balzac's Saumur can be seen as incorporating History 1, the *chronotope* of Andrić's Sarajevo in the turbulent times of WWI, the dissolution of the Empire, and the establishment of the new state (the Kingdom of Serbs, Croats, and Slovenes) still contains enough elements of History 2 that are connected with traditional forms of community, mutuality, and that – one dares to think – allow for an anti-capitalist critique.

What people expect from Rajka – a sense of belonging – is structurally related to what society expects from Eugenia – a sense for spending. They both should partake or 'have a share' in the community. Now, whereas 'community' in Andrić's novel refers to a collective being or being in common that does not exclusively rely on a notion of having, property, or possession (Esposito 6), within the framework of financial capitalism, the 'share' in the community is expressed via one's duty to spend *for* the community. The duty to spend renders the subjects obligated so that they are not "masters of themselves" (6). One concludes that the traditional community and the utilitarian 'community of consumers' in fact similarly expropriate their subjects' initial property, both material and psychological ("their very subjectivity", 7). Logically, being obedient to the rule "leave the world; or, conform to its usages" (*Eugenia* 26), Eugenia considers entering a convent or even death. However, the pastor advises her not to forget about her social duties and responsibilities:

> Death! [...] Miss Grandet, you have high duties toward society to fulfil. Are you not a mother to the poor, to whom you give food and clothing in winter, and employment in summer? Your large fortune is but a loan, which you must restore, and thus far you have holily accepted it as such: but to bury yourself in a convent would be only selfishness. At the same time you ought not to remain unmarried; for in the first place, even if you were capable of managing your immense property, you would perhaps lose it all: you would have a thousand law-suits and be exposed to inextricable difficulties. Believe your pastor; a husband is essential to your interests, for it is *your duty to preserve what God has bestowed upon you.* (26, italics mine)

This advice corresponds to Franco Moretti's observation that by the middle of the 19th century capitalism had become too strong to be preserved only for the small circle of those who gained immediate profit from it. Capital was expected to socialize, that is, to appear useful to everyone. In this matter it was confronted with the necessity of its public justification. Only by means of this maneuver could the bourgeoisie gain not only financial but also political power. Therefore one may conclude that while *Eugenia Grandet* is a narrative on the prudent, calculated socialization of wealth with the aim to discharge accusations of being 'non-social', *Gospođica* is a narrative on premature greed, literally a narrative on *ill success* that the "minor pasts" seem to be predestined to if they dare to jump from the "immaturity" of *History 2* (Chakrabarty 2000: 101) towards the progressive narrative of *History 1*. Therefore, the questions that remain to be discussed in the final section of the paper read as follows: does Balzac possibly approve of Eugenia's 'apprenticeship' and admire her success? Does Andrić use the greedy heroine to show the misfortunes of *History 2* when it is thoroughly sublated into *History 1* and, thus, to possibly exert an anti-capitalist critique, as indicated above? In other words, does the chronicler of the years 1908, 1912, 1914, etc. assign Rajka's *ill success* to the "inferior" or "marginal" (Chakrabarty 2000: 101) position the academic historian's language is fond of?

4. Two histories of capital

In his article on the "uneven development on a world scale", John Weeks remarks that the transitions in the history of capitalist expansion are by and large dependent on and conditioned by the concomitant "development of capitalist social relations" (Weeks 2001: 27). Similarly, when discussing the preconditions for economic progress or belatedness, Donald J. Harris points to the "social environment" (2007: 6) as a "system of governance by the state, that sets and enforces the rules and norms, including property rights, governing conduct by firms", etc. (7). By employing an "extended framework of analysis" (8) that takes into account this uneven development, it becomes possible to argue that *Eugenia Grandet*, albeit a narrative on alienated, privatized life, is also a narrative on social, i.e. financial, success that was possible at a certain time and in a certain place. By way of contrast, *Gospođica* is a story of those who are "left behind" (8), the drop-outs and peripheral agents who, even if they succeed in 'catching up', are sort of predestined to be 'left behind', to remain doomed to the time of "not now" (Chakrabarty 2000: 9). Now, departing from Weeks' remark on the replacement of "feudal and semi-feudal social relations" by "the social relations of capital" (12), as was underway in countries such as Italy and Japan (which entered the European market only in the late 19th and early 20th century, 28), one may observe Bosnia and Serbia as similarly participating in the second wave of capitalist expansion. One should bear in mind the fact that the major problem of Bosnia and Serbia, that is, of the Kingdom of Yugoslavia (as it was for all new Balkan states after the end of WWI), was predominantly economic and not political, as is usually considered to be the case (cf. Jelavich and Jelavich 1977: 322; Kopsidis 2014). Especially when measured by Western standards, one cannot ignore the fact that "[f]rom their establishment the[se] states were not truly economically viable units on a modern level" (Jelavich and Jelavich 1977: 322; cf. Kopsidis

2014). The situation worsened in the years after WWI, when the financial sector developed rapidly and not necessarily for the benefit of the Balkan lands. Namely, the "sectors of the economy that enriched the investors and not necessarily the country itself were developed" (Jelavich and Jelavich 1977: 323). Charles and Barbara Jelavich, who point to this rarely considered fact, also stress the lack of experience with economic models of Western liberalism and its laissez-faire policy. Namely, the 'progressive' governments made no effort regarding matters such as health, education, extreme poverty, or debt (325). So if Balzac's France was the France of imperial rule and capitalist progression and Andrić's Bosnia the semi-colony of a dying empire, if Saumur was the province of Paris and Sarajevo the province of both Vienna and Belgrade, then it must come as a surprise that the rare literary analyses of *Gospođica* deal predominantly with the hybrid gender identity of the main protagonist and that they do not recognize its, historically speaking, double marginal position (Terzić 2009; cf. Thiergen 1995: 132-133, 136).

While for both novels it can be said that they display the "complex process of translation of diverse lifeworlds and conceptual horizons about being human into the categories of Enlightenment thought that inhere in the logic of capital" (Chakrabarty 2000: 71), it is only *Gospođica* that confronts the reader with disparities, fissures, and gaps that, first, open up between *History 1* and *History 2*, and second, between society and individuals who at an inopportune moment decide to stock up their savings and reduce spending. The "rough translation" (17) of the capitalist models from the *History 1* to *History 2* is best exemplified by Rajka's adherence to an American success story she hears through a newspaperman. An American millionaire allegedly said as follows: "The first million is the hardest, afterwards everything comes easy. It's only the man who doesn't want to be a millionaire who doesn't become one. You have to want to be" (71). Having only this million in mind, Rajka abandons herself neither to the political role of citizen nor to the social role of bourgeois, but to the will of the surrogate father, to a bare mimetic work of rapid enrichment via the American model.

Without considering the political and social context, one could read Rajka's growing avarice and social withdrawal as a final consequence of unsuccessful mourning for the father, whose idealized image leaves a melancholic trace in her hollow identity. But if one reads Andrić's narrative with regard to Sarajevo as a periphery that is, as Chakravarty says of India, "capable of living in several centuries at once" (49), then Rajka's misfortune corresponds to the city's marginal position in the world system of capitalist transitions and translations. If *Eugenia Grandet* thrives on a progressive, stable, and predictable set of institutions and social expectations, *Gospođica* is set against the backdrop of an inconsistent, perturberant, and unpredictable geographical space. Incapable of sustaining 'progress' institutionally and economically, this peripheral space produces monsters whose monstrosity turns out to be more outrageous than the monstrosity that persists in the centers.

Contrary to the time and space of post-revolutionary France, Sarajevo belonged to a land that had been under Ottoman rule for centuries. Modernization entered abruptly, enforcing new social stratifications, the establishment of foreign administration and harsh restrictions on the domestic economy. Not only after the Austrian colonization in 1878 or after the annexation in 1908, but throughout the entire 19th century, Bosnia and Herzegovina carried "an imprint of Austro-Hungarian imperial interests in the Balkans" (Redžić 1977: 307; cf. Rathberger 2009). The agricultural abundance of the land was used in the interests of the centers of the Empire (Vienna, Budapest) and not of the periphery. At the same time, much of the continental capital moved from more developed lands of the Empire to Bosnia and Herzegovina because of the possibility of high and extra high profit rates (Redžić 1977: 308). "These merchants conducted their business based on credit in a country which had not a single bank or credit institution" (Sugar 1963: 17). It follows that the "lack of capital" (17) remained one of the main problems for local merchants and the reason for their economic instability:

> Sarajevo in the year 1906! A city that was the contending ground of influences and overlapping cultures, one in which diverse modes of life and conflicting ideas clashed head-on! Yet all these various and distinctive classes, faiths, ethnic and social groups had one thing in common: all needed money, all needed more of it than they had. (*Gospodica* 54)

Therefore, Sarajevo is not a space of an imagined and mystified pre-capitalist community; undoubtedly, it partakes in the lifeworld of capital. Therefore, the withdrawal to a position of independence, of protection against the 'world' in which people improve their lot not "with work but with thrift" (22) proves to be impossible. That is why, being "an exception and a renegade" (117), Rajka is a kind of anachronism. Being still that old type of non-social miser and at the same time obtaining revenues from usury and the stock market, Rajka rejects both the traditional community of *History 2* (the one the miser cancels but that is, nevertheless, able to tolerate him/her) as well as the minimum of community of *History 1* (the utilitarian community of consumers). Disregarding any kind of "sacrifice" (Esposito 10) for the common good, she proves to be an isolated example of *History 2* that is, however, already colonized by the profit-driven logic of *History 1* and still averse to that minimum of 'community' *History 1* needs in order to constitute a modern capitalist society.

If narrations are understood as interventions in the preconfigured world that due to their potential for epistemological effect do not leave the reality unchanged, then one should examine Balzac's and Andrić's novels with regard to this potential for epistemological intervention. Namely, if narrations are understood as "linguistic articulations of changeability" (Koschorke 2012: 22) and if they may be seen as motors of change that "resolve the states into processes" (21), one should pose the question as to where and how this changeability is incorporated in literary texts. Are these novels something more than objective, scientifically disinterested studies on the 'soul of man under capitalism'?

Whereas Balzac has been characterized as a great portrayer of 19th-century capitalism, his aesthetic adherence to capitalist progress has seldom been subject to critical scrutiny. In a text on Balzac's *The Peasants*, György Lukács notices that in Balzac's eyes the Revolution of 1789, Napoleon's Empire, and the Restoration were "merely stages in the great, continuous and contradictory process of French evolution towards capitalism" (Lukács 1964: 40). Therein one may observe both the proverbial "azure skies" as well as "the mud and puddles of the road" (Stendhal 1969: 289). Although disenchanting, Eugenia Grandet's narrative follows a progressivist path in which the heroine undertakes a successful translation from her isolated childhood towards a profitable and socially acceptable life. Her history undoubtedly contains "mud and puddles" but it contains a fine sense of exorbitant progress as well.[29] This sympathy for progress distinguishes Balzac's narrative structure from Andrić's counter-narrative. While Eugenia's narrative focuses on years such as 1804 (the establishment of the progressive Napoleonic Code), or on purely 'private' years (1806, 1811, 1816, 1826) that are of little significance for history but are milestones of capitalist progression in the private timeline of Eugenia Grandet, Rajka's personal narrative is structured according to economic and political turbulence in local history. The narrator, who proceeds as a chronicler, relies on historical milestones that are anything but markers of stability: 1908 (the annexation of Bosnia), 1912 (the Balkan War), 1914 (the assassination of Archduke Franz Ferdinand), 1918 (the end of WWI), 1930 (the Great Depression), and 1935 (Rajka's death). Whereas Balzac has his heroine stably grow into the logic of political economy, Andrić's novel carries elements of the unexpected, stunning, and monstrous. Still, when considered in the context of the historical development of capitalism in Bosnia, Miss Radaković's monstrosity ceases to be inexplicable. It turns out to be an epitome of the "radicalization of Western ideas that liberates their destructive potential" (Moretti 2013: 168). If *Eugenia Grandet* is an homage to the advent of a new historical era in which the *superbia* of the miser is successfully sublated in the sociability of capital, then *Gospođica* is a critique of a miser's overriding of community. This, however, does not mean that Andrić's novel is necessarily an anti-capitalist narrativization of the resistance of *History 2* to *History 1*, of 'community' against 'society.' The overridden community is not an idealized '*ur*-community' but partly already that utilitarian economic community Keynes places at the core of his theory. Therefore,

---

29 In his discussion of Gobseck, Dolar compares Gobseck to Balzac himself: both occupy a position from where the "horrible truth" can be seen, from where they can penetrate into "people's hearts" and "provide the diagnosis of the society in question" (Dolar 2002: 197).

Gospođica is neither a study on the abstract, decontextualized sinfulness of a female heroine nor a story of resistance to History 1. Instead, it is a narrative on a somewhat excessively rapid and excessively rough translation of the 'pre-capitalist' into the 'capitalist', of the 'commonality of the community' into the 'communism of capital', of 'community' into 'society', and, finally, of a 'miser' into a 'usurer' – and this before the "development of capitalist social relations" (Weeks 1968: 27) is completed. Written from the perspective of the inexorability of economic and political translations, the novel depicts the anachronism of non-social miserliness in times when the communism of capital is already at the door, expecting from the socialized usurer befitting revenue.

Bibliography

Andrić, Ivo (1963) *Gospođica* [1945]. In: *Sabrana djela Ive Andrića*. Zagreb.
Andrić, Ivo (1965) *The Woman from Sarajevo*. Trans. Joseph Hitrec, London.
Arendt, Hannah (1958, 1998) *The Human Condition*. Chicago, London.
Bobbio, Norberto (1989) The Great Dichotomy: Public/Private. In: *Democracy and Dictatorship. The Nature and Limits of State Power*. Cambridge, 1-21.
Chakrabarty, Dipesh (2000) *Provincializing Europe: postcolonial thought and historical difference*. Princeton, NY.
de Balzac, Honoré (1878) *Eugenia Grandet; Or, The miser's daughter* [1833]. New York.
Dolar, Mladen (2002) *O skoposti. In o nekaterih z njo povezanih rečeh. Tema in variacije*. Ljubljana.
Hardt, Michael/Negri, Antonio (2000) *Empire*. London, Cambridge, MA.
Harris, Donald J. (2007) Uneven Development. In: *The New Palgrave Dictionary of Economics*. 2nd edition. London. URL: http://www-siepr.stanford.edu/workp/swp06007.pdf (retrieved July 23, 2019).
Hawkesworth, Celia (1984) *Ivo Andrić: Bridge between East and West*. London, Dover, NH.
Jandrić, Ljubo (1982) Sa Ivom Andrićem. Sarajevo.
Jelavich, Charles/Jelavich, Barbara (1977) *The Establishment of the Balkan National States, 1804-1920*. Seattle, London.
Keynes, John Maynard (1936, 1964) *The General Theory of Employment, Interest and Money*. San Diego, New York, London.
Kopsidis, Michael (2014) Bäuerliche Landwirtschaft und Agrarwachstum: Südosteuropa 1870-1940 im Licht moderner Entwicklungstheorie. In: *Jahrbuch Wirtschaftsgeschichte* 1: 65-92.
Koschorke, Albrecht (2012) *Wahrheit und Erfindung: Grundzüge einer allgemeinen Erzähltheorie*. Frankfurt a. M.

Lucey, Michael (2001) Legal Melancholy: Balzac's "Eugénie Grandet" and the Napoleonic Code. In: *Representations* 76(1), Fall: 1-26.

Lukács, György (1964) Balzac: The Peasants. In: *Studies in European Realism*. New York: 21-46.

Marazzi, Christian (2011) *Verbranntes Geld*. Translated by Thomas Atzert. Zurich.

Marx, Karl (1843, 1956, 1981) Zur Kritik der Hegelschen Rechtsphilosophie. Kritik des Hegelschen Staatsrechts. In: Marx, Karl/Engels, Friedrich: *Werke*. Vol. I. Berlin: 201-333.

Marx, Karl/Engels, Friedrich (1988) *Economic and Philosophic Manuscripts of 1844 and the Communist Manifesto*. Amherst, NY.

Moretti, Franco (1998) *Atlas of the European Novel 1800-1900*. London, New York.

Moretti, Franco (2013) *The Bourgeois. Between History and Literature*. London, New York.

Padua, Donatella (2014) *John Maynard Keynes and the Economy of Trust: The Relevance of the Keynesian Social Thought in a Global Society*. New York.

Pulcini, Elena (2001) *L'individuo senza passioni. Individualismo moderno e perdita del legame sociale*. Turin.

Rathberger, Andreas (2009) Balkanbilder. Vorstellungen und Klischees über den Balkan in der Habsburgermonarchie im 19. und frühen 20. Jahrhundert. In: *Kakanien revisited*. URL: http://www.kakanien-revisited.at/beitr/fallstudie/ARathberger1.pdf (retrieved July 23, 2019).

Redžić, Enver (1977) *Austromarksizam i jugoslavensko pitanje*. Belgrade.

Ross, Kristin (2008) *The Emergence of Social Space. Rimbaud and the Paris Commune*. London, New York.

Rost, Norbert (2008): Der Homo Oeconomicus – Eine Fiktion der Standardökonomie. In: *Zeitschrift für Sozialökonomie* 45: 50-58.

Schor, Naomi (1985) Eugénie Grandet: Mirrors and Melancholia. In: *Breaking the Chain: Women, Theory, and French Realist Fiction*. New York: 90-107.

Shakespeare, William (2006) *The Merchant of Venice*. New Haven, London.

Stendhal [Henri-Marie Beyle] (1969) *Red and Black*. Translated by Robert M. Adams. New York.

Sugar, Peter F. (1963) *Industrialization of Bosnia-Hercegovina 1878-1918*. Seattle.

Terzić, Ajla (2009) Andrićeva Gospođica – netipičan ženski lik ili nešto kao moderna vještica. In: *Motrišta* 45-46: 78-87.

Thiergen, Peter (1995) Ivo Andrićs Roman Gospođica: Psychologie, Symbolik, Textvergleich. In: Thiergen, Peter (ed.) *Ivo Andrić 1892-1992. Beiträge des Zentenarsymposions an der Otto-Friedrich-Universität Bamberg* [Vorträge und Abhandlungen zur Slavistik. Bd. 25] Munich: 131-155.

Vogl, Joseph (2004) *Kalkül und Leidenschaft – Poetik des ökonomischen Menschen*. Zurich et al.

Vollrath, Ernst (1987) *Grundlegung einer philosophischen Theorie des Politischen.* Würzburg.

Weeks, John (2001) The Expansion of Capital and Uneven Development on a World Scale. In: *Capital & Class* 25(2): 9-30.

The Socialist Robber-Baron as a Superfluous Man
Derviš Sušić's Novel *I, Danilo*

Andrea Lešić

> I, Danilo Lisičić,
> A citizen of this country and of the United Nations, occupation: manager at your disposal, have found myself suddenly at the bottom of my career spiral. I am not Sisyphus, and I do not carry the obligations of the myth and the symbol that people have bestowed upon that poor man. I am an ordinary mortal who's crashed from the top of his biographical minaret onto the cobblestones. And remained alone, weakened, old and tired, personally removed from office, materially naked.

The passage quoted above marks the beginning and the end of the first part of the novel by Derviš Sušić *I, Danilo*, and frames the part of the novel on which this chapter will mainly, although not exclusively, focus.[1] The stylistic exuberance with which the novel begins continues throughout the text, and some of my discussion will be dedicated to its stylistic features, particularly where economic terminology takes over as the main reference point for the protagonist's understanding of the world. The second aspect of the novel under discussion will be that of the plot, of the trials and tribulations of the socialist entrepreneur, as embodied in the novel's main character and narrator Danilo Lisičić. The discussion of the second aspect will take into account the interpretative lens through which the novel has been seen in the critical literature, construing the hero as a modern, Yugoslav and Socialist version of the Russian literary archetype of the "superfluous man". As the parallels with the Russian tradition are largely left implicit in the critical reception of Sušić's novel, serving as a kind of interpretative short-hand, the aptness of the comparison is mostly insufficiently discussed, and I shall aim to show that this has also meant that the specificities of the hero's circumstances and the nature of his actions and characterisation have not received the attention they are due. In addition to this,

---

[1] The novel was initially published in two parts; the first part, entitled *Ja, Danilo* (I, Danilo), was published in 1960 (Belgrade: Beletra), the second part, entitled *Danilo u stavu mirno* (Danilo at Ease) was published in 1961 (Sarajevo: Veselin Masleša). All subsequent editions that I have consulted have incorporated the two parts into one novelistic whole, dispensing even with the titles for the two parts of the novel.

and via Gheith's (1996) discussion of the link between the "superfluous man" and the "necessary woman" in the Russian literary tradition, I shall also briefly analyse the ways in which Sušić's novel lays bare the predicament of Partisan women in the post-war period, and the failure of the new Communist society to transform itself out of the old patriarchal gender relations and to make full use of the abilities of its women in the new economy.

The two aspects of the novel, the stylistic exuberance of the narration and the deceptively sparse construction of the plot, are in a strange tension throughout the text, and it can even be said that the former obscures the latter; particularly as the latter is predicated on some fairly complex economic shenanigans of the hero. My aim will be to show how the two are related, and in what ways they shed light upon one another and on the novel's representation of the early economic development of socialist Bosnia-Herzegovina and Yugoslavia in the years after World War II.

The story told in the novel is, at first glance, fairly simple: it begins immediately after the war, when the Communist and Partisan Danilo Lisičić returns to his birthplace of Labudovac in eastern Bosnia. His wartime reputation impeccable, and his political dedication to the Communist cause sincere and authentic, Danilo finds himself at the centre of the new Communist government's efforts to rebuild and modernise the country. War-weary and reluctant at first, as well as fully aware of the wartime machinations and post-war hypocrisy of many of his Labudovac neighbours, he at first struggles to define what his new purpose in life could be, and then, realising that he could either become an idle "peasant ass" who would "poison himself with hatred and vanity" or follow the wartime logic of serving the higher cause, he decides to make himself available for whatever purposes the new authorities see him fit (Sušić 1984: 24). When put under pressure to follow his superiors' plans and orders, particularly where it comes to trade, Danilo discovers his own abilities, and decides to use his self-proclaimed "peasant cunning" and talent for reading people to better the life of his neighbours, regardless of whether they deserve it or, indeed, desire it. Casting aside any personal desire for a comfortable life or for personal relationships, he throws himself into altruistically motivated wheeling and dealing, and into turning a backward village into a modern little town with a large school, new housing, a sawmill, a freight company, and a growing population. As the initial hectic and unruly period of rebuilding and rapid growth becomes replaced by the authorities' demand for order and accountability, Danilo's rule-breaking and willingness to bamboozle anyone he deems to be fair game in his determination to make Labudovac an example of socialist progress come to be seen as problematic, causing a heated argument with a newly appointed president of the County Council, which costs Danilo his position in Labudovac, as well as his membership of the Communist Party. Transferred to another town, and subjected to compulsory and indefinite sick leave, designed to prevent him from doing anything too ambitious in his new environment, Danilo reorients himself towards fatherhood and family life, as he adopts a son of a fellow Partisan who was killed in the war, and marries a woman whom he knew as a nurse in his Partisan unit. The novel ends with Danilo's despair at the revelation that the position of the director of the wood processing factory, which would have finally ended the period of idleness in his life and given him a chance to direct his energies into socially useful work again, is due to his wife's pestering of the local authorities, with what appears to be heart failure caused by disappointment and a loss of faith in the new society, and with his final breath.

The relatively simple central plot of the novel is turned into a vastly more complex text through its stylistic richness and the arabesque employment of a large ensemble of characters and a multitude of episodes, all of which are characterised by richly observed detail and a witty and engaging manner of narration. This narrative and stylistic generosity of spirit seems to produce in its readers a similar effect that Danilo's gift of the gab has on the characters he tries (mostly successfully) to talk into all sorts of economic schemes. Seemingly seduced by Danilo's narrative voice, critical reception of the novel has mostly followed a pattern of interpretation which implicitly links Sušić's hero with the archetype of the "superfluous man" in the Russian literary tradition. As Jehanne Gheith (1996) explains in her inspiring article on "superfluous men" and "necessary women" in Russian literature (to which I shall later return, when we come to some of the female characters in Sušić's novel):

> The superfluous man, variously understood and interpreted, has long been one of the most familiar characters in nineteenth-century Russian literature. He is a "type" as much constructed by critics as by authors of belles lettres, and represents an important cultural category in Russia, that of the dispossessed intellectual; he has commonly been seen as the representative of a generation of liberals, "a man of the forties." Though he has clear affinities to characters and ideas in French and German Romantic literature, the superfluous man was made into a cultural icon, a figure for a peculiarly Russian phenomenon: the desire for reform on the societal and personal level, matched by an incapacity for taking effective action. This incapacity or apathy was largely attributed to Russian social and mental structures that blocked the expression of creative, reforming energies. And so, the superfluous man's alienation from society could be regarded as a positive attribute, a confirmation of his inner nobility; if society could not accept him, so much the worse for society. (Gheith 1996: 229-230)

However, as Gheith notes, the basic type is hugely complicated by the range of characters which have been associated with it:

> It is difficult to pinpoint the moment when the "superfluous man" became important in Russian society and letters, but it is generally considered that Ivan Turgenev brought the term into wide usage with the publication of his 1850 work

> *Dnevnik lishnego cheloveka*. It is clear, however, that the concept existed earlier, for Pushkin used the term in a cancelled draft of Evgenii Onegin. The label has used to describe a wide range of characters including Chatskii, Onegin, Pechorin, Chulkaturin, Bazarov and Oblomov.
>
> Given the broad spectrum of characters subsumed by the term "superfluous man," it is difficult, perhaps impossible, to define conclusively the nature of superfluity, though critics from Dobroliubov in 1859 to Ellen Chances in 1978 have described various schema for grouping these characters under one rubric. In my view, the very flexibility of the concept is important; it can be variously used and understood, and its resistance to sharp delineation allows for an ever-widening circle of interpretation. It is perhaps even detrimental to attempt a strict definition of this motif as it represents a moment, an attitude, a fluctuating mode in Russian literature and culture. Superfluous men represented, among other things, varying forms of opposition, but the specific contours of this opposition shifted with the times changing political developments. (Gheith 1996: 230)

It is clear from the very list of characters associated with the term that the superfluity can range from an unusual proclivity to action (of both an intellectual and an adventurous type, as in, say, Bazarov, on the one hand, and Pechorin, on the other) and an excessive proclivity to inaction (as in Oblomov, Goncharov's eponymous hero of who, famously, spends the first quarter of the novel unwilling to leave his bed). The wide range of possible meanings leaves a great deal of scope for comparisons with various literary works, Sušić's novel included, but the difficulty lies in this particular novel's subtle reworking of the type, and in the attention to the fine detail of its hero's economic adventures that mark him as a completely different kind of beast to the previous tradition. Moreover, the "superfluous man", as far I could tell, is never explicitly stated as a point of comparison, but is visible in the rhetorical strategies with which critics have dealt with Danilo Lisičić's predicament in the context of the early development of the socialist Bosnia-Herzegovina in the post-World War II years. For example, Enes Duraković characterises Sušić's hero thus:

> Impatient, crafty and entrepreneurial, but enclosed within the slopes of his native Labudovac, Danilo upon his return from the Partisans is unable to rest in comfort, whilst waiting for somebody else to remember his backwater; instead, he takes it upon himself to realise his own vision of the "People's Justice and State". His conflict with the social environment flows from his irrepressible urge to act and to create, and the impossibility of channelling that abundant energy into effective action in the environment steeped in lethargic somnambulance. Driven by this greedy strength, Danilo frequently "takes a wrong turn", and the force of the stream starts flowing outside of the river bed of the official policies, which, natu-

rally, show a lack of understanding for the unbroken freshness of Lisičić's efforts and his actions. (Duraković 1985/1998: 533)

I shall return later to Danilo's concrete activities which are hidden behind Duraković's metaphorical formulations on flows of irrepressible energy and its river beds; the vagueness of its rhetorical flourishes is, however, fairly typical of most discussions of the novel. Risto Trifković, for example, sums up the work as follows (and I am afraid that my translation into English will not do justice to the stylistic extravagance of the original):

> A comedian, a jolly fellow, a typical Bosnia-dwelling Don Quixote of our Partisan adventures and situations, Lisičić is a protagonist of the Partisan narrative transplanted into contemporary social conditions. Inevitably, a conflict follows: between the subjective and the objective, the situation as it is and the situation as it follows. Danilo is a victim. Sušić is emotionally on his side, on the side of this warrior of the Ćopić kind. The novel (I, Danilo) is all askew, steeped in a mocking optics of an ossified structure which gains a bureaucraticised form of an inviolability of a free, somewhat bandit-like and neurotic logic which pays no attention to any other kind of order but its own, ideal one, which has a tendency to turn into a likeable disorder, into critique and rebellion. In essence, Danilo is an openhearted, great man, and because of that unsuited to reality. Sometimes even small things can triumph over a man. [...] He is somehow always alone, likeably alone. On the other side is the obedient and submissive majority. And loners and those who are alone have a well-known destiny. They become lone wolves, dreamers, fantasists or tragic enthusiastic individuals who do not belong to the real world. (Trifković 1974/1998: 527)

If we combine Duraković and Trifković's takes on the hero of Sušić's novel, he somehow becomes Evgeny Onegin, Bazarov and Pechorin all rolled into one, with a generous sprinkling of Branko Ćopić's Nikoletina Bursać and Cervantes's Don Quixote added to them. Enver Kazaz, however, also seems to add some Kafkaesque critique of bureaucracy and a veiled demand for Kunderaesque critique of communism to this already heady mix:

> The individual who from the heights of his faith in the revolution crashed "to the bottom of his career spiral" [...] reveals, in fact, the crack between the promised, proclaimed value system and the social reality. It is paradoxical, but this individual still believes in Communist ideology; even though reality has disappointed and denied him, he criticises and mocks, but he does not dispute revolutionary principles, moreover: in the name of those principles he undertakes his futile humorous and critical action. (Kazaz 2004: 244)

Again, we shall shortly return to what that "futile act" was; further on, Kazaz continues:

> The deformation of that [revolutionary] ethics is the main object of Sušić's laughter, with both novels reaching their aesthetic heights only in those moments when the story reveals the lack of balance between human nature and the revolutionary dogma with its radically formulated ethics. The radicalism of the revolutionary ethical demands and human nature which spills over its edges produce situations of discord and misunderstanding in which Sušić's disappointed, yet humorous hero reveals the deeper, essential discord based on the discrepancy between the social bureaucraticised praxis and the revolutionary idea. (Kazaz 2004: 245)

Kazaz places Sušić's novel in the tradition of those literary works which criticised the dark side of the revolution, noting that it refrains from "touching on the essence of its totalitarianism, the horror of its camps, political oppression, the absurdity of its dogma", which would later be fully developed themes in Yugoslav literature, but remains interested on a more superficial level in the "conflict between the revolutionary worker who still believes in his mission and the bureaucratic practice which degrades that mission" (Kazaz 2004: 245).

Although Kazaz's take on the novel subjects it to stronger critical demands, and slants its interpretation towards much darker tones, interpreting it as a critique of the degradation of revolutionary ideals with mechanical bureaucratic practices, the basic idea that the hero is in conflict with a society into which he cannot fully fit, and which ultimately disappoints him, is a variation on the theme of the superfluous man. The notion that Danilo Lisičić is a revolutionary in conflict with the bureaucracy of the new socialist state is also highlighted in Hasnija Muratagić-Tuna's brief review of the critical literature on Sušić's novel:

> The writer wisely chose Danilo Lisičić – one of the first Partisans, a distinguished warrior, manager and man of heroic stance in battle – as a critic of social deviations. The criticism is, therefore, formulated by "a man of special qualities for whom the country's progress and building socialism were close to his heart. He is a warrior who has no illusions about the difficulties of socialist development, but who is determined to correct the mistakes and failures of the new society",[2] that is, bureaucracy, which was still neither very strong nor widespread. Danilo Lisičić, on the writer's behalf, criticises society in satirical form. He is an equal interlocutor, well matched to social developments. Danilo's fall from his position and his loss of Communist Party membership are the result of his conflict with bureaucracy. Danilo is not just a critic, he is also a humane man, willing to help others, to make

---

2 Muratagić-Tuna is quoting: Cvijetić, Ljubomir (1983) *O romanu Ja, Danilo Derviša Sušića*, Predgovor u romanu *Ja Danilo*. Sarajevo: 22.

sacrifices for others, whilst giving up his own interests. That is why he remains "a bright example of a true fighter for the humanisation of human relations in the fight against bureaucracy, regardless of his methods, which are, in essence, also bureaucratic."[3] Danilo dreams, fairly and honestly, about the progress and prosperity of Labudovac, and he subjects everything to this dream. He marches into a future time, although he is dissatisfied with the present, and thus the novel radiates optimism. "Unrestrained optimism and joy that emanates from his work brings us closer to healing than to new wounds [...]."[4] The optimism and activity of Danilo Lisičić stem from his faith in the possibilities of the man of the new age. (Muratagić-Tuna 2012: 358-359)

Of course, it is clear that the views expressed by Muratagić-Tuna and the critics she quotes are nowhere close to Kazaz's interpretation of the novel, which sees in it not a light-hearted critique of a light-hearted bureaucracy, but an indictment of a "dehumanised machine which feeds itself on human contents for the sake of an alleged higher purpose" (Kazaz 2004: 246). Kazaz summarises his view of the novel in the following manner:

> Organised as a mosaic-like series of anecdotes in which a mild joke and a humorous game become bitter irony and sharp satire in line with the change of the focus of the story, from a description of events to a humorous commentary or a satirically intoned ideological analysis, the novels about Danilo Lisičić paint the picture of provincial Bosnian society after the Second World War, within which there is a conflict between the habitual inert mentality with the ideologically led demands of revolutionary action, in order for the latter, in its clash with creative abilities, to reveal itself as an empty value system turned into a bureaucratic norm. (Kazaz 2007: 247)

As we can see, there are a large number of abstract nouns battling it out on Bosnian literary soil in this account of Sušić's novel, and what I shall attempt to do next is peel back the seductive "mosaic-like series of anecdotes", with its vast range of humorous effects, to reveal the basic plot of the first half of the novel (or, if we take the original publication into account, in the first novel).

So what happens in the part of the novel that begins and ends with the quotation with which I started this essay? I have already outlined the basic plot, and that first half ends the moment Danilo loses his Party membership and his position in Labudovac; however, it is now quite important to pay attention to the details,

---

3 Muratagić-Tuna is quoting: Cvijetić, Ljubomir (1983) *O romanu Ja, Danilo Derviša Sušića*, Predgovor u romanu *Ja Danilo*. Sarajevo: 25.
4 Muratagić-Tuna is quoting: Ivan Fogl (1961) Danilo u stavu mirno ili mogući razlozi uništenja žeđi za životom. In: *Život*, 10-11.

not of the witty verbal games and humorous asides and comic portraits and satirical flourishes, but of the actual things that Danilo does to turn Labudovac into an industrial town with all the mod cons for its inhabitants.

The first thing to note is the chaos of the post-war social and economic order, at the micro-level on which Danilo, who is, by his own admission, a fairly uneducated peasant, is actually operating. He is roped in to do things for the county ("srez"; a unit of administrative organisation at the time, one level above the municipality, which was as the smallest), simply because he is around, has shown himself willing, and is considered politically and ideologically trustworthy. He is given the instruction to organise a local co-operative ("zadruga") in his village (Sušić 1984: 34), but that is as far as that instruction goes; he is more or less allowed to work out his duties for himself (apart from having to accompany the local secretary of the Communist Party Committee on his mission to win over any "reactionary elements" lurking in the surrounding villages). He starts out by opening a shop and filling it with everything from agricultural implements to silk stockings (which his then girlfriend and fellow former Partisan Jovanka buys on credit and hands out to local war widows; exactly the kind of delightful and suggestive small detail that can distract the reader from the bigger picture); the shop-keeper he employs in it is the son of a recently deceased local merchant, who immediately starts showing his mercantile flair by both buttering up his customers and cheating them of a tenth of the measure (Sušić 1984: 35). Three officials turn up in front of the shop with a polite written request from a federal minister (it is part of the narrative strategy to be imprecise when it comes to specific titles and job descriptions) for assistance with buying out walnut tree stumps. A much more brusque and laconic note from the secretary of the county governing board was added, which Danilo interprets as an order that this be done at all costs and within a week (Sušić 1984: 37). He sweet-talks the officials and gets them well fed and drunk in the local inn. Then, once they have been effectively put to bed, he sets out on what he calls "a silent class war" which is waged throughout the night. Highly talkative and very willing to describe details of all that happens around him, Danilo reduces the story of the tree stump venture to a very basic and almost unashamedly shifty account:

> I hoodwinked the authorities into giving me some sort of decree on the requisition of tree stumps, gathered three policemen, and went from door to door. Pre-war landowners, who kept their stumps waiting for "the third thing" to sell them, hadn't been expecting an offensive.
>
> All through the night carts creaked and the three trucks that happened to be in the village roared. Twenty members of the Communist Youth did the job faster than two hundred dozy hired hands could have done. I dare not list all the things that happened that night.

At ten in the morning in the church yard the tree stumps lay like peaceful fat oxen, ready to be sold. (Sušić 1984: 42)

To sum up the events even further: Danilo turns the request for a buyout into a requisition, and handles it as a police raid, dragging people out of their beds and probably keeping the whole village and the surrounding countryside awake all night. The amount he receives for his effort is "eight times greater than expected" (Sušić 1984: 42), and the money is stashed away at the police station, under the commissioner's straw mattress, to be used another day.

The reference to "pre-war landowners", however, soon receives further clarification, as on the next page Danilo explains the disparity between the concrete socio-economic conditions of his native village and the Communist theory of class relations:

> I had learned about class war, but there's not a single landowner in my municipality with more than twenty sheep or a pair of horses. When I want to raise my hand to wave away, to forgive the populace of the municipality its class sins, my hand stays itself: wait! Are there so few heads here that shelter that greedy beast, ready to hack its brother to pieces with an axe for a dry plum tree, for a foot of garden fence? And who among these, so convoluted and incomplete in class terms, would refuse if tomorrow they were to be offered two thousand hectares of plough land and a dozen servants? What is to be done to keep the pure landowner in today's pauper tightly leashed? Except for the agrarian maximum? And how can we lead them by the hand, innocent as a bloodthirsty ferret, into the empire of a real feeling for common property? Coercion won't solve this. And kind words can easily become fairy tales and hokum. (Sušić 1984: 43)

However, the complexities of the situation on the ground also imply a certain amount of chaos in which further deals can be made, not unlike the tree stump scheme. Even though the administration begins to tighten up, hinting at "something which has been carefully thought through", the preceding disorder means that the changes primarily involve literate official letters (as opposed to those that read something like: "Give Jovo twenty kilos grain how's things what ya all up to we all fine death to fascism Radiša") and the introduction of banking instead of carrying money from Sarajevo to the countryside in sacks. However, as Danilo notes, the bank director had completed only four grades of elementary school, and there are still some ways to divert money from its official purposes into Labudovac and into Danilo's ventures for the good of his unworthy fellow villagers (Sušić 1984: 45). The idea he comes up with is a fantasy orchard-planting scheme, which would provide him with an agricultural subvention to be used as starting capital for industrial development. He represents Labudovac as having the "same conditions for fruit growing as California" (Sušić 1984: 47), manages to get a large portion of the county's agricultural subsidies for orchards allocated to the village, and then sets to work:

> The county gave me millions to build a fruit farm. I intended that money for something completely different. By God, there's plenty of time for fruit. Whoever feels the need for vitamin C can get as much of it as he wants in the pharmacy. Still, I fenced off an expropriated field and planted a few seedlings. Who knows, that might come in handy. A comrade could turn up and ask: where is your fruit farming development? There's the fruit farming development! [...] It's spring. Electrification and industrialisation roar away somewhere in the distance. And I am suffering from a strange industrial itch. If we have laid down the rule that the countryside should come last in our plans, then, comrades, let's not disrupt the old exception principle. Why should Labudovac not be the exception to that rule? [...] What I want are machines which would start making money with their first rattle. So that I can then let myself loose, and show how one can build a socialist town out of this capitalist village! [...] After I tried several times to turn around all the possibilities for acquiring new money, except for those orchards, and couldn't find a single dinar, I decided to try to get things together without money. The dinar is a mediator between the goods and the needs. Let us try to do without that mediator, or with its minimal contribution! [...] In other words: instead of paying two million, let's pay twenty thousand. And let's fill the rest in with other human values, such as, for instance, my kind words, and the other guy's comradely lack of attention. (Sušić 1984: 51-53)

The way his plan is explained to the reader is as convoluted and seductive as the tree stump story. He tells us he is in Belgrade, performs yet more rhetorical acrobatics on the subject of the relationship between the capital city and the rural provinces, and casually informs us that the Sarajevo part of the plan had already panned out: that there was a poverty-ridden village in Eastern Bosnia which was supposed to be given a sawmill, but they did not have the small sum needed to contribute to the costs; Danilo, however, did, and he was given the main portion of the necessary equipment. The trip to Belgrade really serves to provide him with extras for his little industrial venture; a reader more fully versed in mechanical engineering than I am would be able to tell just how much more he needed on the basis of what he had already received, but the way he puts it makes it clear enough: "I got a tray of baklava. And now I needed Belgrade to give me some spices to sprinkle on top" (Sušić 1984: 54).

He sets out his impressions of Belgrade, both fortifying himself and dazzling the reader with yet more rhetorical flourishes, making it clear that his plan for obtaining the capital to provide him with "spices" is, effectively, to sniff out possibilities and to improvise as opportunities present themselves. There is a distinct sense of adventure and excitement he gets from the buzz of the post-war and politically transitioning city, even as he spells out that he is a country boy at heart. The story he tells of how he marched into a ministry, of the administrative chaos that allowed him to just walk into an office of a commissioner, sell himself as a dumb Bosnian to his surprisingly elegant secretary, and, upon realising that there are greater chances to obtain aid if he pretends to be from Serbia, suddenly change his accent and demeanour in front of the commissioner himself, is full of wit and vigour. Yet it should not distract us from the fact that his little venture is a swindle from the beginning to the end (ending as it does with the staged break down of one of the trucks used to haul the machines obtained in Belgrade to Labudovac; after the "lost" parts have been replaced and the truck itself repainted, said truck is put to use in the "merry service of the homeland within the borders of the Labudovac municipality") (Sušić 1984: 57-66). Once it has been built with less than enthusiastic local labour, the help of a chronically drunk technician and some self-taught mechanics Danilo had "picked up on the road" (Sušić 1984: 72), the sawmill itself stops working half an hour after the ceremonial opening (because the drunken technician falls and cuts the water off, for which he receives a dismissal in the form of a "boot up his behind"). After being restarted, the sawmill proudly "belches up white and grey smoke from its metal chimney, which was prevented from falling down by means of some ropes and wires" (Sušić 1984: 74).

Every other economic venture of Danilo's is equally suspect and equally amusingly and seductively told; there is the story of the rotten chestnuts which he buys, sight unseen, in a drunken haze, and which he manages to sell to somebody else on the Sarajevo black market, whilst making sure that the authorities find out about the identity of his buyers (Sušić 1984: 103-109); the story of his offering an administrative position in the *zadruga* to a young woman he met in Sarajevo by accident, on the basis that she is pretty, literate, fairly cultured and could potentially have a compromised past which would make her doubly loyal to him after he has given her his confidence (although he turns out to have been right about her ability to do the job, the real reasons behind her hiring are revealed by his heroic attempts to resist her flirtation throughout their dealings with each other, for as long as he is her superior; he eventually does give in to their mutual attraction after his position changes) (Sušić 1984: 82-85; and 160); the story of a business trip to Sarajevo during which he "swindled the Ministry" and received a lot more than Labudovac was due, planning in advance to cut double the amount of forest than his permit allowed, "by mistake, of course", and thus earn a lot more money (Sušić 1984: 82); the story of how he returns to Belgrade to "punish" a large civil engineering corporation, which is wasting money and ruining its machinery with bad practice, by talking them into selling him their old equipment, for which he has no intention to pay (Sušić 1984: 118-120). This last scheme creates the Labudovac construction company, but it also sees him in court, as the company sues him for not fulfilling his side of the contract. Even then, he manages to talk himself out of the consciously created and quite serious legal trouble, by guessing correctly that the presiding judge on the council will be emotionally and ideologically susceptible to his story of the wartime heroism of the Partisans (in which he includes the judge himself, although it is quite clear that the man was a pre-war salon socialist who was never an active fighter) and of the need to deliver Bosnian villages, chronically poor and ravaged by the war, into communist paradise by any means necessary. His opening words ("Brothers and comrades!"), purposefully chosen for their inappropriateness in a courtroom, are, as he puts it, delivered with the tragic tone of a man "informing investors of the death of the National Bank of the Federative People's Republic of Yugoslavia", and are followed with a great deal of rhetoric full of pathos, appealing to the Belgrade judge's sentimental regard for the "simple folk" (Sušić 1984: 126). Even though Danilo is, legally speaking, obviously in the wrong, the judges decide that his *zadruga* should pay a minimal fine, and surrender the machines to the ownership of the initial corporation, but on the spot where they stood at the time of the ruling (which effectively means they remain where they are) (Sušić 1984: 124-130). After the trial, in a conversation with the corporation's lawyer, who is bewildered by the loss of the case, which seemed absolutely straightforward, Danilo ascribes his legal victory to his peasant's cunning, and wishes him "never again to come up against a descendant of the peasants who, in the absence of Austro-Hungary, cheat their own mothers, for whom they are otherwise ready to lay down their lives" (Sušić 1984: 130). Upon returning to Labudovac, Danilo is greeted as a hero (Sušić 1984: 130-131), but promptly returns to his one room above the local inn and to his solitude; what is subtly underlined throughout the narrative of his tricks and schemes is the fact that he does not take any of the proceeds for himself personally, nor seek any comfort, but, instead, uses all his gains to develop Labudovac's industry.

There is nothing here that points to some inhumane bureaucratic machine stifling the idealistic revolutionary; what we have instead is a socially-minded and ascetically inclined robber-baron who knowingly uses the possibilities opened up by insufficient administrative order to further his altruistic industrial ambitions. It is a very unusual motivation for a literary character, and a rather singular plot logic for a novel, especially when we also take into account the way that the plot is buried under the rhetorical fireworks with which Danilo blinds both the reader and all the characters surrounding him. As Danilo uses his gift of the gab to con the various officials and superiors into giving him what he needs for the development of Labudovac, his seductively talkative, both stylistically exuberant and emotionally honest narration obscures the nature of the deeds he relates. He is neither a romantic dreamer nor a man of action confronted by an excessive bureaucracy; if we feel for him, it is because he has conned us into believing in him, the way he has conned everyone he has met. The chaos he leaves behind through his unchecked need to create rapid progress is not a good chaos, and it is the same chaos that allows the various inept characters to occupy positions of authority or power in the world depicted in the novel.

His fall, however, comes soon after his position in the rapidly growing little town becomes less central. He notices that children are not greeting him when they meet him, and that more and more things are happening in Labudovac that do not require his input and approval; he sees it as a sign that he has succeeded in his aims, and that Labudovac has become what he wanted it to be (Sušić 1984: 132). After the "reorganisation" takes the sawmill, the construction company and the trucking business out of his hands, appointing "a tailor, a registrar, and a former priest" as the new directors of those enterprises, he even tolerates their immediate and crude attempts to take advantage of their new positions, commenting only that "they don't know even how to steal" (Sušić 1984: 134). What he finds much more intolerable is the sense of purposelessness, now that he has managed to create "a socialist town out of the capitalist village". Although the novel is not very clear on the passage of time, it does indicate – based on the years since Jovanka and Danilo ended their relationship – that it took some six years since the building of the sawmill for Labudovac to come this far (Sušić 1984: 143); another number Danilo mentions in passing is 11 years, but that could refer to the period that includes his time with the Partisans in the war (Sušić 1984: 135). Whichever it is, the achievement is impressive; however, its very haste also points to the problems that will bring about Danilo's downfall.

After the economic reorganisation takes most of Labudovac's economic activity out of his hands, the next big change is political and administrative (at long last): the arrival of a new president of the county council. Danilo describes his first attendance of the council meeting as follows:

> He sat like an ordinary citizen who sits at the table and listens. But I concluded that this was a fellow far superior to the rest of us, that he remembers, sees, and hears everything, that he's making conclusions, comparing, checking the speakers against some unknown reports that he has read. This buddy knows what he knows and it is certain that at one fine day's meeting he will carefully, calmly, slowly, yet firmly, and at the same time unrelentingly implement what he wants. He belonged to that class of thin and slow people whose gaze is made of icy steel, and whose every movement, glance and blink of an eye are perfectly controlled by the inner omnipotent boss: his brain. (Sušić 1984: 145)

Here, finally, we have someone to a certain extent resembling the image of the bureaucratic machine that several analyses of the novel mention. However, it is hard to conclude that he is entirely in the wrong when he gives his instructions at the end of that first meeting:

Comrades, the economy and the politics in your county are the same as you are. I shall not allow anyone to attend the next meeting without a tidy suit, a clean shirt and a neat tie. The war ended more than a decade ago. This is the county's parliament, and not a village get-together. I propose to have the secretary sanctioned for not preparing the meeting properly by deducting twenty percent from his pay. Next time, I want the room spotlessly clean, all the paperwork neatly typed out in front of every councillor, and all councillors on their seats a minute before the meeting. Also, no smoking during the meeting, since this is not an assembly of sailors from the October Revolution. (Sušić 1984: 145)

Danilo, along with everybody else, wonders "what's comrade going to say about the budget when he's this strict regarding suits and smoking!"; moreover, the fact that everyone is talking about his careful combing through the accounts of all the county companies (causing directors to "enter his office with rosy cheeks, and leave looking green") does not bode well. The catastrophe for Danilo comes about that very evening, as the new president summons him, with the warning that he should be ready for a long discussion.

The discussion that takes place that evening is probably the central point on which critics like Enver Kazaz base their interpretations of the novel as depicting idealistic humanity against dry bureaucracy. The new president of the county council is portrayed by Danilo as being "one of those people" whom he had "recently noticed quietly infiltrating the communes" who are "taciturn, icy and resolute", "capable of fine-tuning the bulkiest *kombinat* and making it march to the beat of the law", who "respect order more than they respect abstract consciousness", who "hate noise and large gestures and are faster to forgive snobbism than anarchy", and who "will implement Swedish order" while "somebody else will have to apply Yugoslav love" (Sušić 1984: 147-148). At the start, the president also rebukes Danilo for coming to the meeting unwashed, unshaven and without a suit, pointing out that his "inner purity is made dirty with outward primitivism". However, the main thrust of his criticism is directed at huge financial malfeasances in the *zadruga*, of which Danilo has informed his readers from the start of the novel. He also points out that the fast growth in Labudovac is "nothing to boast about", as the town is like "a cabin thrown together using an axe", with toilets in outhouses, and that a good part of it will need to be demolished because of the new town planning. Money was wasted, because Danilo was suspicious when it came to experts, and because he wanted to do everything himself; the paperwork contains many forgeries, signed in his own hand (Sušić 1984: 148-149). All of this the reader knew, or should have known, or suspected: that chimney on the sawmill, propped up and held together with ropes and wires, should have been, even taken on its own, a clear indication of how dubious Danilo's industrial achievements were from the beginning. The discussion as represented by Danilo is by the very virtue of the fact that it is represented by him skewed towards his point of view on the matter. However, even though the president is presented as "poisoning [Danilo] with his eyes" and being deserving of his hate (Sušić 1984: 148), once we take his words (and his actions) away from Danilo's point of view, there is nothing he says that seems either disrespectful towards Danilo or particularly unfair to him. The president points out that the *zadruga*, thanks to Danilo's leadership, owes one hundred and sixteen million dinars to "others", and that that money needs to be paid back (Sušić 1984: 150). He acknowledges that Danilo is "capable", that he "could have built wonderful things had there been a firm hand" to keep him in check, and that he "wouldn't exchange him for a hundred others" (Sušić 1984: 149), but that now Danilo needs to wash, shave, dress appropriately and give up the absolute power he had over Labudovac, by being transferred "into town", and by having his "primitivism" driven out of him by being made into an "executive", rather than a mastermind of all progress (Sušić 1984: 150). We, as readers, have known from the beginning that the things Danilo is doing are both morally and legally problematic, and it is a sign of the president's benevolence towards him that he is giving him a second chance, and not delivering the dossier of his misdeeds to a prosecutor. Danilo himself, however, reacts first with "unstoppable hot tears", and then with rage, and a fiery "Where were you when we starved and struggled?" speech, which finally results in the reason for the downfall alluded to in the quotation which opened this chapter: Danilo slaps the president, and ends up being stripped of his Communist Party membership (with an open option to regain it at some later date) and transferred out of Labudovac. As bitter as this exile is, later in the novel he will choose his new place of residence, following a woman who will also become his wife, where the main problem he will face is the local authorities' reluctance to give him anything meaningful to do.

I shall say a few things about this a little later. What is important to understand about the main point of crisis, however, is this: the president's view of Danilo is very precise and grounded in the same kind of knowledge that the reader has. Danilo's view of the president and his use of the term "philosopher" as in insult in relation to him is, however, based on prejudice, and not on any certain, or at least expressly stated knowledge. When he categorises him as some kind of dry apparatchik who never directly experienced the hardships that Danilo had to overcome, our only guarantee that he is right is the impression he has given us up to this point in the narrative about his ability to read people. However, all of those people he knew how to read were people he was about to trick or defraud in one way or another. As I shall show in the last part of this chapter, when it comes to people who wish him well and who hope to make a deeper connection with him, he is far less reliable a judge of character. That aspect of Danilo's relation to other characters will take us to the novel's women. When it comes to the president and his words, however, Danilo's reaction the next morning, after swallowing the bitter pill of criticism, is, effectively, acceptance of its (at least partial) justness:

Ridiculous dirty old man, with his elementary school certificate and a lack of taste, wit and sense all set in concrete, wanted not only to march to the rhythm of the times, but also to be their conductor, convinced that it was enough to wave your stick at the cows to be able to conduct a symphony orchestra. [...] I have no one to blame for this. [...] I'm not losing any privileges or benefits, for I never had any. I am losing only myself. And along with that, the faith in our ability to stimulate virtue, which is more humane and efficient than these cruel attacks on human faults. [...] I know how my fall will look in practice. To the detail I can predict everything, from the vengeful chuckles of those I persecuted to the organised indifference of those who used to pester me with their loyalty. (Sušić 1984: 152)

Yet again, we see his rhetorical acrobatics. On the one hand, his pleas to the "humanism" of "stimulating virtue" as opposed to criticising faults, and on the other, his own ready criticism of the people around him, and his easy, and almost completely unconscious, admittance that he himself was prone to persecuting people and brushing off the loyalty of others. As someone who was aware that he was perceived in his community as a stern fanatic with no recognisable human desires (and who, effectively, carefully fashioned himself as such), Danilo's dislike of the new president borders on sheer projection. Furthermore, the conflict he envisages as taking place between them is rather artificial and disingenuous: he claims to stand for "the wide Partisan soul" and "Yugoslav love" in opposition to the President's "Swedish order" that can lead to indifference, but he himself had up to that point lived a completely ascetic life which isolated him from any real human relationship, and which was dedicated entirely to the transformation of the "capitalist village" of Labudovac into a "socialist town". He had turned himself into a machine for creating profit and progress, and the president's criticism of the results of his efforts is more wounded pride than anything else. His "Where were you earlier?" speech is a fairly fine example of whataboutery as a rhetorical strategy. As for his own practice of love as opposed to frigid order ... Well, this is where we come to the female characters in the novel.

I have already mentioned them in passing; there are three main ones, all three being love interests (or objects of lust). The first is Jovanka, a woman from his village whom he knew all his life, and who, just like him, was in the Partisans; the second the young nameless secretary whom he lifted out of her potential wartime notoriety and into respectable socialist service on the basis of her nice manners and modest clothes; and the third is Malinka, the former nurse in the Partisans, whom he meets again after his fall, and who in the second part of the novel becomes his wife, and, eventually, whom he feels to be a petty-bourgeois ball and chain around his neck and the cause of his final disappointment (after he discovers that the second chance he is given to lead a company was due to her pleading with the authorities, and not to his, finally recognised, abilities).

The young secretary differs from the other two by being younger and an enticing combination of seeming innocence and naiveté on the one hand and hidden corruption and sensual knowingness on the other. She is both an object of lust and forbidden fruit. His eventual succumbing to her skilled seduction (or real affection, it is never entirely clear which) later becomes implicitly linked with her death, possibly by suicide (Sušić 1984: 333). She had told Danilo when she last saw him (and when they slept together for the first and final time) how unhappy she was with her highly suspicious and jealous husband, and yet his main thought upon their parting was the same kind of suspicion of her motives and past sexual experience. He also accused her of using her body to get what she wanted, which, when entertained by her husband, had made her marriage so miserable. It is quite clear that Danilo would have been unable to behave any less destructively towards her had he decided to indulge in his own lust and affection for her earlier (Sušić 1984: 152-162). The fact that she is unnamed throughout (and referred to as "the little clerk girl" by almost everyone who mentions her) adds to a certain lack of substance which is the main feature of her characterisation. She is the nymph of the Labudovac administration, and more a wet dream made of flesh than a woman seen as real by anyone around her (including both Danilo and her husband later in the novel). As such however, she signals what the main problem is that Danilo has with the other two women in his life.

Both Jovanka and Malinka are former Partisans. They both proved their worth in the war through heroism and strength which should, in theory, make either of them a perfect partner to Danilo as the vigorous builder of socialism. This is how he describes Jovanka:

> When I rub my eyes, blinded by problems, I always find myself amazed: a solid and healthy woman stands before me. [...] She is not afraid of god, or mice, or snakes, or of any burden, she goes to the committee to shout at people, she cries only when she hurts herself, she knows how to take an automatic rifle and a pistol apart and how to reassemble them, and, should the need arise, she would yet again put on the trousers and slap the Partisan cap on her head ... (Sušić 1984: 45)

Jovanka is also quite direct about what she wants from him: when he half-jokingly accuses her that all she wants is to get married, she says that she "doesn't need a carcass to drag itself around her house in its underpants" (Sušić 1984: 70), and that she needs him as a lover while she is still young. However, it is not clear that that is all she wants, as she clearly loves him dearly and knows him well. For example, she sees his industrial ambitions as a folly, and after the inspiring speech on the future of Labudovac he gives to the workers building the sawmill, she gives him a pretty accurate prediction of how it will all end:

Dane, you run away from me. Why, Dane, when I know I'm dear to you? You've made yourself believe in this nonsense, and you can't see where you're headed. You think you'll accomplish all you've planned? And even if you do, do you think anyone will say: "Thanks"? Go ahead, build palaces for everyone, sprinkle gold on the roof tops, lay down a river of milk and honey! And who will do the same for you? No-one! They'll drive you away from their doorsteps, and it will be too late for you to start afresh. My old fool, come to your senses! (Sušić 1984: 71)

Danilo is, however, too busy to pay attention to what she is telling him, and or to stop and ask her what she wants from him in terms of a relationship, apart from sexual contact (even though the very fact she is open about that is a fairly revolutionary thing in itself, considering the strict sexual morality of the wartime Partisan movement, and considering the old-fashioned patriarchal village they live in; Jovanka does not even seem particularly bothered by the fact that everyone is gossiping about them). As the story is told by Danilo himself, and as he is fairly oblivious when it comes to what Jovanka might want (as in the scene where she parades in front of him half naked while he is engrossed in some official documents; Sušić 1984: 49), but quick to accuse her of wanting marriage or being proprietary when she expresses a desire to see him (Sušić 1984: 71), the reader does not really get the chance to hear her side of things. But it would be possible to imagine that Jovanka, sexually liberated, marriage-averse, unwilling to be impressed by Danilo and his ambition, but knowing him well and willing to love him, might have wanted to try and create, in this new society, and with an entirely new wartime experience of (at least potential) gender equality (hence the vision of her in trousers and handy with a gun), a new type of relationship between a man and a woman. Their relationship, undefined as it is, ends when Danilo jokingly refers to one of the village men as a "marriage customer", offering him to her as a replacement for himself; Jovanka takes great offence at this, slaps him, and forbids him from ever coming to her again (Sušić 1984: 73). Danilo is too engrossed in his sawmill building plans to try and understand what has happened, attributing the whole incident to female irrationality and need for sentimentality, and allowing her emotional wound to remain unhealed and their relations to remain unrepaired, and for years to pass before they meet again in the same room. That is after he has become ill, just before the final crisis which will drive him away from Labudovac, when she comes to clean his room and give him clean clothes – and, yes, the intense irony of the almost aggressive nature of the gender stereotype in this scene has not escaped me, although I am not sure Sušić was aware of it – threatening him with another slap should he try to touch her (Sušić 1984: 143-144). It is quite significant, however, that the man he jokingly tried to marry her to was the man who had told him just seconds before that he hoped to get married but was afraid he would come across a member of the Antifascist Women's Front (AFŽ), who would demand her rights, and allow his own "to go to hell" (Sušić 1984: 73). That little detail is extremely telling about the position of women who had experienced the changes in gender relations during the Partisan struggle, only to find them revert back to the old patriarchal modes of understanding how men and women were supposed to act,[5] and is doubly poignant when it comes to Jovanka herself. She had fought for a better and freer society, alongside men. Yet the possibilities of what that could develop into in peacetime became depressingly curtailed when it became clear that old patriarchal gender habits were hard to break, and that imagination failed when it came to conceiving of new ways of being a couple in the new society.

Jovanka is not the only victim of Danilo's inability to imagine his old Partisan comrades as anything other than women eager for home and marriage, or, alternatively, as women whose sexual attractiveness should be put into the service of the new society (or at least into the service of his schemes). His "little clerk" falls into this second category, and his second girlfriend, and then wife, Malinka, falls into the first.

He meets Malinka at the start of his exile from Labudovac, and recognises in her the Partisan nurse he knew in his unit during the war. Unlike the peasant Jovanka, Malinka was a city girl (at least that is what is suggested by the reference to her being a grammar school pupil who came to join the Partisans equipped with hiking gear and a toothbrush; Sušić 1984: 178), but the story of her wartime strength and heroism is almost identical to Jovanka's. As they travel together to the town of Vilenica (where Malinka has been appointed as the head of the education department; Danilo decides to follow her there, even though he himself has been allocated to another town; Sušić 1984: 180-181), Danilo sets himself to woo her by praising her bravery and strength in the war:

> All the women in the world fought their wars by writing letters to their husbands on the front, or by parading around with the Red Cross [...]. While you carried bandages and meds, and often the ammunition as well, in the columns of units which were, probably, of all the units on this earth the most attacked and which spent the least time bivouacking. And you crawled with me to the trenches, and when I moaned when wounded, you carried me out on your delicate arms. And when I had a headache or was down with the fever, you propped me up, for you had no right to be tired or sick. (Sušić 1984: 182)

The image Danilo paints of her (and this is where Malinka differs from Jovanka, who is all strength and vitality) is that of a fragile and delicate creature forced by circumstances to find in herself reserves of almost superhuman strength. However,

---

5 On the tensions between the legal and ideological framework of the "women's question" and the situation on the ground, see the online archive of the Antifascist Women's Front, and in particular Katz 2011 and Bonfiglioli 2016.

when trying to find a way to make her believe in herself again (as he discovers her wartime husband had left her for another woman, and noting how much she had aged as a result of her post-war personal disappointments), Danilo does not appeal to that strength, although he, as we have seen in the quotation above, does mention it. Instead, he appeals to her past sexual attractiveness, to the fact that her entire Partisan unit was in love with her, that he himself during the war had once secretly watched her bathe in a river, and had to restrain himself from "pouncing on her" while she was naked (Sušić 1984: 182-183). A woman who once pulled soldiers out of the trenches in her arms and who is about to be the head of the education department is for the rest of the novel described purely in terms of her sexual attractiveness (which she regains thanks to Danilo's earth-shattering advice to get a new haircut and wear make-up and nice clothes; Sušić 1984: 183-184, 212-213), feminine wiles and "female business" (i.e., the apparently unavoidable need for marriage and children; Sušić 1984: 277). He succeeds at doing with Malinka what he failed to do with Jovanka. The woman who had tasted of gender equality during the war, and who had known herself to be an active agent of her own life, is turned into a picture of traditional femininity, into a mother and a homemaker, in considerable part due to his own determination to treat her as such, and his lack of ability to imagine her as anything else. Jovanka, the once-married peasant woman, seems to have been perhaps less articulate in her own desires and visions of the future, but more aware of the dangers of reverting to traditional gender roles; Malinka, a former grammar school pupil who joined the Partisans with a thermos and a toothbrush, and who had grown up in a middle class family (Sušić 1984: 323), seems to have been far more susceptible to a relapse into the pre-war bourgeois femininity, satisfying herself with supporting her husband's career rather than pursuing her own (what does she do as the head of the education department? – the novel does not say, and Danilo clearly does not care), and busily nesting into a traditional hearth and home.

The three women, Jovanka, the young clerk and Malinka, all represent different variations on the type of female character which Gheith (whose definition of the "superfluous man" I cited earlier) calls "the necessary woman". Gheith's discussion of the critical debate regarding that figure in Russian literature is significant for my interpretation of how female characters function in Sušić's novel, hence I quote it here in full:

> [C]entral to all superfluous-man texts is a romantic relationship and separation. The superfluous man is always, at some point in the text, paired with a heroine, or, more accurately, not paired, for his is a love predicated on failure. The heroine, whom I have provisionally titled the "necessary woman," generally functions as a kind of foil for the superfluous man (with, perhaps, the exception of Pushkin's Tat'iana). Some critics, notably Vera Dunham, have argued that these narratives valorize the heroines because they represent moral superiority and *tsel'nost'*

(wholeness). But others, including Abram Terts and Barbara Heldt, have focused on the ways these texts limit the heroine's role. In his wonderfully ironic discussion of superfluous-man texts, Terts argues that these heroines serve as an image of the "ideal" for the "hero," his "goal" (*tsel'*) and a way to regain his lost sense of unity (the heroine herself is "passive, waiting"). As Terts indicates, in most superfluous-man tales, the "hero's" story is primary and the heroine serves as an episode or series of episodes in the narrative of his development. Other critics have claimed a positive role for this heroine in social or political terms, rather than the moral terms Dunham invokes. In a chapter dealing with Turgenev's *Nakanune* (1860) Victor Ripp proposes that female characters in Turgenev were a political articulation specifically of the *obshchestvo* view that women, because they were removed from society, were pure, uncorrupted and, consequently, a potential source of redemption for society. But if being removed from society is the source of women's power, how can they act on society? Ripp's answer is that (at least in Turgenev) women's only means to social action is by facilitating men's participation in the polity: "Woman requires man to enact her ideals for her and man requires woman to sanction his efforts." As feminist critics have argued in other contexts, this vision gives women no independent agency; it also assumes that the only way to affect society is to participate as a citizen in specific, predetermined ways. (Gheith 1996: 230-231)[6]

All of this, of course, refers to female characters in 19th-century Russian novels. And yet it also depicts quite accurately Danilo's attitude towards the women he encounters, and the text's treatment of its female characters. The three heroines are, indeed, episodic characters in the story of his development; they are also seen as somehow set apart from the building-of-socialism story that Danilo tells, even though, at least in the cases of Jovanka and Malinka, they were active participants (and equal agents) in the wartime period of the start of that society. What distinguishes them from the "necessary women" of whom Gheith and other critics quoted by her write, is that they are, paradoxically (and somewhat maddeningly) presented as passive and reactionary (sexual) distractions on Danilo's quest to create the new industrialised socialist society. Russian 19th-century fictional "necessary women", who for reasons of realistic character motivation and portrayal could not do much in terms of any active participation in the fictional societies to which they belonged, seem to have been more "necessary" to the superfluous heroes to which fate bound them, than are Malinka and Jovanka to Danilo's superfluous man, even though they are depicted as being politically active Communists, former wartime nurses and combatants, and, at the time of the main story, financially independent

---

6 I have omitted Gheith's references to the secondary sources quoted, as they are not essential to my discussion.

working women. They should be Danilo's comrades and partners, yet they are depicted as a ball and chain around his neck, rejected either for being too demanding and distracting in their desire to search for an untraditional form of relationship (in the case of Jovanka), or for being too willing to fulfil his expectation of a woman's traditional role as wife and mother, or for being a feminine little charmer and schemer (also in the case of Malinka, as well as in the case of the young clerk). All of them, especially the nameless little clerk (who, as a woman with a dubious political and sexual past, could have been redeemed by her career in the administration, and by the fact that she was good at her job), remain defined purely by their sexual attractiveness and ambiguity, and by their feminine wiles, even when, as in the case of Jovanka, they actively reject that role.

What the novel does in depicting the degradation of these women from necessary political and military comrades and partners to superfluous reactionaries reduced to their sexual function and traditional gender roles is a question not just of gender identity, but also of wasted human potential. That, arguably, is the novel's main theme. The tragic destiny of Danilo the socialist robber-baron, in my view, is not the greatest tragic fate which this novel depicts. Nor, in my view, is Mićun, a boy whose neck, half cut with an Ustaša knife, Danilo bandaged at the start of the novel and whom he meets again at its end as an angry and disappointed young man, wrecked with alcohol and rage at the hypocrisies of the new society, and whose story provides Danilo with the final tipping point into despair, its most significant tragic figure. The novel's most poignant characters, figures of wasted human potential and desperate disappointment made invisible and insignificant, are its women, who tasted the possibilities of a different future, and who were reduced back to insubstantiality and superfluity with mindless cruelty.

The new society could have been quite different, the novel whispers behind its narrator's (and, possibly, even its author's) back, had the Danilos who insisted on building it alone allowed the Jovankas and the Malinkas and the pretty little clerks to be equal partners in its creation.

Bibliography

Bonfiglioli, Chiara (2016) Biografije aktivistkinja AFŽ-a: intersekcionalna analiza ženskog djelovanja. Translated by Selma Asotić. In: Dugandžić, Andreja/Okić, Tijana (eds.): *Izgubljena revolucija: AFŽ između mita i zaborava*.Sarajevo: 16-39.

Duraković, Enes (1985, 1998) Književno djelo Derviša Sušića. In: Duraković, Enes/Nametak, Fehim/Buturović, Đenana (eds.): *Bošnjačka književnost u književnoj kritici: Novija književnost – Proza*. Sarajevo: 531-543.

Gheith, Jehanne M. (1996) The Superfluous Man and the Necessary Woman: A 'Re-Vision'. In: *The Russian Review* 55(2): 226-244.

Katz, Vera (2011) O društvenom položaju žene u Bosni i Hercegovini 1942-1953. In: *Prilozi* 40: 135-155. URL: http://www.afzarhiv.org/files/original/43d0baa6f64e582272f6f63724313065.pdf (retrieved July 23, 2019).

Kazaz, Enver (2004) *Bošnjački roman XX vijeka*. Zagreb.

Muratagić-Tuna, Hasnija (2012) O imenu i govoru glavnog junaka romana *Ja, Danilo* Derviša Sušića (lingvostilistička analiza). In: *Godišnjak Bošnjačke zajednice kulture "Preporod"* 1: 357-372.

Online archive of the Antifascist Women's Front of Bosnia-Herzegovina. URL: http://www.afzarhiv.org/da-zivi-afz (retrieved July 23, 2019).

Sušić, Derviš (1984) Ja, Danilo. In: *Ja Danilo; Uhode*. Sarajevo.

Trifković, Risto (1974, 1998) Skica za književni portret Derviša Sušića. In: Duraković, Enes/Nametak, Fehim/Buturović, Đenana (eds.): *Bošnjačka književnost u književnoj kritici: Novija književnost – Proza*. Sarajevo: 525-530.

Narration as Misunderstanding
The Economy in Borislav Pekić's
The Pilgrimage of Arsenije Njegovan

Davor Beganović

1. Economy between mania and rationality

Borislav Pekić's *The Pilgrimage of Arsenije Njegovan*[1] is the second novel by the Serbian author[2] and the first to mention the Tsintsar family of the Njegovans, whose history was later to be elaborated in the huge, seven-volume saga *The Golden Fleece* (1978-1986). Still, *The Pilgrimage* should not be read as any sort of introduction to this vast reconstruction of the historical period spanning from 1361 until 1941. The main, but not the only reason for this is that *The Pilgrimage* does not follow any chronological line that could be found in *The Golden Fleece*. It is an autonomous novel whose hero's actions are presented as independent of his ancestors and their

---

1 An English translation was published in 1994 under the title *The Houses of Belgrade*. It is inexplicably abridged, which prevented a thorough reception of the book. In the following I will quote from this edition but whenever necessary come back to the original text.
2 Borislav Pekić (1930-1992) was one of the most important authors in the generation that dominated Yugoslav literatures in the 1960s. In literary criticism he is usually considered a member of a group that included such important authors as Danilo Kiš, Filip David and Mirko Kovač. Pekić's first novel was *The Times of Miracle* (*Vreme čuda*, 1965). After the publishing of *The Pilgrimage of Arsenije Njegovan* in 1970 he emigrated to London and remained in British exile until the end of his life. He regularly returned to Yugoslavia and tried to become involved in politics, but more or less failed. He permanently left the country that had already fallen apart in 1991 and died in London in 1992. Pekić's opus is enormous. It consists of some nine novels, seven volumes of *The Golden Fleece*, radio dramas, short stories, memoirs, diaries, philosophical and literary essays and correspondence. It is still being published by authors following his legacy. His personal biography was anything but uninteresting. Shortly after WWII he was arrested as a member of anti-communist Yugoslav Democratic Youth and sentenced to fifteen years in prison. He served five years. His memories of the trial and subsequent years in jail were kept in the hybrid book *The Years the Locusts Devoured I-III* (*Godine koje su pojeli skakavci I-III*, 1987-1990). Written in the manner of Solzhenytsin's *The Gulag Archipelago*, this book switches between memoir and anthropological study of totalitarianism and, specifically, its system of justice, prisons and camps. Pekić quotes broadly from scientific anthropological literature, giving his text the appearance of scientific work, but it is impossible to oversee its merging with fictional elements in this prose.

heritage – of course only within the framework of this literary text. The plot of the novel itself is relatively simple. A 77-year-old landlord decides not to move out of his house for 27 years. This period is characterized by two events. On the one hand, there is the coup d'état that is followed by the revolt led by the Communist Party on March 27th, 1941, the event that led to the immediate outbreak of war in Yugoslavia. On the other hand, there is the student rebellion of June 1968.[3] Everything that happens in the intermediary period is omitted. Time stands still and Njegovan lives in a closed and narrow world that is isolated not only in space (his sojourn within the four walls of his home on Kosančićev Venac in Belgrade), but in time, too. According to the concept developed in the novel, there are only two time dimensions: the past and the future. The present is excluded from the construction. A paradoxical consequence of this is that Njegovan's presence at the moment of narration lasted twenty-seven long years. The moment of its collapse is the moment of Njegovan's death. A heart attack terminating the eternal presence inscribes itself in the tormented body of the loser of the transition from a capitalist to a socialist economy. The novel itself reconstructs the events from the narrator's pre-war life, told in his own words, mainly those concerning the economic rise of the Njegovan family.[4] At the same time, one crucial but unexplained event from the past appears, but is only mentioned in passing. Obviously it is a massacre from the early phase of the Russian Revolution that took place in Solovkin in 1919. It seems to be a trauma which Arsenije Njegovan has systematically dealt with, but only acted out, and which obsesses him more than anything else that has happened in his life. He was involved in it against his own will, but did not suffer any physical harm. The damage came only afterwards in the form of a serious psychological disorder. We do not know how or why he went to Solovkin either, or what he did there. All that is left are the memories of hanged Russian-Jewish merchants, framed within the sight of the overall destruction of personal goods, property and people's lives.[5]

Apart from this, Arsenije acts and narrates in the mode of utter rationality. He causally connects his own family with some crucial developments in the process

---

3 On the role of student's revolts in *The Pilgrimage*, cf. Richter 2009.
4 Of course, the Njegovans are not so short-sighted as to neglect the other dimensions of social life leading to the increase in their influence. Arsenije randomly mentions his brothers, Đorđe, who is a general, and Emilijan, who is a priest. Both of them cover the military and religious part of the "superstructure". The politicians are to be sought in the other branch of the family, the so-called Njegovan-Turjaškis, who settled in Slovenia and look after the industrial and political family network. Jasmina Lukić (2001) considers *The Pilgrimage* in a broader context, as part of *The Golden Fleece* saga, a position she defends by contextualizing the complex work on the Njegovans as part of the specific metafictional poetics developed by Pekić.
5 Pekić himself indicates the triple construction of his figure and the narrative he builds around him. The first violent event (Solovkin 1919) is a tragedy, the second (the Yugoslav March of 1941) grotesque, and the third (the student rebellion of June 1968) a farce (Pekić 2005: 64).

of Serbian modernization. The historical reconstruction of these events is followed by his awakening and outburst in the world of Belgrade he knows only from his window and with the help of the powerful binoculars he uses to watch the construction on the opposite bank of river Sava. Of course, the reader knows that these construction sites are a part of socialist building activities following the growth of the city. But Njegovan, and that is the essence of the initial misunderstanding,[6] is not aware of the political changes – or more precisely, he does not want to know anything about them and his inner circle declines to give him any information, justifying their refusal through concern for his weakened health. His departure from the house is thus an action which requires the ability to produce the most complex intrigue. Njegovan has to be left alone. He has to convince his wife that she can go to the spa for a couple of days and that he can take care of himself alone, with a little help from the French nurse who cared for his late brother. After her departure, he makes an excursion to the streets of Belgrade, initially to look after "his"[7] houses. Unfortunately, Arsenije is involved in the tumult caused by the student revolts. He returns to the safety of home, proceeds to write his memoirs and will and dies of a heart attack while doing so. His work is left unfinished and the notes written on the back pages of invoices and receipts are collected and edited by an author, Borislav Pekić. In this way, the narrative level of the novel is constructed from three different parts. The first and the opening part is the will that contingently interferes with the further unfolding of the story. The second is the story itself, told in a fragmentary manner, switching freely between the past and present and anticipating the future. The final level is the Epilogue, which sums up the scattered traces and provides some sort of closure, a component that Njegovan's story in its fragmentarity is largely missing, even resisting.[8]

Thus the ellipse inscribed directly in the narrative structure of the novel forms its core. Marked by multiple loss but still unaware of it, Njegovan tries to reflect on his situation in the present, to reconstruct his past and to foresee, or at least

---

6 As I will show later, the misunderstanding develops into the central rhetorical figure dominating the narrative structure of the entire novel.
7 Njegovan is not aware that his property has been expropriated by the communists. He lives in the world of lies and half-truths constructed by an environment holding him back from the new political reality.
8 The majority of Pekić research concentrates on the urban or urbanization component of *The Pilgrimage*. A prime example of such texts is Tomić (2009). Pijanović (1991) considers *The Pilgrimage* only in the broader context of *The Golden Fleece*, while Mustedanagić (2002) insists on the grotesque elements in the novel. Only Šukalo (2009) touches upon the elements of economics, combined with Njegovan's urbanizing and building activities. But he mentions these only in passing and does not develop the promising theses about Njegovan as a figure split between "grotesque and bourgeois ownership" (261).

tame, the unpredictable future. There is one genre that is appropriate for bridging the gap between three different time dimensions. It originates in a juridical discourse but it is widely used in literature itself, albeit predominantly metaphorically: the last will.[9] As a document, the will possesses the ability to regulate the afterlife, particularly in the economic dimension, of the deceased person. In a sense, it represents the rewriting of a lost story from the past. In another way it is the settling of accounts with the world. An ambitious will could lead to a text bordering on an autobiography. Now, I think it would not be faulty to state that *The Pilgrimage of Arsenije Njegovan* exactly represents this usage of the juridical mode in creating an aesthetic text. The possibility of pseudo-objectivity embedded in bureaucratic discourse gives way to a very specific grotesque element that features as the most important characteristic of the novel as a whole. Still, the form of the last will opens up one more relationship between literature and outer-literary discursive practices, namely the economy, to which it has, as already mentioned, an intrinsic relationship.

Let us briefly consider the economic side of Njegovan's will, which functions as a mirror image of the juridical one. It is impossible to deny that the first aim of this document is (foremost) to regulate the economic circumstances in the family and the remaining closely related persons (friends, business partners and so on) surrounding its creator. In this sense, it is an attempt to coordinate the inevitable dissemination of private property. The private property of the deceased is also endangered by his predictable death. It could be at least partly rescued by the testamentary act carried out in the written form. This written document is a crucial element that gives an official form to an otherwise highly personal issue. One text crosses borders. It becomes its own adversary. The document changes its substance and takes the form of a confession, or even justification. Again, we are on the juridical premises bordering the economy. We can say, then, that the text is based on three different strategies. On the first level we have the notarial act, whose execution is left unfinished; the document does not have juridical force. On the second level, the economic issue is elaborated, consisting of Njegovan's material property that is to be bequeathed to some specific physical persons. And on the third level, we encounter the narrative text in its literariness.[10] In this way, the testament un-

---

9 One extraordinary example of the literary usage of the last will in the Yugoslav literatures is certainly Danilo Kiš's *Hourglass*. E. S., the father, wants to regulate his possessions. However, his testament is not of an economic kind for one simple reason: its creator does not have anything precious to bequeeth. His values are only symbolic. In this sense, he leaves nothing material, only scattered words, mostly in the form of advice, are there to distribute his scarce legacy.
10 Here I use the term "literariness" in the sense that it lends a certain autonomy to the literary text itself. It is, then, to be seen as contrasting the other two areas (law and economy) as context bound. It supplements them and serves as a buffer embedded between two related but still antagonistic discourses. "Literature has become less a distinct object, fixed in a canon, than a

folds as a threefold narrative containing the microstructure of different discursive strategies. Law, economy and literature make it a hybrid construction, whereby it is impossible to determine which is dominant. Its creator himself floats between the three without making a substantial decision concerning their hierarchy.

However, that is not all. The will is only one part of Njegovan's narrative and it performs in its microworld the macrostructure of the entire novel. In a sense, it is a gloss reflecting the events that took part in a period in which the accumulation of capital took place for the first time in pre-modern Serbia. On this narrative level, *The Pilgrimage of Arsenije Njegovan* appears to be a family novel in nuce. It does not seek to reconstruct the entire history of the Njegovan family – the task, as I indicated, undertaken by *The Golden Fleece* – but represents one of the crucial moments of its development: engagement in the process of transition from the largely backward and underdeveloped Serbian economy, based on feudal and patriarchal premises, to a modern capitalist one, a process that was connected with industrialization and urbanization.[11] The second moment is inevitably intertwined with the development of the construction sector, the area of economic life vastly influenced by Arsenije's ancestors. In order to understand this, we have to look to the past, specifically to the volatile time of the transfer of power from Ottoman to Serbian hands. The newly founded (or re-founded) Principality of Serbia was on its way from a predominantly oriental to a modern European state. Only after the withdrawal of Turkish troops from Belgrade in 1862 did the modernizing urbanization of the capital become possible. Mixing historical fact and fiction, Pekić elects the

---

property of discourse of diverse sorts, whose literariness – its narrative, rhetorical, performative qualities – can be studied by what were hitherto methods of literary analysis. And the values that are often taken for granted in literary reading of non-literary materials are frequently literary values: concreteness, vividness, immediacy, paradoxical complexities" (Culler 2007: 18).

11 In an extremely important study *Kaldrma i asfalt (Cobblestone and Asphalt)*, Dubravka Stojanović follows the process of Belgrade's modernization and urbanization in the roughly same period that concerns the memoirs of Arsenije Njegovan. She states: "Winding streets; blind alleys; representative buildings in inadequate locations; central locations without clear urban planning; single-story, crooked shacks leaning on modern multi-story buildings; almost unsolvable traffic problems ... Such a situation in present-day Belgrade is a result of specific modernization processes that affected the look, urbanization, and infrastructure development of the capital of Serbia. At the same time, that specific modernization of the capital was paradigmatic for overall process in the country: it marked two centuries of her attempts to catch up with European trends, and, furthermore, its stopping, giving up on her aim, blocking her total Europeanization and quite often, her self-isolation. That is why understanding the controversial modernization processes of Belgrade is also a path to understanding the initiatives and obstacles Serbia went through, and is still going through, in her attempts to find her place in the contemporary world" (Stojanović 2009: 383). It is essential to see how Stojanović, following Braudel's longue durée approach, connects Belgrade's past with its troubled present. In a way, her historic work echoes Pekić's fictional story of the glorious age of emergence.

Njegovan dynasty as a leading power in the new-born Serbian economic aristocracy. They are the carriers of the spirit of newly won optimism. Pekić unites in two central figures two streams or two possibilities of development. On the one hand, there is a calculating merchant, represented by Simeon Njegovan, the grandfather of the narrator, and the stereotypical figure from the *Gründerzeit*. On the other hand, there is the other moony artist and architect Emilijan Josimović, a real historical figure.[12] Both of them can function only in a symbiosis, as symbols of divergent and ambiguous but still compatible paradigms. Simeon is representative of the cold economic way of thinking, while sensitive Emilijan stands for an aesthetic approach to construction. His erratic and random wish to accomplish everything at once anticipates in a strange way the future activity of Arsenije. Therefore, the contention between the two partners and then antagonists is the inevitable result of divergent approaches to the problem of Serbian modernization.

> Nevertheless, as is often the case when commerce and science come together in a development project, interests were common but not identical. Quickly it became known that Simeon Negovan, personally or through intermediaries, had bought up the major part of the land along the projected park, exactly that area which Josimović had categorized as of prime value [...] Breaking off family relations and repudiating his role as a godfather (to which their friendship had brought him in the meantime), the now furious architect showered my grandfather with imprecations [...]. (Pekić 1994: 145)

In a sense, it is again a performative repetition of the novel's structure itself. Two persons symbolize and anticipate the split in the figure of Arsenije who, in a process of increasing madness, loses contact with reality (represented by capitalist economy) and becomes a sort of artist (this function is represented by his affective relation to the houses he owns, or thinks he owns). At the same time, this split testifies to Arsenije's inability to construct his story as a continuous processing of events he reports about. Of course, that means that Arsenije is not able to comprehend this split in his personality. This means that he cannot create the ironic (or any other) distance to the narrative he tells. Obviously, the comic is the effect of an instance that is to be sought at the margins of the text. The implied author mildly laughs at his figure and turns the ironic spear toward *societies* unable to understand that Njegovan is lost in his own world.

---

12 Emilijan Josimović (1823–1897) was the first Serbian city planner. He studied in Vienna, returned to Serbia, taught at a high school and elaborated a plan for Belgrade's urbanization which was realized after the Turkish withdrawal in 1867.

2. Property vs. money. The Anti-Semitic economy

The economic theory of Arsenije Njegovan is presented in his putative speech that is to be held in the Foundation of Ilija Kolarac[13] in Belgrade, on the occasion of the regular meeting of the organization Kolo Srpskih Sestara (Circle of the Sisters of Serbia).[14] Of course, this organization is a charitable one and accordingly inappropriate for Njegovan's aim. Nevertheless, he tries to justify the relatively humiliating circumstances of his speech by the possible influence of powerful men's wives upon their husbands. His theory shall, in an indirect manner, find its way to the ears of those who are interested in its practical application. Again, failure is inscribed in Njegovan's actions.[15] His plea for a market economy, but one freed from, in his opinion, the exhaustive influence of banks, does not even have a chance of being expressed. In distinction to his contention and following a verbal and bodily confrontation with the masses, he cannot even begin to deliver the speech. After he has heard the concept, the organizer kindly refuses to permit Arsenije's appearance. What is so controversial about this concept? Njegovan is seemingly always out of place and out of time, no matter in which social system he lives and acts. One reason for this could be that these theories about ownership are all too idealistic to be efficient in the pragmatic world of entrepreneurship. In a sense, he collides with himself. Unstable personal identity is reflected in unstable economic identity. The only escape from this imbalance could be found in the projection of his affects onto the houses he owns. It is at the point of intersection between the affective and the narrative economy that his text appears to take on a form of madness, which is the primal cause of misunderstanding finally leading to collapse.

In a word, it seems that Arsenije Njegovan is unable to develop empathy for the people surrounding him. From this puncture emerges the expected vicinity to objects that substitute living creatures. The first act of substitution is naming. He names each of his houses after a woman. He uses all sorts of associations while

---

13 Serbian merchant Ilija Kolarac donated his wealth to the education of the population. His will was executed after 1868, culminating the opening ceremony of the "Kolarac People's University" in 1932, which from the outset functioned as both an education and cultural centre.
14 It is important to note here that his cancelled speech is repeated on the occasion of the 1941 demonstrations. Again, it is misunderstood. Failing in tone and in location, it causes only trouble for Njegovan, who is thrashed by the irritated masses. The masses consist mostly of communists and nationalists. They do not follow his elaborate scholarly lecture. Bloodthirsty and ready for the overthrow of the government, they are easy to mobilize for a physical attack on the proprietor and his complicated presentation. He and his critique of the bank system are not needed. Violence is an appropriate answer to the state crisis and turbulences following Yugoslavia's association with the Tripartite Pact.
15 It would not be faulty to assert that each of his discursive undertakings is doomed to disaster. It is as if he incompetent, although it is obvious that his rhetorical capabilities are considerable enough for him to present his arguments before an audience.

doing so: historical, personal, geographical. In this way, he constructs a complex emotional relationship by giving the houses an identity equal to the one we are used to giving to living beings. The houses supplement the loss of emotional commitment. He is not aware of it, but it is present everywhere, above all in economic theory, specifically the economic theory he develops himself. In a strange way, it echoes the discussion on the role of the banks that dominates the contemporary economic discourse. Njegovan anticipates the critique of banks, which can be heard today from all sides of the political spectrum. Yet his critique is at least twofold. Apart from the banks (and I will briefly consider this aspect in a moment), he also considers the proprietors who do not share his pseudo-philosophical view to be his foes. "Such men increased their possessions either through inertia, to be secure in old age, or simply to strengthen and solidify their personal or social integrity" (Pekić 1994: 56). This pragmatic stance does not mirror the position of Njegovan, who can also be pragmatic, but who, as I have already noted, balances between an economic and an artistic position. He becomes vulnerable when he tries to perform an act of perfect harmony between the transcendental and the immanent in his almost aesthetic economic concept, or, more precisely, in the specific aesthetisizing of the economy:

> They didn't do it to augment their property as such, or in any way to become identified with the things which belonged to them, so that they should merge with these objects of commercial control into an indivisible whole, be absorbed into a mutual lymphatic system for the flow and flood of capital, feeling, will, rent, ideas, instinct, profit, hope, beauty, revenue, passion, and the remaining forms of living – a unity of two otherwise opposite beings in which, as in ideal love, it would no longer be possible to distinguish possessor and possessed, owner and owned, and where the very act of possession would be so completely reciprocal that sometimes, perhaps in some perfect world, it would become one with the act of self-perception. (56-57)

It suffices to concentrate only on the accumulation of the words concerning the affective in order to see how Njegovan trespasses the border of proper economic discourse and ventures to the aesthetic one, to the creation of the harmonic world without differences. At the same time, he makes use of organic metaphors[16] to compare capital with the human body. This is a well-known strategy often used to denote the alleged concordance between nature and a broadly understood notion of culture. But he goes one further step. His concept sounds like a peculiar *unio*

---

16 Cf. "She [his wife – D. B.] couldn't understand that possession, like any other living thing – like love, for example, love or fame, power or capability, vice or virtue – must be fed, must grow, become fruitful and multiply, if it wishes to go on" (68).

mystica abolishing all the discrepancies between two sharp opposites and fusing antinomies into a quasi-religious synthesis.

The nuisance factors in achieving this harmony are the banks and their system concerned only with money, that is: with pure abstraction. In a long passage that I quote in full because of its importance, Njegovan still explains his rejection of the bank system in rational terms:

> Certainly those other possessors would not be capable of such things [love of their property – D. B]. Indeed, can I call them by that honourable name? They have become so alienated from their own possession that, since no other direct or personal link binds them, they no longer *possess* at all in the popular sense of the word, nor does the possessed have any right over them. These men no longer operate in real objects belonging to them, but in their vague, alien, shadowy affairs, such as acquisition on the stock market whereby industrial and agricultural products, immovable assets, land, mineral wealth, ores – in a word, all the wealth of this planet – are transformed into paper values, barely perceivable in concepts of rent, dividends, shares, loan extensions, cash and term of work, or agreed-upon deferred payments [...] Inevitably, that abandoned trace of reality is finally lost by its owner. Yet it's quite inappropriate to call them owners, for they have acquired only echoes of those shadows – in fact, their formless movements up and down, movements defined by the stock exchange index, by the possessor who, speculating *à la hausse*, on the rise of shares, or *à la baisse*, on their fall, in fact possesses only disembodied difference between changeable and similarly disembodied sums, nuances which themselves are exceptionally inconstant and changeable. (57-58)

This diatribe against banks does not slip into pure hatred. But there is one indication that prophesizes such a development. That is, of course, the slight mention of the organic moment connected with healthy business and inorganic degeneration (which is the sign of future illness), and definitive collapse. It is condensed in the word "disembodiment". "Disembodiment" frees the way for the future considerations about the banking system that will anticipate the worst racist offences.

Njegovan still has some more time to develop his real nature. This step is prepared carefully. Pure hatred appears in the central moment of the novel, its breaking point after which the hero cannot find the way back to rationality and consequently falls ever deeper into his madness. This could only be terminated by his death, which does not come immediately. In a replica of Adrian Leverkühn's dialogue with the devil in Thomas Mann's *Doctor Faustus*, Njegovan holds a conversation with an unknown collocutor. It is possibly that the devil provokes him to tell things that he would otherwise refrain from telling. Furthermore: the imaginary dialogue occurs after his failed attempt to go to the auction taking place at the house of his cousin. His *idée fixe* is to buy that very house – the object of his crazy love. In this last act of completing his property, he is obstructed by the mob demonstrating against the Yugoslav government on 27th March 1941. Elevated by the masses, he delivers his speech prepared for the Circle of Sisters of Serbia. While reminiscing on this occasion he supplements his never-held speech with strong affective elements: "I hated banks, I have always hated banks and bankers. I even hated bank notes. From the bottom of my owner's heart I despised everything placed wilfully between the Possessed and Possessor, everything which transformed true possession into more power over empty, hollow, emaciated figures" (99). The peak of this extremely strong emotion can be found in the revelatory exclamation: "It is the fault of the Yiddisher banks!"[17] (Idem) This first revelation of anti-Semitic hatred is followed by others, further amplifying the initial position. The most prominent, and the most evil, is that equating the whole banking sector with Jewry: "I've always maintained that those damned Yiddisher banks would be the end of us! On no account should they be allowed to make a middleman's Profit"[18] (174).

The Jewish economy is the bank economy – for Njegovan there is no doubt in this assertion. Njegovan constructs his theory in agonistic and antagonistic categories. All of his concentration and passion is dedicated to showing that the world is clearly divided between two economies that cannot interfere with each other – the property economy is sharply opposed to the money economy. The first is the incorporation of positive and the second of negative values. Njegovan declines the abstract value of money and accepts only the hard value of things that can be touched, that can be possessed as a property, not as a piece of paper. In this sense, he is the obstacle on the Serbian path to a modern capitalist economy, which must be understood as a mixture of the two abovementioned economies.

3. Aesthetic-Economic Market Economy

It thus makes sense to now ask if there is any historical economic position that Njegovan could claim to be his own – that would be free of the repulsive domination of money? Certainly, there is. It is the economy of the Tsintsars, *nota bene* in his one-sided interpretation. His allegedly ideology-free defence of the mixed aesthetic-economic market economy is unmasked as a narrow and crucially racist view of the Other as inferior. He must be excluded from an exchange that functions on the principle of secret signs, gestures and apotropaic symbols that both hide the real meaning of the actions (in other words, excluding the Other) and eliminate

---

17 In the original the phrasing is even more offensive: "Za sve su krive čivutske banke!" (Pekić 1984: 103).
18 In the English translation, the following words of Njegovan are omitted: "If I had been asked I wouldn't have allowed them to carry out the credit policy either, let alone allow them, yes, sir, allow them by state law to earn their money as the middleman of the class of proprietors ... ordre de propriétaire ..." (1984, 223).

or repel evil. The narrative strategy Pekić uses to represent Njegovan's ostensibly contradictory way of acting is to use the words of the Other: Njegovan does not formulate the quintessence of the Tsintsar economy, rather he has his nephew, the westernized Stefan, do it. The background of the story is Stefan's house. Arsenije fell in love with it and will buy it at any cost. Stefan opposes his offer vehemently for two reasons: on the one hand, he is sceptical about the real aims of his uncle; on the other hand, he acts in defiance of somebody's determination to throw him out of his own home. He explains his decision in a long letter to Arsenije, who in turn transmits Stefan's message doubly: in a direct quotation and in a summarization, thereby using the narrative technique of free indirect discourse. The result of this strategy is the exposure of Arsenije's double standard that reveals his essentially unethical position. His hatred is projected upon every surface that tries to oppose his strange energy consisting in a mixture of affect and ratio. Here is his re-formulation of Stefan's words. It is, again, sadly omitted from the English translation:

> 'Until this meeting I kept receiving you into my house in esteem, even though I never had any particular liking for you – nor you for me, no doubt, that's something we both agree on' and he, if he now adds everything together, all this cleaned of my tantrums and screams for help, and he doesn't give a dime for them, if he makes the account balance between the two of us *conto a metà*, simply, as our Walachian, Tsintsar, Moskopol great grandfathers did, counting on fingers, on a tally board, tying the knots on a scarf, horse halter or tail, he can't but see some hidden agenda in my biased, hysterical offer [...]. (Pekić 1984: 82)

It is evident that Stefan maintains a double position. The first is connected with fidelity to his kin. It is impregnated with politeness. The second appears when politeness is abolished. It uncovers the ineffable economic praxis of the Njegovans. Under the surface of the modern economy there is a barely hidden layer of tradition operating without the abstractions of money, bonds or securities. He has to touch his property in order to possess it. Only the feeling of material things can fill him with satisfaction. And Stefan, a Njegovan himself, can break the carefully built phantasm. He can see how Arsenije is split between his affects and his sense of business. This split appears as an insurmountable obstacle to the construction of a coherent identity. Just one event is sufficient and he slides into autistic madness. This event, as I have already said, is the March demonstrations of 1941, followed by the coup d'état and subsequent war. The only way to avoid the complete and definitive madness is to retreat to enclosure, a place where he is protected by his close relatives. Still, this protection is maintained only through seclusion that leaves him prone to all the wrong conclusions, which themselves are a source of narrative (and not only narrative) misunderstanding.

As we have seen, the contradiction appears as a necessary consequence of the discrepancy between Arsenije's affective relation to his houses, and to houses in general, and the imperative of rationality inscribed in economic behaviour. Still, there is one small window opening onto reality, at least in his consciousness. It is his nephew Isidor, a talented architect and interlocutor.[19] Arsenije sees in Isidor his heir, somebody who would be able to realize the philosophy consisting in a mixture of aesthetics and economy. There is obviously a grain of truth in this assumption. But the rational economist overlooks a simple fact. Specifically, his nephew is broken on an inexplicable and, ultimately, unsolvable dichotomy, a rupture gaping between two irreconcilable worlds: art and business. He must make a decision and it is no wonder that it is in favour of architecture. Paradigmatic for this stance leading to the breakdown of the protagonist and his suicide (of which Arsenije knows nothing) is his being commissioned to build a memorial for the Yugoslav revolution in Belgrade.[20] Again, the story of Isidor has a prehistory. His father Jakov, an architect himself, designed the House of German Culture in Belgrade during WWII. For the communists it was an act of treason and he had to emigrate in order to escape trial. His son became an architect who denied the ideology of his father and accepted the new employer. Was his decision treason? Did he betray, not only his father, but the Njegovans too? Is suicide a way out of dire straits? All of these questions seem, at least if we adopt Arsenije's point of view, obsolete. For him, Isidor is the interlocutor who helps him find confirmation of his hybrid theory. Isidor is important insofar as he abolishes a moral dilemma and concentrates on his work, his building: "'I would build hell [...] only if I had freedom of action. Anyway, I have already given an answer.' He waves the photograph of the monument. 'Here it is ... My answer is MY building'"[21] (Pekić 1984: 255). In this way, he denies any concept of the immanence of architecture. For him it is just business as usual. If he were commissioned by the devil himself, he would accept. In a strange way, he is capable of denying his uncle's turbulent hybrid of aesthetics and economy, but through this

---

19 What Arsenije does not know is that Isidor committed suicide a couple of months before he started to make his notes, write down his life story and construct his legacy. It is, again, proof that he lives in a parallel world projected out of his phantasms.
20 It is possible that the model for Isidor was Bogdan Bogdanović, a well-known Yugoslav architect and mayor of Belgrade, also of Tsintsar origin. He built many monuments to the revolution all over Yugoslavia in specific late modernist style, as well as writing a number of books in which he elaborated his poetics and, later, sharply criticized the politics of Slobodan Milošević. He characterized the Serbian warfare as "urbicide". It is quite possible that Pekić, who himself was a royalist and anti-communist, parodied the figure of the state architect in the guise of Isidor.
21 It is important to mention that Isidor is thoroughly sceptical about the idea of architecture as art. In his opinion, "*buildings aren't architecture*. If what can be seen is art, then it isn't architecture. And if what can't be seen – emptiness, a system of hollow spaces and nothing – if that again isn't architecture, then architecture doesn't exist, at least it doesn't exist *yet*" (Pekić 1994: 197).

denial he paradoxically accepts and even broadens it. Arsenije can appropriate his opinion because he rejects art as a pure entity and emphasizes its utilitarian value.

But how, and this seems to be the most important question, can we bring together the (not so) free act of creation and the economic moment that, for Arsenije, lurks behind it? This act is executed in a symbiosis that transcends Isidor's utilitarianism. Arsenije, as the unreliable narrator, makes an involuntary synthesis that connects another component which I have consciously left out of the discussion so far – life itself. Life synthesises an apparently insurmountable difference between art and the economy. What is the price of this? The economy itself definitively becomes fiction. That is the last change one can notice in the series of transformations of Arsenije. His economic theory reveals itself to be far removed from practice. If it had the same practical use (and that was obviously the case in the past, otherwise he would not have been that successful), it was in a time of different social relations. Yet as we have seen, even then it was not generally adopted or accepted. Now it becomes obsolete in all its facets. Life is economy. Economy is fiction. Fiction is misunderstanding. Economy and life are, in the last instance, misunderstanding. That is the sad message delivered by Borislav Pekić, who reveals his own narrator-position as yet another misunderstanding in this fictional economy. As the editor of the manuscript, he is not able to decipher the last words Njegovan wrote before he was struck by a heart attack. "Tout cela... est... UN... MOD..." (Pekić 1984: 284). Unfinished words create a riddle which remains unsolved beyond the end of the narrative. He can only speculate about the idea the old man wanted to express. He tries out all the possibilities but the only answer he gives is that "each of the written sequels coincided with the condition of the spirit of Arsenije K. Njegovan, the landlord" (ibid.). Just as Njegovan is not able to solve the interaction of life, the economy and fiction, the (fictive?) editor of the (fictive?) manuscript is not able to decide whether the last words of its author are aimed at the model, modernization, moderation or some other possibility the French language offers. He leaves the last question open, just as Arsenije did not give a plausible answer to his retreat. The narrative itself is definitively constructed as misunderstanding.

It seems that the anonymous narrator/editor who appears in the text in person for the very first time perpetrates the last turn in this extremely intricate text. It is as if in refusing to take an unambiguous position related to the text he openly supports its subversive nature. Arsenije Njegovan operates as an instance that is not capable of dealing with changed reality. He is, moreover, in exactly this position of somebody whose reflective, and not acting, self cannot circumscribe all the complexity surrounding him. Now, with precisely this incapability he helps the narrative voice sounding from the last pages leave an unmarked lacuna in the middle of the possible interpretation. In this way, the text turns against its main "speaker". The precarious relationship between the text and the storytelling is definitively subversive here because Arsenije does not have the skill to bring the narrative to an end.

Even if he did not die, he would not be able to finish the story because he does not possess the power to skip the hopeless anachronism rooted in obsolete economic theory as well as in aesthetics and, more concretely, in the art of storytelling. In a word, he masters everything and in this everything he masters nothing. The narrator/editor only confirms this irresolvable situation.

Bibliography

Culler, Jonathan (2007) *The Literary in Theory*. Stanford.
Lukić, Jasmina (2001) *Metaproza: čitanje žanra. Borislav Pekić i postmoderna poetika*. Belgrade.
Mustedanagić, Lidija (2002) *Groteskni brevijar Borislava Pekića. Groteskno oblikovanje romana. Hodočašće Arsenija Njegovana, Kako upokojiti vampira i 1999*. Novi Sad.
Pekić, Borislav (1979, 1984) *Hodočašće Arsenija Njegovana*. Belgrade.
Pekić, Borislav (1994) *The Houses of Belgrade*. Translated by Bernard Johnson. Evanston.
Pekić, Borislav (1996) *Skinuto sa trake. Dnevničke beleške i razmišljanja 1954-1983*. Belgrade.
Pijanović, Petar (1991) *Poetika romana Borislava Pekića*. Belgrade, Gornji Milanovac, Titograd.
Richter, Angela (2009) Roman "Hodočašće Arsenija Njegovana" i šifra 1968. In: Pijanović, Petar/Jerkov, Aleksandar (eds.) *Poetika Borislava Pekića. Preplitanje žanra*. Belgrade, 99-107.
Stojanović, Dubravka (2009) *Kaldrma i asfalt. Urbanizacija i evrpoeizacije Beograda 1890-1914*. Belgrade.
Šukalo, Mladen (2009) Pekićeve slike urbaniteta. In: Pijanović, Petar/Jerkov, Aleksandar (eds.) *Poetika Borislava Pekića. Preplitanje žanra*. Belgrade, 265-278.
Tomić, Lidija (2009) Književni postupci u romanu "Hodočašće Arsenija Njegovana" Borislava Pekića. In: Pijanović, Petar/Jerkov, Aleksandar (eds.) *Poetika Borislava Pekića. Preplitanje žanra*. Belgrade, 257-264.

The End of the Socialist (An-)Economy, Money, and the Beginning of Literary Narration
On Miljenko Jergović's *Buick Rivera* (2002)

Jurij Murašov

Since the 1990s, literary texts addressing economic subjects following the end of socialism in Eastern, Central and Southeastern Europe have primarily focused on the immediate presence of the neoliberal transition process and the entanglement of economic (and monetary) and linguistic or literary forms of communication. Only very few texts show – and if so only *en passant* – a retrospective interest in the semiological and cultural peculiarities of the socialist economies of the respective nations.

Miljenko Jergović's novel *Buick Rivera* (2002) follows precisely this approach. It is set in the provincial American town of Toledo and relates the coincidental encounter between the eloquent Serb Vuko and the quiet Bosnian Hasan, who become involved in a bizarre car sale. With this Serbian-Bosnian deal displaced into the world of the American rationale of money and law, Jergović constructs an experimental narrative arrangement in which – conveyed through the experiences and memories of the protagonists – the socioeconomic culture of Yugoslavia is explored in its mental and communicative effects, putting into context internal Yugoslav confrontations carried out in the name of ethnicity. In this respect, Jergović's novel can be analyzed as an etiology of the violent collapse of socialist Yugoslavia emanating from economic and semiological circumstances.[1]

---

1 So far there have only been a few articles about Jergović's *Buick Rivera*, like Hansen-Kokoruš, Renate (2001) Das Auto, der Raum und die Zeit: Miljenko Jergović' Romantriologie Buick Rivera, Freelander und Volga, Volga. In: *Anzeiger für Slavische Philologie* 11/2011 (39): 75-93; or Jakiša, Miranda et al. (2009) Kontingente Feindschaft? Die Jugoslawienkriege bei David Albahari und Miljenko Jergović. In: Borissova, Natalia (ed.) *Zwischen Apokalypse und Alltag: Kriegsnarrative des 20. und 21. Jahrhunderts*. Bielefeld: 221-236; one of the most researched topics concerning Jergovićs prose and contemporary Bosnian prose is the issue of memory; see for instance Lešić-Thomas, Andrea (2004) Miljenko Jergovićs Art of Memory: Lying, Imagining and Forgetting in Mama Leone and Historijska Čitanka. In: *Modern Language Review* 4/2004 (2): 430-444; or Vervaet, Stin (2011) Writing war, writing memory. The representation of the recent past and the construction of cultural memory in contemporary Bosnian prose. In: *Neohelicon* 2011/38: 1-17; in this context see

This argument shall be further pursued in five steps. First, I show how the socialist economy, including the Yugoslav variation in its fundamental principles, corresponds with the form of gift economy the ethnologist Marcel Mauss described in his essay *The Gift* in the 1920s. In a second step, drawing on Derrida's critique of Mauss' notion of gift, I focus on the two protagonists Vuko and Hasan, who represent two complementary positions in the system of the asemiotic socialist gift economy. How the figures Vuko and Hasan embody a semiotic aporia inherent to the communist project will be shown in the third section. In the fourth section I explore the regressive logic of violence in the (an)economic interactions between the protagonists. Finally, the fifth segment addresses the cathartic and therapeutic role of money as a means of abstraction, sublimation, and fictionalization which may bring about conditions which enable us to break through the vicious circle of the self-destructive (an)economy of socialist gifts and esthetically overcome biographic and historical trauma.

1. The (Yugo)socialist gift economy

The socialist structures, initially a Soviet plan economy and then after 1945 in various deviating forms that shaped the economies of the Eastern European systems, including Yugoslavia, demonstrate in semio- and mediological terms notable analogies to the gift economy the French ethnologist Marcel Mauss described in his 1923/24 essay *The Gift* for archaic, illiterate cultures.[2] This pertains, in particular,

---

also Beganović, Davor (2009) *Poetika melankolije, Na tragovima suvremene bosansko-hercegovačke književnosti*. Sarajevo; especially on Jergović, 319-357.

2 Mauss, Marcel (1925; 1950) *Essai sur le don, forme et raison de l'échange dans les sociétés archaïques*. Paris. The analogies between the gift economy of primal societies and modern and thus also socialist economies, which were referred to in various ways, are reflected throughout Mauss' ethnological essay by its critical social statements. With regard to archaic forms of exchange of goods and services, he writes: "And as we will ascertain that this ethics (*morale*) and this economy continue to function in our own society in a lasting and, so to say, underlying way, and as we believe to have found here one of the human bedrocks on which our societies are built, we can draw some ethical conclusions to several problems posed by the crisis of our law (*droit*) and the crisis of our economy; and there we will stop. This page of social history, of theoretical sociology, of ethical conclusions, of political and economic practice, simply leads us, in the end, to ask once more, in new ways, some old but ever new questions." (Marcel Mauss, *The Gift*, Expanded Edition, Chicago 2016: 59). As a committed socialist, Mauss initially observed with great interest the Soviet attempts to create a new economic order in the 1910s and early 1920s, but then is increasingly critical of the development of the plan economy in the 1930s. See also David Graeber on the connection between Mauss and Marx: "All in all, Mauss' work complements Marx because it represents the other side of socialism. Marx's work consists of a brilliant and sustained critique of capitalism; but as Mauss himself observed, he carefully avoided speculating about what a more just society would be like. Mauss' instincts were quite the opposite: he was much

to the central notion of Mauss' empirically well-founded ethnological analysis, which argues that the gift economy constitutes a process involving all areas of the community. The exchange of goods and services in archaic societies constitutes a "total social phenomenon" which simultaneously comprises economic, judicial, moral, esthetic, religious, mythological and socio-morphological dimensions and transcends far beyond the ideal of the rational *homo oeconomicus* and his economic activity calculated by means of money:

> In those economies and legal regimes that have preceded our own, we never, so to speak, see the simple exchange of goods, wealth, and products that occurs in individual trades. First of all, it is not individuals but collectivities that mutually oblige one another, make exchanges and contracts; the persons present at a contract are moral persons: clans, tribes, and families, which confront and oppose one another, either in groups face to face in the field itself, or through the intermediary of their chiefs, or in both fashions at once. In addition, what they exchange are not exclusively goods and wealth, movable and fixed goods, or economically useful things. They are above all pleasantries, banquets, rites, military services, women, children, feasts, fairs, of which the market is only one aspect, and where the circulation of wealth is only one term of a much more general and much more permanent contract. Finally, these prestations and counterprestations are entered into somewhat more voluntarily, by way of presents and gifts (*cadeaux*), although ultimately they are strictly compulsory, on pain of private or public war. We have proposed to refer to all this as the *system of total prestations*. (60 et seq.)

Referring to a Chinook expression which "has become part of the everyday language of the whites and Indians from Vancouver to Alaska", Mauss describes these "total prestations" realized by means of the exchange of goods with the term *potlatch* (see 23). The economy is no highly differentiated functional system in this case; rather each individual economic transaction activates and involves as a *pars pro toto* the entire cultural system in its social as well as its ethical dimension and enhances its cohesive forces. The person and object are mixed during the exchange of gifts, which is diametrically opposed to the objectification, alienation and differentiation effects to which the human sphere is exposed in the money-based economy according to Hegel, Marx or Luhmann. The gift economy does not have an externalized sphere of discrete signs. Humans and objects penetrate one another in a timeless flow of senses.

> And all these institutions express only one fact, one social regime, one definite mentality: that everything – food, women, children, goods, talismans, the soil,

---

less interested in understanding the dynamics of capitalism than in trying to understand – and create – something that might stand outside it" (Graeber, David [2001] *Towards an Anthropological Theory of Value. The False Coin of Our Own Dreams*. Basingstoke: 163).

work, services, sacerdotal positions, and ranks – is material to be passed on and used in settling accounts. Everything moves back and forth as if there were a constant exchange of spiritual matter, comprising things and people, between clans and individuals, across ranks, sexes, and generations. (39)

At this point, we can observe structural similarities with regard to two aspects between the aneconomic gift economy of archaic societies studied by Mauss, on the one hand, and the socialist economies which were politically imposed during the 20th century in various regions of Europe, Asia, South and Central America and Africa on the other.

The first aspect refers to the concept of property, with which individuation becomes dominant over the collective and symbolically sanctioned by various means. Primary cultures do not have a concept of individualized property. Both the production and the purchase and exchange of goods are always a matter of the entire tribal community:

> [...] As a consequence, one gives because one is forced to do, since the recipient has a kind of right of property over everything that belongs to the donor. This property is expressed and conceived of in the form of a spiritual bond. (74 et seq.)

Analogously to this, the communitarization of the means of production and the profit generated in the agrarian as well as the industrial sector are a basic demand of all socialist economies. In this respect, the Yugoslav model of worker self-administration established in the 1950s constituted a particularly resolute, participatory form of implementation of the idea of communitarization *vis-à-vis* the bureaucratic Soviet planned economy system intermediated by delegates.

The second point pertains to economic communication in a narrower sense and money as its medium. Primary cultures indeed also operate with cash-like symbols and exchange equivalents, but these signs do not function as exclusive, abstract means of the economic process, rather they are incorporated into verbal and social practices in which the actors wholly participate. Ad valorem equivalents do not constitute a system of abstractions here, but rather result from an unstable balance, which is performatively constructed in a "system of total prestations". The (an)economy of archaic cultures analyzed by Mauss is not familiar with symbols of money in the form of exchange of goods in the sense of Niklas Luhmann's "symbolically generalizing media".[3] A reservation towards the abstraction of money is also particular to socialist economies. In his future visions, Marx already assumes that services and goods will be exchanged not mediated by monetary symbols, but

---

3 Luhmann, Niklas (1997) *Die Gesellschaft der Gesellschaft*. Frankfurt a. M.: 316-332; see about money: 347-351.

directly bound to the possibilities and needs of people. The Russian-Soviet economists also espoused this vision after the revolution of 1917 with their attempts to turn a moneyless economy into historical reality.[4] These attempts indeed failed very quickly, but a fundamental skepticism of the socialist systems towards money remained, which is associated with the coupling of the exchange of goods and services to social status, biographies and the ideological stipulations of actors. This ideologization went hand in hand with a devaluation of monetary symbols in socialist systems in principle. While money is always a scarce commodity in relation to goods and services in a monetary market economy, this relationship is reversed in a socialist economy: the scarcity of goods is juxtaposed with an abundance of money. The Russian authors Arkadij and Boris Strugatckij pointedly express this situation in their novel *Monday Begins on Saturday* (*Ponedel'nik načinaetsja v subbotu*, 1965), in which Soviet scientists invent a "Kopejke" that cannot be spent and returns back to the pocket of the payer time and time again. An expression of this relative abundance of socialist currencies is the blatant difference in value between the regulated domestic economies of socialist systems and the free foreign exchange market. Although the Dinar achieved free convertibility, the extensive possibilities of (corporate) credit lending provided by the system of worker self-management ensured that money, in principle, was not scarce, but was permanently available. This was consistently guaranteed by both the active and the ideological participation of the borrower in the collective corporation. This socialist abundance-Dinar also constituted a decisive cause of Yugoslavia's debt crisis from the 1980s on.

2. The aberration on this side of the semiosis: "hypermnestic capitalization" and "expenditure"

This tendency towards the lack of signs which combines Mauss' exchange of gifts with the socialist economies is also the focus of Jacques Derrida's critical analysis of Mauss' theory of the gift.[5] Derrida is concerned with the fundamental question as to how the phenomenon of the "gift" is conceived semiologically and medially and can be grasped under the conditions of economic reciprocity and rational cal-

---

4 The protagonists of such a socialist moneyless economy were Michail Tugan-Baranovskij (*Bumažnye den'gi i metall*, 1917), Nikolaj Bucharin (*Ėkonomika perechodnogo perioda*, 1920), Evgenij Preobraženskij (*Bumažnye den'gi v ėpochu proletarskoj diktatury*, 1920) and Stanislav Strumilin (*O trudovoj edinice učeta*, 1921); on the early Soviet economy, see Barnett, Vincent (2004) *The Revolutionary Russian Economy, 1890-1940: Ideas, Debates and Alternatives*. London, New York: 49-66.
5 In this study *Given Time: I. Counterfeit Money* (1992) Derrida addresses the question from the standpoint of Marcel Mauss' *Essay sur le don* (1923/24) and with regard to Baudelaire's prose poetry *La fausse monnaie*.

culation. Derrida's analysis seeks to verify that the gift must prove to be "the figure of the impossible" under these conditions:

> One cannot treat the gift, this goes without saying, without treating this relation to economy, even to the money economy. But is not the gift, if there is any, also that which interrupts economy? That which, in suspending economic calculation, no longer gives rise to exchange? That which opens the circle so as to defy reciprocity or symmetry, the common measure, and so as to turn aside the return in view of the no-return? If there is gift, the given of the gift [...] must not come back to the giving [...]. It must not circulate, it must not be exchanged, it must not in any case be exhausted, as a gift, by the process of exchange, by the movement of circulation, of the circle in the form of return to the point of departure. If the figure of the circle is essential to economics, the gift must remain aneconomic. Not that it remains foreign to the circle, but it must keep a relation of foreignness to the circle, a relation without relation of familiar foreignness. It is perhaps in this sense that the gift is the impossible. Not impossible but *the* impossible. The very figure of the impossible. (Derrida 1992: 7)

This aporetic confrontation between the economy and rationality, on the one hand, and the different forms of dissolution of economics, on the other hand, is also the semiotic starting constellation in Jergović's novel *Buick Rivera*. Two Yugo-socialist figures emerge here, the Serb Vuko and the Bosnian Hasan, whose way of dealing with things and words turns out to be *"the* impossible, the figure of the impossible" in the milieu of American economic rationality and binding obligations.

The self-confident and aggressive Vuko makes himself "impossible" by leaving his American wife during an absurd dispute and thereby stealing 15,000 Dollars from her in cash plus a credit card and taking off with her Mercedes. Hasan melancholically and introvertedly maneuvers within the sphere of the "impossible". He undermines American rationality and economic efficiency by – instead of following his German wife's wish for a cheap small Japanese car – buying a useless Buick Riviera with exorbitant gas and oil consumption and on which he wastes time and money to the jealous chagrin of his wife.

Yet the peculiarity of the figures and their significant complementarity, which give rise to the dynamic of the novel, appear to be a symbolization of the lines of argument Derrida develops in his critique of Mauss when exploring the consequences which result from the attempt to engage with the "gift" as a "figure of the impossible". An essential moment for Derrida is the temporal structure which is so striking for the gift and in which the recurrences, i.e. the retroactivities constitutive of economic exchange processes, are revoked. Forgetfulness reigns here: "Forgetting and gift would therefore be each on the condition of the other (18)." The gift itself aims for self-forgetting communication, on this side of all self-observation. Hence "the structure of this impossible gift is also that of Being [...] and of time (27)" as well:

> The gift is not a gift, the gift only gives to the extent it gives time. The difference between a gift and every other operation of pure and simple exchange is that the gift gives time. There where there is gift, there is time. What it gives, the gift, is time, but this gift of time is also a demand of time. (41)

At this point Derrida makes it clear that Mauss' concept of the gift constitutes a linguistic-textual formation which works against the effects of differentiality and recurrence, abstraction and spatial-visual, architectural (terminological) orderliness, which consistently brings about the text-based discourses. The talk of the gift introduces poetics which insist on the presence of the experience of language and the senses. The rationality of writing is suspended, while semantic references are "destroyed" and dissolve in two forms of "madness":

> [...] this madness is surely double since it threatens a priori the closed circle of exchange in rationality as well as frantic expenditure, without return, of a gift that forgets itself: madness of keeping or of hypermnestic capitalization and madness of the forgetful expenditure. But because it wreaks havoc on the two sides of the circle, this madness manages to eat away at language itself. It ruins the semantic reference that would allow one reasonably to say, to state, to describe this madness, in short, it ruins everything that claims to know what gift and non-gift mean to say. (47)

Precisely such an opposing constellation of madness on this side of the semiosis, the "madness of keeping" and the "madness of forgetful expenditure" are embodied by Jergović's protagonists Hasan and Vuko.

The names already reveal that the rivals, the Serb Vuko Šalipur and the Bosnian Hasan Hujdur, are complementary figures of aberratio, as the first two syllables of Vuko's family name are derived from the verb "šaliti" (= eng.: "to joke") and Hasan's final syllable from "duriti se" (= eng.: "to pout"). Both protagonists represent an opposing comical duo in terms of temper and character – similarly to Harlekin and Pierrot in the *commedia dell arte* or the witty and the sad clown from the circus ring. In the details of their aberrational thinking and aneconomic actions, Vuko and Hasan respectively follow Derrida's two contrary types of aneconomic behavior for the exchange of gifts.

Hasan's (an)economic way of dealing with words and things is characterized by a "madness of keeping or of hypermnestic capitalization". This is reflected in Hasan's total relationship to his old Buick Riviera. From an economic and technical standpoint, the car is almost worthless, but it therefore constitutes all the more an object of "capitalization" of Hasan's temporal, emotional, mental and physical resources. The author depicts in detail how during adverse winter conditions Hasan devotes himself to his Buick Riviera with long, precise hand movements to meticulously free it of ice and snow. The entire procedure is compared with Muslim ritual when the author describes how the equipment for cleaning the car is spread out on sheepskin "as is used in Eastern Europe for Islamic prayers" (5-6). The ironic narrator leaves no doubt that Hasan's personal identity is immediately linked with the Buick Riviera, but not in the form of a metonymic fetishization of the car as a phallic symbol,[6] but rather as a psychomental objectivization – entirely analogously to a *totem* by which an individual ensures his position in the social cosmos of an archaic society. Hasan experienced such a totemic consolidation of himself by purchasing the Buick Riviera, as the narrator writes in allusion to Ivo Andrić's *The Bridge over the Drina:*

> From this day on Hasan Hujdur was immune to most disappointments. He reacted to angry words like a mystic, full of profound inner peace. He absorbed the nervousness of others like a bridge over a river: while the river roared, the bridge stood calmly over it. The Buick Rivera [sic] became a place of his inner composure; one was devoted to the other, the man and his car gave each other what people cannot give one another, as long as they are not clergy or psychiatrists. (7-8)

Hasan's total relationship to his Buick Riviera, of which he knows himself that the "truth about it can only be said in a madhouse" (25), is further demonstrated in how he deals with objects of remembrance, into whose coincidental accumulation in drawers in the house (207 et seq.) or in Hasan's wallet (80 et seq.) the reader is given an insight in longer passages. This completely unorderly accumulation of objects whose sheer quantity reinforces their sentimental value but does not assemble them into any consistent personality-forming narrative, corresponds precisely with the sentimental-aneconomic collecting mania that the Soviet artist Il'ja Kabakov depicts in his installations on the "man who never threw anything away"[7] and which Derrida defines in his semiotic analysis of the (an)economic exchange of gifts as "hypermnestic capitalization". In his "madness of keeping", Hasan is miserly not only in terms of objects, but also in terms of words and deeds. Trapped in his world of ideas, he cultivates states of silence. The spheres of active action, communication by language and interactions are foreign to him. This is also the reason he already emigrated to the USA before the outbreak of military confrontations between the Yugoslav Republics. He experiences personal and political history as a chain of misunderstandings and coincidences; for him, a fatal, diabolic dynamic prevails which eludes any constitutive access. And while Hasan retreats

---

6 As it is, for example, in the case of the young protagonist with the red Alfa Romeo Spider in Mike Nichols' 1960s cult film *The Graduate.*
7 Wallach, Amei (ed., 1996) *Ilya Kabakov, The Man Who Never Threw Anything Away.* New York; see in particular "Works with Garbage": 171-177.

to the immanence of his conscience, the category of time also loses its structuring and symbolic relevance for him:

> He needs the boredom, which he endured well, and the waiting for nothing to happen, while time passes and simply does not go by, to the dismay of physicists [...]. If a man is alone and banishes all worries and compulsions from his mind, time vanishes as well. You can then think about anything because every thought is faster than time. If nothing drove you from within, you would never move again. (28)

With his ever so solipsistic "madness of keeping", Hasan, a former filmmaker from an urban environment, represents the intellectual character of his Yugo-socialist culture of origin, which his adversary Vuko immediately and very instinctively recognizes (see 170).

Complementarily to the "madness of keeping", the extroverted, extremely communicative and active Vuko embodies the "madness of expenditure". The value of his personality is defined in the performative here and now of talking and acting. This is also the constellation which motivates Vuko to help Hasan when his car breaks down during the night: he "needed success, hungered for admiration. [...] Admiration was his drug" (55). Vuko's self-worth results from the reactions of his counterpart. Words and meanings are unbinding in Vuko's communication. It instead consists of constant deceptions, which are not aimed at swindling anyone however (164), but which rather occur "without any recognizable benefit" (163), because Vuko has "as many faces [...] as there are people whom he was able to meet. He shows everyone the face that he or she expects" (164). "What was not reflected in the eyes of others did not exist for him". (170) Vuko experiences the affirmation of his current self-worth as an immediate physical experience:

> Vuko Šalipur [...] did not have to prove anything to himself. If he did not feel any need to do so, what could he have told himself that he already had not known for a long time? That is why he needed others who observed and admired him and to whom and to him was clear that [...] he had earned everything himself and *experienced every truth with his body.* (170; emphasis – Ju. M.)

Just as Hasan's identity is lost in the clutter of coincidental objects (of memory), Vuko too does not have a word-based memory and thus a biographic narrative; rather his past life is a physical certitude without a concept. The primal scene of this meaningful embodiment is the corporal punishment he received from his father as a child. The words of his father trying to apologize to him at the moment of his death do not remain in his memory. Instead, it is the "scars on his back" which shape his self-perception:

He understood what his father wanted to say, but that was evermore so a reason for him to defend the father inside himself the way he was. It was easier to believe that he was doing good when he beat him – and left more scars on his back than words to remember him by –, than to recognize the truth in what he said before his death. If that were true, then this life would not have had any meaning, neither for the one nor for the other, and all the suffering would have been for nothing at all. Vuko Šalipur could not live with this truth. (174)

In contrast to Hasan as an intellectual, urban figure of "hypermnestic capitalization", it is in particular this accentuation of the body over the words which marks Vuko as a non-intellectual, farmer-like character with his "madness of expenditure". Hasan reacts to Vuko, who previously made his contribution to the construction of the socialist transport system in Bosnia as a bus driver before joining the Serbian army in an act of fervor, with the same resentment with which Vuko confronts the intellectual Hasan in their first encounter.

If one assumes that socialist economies essentially tend toward the aneconomic principle of the gift and thereby considers Derrida's semiological analysis in this regard, Jergović's novel with the two protagonists trapped in complementary forms of "madness" sets up a constellation which aims for a structural moment of Yugo-socialist economic culture that far transcends Bosnian and Serbian ethnic issues, specifically the antagonism of two forms of overcoming economic rationality inherent to it.

3. The aporia of the (communist) notion of state and socialist (an)economy

Independently of their respective social and intellectual status and level of education, conceptual abstractions are equally foreign to both protagonists. This constitutes an additional moment in Jergović's etiology of the disintegration mechanism of the (Yugo-)socialist economy.

In the modes of "hypermnestic capitalization" and "expenditure" in which Vuko and Hasan act with words and objects, "symbolically generalizing media" (Luhmann 1997: 316-332) such as money, love, power, law, politics and truth lose their binding character; processes of sign formation and differentiation are blocked. This is clearly reflected in how Vuko and Hasan remember the war in Yugoslavia and thereby imagine socialist Yugoslavia as a political entity. The Serb Vuko relates the war against Bosnia to his very personal experiences in village life, in order to simultaneously emphasize that he was never a "nationalist", because "he doesn't hate anybody simply because he has a different belief. He places great value on that" (58). At the same time however, the political idea of a socialist Yugoslavia of "brotherhood & unity" is entirely foreign to him.[8] For him this is only "chatter" and "nothing but a distraction maneuver":

> They had sharpened their knives and oiled their rifles for fifty years, but it never occurred that they hated others only because they were Muslims or Catholics. Even during the war and even among the biggest hotheads whose faces could not be seen behind their fur hats, beards and cockades. (58)

For Vuko, the war was the "clarification of misunderstandings": for him it was definitely not a matter of a Serbian strategy and policy to destroy the Bosnians or a genocide. For Vuko, this is an invention of books, of the world of American individualism in which mutual hate is disproportionately crueler:

> We never hated each other the way they hate here. We only clarified misunderstandings. There were villages where thousands of Muslims with depraved characters lived, demonstrably and unambiguously depraved Muslims. Just as there certainly are villages with depraved Frenchmen, Germans and Americans in the world. Just as there are also villages with depraved Serbs. What do you want to do if you come from such a village, but are neither Muslim nor depraved. There were ten, maybe twenty such villages. Thus, they clarified misunderstandings in the only possible way. The Serbs did not hate anyone. But Vuko knew that these ten, maybe twenty villages would suffice to cause a disaster, as soon as strangers came and interpreted everything their own way; they saw houses burnt down and people fleeing, crying grandmothers and tanks moving around, and then they looked in their books, and browsed through them and said: that is genocide. What genocide, for God's sake? (58-9)

Just like Vuko, whose self is defined by the community, but to whom any ethical abstraction is foreign, Hasan's solipsism does not have a concept of ego. He reacts with an according lack of understanding for his wife Angela's efforts to deal with her own biography by attempting to come to terms with a childhood trauma with the assistance of a psychotherapist. Psychological concepts and abstractions are worthless for Hasan. This includes, above all, the concept of sadism, which he will not let stand and which dissipates into an endless series of individual violent actions for him:

> What is called sadism in the West had much simpler and more banal names in his world. Braggers, perpetrators of violence, neighbors who pulled children's ears as

---

8 On socialist "brotherhood", see Zimmermann, Tanja (2014) *Brüderlichkeit und Bruderzwist. Mediale Inszenierungen des Aufbaus und des Niedergangs politischer Gemeinschaften in Ost- und Südosteuropa*. Göttingen; and especially the article by Andrea Zink and Tatjana Simeunović, "Verlorene Brüder? Miljenko Jergović jugoslawische Spurensuche", 519-542, where the communitarian and the biological aspects of brotherhood are discussed, 531-533.

soon as a soccer ball landed in their yard or they caught them stealing cherries, drunken husbands who beat their wives, fathers who lost their temper, militiamen in night-time attacks on random passers-by, mailmen who intentionally brought important letters to the wrong address or joyfully delivered telegrams with the news of someone's death, secret police and gravediggers who stole everything gold from dead bodies, unmarried math teachers, Chetniks who were still hiding in the caves in karst twenty years after the war, school janitors who assaulted the girls, majors in the barracks of Eastern Serbia, rapists and murderers, snitches outside the mosques, fortune-tellers who shook peas on the table and predicted firedamp in the mine for tomorrow, in three months or in five years [...] and mothers who told their children: "touch this – isn't that nice!", while holding a hot iron in their direction. The little ones had to learn sooner or later [...]. (109 et seq.)

From a personal talking perspective, the abstract term "sadism" is concretized in a never-ending list of various cruelties, in order to ultimately disqualify the term itself together with the central political concept of Yugoslavia, the concept of communism:

[...] but neither were all these people sadists, nor were their actions sadistic. Sadism was something different. Like communism. A word that can mean everything and nothing, that is easily uttered when people want to say something but when they open their mouth they say nothing. (110-111)

Hasan's "hypermnestic capitalization" and Vuko's communicative "expenditure" shield themselves from conceptual abstractions. In Vuko's case this primarily pertains to the ethnic, in Hasan's case to the psychological sphere. Thus for both of them, this goes hand in hand with the rejection of communism as an abstract entity of statehood. Precisely this embeddedness of Vuko's and Hasan's lack of understanding of the concept of "communism" in a fundamental rejection of the concept makes it clear that neither figure formulates critique of communism; rather the idea of statehood as a result of abstraction, agreement and contract is inconceivable in the asemiotic cosmos of both of them. In allusion to Derrida's semiological analysis of Mauss' concept of the gift, one could say that the madness, the aberration of aneconomic things, also "eats away at language itself" (Derrida 1992: 47) in its conceptual formation in the case of Vuko and Hasan; for both of them, the abstraction potential of language is eliminated. In Hasan's "madness of keeping", the linguistic word signs nominalistically cling to the defined, external or mental realities. However, in the case of the swindler Vuko, who overexerts himself in communicating and speaking effects, language entirely loses any semantic bindingness. In Vuko's and Hasan's world of language, no conceptual consolidations of meaning occur which escape the maelstrom of nowness (Vuko) or diffuse timelessness (Hasan). In this case there are no "special semantics"[9] and no ideas. Terms such as "genocide", "sadism" or "communism" are essentially foreign to this world of language; they do not have a discursive place in it.

If we consider the structural relationship and similarities between the socialist economy and Mauss's concept of gift, the semiological nonsense inherent to the communist project and its historical attempts at realization become visible in the character constellations of Hasan and Vuko, which Jergović designs to be both comical and meaningful. This consists, on the one hand, in the continuation of the modern, abstract idea of the state with its foundation in the concept of contractuality, but also, on the other hand, in the breakdown into a countermovement of its conceptual structure by the proclaimed and programmatically pursued socialist economic culture, which tended towards the principle of the gift, with its aberrational dynamics which blocked mechanisms of abstraction. The aporia of an abstract, contract-based concept of the state and a concept denying (an)economy is embodied by the two figures of Vuko and Hasan.[10]

4. The (an)economy of the gift between rules and violence

Mauss points out multiple times that the (an)economy of the potlatch is based on the "principle of rivality and antagonism" and that enormous potential for violence is inherent to the exchange of "total prestations" involving things and people. The "destruction of accumulated wealth" and the tendency to go "so far as to fight, even killing chiefs and nobles who confront each other in this way" (63) constitute essential elements of the (an)economy of gift.[11] Archaic exchange processes take place in states of homeostasis of social cohesion and antagonism, of rules and violence. Precisely this unstable equilibrium characterizes the Yugo-socialist culture, which

---

9 Luhmann (1997: 536-556) "Ideenevolutionen".
10 This aporia refers to the communist project from two prominent historical perspectives, one of which that is inherent to the communist project itself speaks of the dismantling of the state in an advanced phase of a socialist economy. The other consists in a general resentment of the incompatibility of the communist idea, which in itself was positive, with historical practice.
11 Mauss speaks about "total prestations of the agonistic type" (63) or about "exchanges comprising acute rivalries" (64); see also Mauss' statements like "To refuse to give, to neglect to invite, as to refuse to take, is equivalent to declaring war; it is to refuse alliance and communion" (74), or "Everything is based on the principle of antagonism and rivalry. The political status of individuals, in the brotherhoods and clans, and in ranks of all sorts, are obtained by 'war of property', as by real war, or by chance, inheritance, alliance, and marriage. But everything is conceived of as if it were a 'contest of wealth'" (115), or "The potlatch is also a phenomenon of social morphology: the gathering of tribes, clans, and families, even of nations, produces a state of agitation, of remarkable excitement. They fraternize, all the while remaining strangers; they communicate and confront each other in a gigantic forum of trade and a constant tournament" (120).

Jergović resurrects with the coincidental encounter between Vuko and Hasan. This constitutes an additional essential element in Jergović's etiology of the violent collapse of the Yugoslav system.

While Mauss' ethnographic interest is aimed at extracting from the (an)economy of the potlatch any morphology and logic on the basis of which the potential for violence in the cultural and historical economic development process could be sublimated by social institutions and rules,[12] Jergović initially exhibits a different dynamic in his novel. Vuko and Hasan are incorporated as embodiments of the Yugo-socialist culture of the gift into an exchange process of words and things in which the antagonism develops a significant potential for violence with dynamics of its own.

The first encounter between Vuko and Hasan is marked by a primeval violent atmosphere of *homo homini lupus*:[13]

> He mistrusts me. The one thinks like the other and puts on a wolf's smile that one wolf shows to the other when they are trapped together: I am not dangerous and have no evil thoughts. Actually it is not mistrust. One just suspects that the other could be mistrustful whenever one shakes someone else's hand, both in Oregon and the Balkans; one would be more likely to die for the other than biological brothers in the rest of the world, but one would also kill the other more quickly, and there would be numerous reasons for doing so. Everything depends on the location and time of the plot, and the causes for love and hate are the same. One exchanges victims in the same way that the other exchanges greetings in other places, just as thoughtfully and according to a comparable protocol. [...] One would extract a glass of blood from the other's carotid artery, just as one would not even pour a glass of water in a more moderate society. (53)

Then the perfidious, communicative competition between the two protagonists begins, whose tragicomical dynamic consists in the fact that each statement by the one draws attention to the fundamental and irreconcilable otherness of the other against which their own selves are constituted. Each reply, each gesture, and each action aggravates the antagonism through which both – reinforced by external circumstances – are joined in an ever closer and thus more aggressive and ultimately self-destructive bond.

For example, the failure to rescue Hasan's Buick from the ditch along the road is equally degrading for both of them, albeit for different reasons: the solipsistic

---

12 Mauss' ethnographic interest simultaneously demonstrates a time-critical component which consists in the gift economy with its social obligation mechanism as an ideal and, so to speak, as an intermediate third way between states of violence of the potlatch economy and the alienated, individualistic money economy, which means the "stage of the purely individual contract, or the market in which money circulates, or sale in the strict sense" (144).
13 Consider also the first name Vuko from "vuk" (Engl. wolf).

and introverted figure Hasan is ashamed because "someone helped him that recognized and knew how to interpret each of his movements and allusions" (55). Vuko's failure to assist Hasan means a personal defeat for him who always "hungered for admiration". The subsequent ride together in Vuko's car turns into a communicative disaster. The talkative Vuko experiences Hasan's intellectual, introverted silence as an intentional refusal to engage with an outgoing partner in conversation, which Vuko ultimately even generalizes as being symbolic of the violent collapse of Yugoslavia:

> [...] you were all for brotherhood and unity, but you understood it this way: everyone for you, and you against everyone. That's not how things work, buddy. Neither on a biological nor on a social level. If you ask why it exploded [...], here is the answer: I have told you everything and you don't tell me anything. (66)

By contrast, Hasan experiences Vuko's offensive willingness to talk as a form of physical pressure: "It became too tight for him, his seat was too close to Vuko, their knees almost touched each other [...]" (63). Deeply trapped in the situation, Hasan is also unable to assess how realistic Vuko's flood of words is: "It did not dawn on him that Vuko was performing a comedy on him and completely fooling him" (67). Yet Vuko also lacked any reflective distance to the communicative action. Although he rhetorically dominates the situation, he is "not certain what effect it would have on Hasan and how much strength he invested in this man and when he would start defending himself" (70).

This antagonistic communication reaches a further level of escalation when Hasan loses his wallet in Vuko's car. This second coincidence makes Hasan's silent loss of self-worth in the encounter with Vuko equally evident as he simultaneously provides a motive for Vuko's further action. He searches for the Bosnian to give him back the found item, which in turn obligates Hasan – subject to pressure from his wife – to invite Vuko for dinner to his home to thank him. In this cycle of loss, selfless reimbursement, and giving thanks, the self-assertion struggle escalates in the presence of Hasan's wife into mutual imaginations of satanic and deadly threats:[14]

> It made him [= Hasan, Ju. M.] furious how this man conquered the world and filled entirely different people with enthusiasm for him.
> [...]
> He is Satan, thought Hasan. Satan, Satan, Satan ...

---

14 See also: "Life is not mathematics or physics. Probability theory, whatever it tells you, and how often the moon really may have turned around the earth, doesn't count for us. People are not celestial bodies, not Bosnians and definitely not Bosnian Muslims. They cannot produce anything with probabilities. They are only making a fool of you with probabilities. That is why we lost the war, even though we should have won it according to mathematics and physics" (199 et seq.).

> [...] He was certain that Satan existed and his fingers combed the world. When the worse possibility turned out to be more frequent, even though it appeared much less probable, when one coincidence followed the next coincidence, then Hasan believed it was Satan at work. [...]. Satan habitually rules over all coincidences every day, because there are not and cannot be any good coincidences, and everything that he does is banal and not worth being told. It is no good for making legends. (162 et seq.)

Vuko accordingly identifies Hasan's "hypermnestic capitalization" and his silence as a religious principle of Islam, which includes a deadly strategy of violence:

> What does this whiner have against me, he thought and looked at Hasan, who shoved grains of rice over the table cloth with his small finger like a snowplow. He remained silent in the bar. Now he is silent and just lurking for the right moment [...].
> Air, dear Hasan, you have nothing but air in your hand and are sweeping grains of rice off the table cloth. As long as it's clean for me. Let the world end if it's fun. [...] The fact is that you have always been clean. It was always your subject how to wash your behind. [...] Is there actually anything that your faith does not ban you from doing? Are you allowed to do anything for a change? And is there a spot on the globe where there are none of you? Can one go anywhere where you leave people in peace and where they can recuperate from your hygiene and what you think while you're being silent, and from the jackknife in your pant pockets that is – ouch – jammed in our ribs just after we have turned around! (169 et seq.)

With these mutual illusions of threats and violence the antagonism, which nature-like reigns over Vuko and Hasan from the very moment of their first coincidental encounter, reaches its climax and turning point.

5. Total losses and esthetic gain

While the volatility of the spoken word dominated up to the escalation of the struggle for self-assertion between Vuko and Hassan, the communicative exchange between the two adversaries takes on a new quality the moment money comes into play via the deal with Hasan's Buick Riviera. This motive of money has a double effect for the self-worth of the protagonists, but also for the further course of action and ultimately for the poetics of the text itself: on the one hand, the protagonists are confronted with the aberration and the "impossibility" of the Yugoslav gift economy on the basis of the monetary (and written) symbols; money functions as a means of reflection and thus of the experience of the loss of Yugo-socialist identity – entirely in line with the laconic remark of the narrator at the end of the novel:

"Symbols are evidently recognized with a delay and only serve to confront people with their mistakes" (225). On the other hand, this exchange of works, things and services, which is now regulated by symbols and "symbolically generalized media" (Luhmann 1997: 316-332), opens new perspectives for fictional designs of the ego and the world and thus also for the prospect of overcoming historical traumas by esthetic and literary means. In the final part of the text, the existential motto proclaimed by Vuko at the beginning of the novel "You have to lose everything in order to win" turns out to be a philosophical sentence on the (esthetic) surplus of value by means of abstraction.

The novel deals with this rationalizing virulence of money in its rapidly narrated conclusion. First the deal regarding Hasan's Buick is cunningly initiated by Vuko, who mimics Hasan's passion for vintage cars towards his wife and reinforces this by claiming that he is willing to put up all his ready cash of 15,000 Dollars for Hasan's Buick. While Hasan's wife acknowledges this with smiling admiration, "what a gesture" (178), Hasan not only insists that his Buick is not for sale, but on his part disqualifies Vuko's offer as a bluff:

> "Don't lie to me. You do not have 15,000 Dollars and even if you had all the money in the world, I would not sell it to you. And do you know why? Because I would not bear anything from my possession coming into your hands. I would not even leave you a burnt match. Not for all the money in the world, Vuko, if you had it, but you don't have the money." (185)

When Hasan ultimately angrily asks his guest to stop the "contortions" and aggressively demands that Vuko "get his ass out of here" (186), Vuko proves the power of his "gesture" and puts the amount of money on the table. The two men's struggle for self-assertion takes a decisive turn when Hasan's wife becomes involved in the deal by remarking that Vuko can take both the "old pile of junk in front of the door" which she hates and only guzzles gas as well as the horrendous amount of 15,000 Dollars. Since Hasan's "unsellable" object is disqualified as being worthless by his own wife, Hasan has no other choice than to secure the discussed amount of money by succumbing to the logic of the deal, and handing over the car key and car papers to Vuko, who leaves behind his 15,000 Dollars for the car.

It is the money which both stimulates the deal and makes the aneconomic mechanism obvious, while thus bestowing on both protagonists, who are fighting for the "total power" of their own self-worth, a "total loss".[15]

For Hasan, the sale of the Buick Riviera signifies the loss of his spiritual self-worth. Now he also feels compelled to leave his wife, who took the side of his adversary during the deal. He also now rids himself of his diverse objects of remembrance from his previous Yugoslav times, which he had accumulated in the drawers.

---

15 See also the comment by Vuko elsewhere: "You have to lose everything in order to win".

He stuffs them in a garbage bag, which he disposes of in what is not an analytical (ecological), but rather a "total" act:

> He dragged the full garbage bag for more than 100 meters behind him before he realized that he could not throw it anywhere. He would have to have gone to the container in the city center and separated every memory according to strict environmental requirements. He was not willing to cleanse his life so thoroughly. Do the Polaroid photographs taken in front of his parents' home in Herzegovina go in the paper waste or plastic waste? And what about the things that were composed of materials for all five containers, and not just of paper, glass, metal, plastic or fabric? In an ideal world each thing would have had its place, but in a world in which everything is made of a piece of something, there is no place for what consists of several materials and for which no container is provided. He ultimately throws the bag down the road embankment. (208 et seq.)

By eliminating all objects of remembrance, Hasan also physically disappears from the city of Toledo and thus also as a figure from the cast of actors in Jergović's novel: "Finally he could go away. Nobody who previously knew him ever saw him again" (209). Yet what remains of Hasan (and his real existence in the novel) are only dead written symbols from a farewell letter in which he documents his disappearance with the cryptic sentence that he has taken off for Kandahar.[16] However, this sentence in which the figure Hasan vanishes from the plot of the novel results in a semiologic quantum leap which is decisive for the development of the text, because it leaves a trace of symbols through which the imagination of the reader and, in particular, his adversary are able to generate new stories.

Yet before Hasan's cryptic written testimony can become a means to Vuko's (economic) success in the American media world, the absurd car deal also proves to be a complete experience of loss for Vuko. He is only able to briefly enjoy the effect of his wasteful gesture and is soon no longer certain

---

16 The deal also signifies a total loss for Angela, who is abandoned by her husband forever. The 15,000 Dollars left behind on her table are not a monetary gain, which may have been a small consolation for her vanished husband. On the contrary: "[...] she was no longer interested in the money later. Her conscience pricked her over it and the mere thought of the 15,000 Dollars seemed like adultery to her. It will probably lie forever in the drawer with the wiping cloths, under the shelf with the herbs, which already had lost their aroma [...]." (223) – Angela overcomes her neurotic purpose-oriented rationalism, begins to appreciate Hasan's totemic bond with his Buick Rivera and immerses herself nostalgically in a fictional image of the real Hasan: "[...] Hasan became better and better and kinder and kinder in her mind and no longer had any similarity with the living Hasan Hujdur who had lived with her. During her night-time conversations, when she turned out the light and the tears ran over her ears, she explained to him, the ideal Hasan, that he should have told her how much this car meant to him [...]" (222).

[...] who was fooled by whom and whose game had been played. It was indeed possible that Hasan returned home overjoyed, because he had palmed off a wreck to a dumb Serb for 15,000 Dollars. Maybe it was all a contrived game between him and his wife to trick him. (198 et seq.)

The feeling of loss compels Vuko to take action once again. In a state of anger he drives back to Hasan's house and barges in to brutally cancel the car deal and demand his money back. Yet all he finds is Hasan's farewell letter with the ominous reference to his departure for Kandahar. Vuko's notorious storytelling skills give him the idea for a new story – namely to call the police and tell them that he has tracked down a Muslim terrorist who remained hidden in the American city of Toledo before he set out to Afghanistan to the Taliban. In contrast to the personal dialog partners in the face-to-face-situations, in which Vuko always cleverly knows what they wanted to hear, the police react as an institution which does not attach any informational value to Vuko's story but rather establishes the judicial fact that he illegally entered a house in order to put him behind bars as a burglar. It is this intertwining of the experienced relativization of the self by means of money, on the one hand, and the institutional safeguarding of property and the associated disciplining of selfish action, on the other, that compels Vuko to shift his combative desire for performative self-assertion from *face-to-face* action to the sphere of fiction. When he is released, Vuko turns to the press and media to spread his Hasan story. He tells the American public about a man named Hasan Hujdur "who they believed came to America over twenty years ago and completely adapted", but now "went to Afghanistan in order to destroy your houses, poison the waterfalls and capture your children when they come home from school while operating from over there" (240). Vuko evolves into a terrorism expert with his Hasan Hujdur story, "esteemed and respected as an important person for all of Oregon" (217) and "[...] worked very hard to ensure that the public did not lose track of Hasan Hujdur" (218). It is now about generalizations for Vuko: "Maybe Hasan Hujdur is not a bad person, but we are talking here about what Hasan Hujdur means" (219 et seq.).

Vuko overcomes his traumatic memories to the extent that he immerses himself in the fictional ideas of Hasan Hujdur's (assumed) world; his work on fiction transforms his "self" and liberates him from the constraints of the repetition of traumatic primal scenes of his Yugoslav past:

> Within a few weeks, more things moved further in the past than in five full American years. He did not recognize himself in the roles of his previous lives – bus driver and warrior – anymore; they resembled so many other images, both real and imagined, which did not concern him. Two months of fame in Portland spared several of his most important principles of life, those for which he [...] went off to war. He did not know how that had happened to him, when and where he had become softer, but the more he lied and invented stories and ultimately read the

newspapers, the weaker his anger became. The more he talked about Muslims [...], the more traits he imputed and attributed to the figure of Hasan Hujdur [...], and the more he pushed the illusion that Hujdur was not an individual case, but symbolic of an entire society, the more Vuko forgot him. (220 et seq.)

This work on the fictive Hasan Hujdur ultimately completely detaches itself from the direct communicative context of the public when Vuko begins to invent stories from details and trivialities, for example a story about Hasan's grandmother:

> No matter how rare it may be, Vuko was proud of this story and himself, because he invented it from something. Actually he did not invent it, but elaborated it, because this story definitely existed. It was part of his world. [...] Thus a narrative grew [...] which [...] did not mean anything for anyone, but from which the new life of Vuko Šalipur peeped, saturated with reality and more credible than his old life, even if it was a life in which he did not have a share himself. Yet the calmer he became, the more seldom he was happy. (221 et seq.)

The figure of Vuko thereby transforms into the image of a literary author. He is no longer a media actor who illustrates his moral phantasms towards the public on the basis of allegedly true stories, but an intrinsically motivated author who "elaborates" narratives of others' lives from details and findings from reality in order to overcome his own traumatic past in the immanence of esthetics and by working on the artistic form, also to atone for his guilt in his first Yugoslav life, when he burned down Bosnian villages as a Serbian soldier. Instead of Vuko's previous naive and narrow-minded zest for life and self-assurance, which during Vuko's time in Yugoslavia as well as in America was based on the notorious repetition of the performative affirmation of his personal self-value, a "new life" emerges after the struggle over the Buick Riviera objectivized in monetary symbols. "Saturated with reality", this new life gains its value through representation of the narrative devised in the abstract text and writing design. Just as Vuko triggered a painful abstraction and reflection process by wasting the enormous amount of 15,000 Dollars (in conjunction with legally and institutionally ensuring and sealing off the car deal), this process ultimately results in the creation of a value of the constructed history from insignificant details, which tells of the "second life" of Vuko as a whole. The image through which the narrator again addresses the Buick at the end of his novel, which is now a worthless and meaningless piece of junk lying on the side of the road, but from which a strong, and therefore esthetic effect on the observer emanates, also tells of this mechanism from which the monetary and esthetic values equally result from a semiosis abstracting from materiality:[17]

---

17 A very similar definition of esthetics, according to which art is compared with a worthless metal sheet which acquires semantic value when it is able to attract the interest of the beholder upon closer examination, is given by the Russian writer and social revolutionist Nikolay Cherny-

The Buick Riviera still lies beside the road, half-way between Toledo and Portland, at the place where he ran out of gas the last time, after Vuko, now released from prison, embarked on his new life. When it is cloudy, it appears like a dead pile of junk, but as soon as the sun comes out, it shines light silver, so that the passengers in the bus turn around to look, and those who keep looking at it have tears in their eyes. (225)

Bibliography

Andrić, Ivo (1945) *Na Drini ćuprija*. Belgrade.
Barnett, Vincent (2004) *The Revolutionary Russian Economy, 1890-1940: Ideas, Debates and Alternatives*. London, New York.
Beganović, Davor (2009) *Poetika melankolije, Na tragovima suvremene bosansko-hercegovačke književnosti*. Sarajevo.
Černyševskij, Nikolaj (1974) *Sobranie sočinenij v pjati tomach*. IV, Moscow.
Derrida, Jacques (1992) *Given Time: I. Counterfeit Money*. Chicago, London.
Graeber, David (2001) *Towards an Anthropological Theory of Value. The False Coin of Our Own Dreams*. Basingstoke.
Hansen-Kokoruš, Renate (2001) Das Auto, der Raum und die Zeit: Miljenko Jergović' Romantriologie Buick Rivera, Freelander und Volga, Volga. In: *Anzeiger für Slavische Philologie* 11/2011 (39): 75-93.
Jakiša, Miranda et al. (2009) Kontingente Feindschaft? Die Jugoslawienkriege bei David Albahari und Miljenko Jergović. In: Borissova, Natalia (ed.) *Zwischen Apokalypse und Alltag: Kriegsnarrative des 20. und 21. Jahrhunderts*. Bielefeld: 221-236.
Jergović, Miljenko (2004) *Buick Rivera*. Zagreb.
Lešić-Thomas, Andrea (2004) Miljenko Jergović's Art of Memory: Lying, Imagining and Forgetting in Mama Leone and Historijska Citanka. In: *Modern Language Review* 4/2004 (2): 430-444.
Luhmann, Niklas (1997) *Die Gesellschaft der Gesellschaft*. Frankfurt a. M.
Mauss, Marcel (1925; 1950) *Essai sur le don, forme et raison de l'échange dans les sociétés archaïques*. Paris.
Mauss, Marcel (2016) *The Gift, Expanded Edition*. Chicago.

---

shevsky in his famous essay *Aesthetic Relations of Art to Reality* (1855): "Golden coins are thrown about all over our road of life but we don't notice them because we only think about the destination without paying attention to the road lying underneath our feet; even if we do notice them, we cannot stoop to pick them up because the 'cart of life' unstoppably carries us forward – this is our attitude to reality; but when we get to a station and are walking around dully waiting for horses, *we fasten our eyes on every metal shield which is probably not worth our attention at all – this is our attitude to art*" (Černyševskij 1974: 95; emphasis Ju. M.).

Vervaet, Stin (2011) Writing war, writing memory. The representation of the recent past and the construction of cultural memory in contemporary Bosnian prose. In: *Neohelicon* 2011/38: 1-17.

Wallach, Amei (ed., 1996) *Ilya Kabakov, The Man Who Never Threw Anything Away*. New York.

Zimmermann, Tanja (2014) *Brüderlichkeit und Bruderzwist. Mediale Inszenierungen des Aufbaus und des Niedergangs politischer Gemeinschaften in Ost- und Südosteuropa*. Göttingen.

Zink, Andrea/Simeunović, Tatjana (2014) Verlorene Brüder? Miljenko Jergović jugoslawische Spurensuche. In: Zimmermann, Tanja (ed.) *Brüderlichkeit und Bruderzwist. Mediale Inszenierungen des Aufbaus und des Niedergangs politischer Gemeinschaften in Ost- und Südosteuropa*. Göttingen: 519-542.

Beyond Economy
Social Misery and Masochism in Post-Communist Serbian Society (Nikola Ležaić's Film *Tilva Roš*)

Tanja Zimmermann

1. Depicting social misery in Eastern Europe

During the communist period, depictions of social misery in East and Southeast Europe remained mostly hidden, and people on the brink, perceived as useless "parasites", were banished from the public sphere and even sent to jail or to a labour camp (Zubkova 2010; Jahn 2010: 135-147; Neuheiser 2011: 109, 110). After the end of communism, they returned to the visual sphere, but their images – especially in photographs by Boris Mikhailov (*Case History*, 1999) or Andrej Krementschouk (*No Direction Home*, 2009; *Come and Bury me*, 2010) – revealed an indissoluble contradiction: on the one hand, they announced the end of the period of the "proletarian dictatorship" that had failed to liberate the miserable, even though it had begun by proclaiming their victory. On the other hand, they revealed the inevitable subjection of the whole of society under the capitalist rules of profit and consumption. Amid the economic restructuring according to the rules of profit, numerous workers lost their jobs and were not qualified to find new ones. The privatization of state-run business in post-communist countries was carried out in a spirit of socially untamed liberalism and 'wild' capitalism and there were no traditions of establishing workers' rights or social policies. Poorly developed healthcare systems and social security networks contributed to the misery of the growing masses of the unemployed. As the struggle for social equality was not at the top of the agenda of the arising national and nationalistic political programs, art – especially photography and film – became the principal and sometimes the only advocate of the miserable.

As early as the 19th century, during the period of realism and naturalism in Europe, people on the brink had become a central topic of art (Clark 1982), first in physiognomic sketches in the illustrated press and later in literature (Zola, Dostoevsky) and painting (Millet, Courbet, the wandering artists Peredvizhniki in Russia). Some images depicted them as dehumanized, animalized products of their milieu and their physical state, characterized by temper and heritage. Others, on the contrary, elevated and even sacralized them as martyrs imitating Christ in their misery and degradation (Auerbach 1994; Kridl Valkenier 1990). At the same time, physiognomic and phrenological studies by anthropologists, ethnologists, physicians (Lombroso) and eugenicists (Galton) classified people on the brink according to different taxonomies, dressed not only for scientific purposes, but also for institutional control and social exclusion (Uerlings 2010; Nicolosi 2016). In the late 19th and early 20th centuries, the period obsessed with the documentation and statistical recording of populations, misery was captured by documentary photography (Jacob A. Riis, August Sander, Walker Evans, Dorothea Lange) and film (John Grierson, the New Deal filmmakers), which laid bare the suffering of the lower classes. The photographers thereby refused to sentimentalize them by poetic or moralistic means, in order to confront the spectators with their corporeal presence (Schäffler 2010). After the October Revolution, the Russian avant-garde and the painters of Socialist Realism even transformed the poor into Promethean victors. The suffering of the miserable, as in Dziga Vertov's propaganda film *A Sixth Part of the World* (1926), was shown to exist only abroad, beyond the borders of the Soviet Union, for example in Africa, which was exploited by colonialist powers.

Art in the post-communist period from the 1990s onwards has thus been confronted with different western and eastern iconographical traditions, representing people on the brink as crude, inhuman "animals" in a naturalist manner, as holy martyrs in sentimental idioms often using religious motifs or as invincible, glorious victors in the manner of Socialist Realism. Under the new condition of subjection to neo-liberalist conditions, which were only initially perceived as a voluntary liberation from a fatalist adaptation to socialist dictatorship, traditional models of depicting misery became increasingly contradictory. The new miserable were not only the traditional groups such as the poor, the homeless and the sick, but after some time also the loser type of the middle class. Artists were challenged to find new, original ways of representing people on the brink.

One of them was the Serbian filmmaker Nikola Ležaić in his film *Tilva Roš* (2010), which won the "European Discovery" award that same year. The movie is a mixture of a feature film and amateur video clips made by teenagers from the city of Bor in Eastern Serbia. They filmed themselves performing dangerous stunts or even deliberately torturing and injuring their bodies. A copper mine that went bankrupt provides the background for their painful, sometimes even dangerous performance. After several unsuccessful attempts at privatization, during which a dangerous sublevel mining method was used, the shafts were abandoned and flooded. Their parents lost their jobs and tried to find new employment, mostly without success. The film deconstructs the neo-liberalist promises of modernization by confronting the failure of the economic transition with the anti-economy of masochism and self-destruction of the teenage generation. The first part of this paper is a survey of psychoanalytical studies of different forms of masochism whose insights will be useful for analyzing the film. I will then discuss masochism as way of acting out misery in the context of different visual traditions representing people on the brink.

2. From erotogenic to social masochism

In his article "The Economic Problem of Masochism" (1924), Sigmund Freud presented his extensive studies on the puzzling phenomenon of love of pain, a phenomenon "mysterious from the economic point of view": "For if mental processes are governed by the pleasure principle in such a way that their first aim is the avoidance of unpleasure and the obtaining of pleasure, masochism is incomprehensible" (Freud 1998: 158). Freud linked the dark desire to the "economy" of excitation: "Pleasure and unpleasure, therefore, cannot be referred to an increase and decrease of quality", but most probably depend on "qualitative characteristics", on "the rhythm, the temporal sequence of changes, rises and falls in the quantity of stimulus" (ibid.: 159). In his early writings "Three Essays on the Theory of Sexuality" (1905) and "Beyond the Pleasure Principle" (1920), Freud derived masochism from primary sadism, an aggressive, extroverted "death instinct" which has been transformed into an introverted one, turned back in on itself. In his later writings published in 1924, he observes that the "pleasure instinct", the "watchman of our life", is paralyzed in masochism and has undergone a modification. This modification is of such a high degree that "we shall avoid regarding the two [sadism and masochism] as one" (ibid.: 159). Masochism is, as Freud claims, a loss of balance in an amalgamation of the death and pleasure principles. It is an intensification of the sadistic expressions of the death drive, but turned back against the self in the course of the cultural suppression of instincts. He therefore distinguishes between a single manifestation of sadism on the one hand and three different sorts of masochism on the other – a primary or "erotogenic" one, experiencing erotic satisfaction through pain, which serves as a foundation for the two further, secondary forms of masochism – a "feminine" and a "moral" one. The so-called "feminine", passive form of masochism, containing several infantile features of regression, places the subject in his/her fantasies in characteristically female situations of being castrated, or copulated with, or giving birth to a baby. The third form of masochism, the "moral" one, is – according to Freud – a product of an unconscious sense of guilt demanding supervision and punishment. Its form of ultra-morality has already loosened the direct connection to the libido. Freud therefore declares the categorical imperative postulated by Kant to be the direct heir of the oedipal complex, which has lost its link to the erotogenic source. As in "moral" masochism, the source of pain is no longer important and the person causing it can also be replaced by impersonal powers or by living circumstances: "The true masochist always turns his cheek whenever he has a chance of receiving a blow" (ibid.: 167). In "moral" masochism, suffering itself becomes what matters.

The Jewish-Austrian psycho-analyst Theodor Reik, Freud's pupil, who immigrated to the United States in 1938, further developed the concept of "moral" masochism and transferred it to the social life and behaviour of individuals, communities and institutions such as the Church. In 1940 he published in London the book *Aus Leiden Freuden* (*Pains for Pleasures*), which was translated into English in 1941 under the title *Masochism in Modern Men*. His reviewers at that time did not recognize the importance of the cultural and anthropological dimension of his study and perceived him as an epigone of Freud (Israel 2013: 454). Reik emphasized the importance of three productive elements increasing masochist satisfaction – the imagination, the moment of suspense and the demonstrative character. The imagination, the most important element provoking masochist excitement, decorates the scene and arranges the procedure to an almost sacred, slowly performed ritual or martyr cycle. The moment of suspense, a delay in the theatrical direction of the masochist performance, enables the subject to momentarily escape from fear, but at the same time also prolongs the procedure by expectation, which arouses tension and intensification. The third feature, the demonstrative character, prepares the body to exhibit its pain and exposes it to voyeurism.

"Social" masochism is, according to Reik, less motivated by an unconscious guilt and the wish to be punished, motivations Freud had claimed for "moral" masochism. It is instead provoked by social fears, triggered by great social changes in the course of modernization. It manifests itself in arranged humiliations and self-provoked failures in everyday life which are paradoxically experienced as victories. In comparison to the erotogenic form of masochism, the social form is characterized by the reinforced moment of suspense, which becomes a living condition. In favour of higher goals and their postponement into a far future – even after death – satisfaction never really comes to matter.

> The masochist character enjoys the idea that he will finally carry through his will despite of everything, that he will conquer all his enemies and then suppress them, that he is going to be acknowledged by the very society which neglects and rejects him now. The aggressive and ambitious, revengeful and violent instinctual aims, the parrying of which resulted in the genesis of masochism, rise again in the expected and phantasied satisfaction. (Reik 2013 [1941]: 285)[1]

---

[1] Reik 1940: 310, 311. "Der masochistische Charakter genießt die Vorstellung, dass er seinen Willen am Ende doch durchsetzen, all seine Gegner besiegen und dann unterdrücken wird, dass er gerade von der Gesellschaft anerkannt werden wird, die ihn jetzt vernachlässigt und verwirft. In der erwarteten und phantasierten Befriedigung kommen die aggressiven und ehrgeizigen, rachesüchtigen und gewaltigen Triebziele wieder herauf, deren Abwehr zur Entstehung des Masochismus geführt hat."

In the same way as suffering is reinterpreted as the future triumph, the masochistic behaviour anticipates subjection and obedience as forms of belonging to a society by destroying his very chances of being presently integrated into it. Both Freud in *Civilization and its Discontent* (1930) and Reik in *Masochism in Modern Men* link technical and cultural progress with suffering and pain, because they demand subjection to the new technologies and economic rules which change the entire network of social relations. Social masochism is thus a phenomenon accompanying economic crisis and social restructuring.

3. The anti-economy of masochism in *Tilva Roš*

In the film *Tilva Roš* (2010), which – as explained in the film – means red earth in the language of the local Valahian minority, the devastated, wasted landscape around the copper mine of Bor provides the scenery for a group of young people who have finished secondary school and now have to find work or continue their studies at universities away from their hometowns (Fig. 1).

Fig. 1 Devastated landscape around the copper mine of Bor in Eastern Serbia.

The boys and one girl spend most of their time at a closed mining facility, which they use as a skating rink (Fig. 2).

Fig. 2 Closed mining facility serving as a skating rink.

Its circular form embodies the void rotation of the adolescents on the threshold between childhood and adulthood, who are unable to find a way out of the limits of their town – and of their adolescence. Two boys, Marko Todorović – Toda and Stefan Đorđević – Seki, perform dangerous stunts in front of their friends, violate their own bodies or allow themselves to be hurt by other people. Seki throws himself into the depth of the mine; Toda jumps from the skeleton of a mining facility and throws himself from a driving car (Fig. 3).

Fig. 3 Toda performing a stunt on a driving car.

He provokes other people to hit him (Fig. 4) – with a bunch of flowers, he teases an unknown man into punching him in the face.

Fig. 4 Toda hit by a man whom he provoked by giving him a bunch of flowers.

He asks his friends to hit the bucket he has put over his head (Fig. 5).

Fig. 5 Toda with a bucket on his head, hit by his friends.

Toda is not looking for a fight. He just wants to be hit, without trying to protect himself. Further strategies of self-harming are piercing, jumping through fire, hitting each other alternately with a rod and a leather strap, throwing themselves into nettles and rasping their skin with a grater (Fig. 6).

Fig. 6 Toda rasping his skin with a grater.

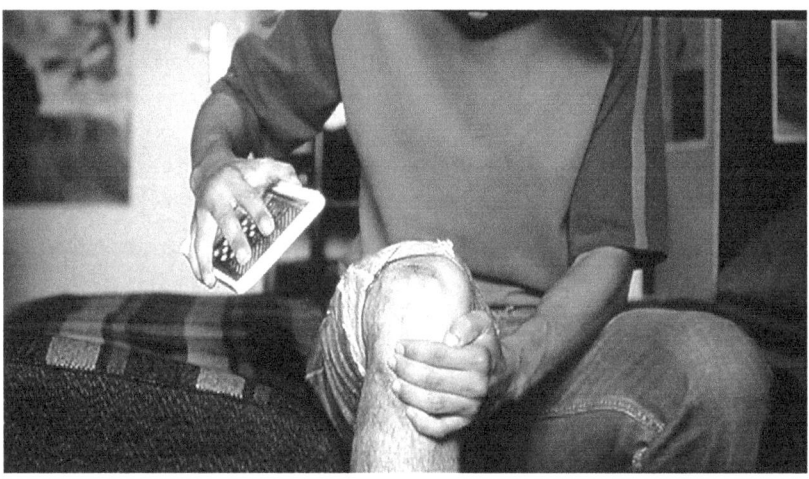

In artistic performances and in body art, pain is often used as a way of conveying transgressive, liminal experiences leading to catharsis (Fischer-Lichte 2004: 305-308, 312s.). The cathartic effect can be experienced not only by the artist, but also by the spectators in a community surrounding the "martyr" and witnessing the actions of self-injuring. Suffering can evoke empathy and provoke ethically motivated actions in which the artist is "saved" by the spectators (Beganović 2017), who experience a process of community building and shared identity. A pain performance is thus close to religious rituals of passage, kenosis and sacrifice, destined to strengthen the group in a mental and even in a physical sense (Meyer 2004). If the spectators fear that the artist is going too far, so far that she/he can lose her/his life, they can intervene – such as in the performance *Rhythm 5* (1974) by Marina Abramović, who lay down in the middle of a five-pointed star set on fire. When she lost consciousness, the spectators in Belgrade rescued her by carrying her body out of the fire surrounding her. The viewers can, of course, also act aggressively and increase the violence of the performance, as in *Rhythm 0* (1974), when Abramović was hurt by them (Enßlen 2003).

The young people who injure themselves in Ležaić's film do not expect any reaction from their audience. The teenagers, observing the actions of their two friends, remain mostly passive and do not try to intervene. The painful and dangerous performances of the protagonists do not have any observable cathartic effect and can hardly be read as a form of rite of passage. The boys, especially Toda, repeat their actions without breaking out of the circle. Although the teenagers find a new method of self-mutilation every time, their reproduction of pain is reminiscent of compulsive repetition inclined to yearning for death.

In the same year when the film *Tilva Roš* was produced, the Serbian writer Sreten Ugričić used the city as a metaphor for economic, political and spiritual death in Serbia. In his novel *To an Unknown Hero* (*Neznanom junaku*, 2010), Bor is depicted as a place where people are subjected to an inevitable yearning for death and commit suicide one after another. The domino effect begins with a bankrupt accounts clerk responsible for the closing of a copper mine.

> Suicides have become very popular. Suicides are a Serbian tourist attraction. The most recent statistics, from this year, reveal that in that year more than seventeen thousand servants of the middle and lower class committed suicide, and that the number of suicides both in remote areas and at primary and secondary schools is on the rise, well above usual and forecasted indicators. [...]
>
> The most recent case was in Bor, where a bankrupt accounts clerk, who used to work for the mine, drank a bottle of acid for dissolving mullock and collapsed prone in front of a mud hut, leaving behind a sickly wife and two half-blind sons who never leave the turbo-folk bars on the seventh horizon. City sanitation workers dragged the body down the main street, right to the end, and bundled it into the enormous crater of what was once a strip mine. The fall to the bottom took a whole minute, and as always, you couldn't even hear the body hit the ground. It was tossed there for a reason: to glisten from the deep.
>
> Then the best man of this guy, the bankrupt clerk, killed himself. Then the sister of the bankrupt clerk's best man, she killed herself. Then her mother and father killed themselves. Then their second eldest daughter killed herself, a girl by the name of Persida [Peach]. Then a neighbour who was secretly in love with Persida killed himself, even though he was married to another woman and the father of a boy. Then the boy killed himself too. Then his teacher killed herself. Then the teacher's lover, who worked at the Bor Post Office, killed himself. Then the postal worker's father killed himself. Then his brother killed himself. Then both the wife and the mistress of the brother of the father of the postal worker, they killed themselves. And this mistress was the neighbour of the best man of the bankrupt accounts clerk from the mine, the one who drank a bottle of acid

for dissolving mullock and collapsed prone in front of a mud hut.[2] (Translated by David Williams)

Bor is depicted as a place of total bankruptcy where not only the copper mine, but also the lives of the people have lost their value. The "life principle" has been replaced by a hypertrophy of the desire for death, which is first provoked by unemployment, but then also by the loss of loved ones. The place thus took on its symbolic geography as a post-industrial landscape in which love does not reproduce life, but converts to death. The filmmaker, born himself in Bor, described in his interviews the landscape as "ruined, desolate places abandoned by the people, but where you can still feel their presence" (Ležaić 2012). Film critics compared it with the photographs by William Eggleston, who documented industrial and urban decay in Pittsburgh and other old American industrial cities.

Ležaić received the self-made videos with the stunts and self-injuries of the teenagers from a friend on a home DVD and embedded them into his feature film, giving them a socio-economic background – the impact of the neo-liberal economic system on the bankruptcy of the old industrial branches and the emergence of a western consumerist lifestyle in the Serbian province.

Well, a friend of mine gave me a DVD of a homemade "Jackass-like" film called "Crap – Pain is Empty". It was a compilation of crazy stunts done by Kolos, a group of skaters from my hometown, Bor. It was totally crazy and unexpected to see [sic] coming from out there. It made me think that it would be great to make a real film with them in which they did the same stunts, but where I would think up a story around them. So I met Stefan and Toda, and I started hanging out with

---

2 Ugričić 2010 : 148, 149. "Самоубиства су постала туристичa атракција Србије. Последњи подаци, из две хиљаде дванаесте, показују да је те године самоубиство извршило више од седамнаест хиљада службеника средње и ниже класе, а да је број самоубиства у забаченим крајевима и по основним и средњим школама у порасту, прилично изнад уобичајених и очекиваних показатеља. [...] Последњи случај догодио се у Бору, где је један стечајни рачуновођа РБ-а, Рударског базена, попио флашу киселине за растварање јаловине и сручио се ничице пред кућицом од блата, оставивши за собом болесну жену и два полуслепа сина који никад не излазе из турбо-барова на седмом хоризонту. Тело су службеници за јавну асанацију пронели главном улицом до краја и одгурнули у огромни кратер некадашњег површинског клопа. Пад до дна трајало је читав минут, да би ударац о дно био, као и увек, нечујан. Бачен је тамо с разлогом : да блиста из дубине. Онда се убије кум овог човека, стечајног рачуновође. Па се убије сестра тог човека, кума стечајног рачуновође. Па се убију њен отац и мајка. Па се убије и друга њихова кћер, девојка по имену Персида. Па се убије комшија који је тајно био заљубљен у персиду, иако ожењен другом женом и отац једног дечака. Па се убије и тај дечак. Па се убије његова учитељица. Па се убије љубавница учитељице, запослена у Борској пошти. Па се убије отац ове поштанске службенице. Па се убије његов брат. Па се убију жена и љубавница тог брата оца поштанске службенице. А љубавница је била комшница куму оног стечајног рачуновође рударског базена који је попио флашу киселине за растварање јаловине и сручио се ничице пред кућицом од блата."

them, listened to their stories and I wrote a script based on the stuff I saw and I heard. It was fun making the script because basically it was made like a collage of real events glued together with some made up stuff in the manner I think was appropriate. (Ležaić 2012)

Ležaić narrates a background story of mass layoffs and strikes, followed by training courses for the unemployed to present themselves successfully in job interviews. The economic transformation is accompanied by the introduction of new forms of earning money, such as buying large amounts of cosmetic products in the hope they can be sold to friends and acquaintances. At the same time, when people lose their jobs in masses, the supermarkets and shops are flooded with new consumption products. While the suffering of the teenagers reveals an absurd, repetitive character, having no goal, bringing about neither catharsis nor leading to a new quality of thinking, the filmmaker Ležaić put the homemade videos into the framework of the fictional film, telling the story of the closed copper mine. He offered a motivating context and made a coherent, logical story. The teenagers' destructive attitudes towards their own bodies and lives start to reflect the hopelessness of the young generation of jobless people sinking into despair after having finished school. In 2010, youth unemployment in Serbia in fact amounted to around 46%, similar to in Spain, Portugal and Greece (MDGIF/International Labor Office 2010). The economic decline of the city, the fear of unemployment on the one hand and subjection to the neo-liberalist market rules on the other seem to provoke an extreme, excessive form of social masochism.

In 2012, Stefan Đorđević, one of the main teenage actors, who started studying film direction at the University of Belgrade after having worked with Ležaić, made a 30-minute video entitled *Making of Tilva Roš* and uploaded it to YouTube. The short film shows another perspective on the group of teenagers: it presents them as a closely linked community of heroes, representatives of the Serbian alternative subculture. Their self-hurting performances are assembled together with other pleasant activities such as skating, dancing and partying, accompanied by different sorts of music from rap to heavy metal. The music and the unbroken rhythm of dynamic scenes compose a rough "symphony" of Bor, permanent motion without any goal, where pain and pleasure, aggression and self-aggression are exchangeable. Beside the already known pain performances from Ležaić's *Tilva Roš*, the *Making of Tilva Roš* by Đorđević presents new activities such as beating with spoons, pressing a cactus onto one's cheeks, throwing different objects at one's head, mutual slapping, stepping on a spade so that the handle hits one in the testicles, performing stunts on a driving train, etc. Their self-presentations, documented by the camera, recall the three fundamental elements of masochism described by Reik – imagination, suspense and the demonstrative character. The boys work at inventing new ways of suffering and prolong their duration by repetition. They not only document their suffering but also ornate it with music and different film editing strategies. Finally, they exchange the role of the "actors" with those of the spectators: they enjoy watching themselves and perceive themselves as heroes, not as losers.

In Ležaić's film, the young people are not presented as politically motivated communists or anarchists but as teenagers with a split attitude towards the new consumer world. On the one hand, they dislike it and damage a supermarket and a new car. On the other hand, they are seduced by new technical 'toys'. They communicate the whole time via new media – by taking pictures with their cell phones, video cameras and editing them with music (Fig. 7).

Fig. 7 Toda filming Seki, throwing himself into the depth of the mine.

Taking pictures seems to trigger the absurd play of self-mutilation; the wounds are destined to be transformed into images. For the philosopher Jean Luc-Nancy (2006: 31-50; 2007), human violence is always closely related to images. First of all, the very impact of violence on the body produces a kind of corporeal picture and transforms the body into a bearer of evidence and of signs – the wounds. Yet in secondary, media pictures showing the act of hurting and its results, violence is also simultaneously demonstrative (it points out) and monstrative (presents itself as evidence of pain). For Luc-Nancy, violence and pictures enter into a close, perverse partnership – by conveying efficiency to one another. In a monstrous / monstrative way, violence increases the intensity of the media picture (its colour, its surface quality, its performative power, etc.), whereas the media pictures guarantee eternal presence and evidence to violent actions. The videos on the internet showing stunts and self-harm transform the boys in *Tilva Roš* into virtual, self-performing heroes – at once both culprits and martyrs.

The adolescents do not express their feelings directly, but only via new media – through digital photographs and by appropriating the words of others, as in karaoke songs. Instead of talking about their pain, Toda and Seki perform a popular song "Godinama" ("For Years") by the Bosnian singer Dino Merlin to express their scepticism towards material values as well as their disbelief in love and friendship.

> Happiness isn't a bag full of money
> Those who have one know that
> There isn't a path between bodies
> Souls travel towards each other. (Merlin 2016)[3]

Both economies, that of money and that of emotions, are bankrupt. Toda and Seki, but also their ex-girlfriend Dunja, who lives most of the year with her divorced and newly married father in France, suppress their feelings and replace tenderness with roughness (Fig. 8). Pain as a pure sensation, not accompanied by any signs of emotion, enables them to move between a position of being the subject and object of hurt by being hurt.

Fig. 8 Dunja hitting her ex-boyfriend Toda.

Toda finally pushes his self-destruction even further than his friend Seki. While Stefan Đorđević decides to continue his studies at the university in Belgrade, Toda refuses to find a job, even though he has no health insurance and his relationship to his parents is getting worse. Instead of learning how to present himself in the best possible way, he collects more injuries every day and makes it impossible to

---

3 Merlin 2004. "Nije sreća, para puna vreća / to znaju oni što je imaju / nema puta od tijela do tijela / duše jedna drugoj putuju."

be hired. In a training course where he practices for a job interview together with other unemployed people, he does not prepare an application, but instead drops his trousers before an examination board (Fig. 9).

Fig. 9 Toda dropping his trousers before an examination board.

Toda's protest behaviour making the possibility of employment difficult or even impossible corresponds to social masochism and reveals a strong element of suspense, preventing success and transforming failure into victory. The self-humiliation and provocation by nakedness resembles the subversive strategies of the holy fool in the Orthodox Church. The holy fool, who rejects institutionalized religious practices, replacing them by subversive forms of belief, feels like a stranger in this world believed to be governed by the devil (Lachmann 2004). He therefore rejects it completely, together with his body belonging to the material sphere. His practices include self-humiliation, self-punishment and the violation of norms by scandals such as nakedness in public places – in order to provoke being punished by others as well. Feeling strange in this world, the holy fool appears in it like an actor on stage, exhibiting his bare, starving and hurt body. He thus replaces spiritual and intellectual religious practices with brutal physical, corporeal exercises. Such carnevalesque performances reach their effect only if performed in urban spaces before spectators. Toda leads an existence similar to that of a holy fool, rejecting the world and performing a secularized 'religion' of pain, transforming life into a spectacle and exhibiting his 'theatre of cruelty' in the urban space of the World Wide Web.

Unlike the holy fool who remains a scandalous figure on the brink of society, Marko Todorović became a famous young film actor and won first prize for "the best film actor" at the Sarajevo film festival in 2010 ('Tilva Roš conquers the heart of Sarajevo', 2010) (Fig. 10).

Fig. 10 Toda becoming a successful film actor.

Toda became successful in the media world with its strong desire for affect and corporeal, haptic presence (Angerer 2007: 10s, 17s, 24s). New media transformed his anti-economy of pain and self-destruction into the economy of money – into a "second life" as a famous film actor. As a masochistic actor, he succeeded in transgressing the threshold between social reality and the affective hyper-reality of the media, between the real of the economic condition and the real of the unconscious.

4. Conclusion

In his film *Tilva Roš*, Ležaić rewrites traditional representations of misery. The self-inflicted pain and injuries of the teenagers prevent the spectator from feeling any form of sentimentalism. The filmmaker never provides insights into their emotional lives, but let them articulate their pain exclusively through their bodies. Their painful performances are presented as absurd, empty rituals defying rational explanations. The boys are not perceived as martyrs, but rather as sado-masochist, destructive fools. Although psychoanalytical studies help us to understand causes and mechanisms provoking social masochism, the filmmaker never tries to use them as a scientific analytical device. The socio-economic background of the city of Bor does not serve to depict the young people as a product of their milieu or to report about the social problems as in documentaries. Together with the devastated landscape, it serves rather as an embodiment and projection of the invisible inside of images and unspoken tensions. The film thus radically deconstructs the traditional representations of people on the brink, presented as a product of their milieu. The socio-economic laws may still be operative as a mere background to the laws of the unconscious rush to death. The film, however, confronts the spectator only with the very ritual of self-injury, without even alluding to any background motivations. In *Tilva Roš*, the violence of socio-economic crisis is presented as already transformed into the violence of the self against the self. Economic bankruptcy is already compensated by an anti-economy of pain and self-destruction, the only forms of an implied future, paradoxical triumph the actors, or better the players, can imagine. Instead of explaining it, it places the beholders in the middle of a post-communist society, marked by a loss of both tangible and intangible values.

Bibliography

Angerer, Marie-Luise (2007) *Vom Begehren nach dem Affekt*. Zurich, Berlin.
Anonymous (2010) Tilva Roš' osvojio Srce Sarajeva [Tilva Roš conquers the heart of Sarajevo], August 1, 2010. URL: http://www.rts.rs/page/magazine/sr/story/411/Film/745440/%E2%80%9ETilva+Ro%-C5%A1%E2%80%9C+osvojio+%E2%80%9ESrce+Sarajeva%E2%80%9C.html (retrieved July 23, 2019).
Auerbach, Erich (1994) *Mimesis. Dargestellte Wirklichkeit in der abendländischen Literatur*. Bern.
Beganović, Davor (2017) Pathetische Ethik des Körpers. Marina Abramovićs Lips of Thomas. In: Nicolosi, Riccardo/Zimmermann, Tanja (eds.): *Ethos und Pathos. Mediale Wirkungsästhetik im 20. und 21. Jahrhundert*. Cologne, Weimar, Vienna: 397-412.
Clark, Thimoty (1982) *Image of the People: Gustave Courbet and the 1848 Revolution*. London.
Enßlen, Michael (2003) Inszenierung der Selbstentfremdung. Performance und Publikum im "Rhythm 0" von Marina Abramović'. In: *Kritische Berichte* 2: 86-91.
Fischer-Lichte, Erika (2004) *Ästhetik des Performativen*. Frankfurt a. M.
Freud, Sigmund (1924, 1998) The Economic Problem of Masochism. In: *The Standard Edition of the Complete Psychological Works of Sigmund Freud XIX: The Ego and the Id and Other Works*. Translated from German under the General Editorship James Strachey. In Collaboration with Anna Freud. London: 155-170.

Freud, Sigmund (1924, 1999) Das ökonomische Problem des Masochismus. In: Freud, Anna (ed.): *Sigmund Freud. Gesammelte Werke XIII*. Frankfurt a. M.: 371-383.
Israel, Morton/Reik Theodor (2013) Architect of the Subjective Approach to Psychoanalytic Treatment. In: *The Psychoanalythic Review* 100/3: 473-512.
Jahn, Hubertus F. (2010) *Armes Russland. Bettler und Notleidende in der russischen Geschichte vom Mittelalter bis in die Gegenwart*. Paderborn, Munich, Vienna, Zurich.
KZS Production – Kolos (2012) *Making of Tilva Roš*. March 12, 2012. URL: https://www.youtube.com/watch?v=71BbwggYtEo (retrieved July 23, 2019).
Lachmann, Renate (2004) Der Narr in Christo und seine Verstellungspraxis. In: von Moos, Peter (ed.): *Unverwechselbarkeit. Persönliche Identität und Identifikation in der vormodernen Gesellschaft*. Cologne, Weimar, Vienna: 379-410.
Ležaić, Nikola (2012) Interview: October 5, 2012. URL: https://iffr.com/en/blog/interview-nikola-le%C5%BEaic-tilva-rosh-1 (retrieved July 23, 2019).
MDGIF - Knowledge Management Facilities Youth Unemployment and Migration, Geneva/Switzerland; International Labor Office (2010): *Youth Unemployment and Migration: Country Brief: Serbia*. URL: http://www.ilo.org/wcmsp5/groups/public/—ed_emp/—ed_emp_msu/documents/publication/wcms_219635.pdf (retrieved July 23, 2019).
Merlin, Dino (2004) Godinama. In: *Tekstovi.net. Galerija muzičkih tekstova*. February 2, 2004. URL: http://www.tekstovi.net/2,66,906.html (retrieved July 23, 2019).
Merlin, Dino (2016) *For years*. April 24, 2016. URL: http://lyricstranslate.com/de/godinama-years.html-4#songtranslation (retrieved July 23, 2019).
Meyer, Helge (2005) Die Kunst des Handelns und des Leidens – Schmerz als Bild in der Performance Art. In: *Image – Zeitschrift für interdisziplinäre Bildwissenschaft* 2: 34-41.
Nancy, Jean-Luc (2003) *Am Grund der Bilder*. Zurich, Berlin.
Nancy, Jean-Luc (2007) Bild und Gewalt. In: Wolf, Burkhardt/Tyradellis, Daniel (eds.): *Die Szene der Gewalt: Bilder, Codes und Materialitäten*. Frankfurt a. M.: 33-44.
Neuheiser, Jörg (2011) Von Proletariern, Lumpen und Entfremdung: Armut und Arme in sozialistischer Sicht. In: Uerlings, Herbert/Trauth, Nina/Clemens, Lukas (eds.): *Armut: Perspektiven in Kunst und Gesellschaft*. Darmstadt: 102-111.
Nicolosi, Riccaro (2016) *Degeneration erzählen: Literatur und Wissenschaft im Russland der 1880er und 1890er Jahre*. Munich.
Reik, Theodor (1940) *Aus Leiden Freuden*. London 1940.
Reik, Theodor (2013 [1941]) *Masochism in Modern Man*. Translated by Margaret H. Beigel and Gertrud M. Kurth. New York.
Schäffler, Thilo (2011) Sozialdokumentarische Fotografie zwischen Poesie und Propaganda. Amerika während der Großen Depression im Sucher der Farm Secu-

rity Administration. In: Eißler, Franziska/Scholz-Hänsel, Michael (eds.): *Armut in der Kunst der Modere*. Marburg: 124-134.

Uerlings, Herbert (2011) Zigeuner als 'Asoziale'? Zur visuellen Evidenz eines Stigmas. In: Uerlings, Herbert/Trauth, Nina/Clemens, Lukas (eds.): *Armut: Perspektiven in Kunst und Gesellschaft*. Darmstadt: 249-258.

Ugričić, Sreten (2010) *Neznanom junaku*. Belgrade.

Valkenier, Elizabeth K. (1990) *Ilya Repin and The World of Russian Art*. New York.

Vorlaufer, Johannes (2013) Voreilender Gehorsam. Über ein Moment des sozialen Masochismus und die Auf-Gabe der sozialen Arbeit. In: *Soziales Kapital. Wissenschaftliches Journal österreichischer Fachhochschul-Studiengänge soziale Arbeit* 9. URL: http://soziales-kapital.at/index.php/sozialeskapital/article/viewFile/267/416.pdf (retrieved July 23, 2019).

Zubkova, Elena (2010) Na "kraju" sovetskogo obščestva: social'nye marginaly kak ob'ekt gosudarstvennoj politiki 1945-1960-e gg. Moscow.

Economy on Stage
Theatrodicy and Revolution

Miranda Jakiša

> When the invisible fist of the market hits you in the face – you won't even see it coming.
> (Paweł Demirski: Don't be suprised when they come to burn your house down 2010)

1. Introduction: Theatrum Europaeum Precarium

In the past decade, topics dealing with the economy, scenarios of the financial crisis and the critique of precarious working conditions of the new *homo oeconomicus* have become increasingly present in contemporary theater. This economy theater reached its zenith in the time of the financial crisis in 2008 and has not ceased since. Plays paradigmatic of the new economy theater on German stages are, for instance, Elfriede Jelinek's *Die Kontrakte des Kaufmanns. Eine Wirtschaftskomödie* (2009), the theater group Rimini-Protokoll's *Karl Marx. Das Kapital. Erster Band* (2006), Andres Veiel's *Himbeerreich* (2013) and Rene Pollesch's *Tod eines Praktikanten* (2007). They illustrate the ongoing theatrical interest in questions of contemporary economic conditions people in Europe are confronted with: the fall from secure working places into precarious employment and the everyday ambivalence of the neoliberal auspiciousness. These questions concern all European theaters, those in the new capitalist economies of the previous socialist states as well as those that have gradually grown into the neoliberal battlefield since Thatcherism in the 1980s.

Katharina Pewny, Professor of Performing Arts in Gent, labeled this kind of contemporary European economy plays *Theatrum Europaeum Precarium* (Pewny 2009: 39), defining their foremost characteristic as the "precarious", and describing it as an all-European phenomenon at the same time.

Pollesch's play *Tod eines Praktikanten* (Death of an Apprentice) illustrates the topicality of the economy for the theater. Its title alludes to Arthur Miller's *Death of a Salesman* (1949), a stage classic that questions the myth of capitalist materialism in the American Dream. In *Death of an Apprentice*, bride-actresses are staged "as day laborers of the Volksbühne" (Annuss 2009: 30) wearing price tags with the sum each of them is being paid for acting. The play not only deals with people's mistrust of the financial and economic world, but also exhibits the market value and all-encompassing usability of man, theater being no exception to the rule. The title *Death of an Apprentice* even anticipated on stage the real-world headlines on the death of 21-year-old apprentice Moritz Erhardt in London in August 2013.[1] The play brought the topic of self-exploitation under precarious working conditions in which the borders between life and work became increasingly blurred (Annuss 2009: 33) to the stage before the young bank intern's cruel fate went viral. Theater work – this is Pollesch's concern in *Death of an Apprentice* – and the economic reality of today's *homo oeconomicus* have exhaustion and the dogma of self-fulfillment in common. Iconic images of socioeconomic reality, like that of a dead boy in a London shower after three days of overambitious work without sleep, and theater's productive reality – playwrights, actors, and staff giving their maximum while at the same time living on next to nothing – overlap in a stage palimpsest in which the fatal chiastic constructions of both the economy and theater shine through.

While theaters are thus victims of economization, forced savings and barely acceptable working conditions, they also have learned to profit from the economic crisis. Thomas Ostermeier, the director of Schaubühne Berlin, diagnosed that theaters have established a new relevance in turning to the economy, reviving the "umbilical cord with reality" (Ostermeier 2002: 10). According to Ostermeier, in times when theaters are stalemated by cultural politics and by doubts concerning their 'usefulness' and 'relevance' for contemporary society, the turn to contentious and 'real' issues operates as successful legitimization for stage work.

In recent South Slavic plays, the economic threats to the global world that produce the European Theater of the Precarious entered stages too and connected society's issues with theater. Yet when dealing with the problems of the economic and financial crisis in the region, one also has to cope with the painful experiences and the failures and defects that inevitably accompanied the *Big Bang* installation of capitalism in the post-socialist and so-called "transitional" countries. In some stagings, titles alone allude to the enormous meaning the critique of the economy, consumerism and capitalism have achieved here: for example Biljana Srbljanović's *Supermarket* (2001) or its climactic successor title Dino Mustafić's *Hypermarket* (2010). In Srbljanović's "soap opera" *Supermarket*, Leonid Crnojevič converts everything in his mind into dollars. Both plays, Srbljanović's and Mustafić's, are ultimately not mainly concerned with economic issues, but rather with further contentious issues of contemporary Serbian society that are metaphorized and com-

---

1 Moritz Erhardt died in 2013 after working three nights in a row, a practice not unusual during the highly competitive bank internships in London. See "Moritz Erhardt: the tragic death of a City intern", The Observer October 5, 2013.

prised in the negative notion of the "market". The notion of the "market" poses as demon in them, a magnet absorbing all uncanny and frightening components of contemporary life.

2. Economy plays from Serbia and Croatia

In the following I focus on (failing) economies on stage in referring to two fairly recent theater texts that I consider to be crucial for the South Slavic stage debate on economic issues: Ivana Sajko's *To nismo mi, to je samo staklo* (*That is not Us, it's Only Glass*, 2011) and Olga Dimitrijević's *Radnici umiru pevajući* (*Workers Die Singing*, 2011). Adding their perspective to the *Theatrum Europaeum Precarium*, both plays discuss the social issues of unemployment, underpayment, privatization and consumerism and their entanglement with the economic transitions in Serbia and Croatia after the dissolution of Yugoslavia.[2] In both (very different) plays, revolutionary uprising and generational obligations between the young and the old are translated into catastrophic scenarios and presented in the infernal ado that I will interpret as challenging theater's own potentials and abilities (*theatrodicy*). On various levels, the plays intertwine the question of economy and social revolt with revolution in art under today's conditions.

In Sajko's *That is not Us, it's Only Glass*, which was staged in Belgrade's shopping center *Beograđanka* in 2012 and in several international stagings and scenic readings, the domestic audience is mirrored by stage actors named "mi" (us), who are overrun by principals of a ruthless and to them unintelligible economy. The play, designed as a conversation between children and their parents' generation, begins with the words "Let us pray for the future of this country"[3] (Sajko 2011: 71) and ends in a violent riot and the death of the main characters. They are victims of (Croatia's) economic transition and are no longer willing to keep calm or, as Sajko writes: "to keep the social peace with their oafishness" (ibid.: 90). Therefore, they rise up violently in the play. These main protagonists are named Bonnie and Clyde, referring,

---

2 This text is based on a conference paper from May 2013, was written in the same year and has been updated in 2016. Two other theater works from Croatia and Serbia that are of comparable interest here are Vedrana Klepica's *Tragična smrt ekonomskog analitičara* (*The Tragic Death of an Economic Analyst*, 2013) and meanwhile also Olga Dimitrijević's *Sloboda je najskuplja kapitalistička reč* (*Freedom is the most expensive capitalist word*, 2016) as well as others.
3 In the following, I will use my own English translations of Sajko's and Dimitrijević's play, as there is no published English version. The pages in brackets for "That is not Us, it's Only Glass" refer to the original Croatian version: Ivana Sajko (2011) To nismo mi, to je samo staklo. In: *Trilogija neposluha*. Zagreb: 67-96. The pages in brackets for *Workers Die Singing* refer to an unpublished manuscript by Olga Dimitrijević. The Heartefact Fund published the play in 2011 in Belgrade, yet this printed version is, unfortunately, unavailable commercially or in libraries.

of course, to probably the most famous act of rioting in times of economic crisis by representatives of the lower class in popular culture. While the historical couple lived (and died) in the times of the Great Depression of 1929, Sajko's Bonnie and Clyde are angered by the poverty and helplessness in a new year of crisis: 2008. At the end of the play, the couple is shot just like their predecessors, killed by the police in a shopping mall where they run riot and fire guns at the shop windows displaying enticing commodities and their own (miserable) images. Firing at their own desperate reflections in the window, they commit suicide-by-cop, in this helpless way abusing 'the system' that they cannot destroy, let alone change.

Fig. 1: *To nismo mi, to je samo staklo (That is not Us, it's Only Glass*, Ivana Sajko, 2011).

The Croatian Bonnie and Clyde (their nationality being exchangeable) revolt this way to take revenge for "a childhood without shoes" (ibid.: 93). The repeated notion of "shoes that do not fit" not only denominates the economic poverty of many children in capitalist societies, it also alludes to the inability of their parents and society to provide them with an adequate and suitable future to grow into. In the play the children's generation still "insists on growing up" despite being permanently hungry (ibid.: 79). At the same time, their parents are overstretched by the children's needs and wishes they can no longer satisfy. In Sajko's play, people are unemployed, burdened by credits and debts or are outrageously underpaid and exhausted by their multiple exploiting jobs, in this mirroring contemporary Croatia with an unemployment rate of around 20%, even 49% among young people, as well as an average per capita income of less than 700 Euro.[4]

Fig.2: *Radnici umiru pevajući* (Workers Die Singing, Olga Dimitrijević, 2011).

Olga Dimitrijević's award-winning dramatic text *Workers die Singing*, staged so far in Belgrade and Sarajevo and at the important theater festival *Sterijino pozorje* in Novi Sad in 2012, presents a choir of mothers and a group of desperate workers in a privatized factory in Serbia. They radicalize and go on hunger strike because they have no social and health insurance and are not even being paid anymore. They and their children are literally hungry, almost starving to death. Dimitrijević's song-loaded play with many references to popular TV shows and well-known traditional and contemporary folk songs from Serbia is organized on two levels of the stage: a lower level, on which the miserable mothers and workers in hungry agony "sing and put up a revolution" (Dimitrijević 2011: 10) and an "upstairs" level on which the factory owners and corrupt politicians 'reorganize work' from "above", blame the market for the workers' misery and secretly laugh at the dumb people "below" them. The text runs: "While the workers with the mothers thus sing and put up a revolution, the enemies are sitting on the upper level" (ibid.: 10). Before

---

4 For exact figures see: Croatian Bureau of Statistics, April 10, 2015. URL: http://www.dzs.hr (retrieved July 23, 2019). See also: Europe's jobless youth crisis hits Croatia, April 10, 2015. URL: http://www.aljazeera.com/indepth/features/2014/02/europe-jobless-youth-crisis-hits-croatia-201422581849915221.html (retrieved July 23, 2019).

that, Dimitrijević in her staging instructions at the beginning of the play explains that the setting may seem a little black and white, but to her it is just like this in reality. Therefore, the authorial voice of the text suggests "organizing the stage into two levels. On top are those in power, on the bottom are those who ask them for crumbs in the dust. Very simple and trivial. Just as in real life" (ibid.: 3). At the end of the play, after the hunger strike revolution has miserably failed, the mothers burn the factory, the stage and themselves, taking their children and the audience with them. The last sentence of the play explains the scenario: "the fire eats all, the factory, the scene, the mothers themselves, including dead Danica and all of us in the audience, so that we can all together go to hell [in the original: to mothers' cunt]" (Dimitrijević 2011: 43).

The first mother to die is Danica, one of the main characters. While parting with life she repeats twelve times: "I am going to die for I don't want my children to live in this country" (ibid.: 42), inverting the popular motif of the "mother of the nation" who willingly sacrifices her children for Serbia and its prominent, often repeated source: epic poetry on the battle of Kosovo.

3. Theater and Economy: Levels of Entanglement

Let us for a moment turn away from the 'locatedness' of these two economy plays – which while addressing general economic circumstances focus on Croatia and Serbia (very decidedly in Dimitrijević's play, Serbia being mentioned explicitly nine times) – and take a brief look at economy theater in general.

When it comes to economic issues on stage, three levels of economy-theater relations have to be taken into consideration: first, the plain staging of the economy, of the economic crisis and critique of neoliberalism; second, the involvement of the theater (as an institution) with the economy, for theater is also a product on a market of cultural goods. The third level I am interested in here is the *oikos/oikonomia* within the theater event and the theater space itself that relates to the aesthetic economy of the theatrical experience as such. Theater and the theater space as a location of common negotiations set up a household, an *oikos*, within the realm of theater itself. It equates and balances topics, emotions and agency inbetween its participants, establishing an economy of perception, setting compensating flows of affectivity and information within the *theatron* into motion. In this common theater space, actors, directors and the audience actively participate in influencing and constantly changing the event. The ways in which theater sets the crisis of European economies in relation to its own processes of functioning will therefore be considered here as well.

The first and third levels of economy theater listed above play an evident role in Sajko's and Dimitrijević's plays, while the second – so prominent, for example, in German, Dutch and British theater – seems to be less relevant to them at first sight. A reason for this could be the disproportionate claims to art in the post-Yugoslav context. Artistic representations are often expected to negotiate current issues such as homophobia, racism, war traumas and the desolate economic state of the post-Yugoslav societies, with extraordinarily high unemployment rates, immense private and public debts and increasing social insecurity that contradict the glorious promises made by the proponents of economic transition and free market society. The arts refrain from complaining too loudly about the working conditions and forced savings in the cultural sphere in the face of the far more serious economic poverty in general. As we will see, the topic of theater as an economic product nevertheless makes its way into the plays.

Sajko and Dimitrijević, undertaking the (inevitable) task of politicizing their stages with economic problems, both focus first on the ghosts of the free market their protagonists are haunted by. In the plays *That is not Us, it's Only Glass* and *Workers Die Singing* the 'real' economic situation of the audience is reflected and contrasted with the dogma of the market.

4. The delusive religion of the free market on stage

Ivana Sajko's broken and hungry people of glass in *That is not Us, it's Only Glass* "trusted in economic stability" (Sajko 2011: 73) and market growth, they were told "to invest in production" in order to "double the profits" (ibid.: 74). They were persuaded to trust the transition to capitalism by intertwining their re-valorized religious beliefs with the promised market to come: "They taught us that God is just, that he sees and knows everything and in the end distributes to all what they deserve. They told us we will each have our share [...] They explained to us that the laws of the free market do the same" (ibid.: 72). Of course, the promise of a biblically just distribution within capitalism turns out to be false, with the outcome that in Croatia: "All has gone to hell [in the original: gone to cock] and it cannot be expressed differently" (ibid.: 71).

In Dimitrijević's play, the deceitful promises of the questionable transition and the criminal privatization it entailed also play a crucial role. The outcome here is anything but good too. In the introductory staging instructions, Olga Dimitrijević writes: "Now it's already the year 2010, the transition is ongoing and the factory was already privatized long ago. And, of course, like most of the privatized factories it's gone to shit now [in the original: is not good for cock]. The workers in the factory have also gone to shit" (Dimitrijević 2011: 3). Following this drastic summary of their situation, the workers in the play sing: "We had good will / And too much faith in rich people / And all so naïve and beautiful / And all as if we didn't understand" (ibid.: 5).

Sajko's and Dimitrijević's stagings of naïve people led like sheep to trust a destructive economic system change display the widespread notion of the 'transition lie' and are expressions of the immense damage the 'turbo-capitalistic' changes are considered to have caused in the post-Yugoslav regions. Both texts are loaded with commonplaces of neoliberalism critique that are omnipresent in the public discourses of Croatia and Serbia and that even led to a brief but powerful uprising in Bosnia in February 2014.[5]

The philosopher and literary scholar Joseph Vogl in his inspired study on capitalism *Das Gespenst des Kapitals* (2010, Engl.: *The Specter of Capital*) critically tracked down the history of the idea of market exchange processes, best known, of course, from Adam Smith's metaphor of the "invisible hand".[6] Vogl coins the term of the "Oikodizee", *oikodicy* (a German neologism alluding to the term "Theodizee", *theodicy*), describing the phantasm of a market that allegedly balances to the benefit of all with an invisible hand in its more religious than factual dimensions. Vogl writes: "Under the aegis of that ominous invisible hand, our sole responsibility as economic agents is to be responsible for nothing and nobody but ourselves" (Vogl 2015: 29). An according unmasking approach to the 'religion of the free market' and its deceits can be found in the two plays.

The obscure character of market economy and the incomprehensibility of economic laws that are enigmatic to all appear in Sajko's theater text in the topos of intrinsic intransparency. The enigmatic character of economic processes, only legible to the 'priests' of economy, manifests itself in a listing of vocabulary taken from the economy that seems to have more of an ornamental, or even repetitive-meditative, than an informational function. Economic keywords dispersed throughout Sajko's text and recited constantly are reminiscent of prayers or even credos, confessing an unconditional belief that does not ask for intelligibility. The all-encompassing lack of economic knowledge and thorough understanding of financial processes is paratextually commented on in Sajko's play, where she states: "I am endlessly thankful to Sandro for the instructions in economy" (Sajko 2011: 67). The disciple's position she takes up here as the authorial voice of the text indicates the proportions of the economic relationship between the small subject and the huge, dominant and for all times incomprehensible financial system.

In Dimitrijević's play, those in economic power know very well that there is no god in the market. They deliberately fool the people. In conversations with the workers they pretend that economic laws have caused the factory's problems, but aside they openly show their disbelief, for example in the Brechtian "corruption

---

5 On the Bosnian uprising, see Arsenijivić, Damir (2015) *Unbribable Bosnia Herzegovina. The Fight for the Commons*. Baden-Baden.
6 Smith mentions the "invisible hand" twice in his work: in *The Theory of Moral Sentiments* (1759) in part IV, chapter 1, as well as in *The Wealth of Nations* (1776), book IV, chapter II, paragraph IX.

song" titled "pesma o korupciji i preprodavanju zemljišta u privatizaciji" (ibid.: 11), the "song of corruption and of real estate resale in privatization". The character with the telling name "hohštapler Aleksić" (impostor Aleksić), when confronted with his desperate workers in a Serbian factory, makes excuses: "It wasn't me who made the stock exchange prizes, it was the market" (ibid.: 13).

Clearly the binary structure of those in power versus those who are desperate, big versus little and those on top versus those on the bottom organizes both plays. This vertical dimension is intersected by a secondary, horizontal axis running between two generations present in both plays: parents and children, Yugoslav and post-Yugoslav, socialist and post-socialist generations, who reflect on the experience of change they have gone through. The people in the transition processes have been, as both plays suggest, figuratively reduced to small and helpless beings without voice or agency. "They told us a good child has to reduce to a minimum" (Sajko 2011: 73) state the children in Sajko's play, while their parents are told "by the government" to minimize to "mice" and "hide in small holes". In *Workers Die Singing*, not only are people reduced to "mrvice" (crumbs) in size, but also their political commitment is cut down constantly. More than once, they are told by the minister to calm down and not to radicalize (Dimitrijević 2011: 40). Social peace, "socialni mir", a keyword in both plays, is an explicit imperative to those "above" and in power. The plays therefore suggest that to threaten this peace (with an uprising, revolt or even revolution) is the only option left to the people on the bottom of the new societies.

Thus in both plays the thorough critique and disbelief in the new system based on ideas of a raw market economy always has to do with the loss of political power that people have experienced since Yugoslavia's self-management socialism was abolished. Yet the conclusion that things have gone wrong and produced an unbearable tension between up and down, now and then, does not provide any means for productive change or revolution, but only for self-destruction. Dimitrijević's and Sajko's plays cite all well-known and wide-spread points of critique of neoliberalism and stage helpless and bloody revolts that, in the end, seem to emphasize no more than the impossibility of social revolution on the thematic level. In both plays, there can be no doubt that the simple derogatory mention of up and down, a simple negative gesture, will not change circumstances and therefore will not "turn over" anything. Moreover, the victims of the desperate revolutionary acts are the poor and the workers themselves.

Byung-Chul Han, philosopher and critical essayist, interprets this impossibility of revolution as a necessary consequence of today's working conditions. "Burnout and revolution exclude each other" (Han 2014), he states. The actors on Dimitrijević's and Sajko's stage, representing the subjects of neoliberalism, instead of attacking turn their aggression on themselves. Bonnie and Clyde, the mothers and the workers, they all die without achieving any improvement for themselves or those they leave behind.

I will return to the question of social unrest, but first turn to revolutions on stage: in Dimitrijević's and Sajko's plays, the challenge of the market faith and its 'god-given' laws is paralleled with the challenging of the belief in the potential of theater, thus turning to the arena they as playwrights are more competent to fight in. In the same way the economy fails in distributing justly and has to be questioned on stage, the transfer ideas of contemporary theater are in question, both suggest. "O tome se radi" (Sajko 2011: 71), "That is what this is about", Sajko's play informs us on the first page.

5. Challenging *theatrodicy*: the economy of theatron

Ivana Sajko, in the staging instructions right at the beginning of *This is not Us, it's Only Glass*, presents actors standing at the edge of the stage about to jump 'into the audience': "they approach the edge of the stage as one approaches an abyss or a bridge fence or the subway tracks. As if they were about to jump." The text also says such a death would be meaningless, for "tragedies are everywhere, they are banal (trivial) and people are not entitled to them any more" (ibid.: 71). This introduction not only brings the theatrical situation itself to the forefront (e.g. the presence of economic subjects in a theater, sitting beyond the "edge of the stage"), it also reminds us of all recent rejections of the dramatic and its ability to meaningfully represent us in theater that were met with new (meta-)theatrical devices and postdramatic strategies.

While Sajko's stage personnel, questioning the border between stage and reality, jump into the audience, they produce reality effects while committing theatrical suicide at the same time. With this initial threat, Sajko turns to the notions of political theater and reality theater, combined into theater that is expected to be 'relevant' to the world. If theater actually leaps into the audience and therefore crosses the border to reality, or, described from the other side, if actors, by trespassing into the seats, become the audience and therefore real people in (a harsh economic) reality, what happens to theater then? Sajko's imagery here is quite different from Ostermeier's "umbilical cord", where reality is the nourishing mother of the child (theater) that is part of her (or is it the other way round?). Theater and reality at the beginning of *That is not Us, it's Only Glass* appear as distinct realms, collapsing if united.

Here Sajko of course does not aim to eliminate their co-existence, but challenges the concept of it. Theater, exactly because of the co-presence of actors and spectators, has often been considered a place of realness where palpable "presence" takes place. Still, even in documentary or partly documentary theater like Sajko's theater text *That is not Us, it's Only Glass*, the framing of theater, the communicative situation the theater event is embedded in, makes any stage utterance a quotation. Therefore, "to decide over fact and fake is first of all a question of theatrical perception" (Keim 2010: 130) that can either refute or acknowledge the factual dimensions of the performed theater text. This crucial point is already pronounced in the title *That is not Us, it's Only Glass*, which not only refers to Bonnie and Clyde firing at their own images in the glass but also to the fragile people in the transition society. The simultaneous "presentation of social and aesthetic authenticity" on stage, as in Sajko's and Dimitrijević's engaged economy plays, necessarily includes "a moment of deceit" (Keim 2010: 128). Well aware of this problem, according to Keim, stages often deal with it with disillusioning irony. Sajko works with it, while Dimitrijević is disillusioned straightforwardly and without any distancing irony, when explicitly mentioning their stages in their texts. The pivotal question both playwrights raise by mentioning this is: how can a political approach to the economy leave the stage and enter the audience without collapsing the aesthetic 'system' in a suicidal leap (Sajko) or a devastating, all-consuming fire (Dimitrijević)?

This question addresses the economic level of stages that takes place in the processes of exchange and equalization of emotions and of information within theater. Theater has always served certain intentions, ranging from educational efforts to straight-out political claims, reaching out for its audience down from the stage. Since the 1980s, stages have been re-politicized in Brecht's tradition, allegedly with less (political) naivety now, the central question always remaining how to actually become relevant to the world. The new engaged theater demands political involvement of art in Rancière's sense as described in *Le partage du sensible: esthétique et politique* (2000). Political theater, according to the studies on the postdramatic by Hans-Thies Lehmann, has to show the "shaky conditions of the viewer's innocence" (Lehmann 2002: 19) in "interrupting". Translated into the terms of Jacques Rancière's, the latest intellectual source for this kind of stage work, theatre, like any other art, has to contour the border between the excluded and real dissensus to be truly political.[7] This, of course, cannot be achieved by simply staging a political topic, like the critique of privatization and the capitalist market in Sajko's and Dimitrijević's plays. Instead theater, working in recent decades on the objectives described above, 'democratized itself' by dethroning text, directors and actors. Audience participation and breaking through the 'fourth wall' became key notions of a new engaged theater that was to provide a common space in which questions of the community are negotiated by participants with equal rights – no matter which side of the stage they occupy. Sajko's actor-audience leap therefore ultimately models the theatrical perception of her audience from the very outset. Her audience

---

7 On the concept of intellectual equality within the theater space see also Jacques Rancière (2008) *Le spectateur émancipé*. Paris.

is to realize and experience "realness" while keeping a distance to the "liveness"[8] of the presentic experience of theater.

Sajko skillfully combines the critique of the economy with this reflected experience of theater, challenging core concepts of contemporary theater in her own work. *This is not Us, it's Only Glass* brings real life people and the theater audience together in the accusation of double hypocrisy. The sentence "We pretend we do not know how the scene will end", "we close our eyes, keep our breath" (Sajko 2011: 95) relates as much to Croatians in the economic crisis as it does to the spectator. Both are soon identified as one and the same. The text specifies those who "pretend not to know" as those who "knock the back of their heads against the seats" (ibid.: 95). While the desperate act of knocking on one hand illustrates the desperation in the face of economic misery, it authenticates the potential of theater to produce co-presence (in feeling yourself in the seat) on the other. In Sajko's text, Vogl's *oikodicy*, the more or less religious faith in market rules supposedly equating to natural laws meets contemporary *theatrodicy*, the excusatory belief in the potential of theater despite all its shortcomings. Both are intertwined, and both are fundamentally challenged.

One of the limitations of the theater of co-presence and democratized common space, the entanglement of theater and economy itself, comes to the fore here and questions its own "liveness" experience with an economic point: the audience purchased theater as a commodity. It is made aware of consuming its liveness experience when the seats (that 'we' paid for) become palpable beneath them, despite all pretense. "We" not only pretend not to know about the outcome of capitalism, "we" pretend that theater is free from the market too.

Olga Dimitrijević's disillusioned mothers burn the entire theater space, along with the workers, the actors and the audience. The act of burning down everything all together exemplifies the audience's presence in the theater space and breaks the stage-auditorium boundary by equating the poor on stage with the poor in Serbia/the audience in a fashion analogous to Sajko's. But what really distinguishes this last scene of burning everything down in *Workers Die Singing* is its genuine appeal. Olga Dimitrijević's play has, in contrast to Sajko's theater text, an almost classical form. In writing a drama, with characters and stage instructions, the play turns away from postdramatic concerns. While Sajko's stage economy equals information and emotion between stage and audience on an often reflexive, cognitive basis, Dimitrijević has left the skepticism and qualms concerning theater's 'genuineness' behind and operates more openly 'undemocratically' and affectively per

---

8 Liveness is a key notion of contemporary theater and performance studies that is often considered a defining aspect of theater. See on liveness: Auslander, P. (1999) *Liveness: Performance in a Mediatized Culture*. London; and Reason, M. (2004) Theatre Audiences and Perceptions of 'Liveness' in Performance. In: *Particip@tions* Volume 1, Issue 2 (May 2004).

musical and melodrama. Theater itself is reversed to more traditional and populist models in which those on the stage reign, and those down in the audience receive a lesson. Thus here too the initial announcement of those above and those below applies not only to economic inequality, but also to theater's imbalance. As lucidly as Olga Dimitrijević refers to societal inequality, for her theater work she accepts theatrical inequality. The text proposes a binary structure of top and bottom from the outset and adds: "and now that we have clarified this, the song can start. Let's go" (Dimitrijević 2011: 3). This clarification can be read parallel to Sajko's "we pretend".

In today's optimistic and utopian theatrical community that includes theatergoers, theater project workers, directors, and actors, all are imagined as equal participants. The theater spectator in postdramatic theater is even conceptualized as a liberated and empowered *acteur* (person with agency). What Ivana Sajko's and Olga Dimitrijevic's plays, each in its own fashion, show is the chiastic and contradictory structure of the liberated, democratized dramatic form and the de-democratized economic reality in which workers' self-management and participation rights have been replaced by a system of hierarchical exploitation. The post-Yugoslav subject, deceived by the transition lie with religious-like doctrines of capitalism that is presented in both theater texts, profits ambivalently from the economy theater which itself discusses the core concept of equation and balance.

6. Revolution in common space(s): internet, public space and theatron

The extended discussion on participation in theater studies and theater work has its equivalent in contemporary economists' ideas on the sharing economy. According to the economic and social theorist Jeremy Rifkin, the schizophrenia at its core will eat capitalism itself while "the emerging Internet of Things is speeding us to an era of nearly free goods and services, precipitating the meteoric rise of a global Collaborative Commons" (Rifkin 2014: Cover text). In Rifkin's vision of the future, sharing-economy capitalism will disappear after surviving the coming decades in niches of economy at best. Capitalism, he writes, will historically go through a time of transition with a hybrid economy of sharing plus capitalist logic to abolish itself in the end. Analogous capitalism will no longer be needed and when the crowd becomes aware of its power, it will take control in a new revolution, like the factory workers in the industrial revolution, (see Rifkin 2014: 1-27).

This recent discussion on the collaborative economy and the ideology of commons strike a chord in the formerly socialist states, reviving their special history of solidarity and self-organization. *Samoupravljanje* (workers' self-management) in Yugoslavia and the *Solidarność* movement in Poland, for instance, are part of the socialist legacy that occasionally reappear as a loophole of crisis and social strife in intellectual debates. The translation of the solidarity tradition into collaborative commons has even become prevalent in many post-communist contexts today.

In Damir Arsenijević's contribution to a collection of texts on the recent protests in Bosnia and Herzegovina, for instance, the prominent notion of commons culminates in the idea that the anti-separatist upheavals and workers' strikes were actually a formation of the people against capitalism. According to Arsenijević, the people of Bosnia have been subjected to a political agenda of ethnic differences by an elite who had nothing more in mind than to install a neoliberal system without being disturbed. As a reaction, people now revive their solidarity in collective gatherings, called plenums, to "enact emancipatory politics" (Arsenijević 2014: 48). They "have reinvented ways of declaring and enacting their presence in public spaces" (ibid.: 8) in order to put "an end to the everyday terror of ethnic privatized slavery" (ibid.: 45). Antonio Negri and his political philosophy of workerism (operaismo) claim accordingly that the "multitude" as a new revolutionary mass will confront and eliminate "the Empire" (Negri/Hardt 2003) in general. Like the Bosnian activist Arsenijević, he sees revolution as a necessary consequence of the contemporary circumstances.

Even well-recognized economists with far less ideological verve, such as Thomas Piketty, the pop star of contemporary capitalism critique, has convinced the scientific community and a broader public that inequality is a structural feature of capitalist markets. He also argues that the current economies will collapse into social unrest if governments or, even better, a global union of nation states do not reduce the level of inequality by providing access to education and basic requirements of life for all (see Piketty 2014). Thus, in the economic context there has been a serious debate on the dangers (or potentials) of social unrest and revolution that is directly intertwined with the given economic beliefs and circumstances. Dimitrijević and Sajko take up this nexus of economy and revolution and relate it to their stage work. "Is revolution possible?" is a question they raise for society and for theater.

Byung-Chul Han has also reflected critically on the possibility of revolution and social strife in the context of capitalism critique. He decidedly opposes Rifkin's idea that full access within a world of sharing can free the world from capitalism. Quite on the contrary, he argues, community platforms such as "airbnb" transform homes into hotels and turn even hospitality into a business. For Han, the ideology of community and collaborative commons perfects capitalism by selling "communism as a commodity" (Han 2014). Even though Han in his Adornite critique ignores that Rifkin assumes a transitional phase in which capitalism and the commons are intertwined, his main point may well be right: revolution is impossible in a world built on the solitude of the individual, singled-out entrepreneur. As Han elaborates, the solidarity that once existed in societies and within companies has been replaced by exhausted and depressed individuals who cannot be united into upheaval. Or, alluding to the reduced beings from the plays discussed here: "mice" and "crumbs" simply do not qualify for Negri's "multitude".

Olga Dimitrijević's singing workers turn to their loss of solidarity, the minimal requirement for joining in revolt, when articulating the pain of losing identification with the workplace. They mention the immense role of the factory in their lives that even spanned generations within families. The worker Goran says: "My father built this and I worked here a long time." (Dimitrijević 2011: 7). The choir of mothers and Milica sing accordingly: "I worked for a long, long time / And madly, madly loved this factory / And each screw in it. // [...] You were my first love / My beloved factory / First love, my whole life. // [...] I am leaving you, my factory / to my children to keep you / to keep and look after you // My children guard it / this your mother has given to you / it is all she has had in her life" (ibid.: 43). Even though at first sight this love song to a factory seems to be ironic, the prevalent distancing feature is the form of a popular music song it is embedded in. The song on stage reaches its audience emotionally via affects and urges people to join in the singing.

The loss of identification with the workplace that united all workers in former times is replaced here by the common space shared by all in the theater. The audience in both plays is flooded with sound, with music and with affective effects and that, whether they like it or not, makes them participate in the performance, drowning everyone in the ecstasy of the experienced theater event.

The chronic lack of money, resources, and even food experienced by Sajko's and Dimitrijevic's post-Yugoslav *homo oeconomicus*, his confrontation with the doctrine of saving, tightening one's belt and 'minimizing' are ultimately met with a surplus that functions as revolt. In both plays, the failure of distributional justice and the dictate to save, to economize public and private life is opposed on the theatrical level with the display of ample abundance. *That is not Us* presents a violent, noisy and chaotic stage. Bonnie and Clyde run amok, fire machine guns and are killed by gunfire in return. Sajko's copious stage of bursting glass, overabundant sound and a constant flow of words has its equivalent in Dimitrijevic's stage on fire, her stage staff singing at the top of their voices in a performance that embraces all: the culture of mass musicals, the motifs of TV melodramas plus a whole set of cinema images that enter her stage at the same time. Abundance is set against economizing life, words, sound, space.

In the two plays considered here, what could, at first sight, be the illustration of the failure of theater paralleled to economic misery might even prove to be a reinforcement of theater's aesthetic effectiveness in the audience's response.

Ancient rhetoric discussed abundance as a quality alternating between a negative idea of 'too much' and its opposite of a healthy plethora. Ivana Sajko in her work *Prema ludilu (i revoluciji)* (Engl.: Towards Madness [and Revolution]), a theoretical, yet personal "reading" of Antonin Artaud, Michel Foucault, Shoshana Felman, Peter Weiss and others, elaborates on the possibility of revolution (Sajko 2006) –

here, as in the play, refusing to pinpoint thoughts, but circulating them constantly in an eloquent stream of words. Sajko, in *Towards Madness (and Revolution)*, explores the connection between writing, revolution and madness, identifying madness as the (only) key to change. To Sajko, artistic work on the theater text is the gate to both personal and societal revolution. For her, it is the language of madness – the ultimate freedom of utterance – that produces (political) truth. Sajko's theoretical conception of revolution and madness correlates with her pleonastic theater work in *That is not Us*. Revolt, and in its lead revolution, is an imperative to her own writing as well as to the world (Sajko 2006: 55). The madness of a theatrical 'too much' in *That is not Us* functions as a means of persuasion and of reaching one's audience. Cicero, in *De optimo genere oratorum*, when elaborating on how to stir the audience's heart and minds, chooses the motif of abundance as an emblem of oratorical power and charismatic presence. In order to win over his audience, the orator should radiate the "force, muscles and blood" of an athlete, instead of sticking to atticist plainness, he states.

In the playwrights' Asianist interpretations, the market economy and the idealized economy of perception in theater (Pewny 2009: 43) fail. The transitional subject has been disappointed in the hope for a wondrous new world of prosperity as much as Rancière's notion of art, in more than one way, is mocked by theater's reality. Yet even those who purchased their theater experience can, as long as they 'knock their heads against the seats', overcome the destructive impact of a stage burnt down in agony and feel and hear the truth of madness in theater that still carries some power of change. Theatrodicy, as so often in the history of theater, again poses as a first step to revolution.

Bibliography

Annuss, Evelyn (2009) Tatort Theater. Über Prekariat und Bühne. In: Schößler, Franziska/Bähr, Christine (eds.) *Ökonomie im Theater der Gegenwart. Ästhetik, Produktion, Institution*. Bielefeld: 23-38.

Arsenijević, Damir (2014) *Unbribable Bosnia and Herzegovina. The Fight for the Commons*. Baden-Baden.

Auslander, Philip (1999) *Liveness: Performance in a Mediatized Culture*. London.

Dimitrijević, O. (2011) *Radnici umiru pevajući: savremena drama*. Belgrade.

Erhardt, Moritz (2013) The Tragic Death of a City Intern. In: *The Observer*, 5. October 2013.

Han, B-C. (2014) Warum heute keine Revolution möglich ist. In: *Süddeutsche Zeitung*, 02. September 2014.

Keim, K. (2010) Der Einbruch der Realität ins Spiel. Zur Synthese von Faktizität und Fiktionalität im zeitgenössischen semi-dokumentarischen Theater und den Kulturwissenschaften. In: Tiedemann, Kathrin/Raddatz, Frank (eds.): *Reality strikes back II. Tod der Repräsentation*. Berlin.

Lehmann, H.-T. (2002) *Das Politische Schreiben. Essays zu Theatertexten*. Berlin.

Negri, A./Hardt, M. (2003) *Empire – die neue Weltordnung*. Berlin.

Ostermeier, T. (2002) Das Theater im Zeitalter seiner Beschleunigung. In: Müller, Harald/Schitthelm, Jürgen (eds.): *40 Jahre Schaubühne. 1962-2002*. Berlin : 6-14.

Piketty, Thomas (2014) *Das Kapital im 21. Jahrhundert*. Munich.

Rancière, J. (2000) *Le Partage du sensible : esthétique et politique*. Paris.

Rancière, J. (2008) *Le spectateur émancipé*. Paris.

Reason, M. (2004) Theatre Audiences and Perceptions of 'Liveness' in Performance. In : *Particip@tions* Volume 1, Issue 2, May 2004. URL: http://www.participations.org/volume%201/issue%202/1_02_reason_article.htm (retrieved July 23, 2019).

Rifkin, J. (2014) *The Zero Marginal Cost Society: The internet of things, the collaborative commons, and the eclipse of capitalism*. Basingstoke.

Sajko, I. (2006) *Prema ludilu (i revoluciji)*. Zagreb.

Sajko, I. (2011) To nismo mi, to je samo staklo. In: *Trilogija neposluha*. Zagreb: 67-96.

Vogl, J. (2010) *Das Gespenst des Kapitals*. Zurich.

Contributors

Davor Beganović, lecturer in the Slavic Department of University Tübingen; adjunct lecturer in the Slavic Department of University Zurich and Slavic Department of University of Constance. Research interest: theory of literature, especially narratology, studies in cultural memory; contemporary South-Slavic literatures. Recent publications: *Pamćenje traume. Apokaliptička proza Danila Kiša*, Sarajevo, Zagreb 2007; *Poetika melankolije. Na tragovima suvremene bosansko-hercegovačke književnosti*, Sarajevo 2009; *Protiv kanona. Mlada crnogorska proza i okamenjeni spavač*, Ulcinj 2010; co-editor *Krieg sichten. Zur medialen Darstellung der Kriege in Jugoslawien*, München 2007 and *Unutarnji prijevod. Antologija*, Zagreb, Podgorica 2011.

Aleksandar Jakir, professor for Croatian and Contemporary and Modern History at University of Split. Research interest: History of South Eastern and Eastern Europe of 20th century especially aspects of political, cultural and social contemporary history of Dalmatia, Croatia, and Yugoslavia. Recent publications: *Dalmacija u međuratnom razdoblju 1918-1941*, Zagreb, 2018; with Andrijana Perković Paloš: *Djelovanje Matice hrvatske u Brelima od 1993. do 1997. godine*, Split, 2018.

Miranda Jakiša is professor of South Slavic Literatures and Cultures at Vienna University. Research interests: Bosnian, Croatian and Serbian Literatures and Cultures of the 18th-21st century, documentary and postdramatic theater, oral epics and heroic tradition of the South Slavs, aesthetic strategies of dissensus and cultures of resentment, Yugoslav partisan literature and film and (post-)Yugoslav film. Recent publications on: The Evidence of Srebrenica, Ivana Sajko's Postdramatic Theatre of Disjunction, Cinema of Subversion und Affirmation in 1960s Yugoslavia, Mostar's Revised Urban Contract and the Intersection of Time and Space. Co-editor: Jugoslawien-Libanon. Verhandlungen von Zugehörigkeit in den Künsten fragmentierter Kulturen, Berlin 2012. Partisans in Yugoslavia. Literature, Film and Visual Culture, Bielefeld 2015.

Renata Komić Marn, postdoctoral fellow at the Research Centre of the Slovenian Academy of Sciences and Arts, France Stele Institute of Art History, Ljubljana,

Slovenia. Research interests: art collecting, history of collections and art provenance research. How socio-political changes affected private collections in Slovenia in the 19th and 20th centuries are the key research questions, explored also in her PhD thesis. Recent publication: *Strahlova zbirka v Stari Loki in njena usoda po letu 1918*, Ljubljana 2016.

Andrea Lešić, assistant professor at the Department of Philosophy University of Sarajevo. Research interest: literary theory (in particular structuralism, narratology, and Bakhtin, as well as memory studies), cognitive poetics, popular genres, love stories, and vampires. Recent publication: *Bahtin, Bart, strukturalizam: Književnost kao spoznaja i mogućnost slobode*, Beograd 2011. Various journal publications in amongst other: *The Modern Language Review, Paragraph, International Journal of the Humanities, Sarajevske sveske, Novi izraz,* and *Zeničke sveske*.

Anita Lunić, teaching assistant at the Department of Philosophy at the Faculty of Humanities and Social Sciences, University of Split, Ph.D. candidate at Postgraduate doctoral studies in humanities.

Jurij Murašov, professor for Slavic literatures at the University of Constance. Research interests: theory of literature and media, the history of Slavic literatures; orality and literacy; literature and technical media in 20th century; mediatization of body and "symbolic generated media" (money, law, love). Recent publications: *Das unheimliche Auge der Schrift. Mediologische Analysen zu Literatur, Film und Kunst in Russland*, Paderborn 2016; co-editor, with K. Bogdanov, R. Nicolosi, *Džambul Džabaev: Priključenija kazachskogo akyna v sovetskoj strane*, Moscow 2013; with Sylwia Werner, *Science oder Fiction? Stanisław Lems Philosophie der Wissenschaft und Technik*, Paderborn 2017.

Ivana Perica, postdoctoral fellow at the Research Training Group "Globalization and Literature. Representations, Transformations, Interventions" at the LMU Munich. Completed her PhD at the University of Vienna. Current Research: Literary World Politics: Indexes of Historicization 1928 – 1968 – 2018. Recent publication: *Die privat-öffentliche Achse des Politischen: Das Unvernehmen zwischen Hannah Arendt und Jacques Rancière*, 2016.

Tina Potočnik, independent researcher at the design studio Oblika- kot se šika, oblikovanje, arhitektura, raziskave, PhD at the Faculty of Architecture University of Ljubljana. Research interests: architecture and design in the 20th Century, cultural heritage. Recent publications: *Razvoj in preobrazba primestnih naselij s primerom naselja Mengeš*, Ljubljana 2013.

Jelena Rafailović, assistant professor at the Faculty of Philosophy at the University of Belgrade. Winner of the first annual "Awards for research in economic history of the Balkans" in 2014 (Center for Liberal Democratic Studies and Archipelag). Research interest: Balkan history, economic and social history of the Balkans in the interwar period (1919-1939), history of economic institution, comparative studies and entangled history of Balkan states, methodology of historical research. Recent publications: *Razvoj industrije na Balkanu. Tekstilna industrija u Kraljevini SHS I Bugarskoj 1919-1929*, Serbia 2018.

Reana Senjković, research advisor at the Institute of Ethnology and Folklore Research, Zagreb. National coordinator for the research project INFORM: Closing the Gap Between Formal and Informal Institutions in the Balkans (Horizon 2020) and head researcher on the project TRANSWORK: Transformation of Work in Posttransitional Croatia (HRZZ). Research interest: cultural and anthropological theory, anthropology of (post)socialism and of popular culture. Recent publications: *Izgubljeno u prijenosu. Pop iskustvo soc culture.* Zagreb 2008; *Svaki dan pobjeda. Kultura omladinskih radnih akcija*, Zagreb 2016.

Dubravka Stojanović, professor at Department of History, Faculty of Philosophy Belgrade. Research interests: processes of modernization and Europeanization in South East Europe, history of ideas, processes of democratization in Serbia, history of urbanization, history of Belgrade, relation history-memory, presentations of history in history textbooks. Recent publications : *Ulje na vodi. Ogledi iz istorije sadašnjosti Srbije*, Belgrade 2010 ; *Noga u vratima. Prilozi za političku biografiju Biblioteke XX vek 1971-2011*, Belgrade 2011; *Iza zavese. Ogledi iz društvene istorije Srbije 1890-1914*, Belgrade 2013; *Rađanje globalnog sveta. Vanevropski svet u savremenom dobu 1880-2015*, Belgrade 2015; *Populism the Serbian Way*, Belgrade 2017; *Srbija i demokratija 1904-1913*, Belgrade 2019.

Tanja Zimmermann, professor of history of art with a focus on East, Central East and South East Europe at the University of Leipzig. Research interest: memory cultures, art policy, cultural transfer between East and West Europe, Russian Avantgarde art, art in communism, comics. Recent publications: *Der Balkan zwischen Ost und West. Mediale Bilder und kulturpolitische Prägungen*, Wien, Köln, Weimar 2014; co-editor: *Räume der Kunst. Ausstellungspraktiken im 20. und 21. Jahrhundert*, Leipzig 2017; *Ethos und Pathos. Mediale Wirkungsästhetik im 20. Jahrhundert in Ost und West*, Wien, Köln, Weimar 2017.

Ivana Ženarju Rajović, research assistant at the Insistute for the Serbian Culture, Leposović. Research interest: visual culture of the Balkans, with the focus on sacral art in the Ottoman era. Recent publication: *Crkvena umetnost u Raško-prizrenskoj eparhiji (1839-1912)*, Leposavić 2016.

Literaturwissenschaft

Achim Geisenhanslüke
Wolfsmänner
Zur Geschichte einer schwierigen Figur

2018, 120 S., kart., Klebebindung
16,99 € (DE), 978-3-8376-4271-1
E-Book: 14,99 € (DE), ISBN 978-3-8394-4271-5
EPUB: 14,99 € (DE), ISBN 978-3-7328-4271-1

Sascha Pöhlmann
Stadt und Straße
Anfangsorte in der amerikanischen Literatur

2018, 266 S., kart., Klebebindung
29,99 € (DE), 978-3-8376-4402-9
E-Book: 26,99 € (DE), ISBN 978-3-8394-4402-3

Michael Basseler
An Organon of Life Knowledge
Genres and Functions of the Short Story in North America

February 2019, 276 p., pb.
34,99 € (DE), 978-3-8376-4642-9
E-Book: 34,99 € (DE), ISBN 978-3-8394-4642-3

**Leseproben, weitere Informationen und Bestellmöglichkeiten
finden Sie unter www.transcript-verlag.de**

Literaturwissenschaft

Rebecca Haar
Simulation und virtuelle Welten
Theorie, Technik und mediale Darstellung
von Virtualität in der Postmoderne

Februar 2019, 388 S., kart., Klebebindung
44,99 € (DE), 978-3-8376-4555-2
E-Book: 44,99 € (DE), ISBN 978-3-8394-4555-6

Laura Bieger
Belonging and Narrative
A Theory of the American Novel

2018, 182 p., pb., ill.
34,99 € (DE), 978-3-8376-4600-9
E-Book: 34,99 € (DE), ISBN 978-3-8394-4600-3

Wilhelm Amann, Till Dembeck, Dieter Heimböckel,
Georg Mein, Gesine Lenore Schiewer, Heinz Sieburg (Hg.)
Zeitschrift für interkulturelle Germanistik
9. Jahrgang, 2018, Heft 2: Interkulturelle Mediävistik

Januar 2019, 240 S., kart., Klebebindung
12,80 € (DE), 978-3-8376-4458-6
E-Book: 12,80 € (DE), ISBN 978-3-8394-4458-0

Leseproben, weitere Informationen und Bestellmöglichkeiten
finden Sie unter www.transcript-verlag.de